MOON

BUENOS AIRES

NICHOLAS MILLS

CONTENTS

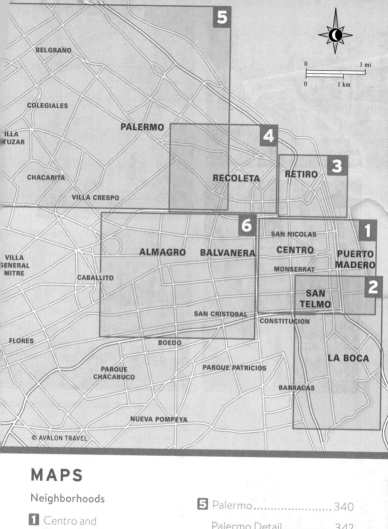

MAPS

Neighborhoods

DISCOVER
BUENOS AIRES

The smells of grilling meat, baking pastries, and blossoming jacaranda trees will follow you everywhere through Buenos Aires.
Every neighborhood has a wildly distinctive smell and flavor, with
the intense central region opening up into beautiful residential
communities, all of which welcome visi-
tors with open arms.

Renowned as the city of tango,
Buenos Aires is culturally explosive.
Walking along the street, you will often
be surprised by people simultaneously
racing to their balconies to cheer or
taunt during *fútbol* matches. A unify-
ing passion in Buenos Aires, *fútbol* is everywhere and everybody has an opinion
about it, as they do with any political
situation, and public debate over both
themes is common. One of the favored
locations for such discussions is a *parrilla*, an Argentine steak house. The
choice and quality of meat in Buenos
Aires is second to none.

The architecture of the city is a diverse mix of ages and styles.
Elegantly carved French buildings sit alongside edifices with a more
Latin American style, producing an eclectic overall aesthetic. Many
hotels and restaurants are found in enchanting old buildings while
the city forges ahead, trying out modern styles and techniques.

The chaos of the city may be overwhelming to a first-time visitor. The roar of ancient mopeds, taxis honking at everyone they can,
airplanes descending into the city airport, the constant rumble of
construction work, protesters banging on drums, dogs barking everywhere, and residents boisterously conversing in the street can
sometimes make it hard to find a bit of peace and quiet. Once the
sprawling parks and woods are found, however, it is easy to sink into
the joyful relaxation alongside the thousands of other people who
flock to such places on sunny days.

The exuberance of Buenos Aires enthralls visitors, many of
whom find it impossible to leave the charm and warm embrace
of the city.

12 TOP
EXPERIENCES

1 Plaza de Mayo: The famous historic plaza gives an instant impression of the city (page 68).

2 **Teatro Colón:** Plush decorations, extravagant architecture, and a volatile history make this South America's most dramatic theater (page 69).

>>>

3 **El Zanjón de Granados:** These underground archaeological sites bring the city's fascinating past to life (page 79).

>>>

4 **Reserva Ecológica Costanera Sur:** Wandering this ecological reserve, it's easy to forget that the city lies just beyond the trees (page 76).

5 **Cementerio de la Recoleta:** The dramatic mausoleums at this cemetery offer insight into the wealth and splendor that once reigned in Argentina (page 86).

6 **Museo Nacional de Bellas Artes:** This museum houses an impressive collection of Argentine art—and faces the cemetery where many of its featured painters are buried (page 87).

7 Caminito:
This street is an explosion of color—and one of the city's most photographed sights (page 78).

>>>

8 Museo de Arte Latinoamericano de Buenos Aires:
MALBA showcases a beloved collection of Latin American art that includes pieces by Frida Kahlo, Roberto Matta, and Antonio Berni (page 90).

>>>

9 **Bares Notables:** The city's ornate bars and cafés are so important to local culture that the government grants them special status for their historical and architectural significance (page 104).

>>>

10 **Parrillas:** Argentine beef is some of the best in the world. Dining at one of these traditional steak houses is a must (page 109).

<<<

11 **Tango:** Experience the dance that defines Buenos Aires by going to a show, participating in a *milonga*, taking a class, or attending the annual tango festival (page 132).

>>>

12 **Soccer:** The city is passionate about *fútbol*. Join in the fun by attending a match of one of the many teams that play here (page 179).

EXPLORE
BUENOS AIRES

THE BEST OF BUENOS AIRES

If you can, align this itinerary so that Day 3 falls on a Sunday, so you can enjoy the myriad pleasures of the Feria de San Pedro Telmo. This itinerary assumes you'll be on foot or taking public transit, but it's often just as easy (and cheap) to take a cab from place to place.

Centro is an ideal home base and starting point for this itinerary. **Milhouse Hostel Avenue** is the city's hottest lodging for backpackers, while **Hotel Castelar** offers classy rooms and old-school charm.

> **DAY 1:**
CENTRO AND PUERTO MADERO

Start at **Plaza de Mayo,** the focal point of the city. It contains a wealth of attractions, including the **Casa Rosada, Cabildo,** and **Catedral Metropolitana.** Stop off at nearby **Café Tortoni** for refreshments during the morning.

Next, take a tour of the fascinating **Teatro Colón,** then walk to Plaza de la República and take a peek at the **Obelisco.** From there, it's time to lunch on the finest beef at **Cabaña Las Lilas.**

the widest avenue in the world, Avenida 9 de Julio

>>> **PUBLIC TRANSIT:** To get to Cabaña Las Lilas from Plaza de la República, take a Subte Line B train from Carlos Pellegrini station to Leandro N Alem. Continue east on Av. Corrientes, then turn south onto Av. Alicia Moreau de Justo.

Puente de la Mujer

Cross the **Puente de la Mujer** and walk down the Costanera Sur to reach the **Reserva Ecológica Costanera Sur.** Work your way north, exploring the coastline and marshy areas and see what birds and wild animals you can spot.

Proceed to the **Colección de Arte Amalia Lacroze de Fortabat** to appreciate an eclectic private art collection. After you're done, stroll down the docks of Puerto Madero until you reach **Rojo Tango.** At this upscale spot, you'll enjoy dinner while watching one of the most luxurious tango shows the city offers.

> **DAY 2:**
RECOLETA, BALVANERA, AND ALMAGRO

Begin at the **Cementerio de la Recoleta,** the graveyard for many of the country's most illustrious historical figures. Next door to the cemetery, check out the current exhibitions on offer at the **Centro**

Cultural de Recoleta before meandering through the pleasant grass squares to the **Museo Nacional de Bellas Artes** and spending a few hours admiring the work of international and Argentine masters.

Following a light lunch on the patio at **Croque Madame,** swing by the **Biblioteca Nacional.** Head up to the fifth floor for a panoramic view of the city.

>>> **PUBLIC TRANSIT:** To get to El Ateneo Grand Splendid from the Biblioteca Nacional, walk southwest one block to Av. Las Heras, then turn east and continue to Las Heras Subte station. Take Line H one stop south to Santa Fe. From the station walk about six blocks east.

Browse through the books in **El Ateneo Grand Splendid,** once an ornate theater. For more shopping, head south toward Balvanera to visit the **Mercado de Abasto,** a four-story mall. A few blocks away is the **Museo Casa Carlos Gardel,** a small museum dedicated to the tango hero.

>>> **PUBLIC TRANSIT:** To get to Mercado de Abasto from El Ateneo Grand Splendid, walk south along Av. Callao to Av. Corrientes. At the Callao Subte station, get on a westbound Line B train. Disembark at Carlos Gardel station, which will deposit you directly in front of the mall.

You've likely worked up an appetite, so have a hearty dinner at one of the city's many Peruvian restaurants, such as nearby **Carlitos,** on Avenida Corrientes, or **La Conga,** a 15-minute walk farther south into Balvanera. Combine your meal with drinks before or after at the classic Almagro bar

El Banderín. From there, it's just a few-minutes' walk to **La Catedral.** Get there in time for the evening tango class or arrive later and watch others dance during the late-night *milonga*.

> DAY 3:
SAN TELMO, LA BOCA, AND RETIRO

Head down to San Telmo for breakfast at **Bar Británico,** which looks out over the morning bustle of **Parque Lezama.** If it's a Sunday, you'll want to eat quickly to beat the crowds to the weekly **Feria de San Pedro Telmo,** where you'll enjoy picking through the antiques on offer in **Plaza Dorrego.**

It's just a short walk of several blocks north to the next stop. Drop into **El Zanjón de Granados** to take a tour of underground tunnels and learn about the earliest moments

in the city's history. Break for lunch at **El Federal,** a few blocks southwest of the tunnels.

Make your way east to Avenida Paseo Colón to see the *Canto al Trabajo* monument. Stroll around the colorful **Caminito** and adjoining streets, with their open-air **tango shows** and rustic shops.

>> **PUBLIC TRANSIT:** To get to Caminito from Canto al Trabajo, take a southbound 152 bus from in front of the statue to the last stop on the route, which is on La Boca's waterfront. Walk west along the waterfront until you reach Caminito.

Walk a few blocks north and take a tour of the **Boca Juniors** soccer stadium and museum (as long as there's no match scheduled). Then head back toward Caminito to peruse the exhibits in one of the city's best art museums,

Tango music and shows are easy to find in La Boca.

BEST VIEWS

view from the Reserva Ecológica Costanera Sur

PALACIO BAROLO
Take the guided tour of this stunning palace for a chance to survey the city skyline during the day or at night (page 74).

RESERVA ECOLÓGICA COSTANERA SUR
Look back at the city from this nature reserve to observe the dramatic contrast between nature and the towering skyscrapers (page 76).

BIBLIOTECA NACIONAL
Recline on a comfy chair on the fifth floor of the national library while surveying the northern section of the city (page 88).

ZIRKEL
Make sure to ask for a window seat at this 21st-floor restaurant in the middle of Centro (page 102).

SKY BAR
Watch the sunset from this 13th-floor night spot while live jazz plays in the background (page 136).

PURO REMO
Head out into the Río de la Plata with this outfitter to see the city from a boat (page 172).

SOCCER STADIUMS
The highest tier inside the stadium of the city's most popular soccer teams, **Boca Juniors** and **River Plate,** afford splendid views of the surrounding neighborhoods (pages 174 and 180).

Fundación PROA. Enjoy the views of the old port from the museum's café before heading back into the city center to explore the Retiro neighborhood.

>> **PUBLIC TRANSIT:** To get to Retiro from Fundación PROA, catch a northbound 20 bus, which passes the museum entrance. Disembark at the bottom of Plaza San Martín (intersection of Av. Eduardo Madero and San Martín).

Once you're at Plaza San Martín, listen for the bells of Torre Monumental, which imitate those at Westminster Abbey. In the southern part of the plaza, you can catch sight of the elegant **Palacio de San Martín** and **Palacio Paz.**

Top off the day with dinner from the *parrilla* at **BASA,** just a block from the Torre Monumental, and a well-earned cocktail from **Florería Atlántico.**

>**DAY 4:**
PALERMO

Sleep in a bit, then head to the Palermo neighborhood. Have a light breakfast of French pastries and coffee at **Le Pain Quotidien** before taking in the renowned collection of art at the **Museo de Arte Latinoamericano de Buenos Aires (MALBA),** just around the corner, when it opens at noon.

It's about a 20-minute walk southwest to **Museo Evita,** today's lunch destination. From here, walk just a short distance south to reach the **Jardín Botánico.** Wander amid the Roman, French, and oriental gardens and enjoy the shade from the botanic garden's many trees. For more greenery, visit the adjacent **Parque Tres de Febrero** and stroll its paths or rent a boat and paddle around one of its lakes. Try and count the number of roses on

Palermo's bars and cafés are popular destinations.

GREATER BUENOS AIRES

Though it's not far from the western edge of Palermo, plan on devoting a half day or more to visiting the hard-hitting Escuela de Mecánica de la Armada (ESMA). On one of their three-hour tours (book in advance), you'll learn about one of the darkest periods in Argentine history.

TIGRE AND THE PARANÁ DELTA

If you have an extra day, heading out to Tigre and the Paraná delta is not to be missed. Pack a picnic and take a train from the Retiro station to Olivos, then the connecting Tren de la Costa to the final station, Delta, which lies in the heart of Tigre.

Browse around the Puerto de Frutos before wandering along the coast to the spectacular Museo de Arte and eating your picnic lunch overlooking the river along Paseo Victorica.

Choose from one of the guided boat excursions at the estación fluvial (port) and head out into the maze of islands and rivers, or simply take the Interisleña, a type of boat taxi, to the end of the line and back again.

Catch the train back to the Retiro train station from Tigre station, which is five blocks south of Delta station. From Retiro, take the Subte to Uruguay station on the red B line for a pizza dinner at Centro's Güerrin.

display in the **Rosedal** or explore the **Jardín Japonés,** the city's large well-kept Japanese gardens.

Once you've had your fill of parkland, cross Avenida Santa Fe to reach the **Palermo Soho** shopping district, where you can explore boutiques and high-end shops.

Jardín Japonés

Have a Mexican dinner at **María Felix** or an Armenian feast at the acclaimed **Sarkis.** Afterward, paint the town red in Palermo Soho at beer haven **Antares** or Paris-themed **Oliver's Club.**

EXPLORE

BUENOS AIRES WITH KIDS

Attitudes toward children are generally more relaxed in Buenos Aires, and it's normal for kids to stay up well into the evening and beyond. Many of the city's squares and parks contain fenced-off play areas and sometimes even musical carousels.

Planetario Galileo Galilei in Parque Tres de Febrero

>SATURDAY

Start the morning off with a look around the **Cementerio de la Recoleta,** with its stray cats and opulent mausoleums before dropping in next door to the **Centro Cultural de la Recoleta** to check out the hands-on science museum for kids. If you have come on Saturday or Sunday, the square out front will be filled with the **Feria Plaza Francia,** an open-air market selling all kinds of goodies. Grab some empanadas from the food section and eat them on the grass while you watch live music, magic, and circus acts.

Floralis Genérica

Head over to watch the *Floralis Genérica* sculpture in motion and then take a passing 67 or 130 bus to the **Planetario Galileo Galilei** in Palermo's **Parque Tres de Febrero** for some afternoon stargazing. Carefully cross over Avenida Figueroa Alcorta and spend a few hours exploring the park's lake and pathways, or rent a bike that carries a whole family.

Take a cab to Plaza Julio Cortázar to peruse the wares at the **Feria de Plaza Julio Cortázar** before dining at **Las Cabras,** where kids (and adults) are encouraged to draw all over the tablecloths.

>SUNDAY

Feed the pigeons in **Plaza de Mayo** with nuts and seeds sold in the middle of the square before walking down Defensa, which on Sunday is closed to traffic and filled with the **Feria de San Pedro Telmo.**

Be sure to check out the collection of puppets at the **Museo Argentino del Títere,** a few blocks northwest of the market. Head east several blocks for lunch at **Desnivel.**

After lunch, walk south for about a half-dozen blocks on Defensa to **Parque Lezama.** Take a

The Caminito is a street known for its brightly painted houses.

southbound 152 bus from the park to the last stop, which will leave you a couple of blocks east of **Caminito.** Watch the street performers, live music, and tango dancers while checking out the colorful stores that fill the neighborhood.

End the day back in San Telmo by choosing from the wide selection of sandwiches at **El Federal,** then try one of the wacky ice cream flavors at **Nonna Bianca.**

>MONDAY

Begin the day in Almagro at **Parque Centenario** with its lake and play areas until the **Museo Argentino de Ciencias Naturales,** which sits alongside the park, opens at 2pm and you can admire its collection of dinosaur bones.

Next, take the Subte (B Line) from Angel Gallardo two stops to Carlos Gardel to reach the **Mercado del Abasto** mall, which contains the **Museo de los Niños.** There is no surer guarantee of wild distraction for children in the city than the vast quantities of toys and indoor fun here. For lunch, head to **Las Violetas** and watch your children's eyes widen at the pastries behind the counter.

Hit Line B of the Subte again and take it to the end of the line to Leandro N. Alem. Wander down to the boat-filled docks of Puerto Madero and enter the **Reserva Ecológica Costanera Sur** from the entrance at the northern end of Avenida Hernan Giralt. After the kids have seen enough birds, trees, and waves, drop into the nearby **Museo del Humor** for a few laughs.

Finish the evening off with an upscale all-you-can-eat dinner at **Gourmet Porteño,** where everyone can mix and match as many plates as they want.

A DAY OF CULTURE

The collection of art museums and galleries is extensive in Buenos Aires. Some of them are huge, some tiny, but all offer fascinating displays and exhibitions. The following itinerary is very immersive; break it into two days by neighborhood or genre, or simply omit one or two of the options if you want a more laid-back approach.

>MORNING: SAN TELMO AND LA BOCA

Contemporary artists that cross the boundaries between themes and mediums all yearn to have their pieces displayed in La Boca's **Fundación PROA,** but only the best are chosen by this modern, eclectic, and revered museum that houses solely temporary exhibitions.

Permanent collections can be viewed at the **Museo de Arte Contemporáneo** and **Museo de Arte Moderno,** which handily lie side by side in nearby San Telmo. Stroll up to **La Poesía** for lunch, a historic meeting point for local poets and writers.

>AFTERNOON: RECOLETA AND PALERMO

Check out the largest public collection of art in Latin America at Recoleta's **Museo Nacional de Bellas Artes,** which includes works by many national and international greats and is free to enter.

For a break from austere exhibition halls, head over to the nearby **Museo de Arte Popular José Hernández** to browse the

gallery in the Museo de Arte Contemporáneo

BEST FOR ROMANCE

a few of the thousands of roses in the Rosedal

STARGAZING
Wander around the docks of **Puerto Madero** at night, where the moon reflects off the water and lovers canoodle on benches (page 40).

JARDÍN BOTÁNICO
Find a shady bench among the wild plants and cats that wander among the foliage in this botanical garden (page 91).

ROSEDAL
This rose garden, with its 20,000 roses, a lake, fountains, pergolas, swans, wooden bridges, and busts of poets, provides an ideal location for meandering hand in hand (page 92).

DINING AT LA CABRERA
Reserve an intimate table at this gourmet *parrilla* and share one of their oversize melt-in-your-mouth steaks (page 117).

WATCHING A TANGO SHOW
While options are endless for watching tango dancers, **Bar Sur** is of the most intimate venues, while **La Catedral** is one of the most unique and bohemian (pages 134 and 142).

LISTENING TO MUSIC
Let the musicians at tiny **Lo de Roberto** charm you with their romantic laments (page 143).

PARQUE TRES DE FEBRERO
Hire a tandem and roam this park on a sunny afternoon (page 175).

inside the Teatro Colón

artisanal works of gaucho culture. Head north a couple of blocks to the city's most popular art museum, the **Museo de Arte Latinoamericano de Buenos Aires (MALBA),** which is home to some of the region's most historic pieces of art, as well as exhibitions by internationally renowned artists.

If you still have energy, catch a D Line (green) Subte to the Juramento stop, which lies just a couple of blocks from two of Buenos Aires's lesser visited yet excellent museums. **Museo Casa de Yrurtia** displays work by Argentine sculptor Rogelio Yrurtia in his former house, while the **Museo de Arte Español Enrique Larreta** presents ancient Spanish art and some beautiful gardens.

>EVENING: CENTRO

Choose between a show at the luxurious **Teatro Colón** or a film at the historic **Cine Gaumont,** either of which is traditionally followed by a dinner of pizza at **Güerrin.**

BEST PEOPLE-WATCHING

Plaza de Mayo

THE CITY CENTER
It's the obvious choice: **Plaza de Mayo** is a gathering place for residents and is often the site of political protests (page 68).

IN A SQUARE
Sit at one of the tables in **Plaza Dorrego** on any day but Sunday (when the popular Feria de San Pedro Telmo makes it impractical) and you're sure to pass hours watching the passersby (page 81).

AMONG THE ROSES
With the sheer quantity of people around the lake in Parque Tres de Febrero's **Rosedal** over the weekend, almost anywhere will do, but setting up near the Greek Bridge will ensure you see an endless stream of people taking photos on the peculiar structure (page 92).

CAFÉ WITH A VIEW
There are few café patios that provide such an ideal spot for people-watching as **La Biela,** where lavishly dressed women sweep down the adjoining avenue alongside wandering musicians and artisans selling homemade bread (page 115).

GREEN SPACES
During the day, the shaded benches in the tree-filled **Plaza San Martín** draw a diverse mix of people (page 175). One of the largest green spaces in an area otherwise deprived of open land, **Parque Centenario** fills with people over the weekend (page 178).

SHOPPERS' HAVEN
The hardest part of people-watching in the crowded shopping district of **Once** is finding somewhere to sit down. Prepare to be amazed at the variety of purchases you'll see tucked under people's arms when you do find an unoccupied bench (page 186).

THE ORIGINS OF THE CITY IN A DAY

EXPLORE

Buenos Aires is a city of fascinating architecture that seamlessly blends early colonial styles with luxurious French grandeur, while modern glass-walled towers sit alongside crumbling mansions. While the various neighborhoods all represent different periods from throughout the city's history, this itinerary focuses on the city's origins and early developments.

> **MORNING**

Start off with a visit to **Parque Lezama,** the widely accepted site of the city's original founding. Explore the statues and monuments in the park, then pop into the **Museo Histórico Nacional,** where you can admire some of Argentina's oldest artifacts.

Parque Lezama

Stroll up Defensa, past **Plaza Dorrego,** which has been a part of the city since the 1580s, until

El Zanjón de Granados

you reach the ancient structures within **El Zanjón de Granados.** Take a tour of the underground tunnels that reveal the literal foundations of the city.

>AFTERNOON
Move on to **Plaza de Mayo** and learn about this site historic importance by visiting the **Cabildo,** the square's last remaining colonial building, and the small **Museo de la Ciudad de Buenos Aires.**

Break for a refreshment at the city's oldest *bar notable,* **Café Tortoni,** before finishing the afternoon with stops at the **Casa Rosada** and **Museo del Bicentenario.**

>EVENING
Head to **El Querandí,** named for the indigenous people that once ruled this area. The show that accompanies dinner covers the history of tango through dance and music.

PLANNING
YOUR TRIP

WHEN TO GO

The seasons in Argentina are the reverse of those in the northern hemisphere. The best time to visit is in **October** and **November,** when **spring** has taken a hold and the picturesque jacaranda trees are blooming across the city. **January** and **February** are traditional **holiday periods** for Argentines and many take the opportunity to flee the oppressive **summer heat** of Buenos Aires for more balmy climes, meaning the city offers fewer cultural activities and festivals during this time. February is also notoriously **rainy.**

The weather cools down from **March** to **May,** meaning that **fall** is another ideal time to visit. During the **winter** (June-Aug.), cold periods alternate with warm sunny ones, but temperatures rarely drop below 0° Celsius and snow hasn't been seen since 2007. Winter also sees the annual **Tango Buenos Aires Festival y Mundial,** which draws hundreds of thousands of people to the city.

ENTRY REQUIREMENTS

Foreign travelers are required to present a **passport** upon entering Argentina, as well as submitting to fingerprint and photo checks, with the exception of citizens from

a busy street corner in Centro

DAILY REMINDERS

- **Tuesday:** La Catedral offers the most tourist-friendly *milonga*.

- **Thursday:** Attend a wine-tasting session at Lo de Joaquín Alberdi.

- **Friday:** Oliver's Club hosts a language exchange, while Niceto Club is home to the popular Invasion party. A moonlight tour of the Reserva Ecológica Costanera Sur occurs on the Friday closest to the full moon.

- **Sunday:** There are free morning concerts in Teatro Colón. The huge open-air market, Feria de San Pedro Telmo, is held, along with smaller markets in Plaza Francia, Plaza Julio Cortázar, and Mataderos.

Mercosur countries (a trade bloc comprising most South American countries). A 90-day **tourist visa** will be issued and indicated with a passport stamp. Upon departure, a similar stamp will be given.

Citizens of the United States, Canada, and Australia that arrive by air are required to pay a **reciprocity fee** (the equivalent of what Argentine citizens are charged to visit these countries) of US$70-140, depending on the country of origin. Travelers arriving by land or sea do not incur this fee.

TRANSPORTATION

Most international planes land at **Aeropuerto Ministro Pistarini** (better known as **Ezeiza**), a 45-minute, US$25 cab ride from the city center. The smaller but more conveniently located **Aeroparque Jorge Newbery** is in the heart of the city.

Ferries from Uruguay and international **cruise ships** dock in Retiro, which is close to the city center. The travel hub for **long-distance buses** is also in Retiro.

The public transit system in Buenos Aires offers extensive coverage at exceedingly cheap prices. All public transportation, including buses, Subte, and overland trains, are paid for with an electronic travel card called the **Sube.** (See page 283 for how to obtain a Sube card.)

Colectivos (local buses) run 24 hours, while the **Subte metro** system operates 6am-10:30pm. The **Ecobici bicycle rental program** is free and allows locals and visitors alike to make use of its thousands of yellow bikes to travel around the city.

Black and yellow **taxis** can be hailed from anywhere on the street (especially the avenues), but it's worth calling for one in advance if possible. Unless you plan on leaving the city center, renting a car is unnecessary, impractical, and expensive.

RESERVATIONS

It's not necessary to book in advance for any of the city's **museums** or **galleries.** When there are temporary exhibitions by internationally renowned artists at museums like the **Museo de Arte Latinoamericano de Buenos Aires (MALBA),** long lines form (especially on weekends), so buying tickets in advance is a good idea. Shows at the **Teatro Colón** often sell out, but tickets can be bought online and

shoppers pausing for a bite in Palermo

picked up on arrival. Tickets for important *fútbol* **matches** must also be purchased in advance.

Making a reservation at many of the city's **restaurants** is basically compulsory, especially on the weekend and in the evening. Some restaurants refuse bookings for the same day, while others will only accept requests on the same day. Additionally, some refuse to accept reservations, operating on a strict first-come, first-served basis. Although all bookings can be made by telephone, not all restaurant employees speak English, so it may be a better choice to email your reservation request. Argentines tend to dine late (from 9pm onward), so arriving at 7pm to any but the most popular restaurants means you're likely to get a seat.

There is such an extensive selection of **hotels** and **hostels** in Buenos Aires that unless you're set on staying at a particular place,

it's hardly ever necessary to book more than a week in advance, although reserving a room early can often mean getting a reduced rate. **Alternate accommodation networks** such as Airbnb or Couchsurfing should be arranged as early as possible to ensure the widest selection of possibilities.

PASSES AND DISCOUNTS

Most of the city's public museums and galleries don't charge admission, and the rest offer a day of either discounted or free entry, although the day in question differs with each venue. Nearly all museums offer **reduced rates** for children, students, seniors, and people with disabilities.

GUIDED TOURS

There are a huge variety of guided tours around Buenos Aires, including those that offer general historic overviews as well as ones dedicated to certain

WHAT'S NEW?

- **A new space: Mash,** the Indian restaurant that specializes in British curries, moved to a new large space in San Telmo.

- **A grand reopening:** The legendary **Confitería del Molino** reopened in 2016, with its ground floor and basement serving their original purpose as a café and pastry shop.

- **A big honor:** In 2014, the **Rosedal** received the Garden of Excellence award—coincidentally, this was also its centenary.

- **A facelift: Teatro San Martín** underwent extensive renovations in 2015, retaining its status as one of the best theaters in the city.

aspects of *porteño* life, such as tango, street murals, or *fútbol*.

Buenos Aires Bus (www.buenosairesbus.com) offers perhaps the most comprehensive and adaptable tour, as it allows participants to view all the corners of the city from its open-top buses with audio guides, as well as the freedom to disembark at any of its stops to explore more before catching a later bus.

Many **free walking tours** are offered around the city center. Participants are encouraged to tip their guide at the end.

CALENDAR OF EVENTS

JANUARY TO FEBRUARY

The hottest months of the year, this is a period when many locals head to the coast on vacation. As a result, there are far fewer festivals and events than during the rest of the year. The main exception is **Carnaval,** which involves music and dancing in the streets every weekend evening throughout February.

MARCH TO APRIL

The pleasant crossover between summer and autumn includes the huge **Buenos Aires Book Fair,** as well as the internationally renowned **Buenos Aires International Independent Film Festival** and the beginning of *fútbol* season.

MAY TO JULY

The city's major art festival, **ArteBA,** is held during May. Smaller festivals during these months include the avant-garde **Polo Circo,** celebrating the circus arts, and the joyous celebration of countryside culture and tradition in **La Rural Agricultural Festival.**

AUGUST TO SEPTEMBER

The coldest month of the year is warmed somewhat by the presence of **Tango Buenos Aires Festival y Mundial** in August, which includes a world dance championship as well as numerous free tango events across the city, drawing visitors from across the world.

OCTOBER TO DECEMBER

Spring is packed with festivals and events, including the acclaimed **Argentine Polo Open Championship; Día de la Tradición,** which celebrates gaucho culture; **gay pride;** the **Buenos Aires Jazz** festival; and the wildly popular La Noche de los Museos.

NEIGHBORHOODS

Centro

Map 1

Centro is the main neighborhood for sightseeing in Buenos Aires. Various **historic buildings** can be found on its **cobbled streets,** many of which are pedestrianized. A wide variety of **museums** are open during the day, while a dense congregation of **cinemas, theaters,** and **cultural centers** provide entertainment in the evening. Centro's restaurants cater to the **multicultural palates** of its residents and workers, offering everything from German to Japanese—and the typical *porteño* cuisine, too.

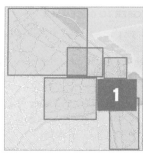

TOP SIGHTS

- Plaza de Mayo (page 68)
- Teatro Colón (page 69)
- Café Tortoni (page 70)

TOP RESTAURANTS

- Güerrin (page 101)

TOP ARTS AND CULTURE

- Teatro Colón (page 151)

TOP SPORTS AND ACTIVITIES

- Buenos Aires Bus (page 171)

TOP HOTELS

- Milhouse Hostel Avenue (page 207)

GETTING THERE AND AROUND

- Subte lines: A, B, C, D, E
- Subte stations: Plaza de Mayo, Perú, Piedras, Lima Saenz Peña (A); Leandro N. Alem, Florida, Carlos Pellegrini, Uruguay (B); Moreno, Avenida de Mayo, Diagonal Norte, Lavalle (C); Catedral, Diagonal Norte, Tribunales (D); Bolivar, Belgrano (E)

- Major bus lines: 2, 5, 8, 33, 64, 111, 152

CENTRO WALK

TOTAL DISTANCE: 4.7 kilometers (2.9 miles)
WALKING TIME: 1 hour

With streets packed full of so much history and intrigue, walking in any direction in the Centro is bound to lead to interesting discoveries. The following route traces the main thoroughfares and stops at major points of interest, but detouring down interesting side streets is strongly encouraged.

The starting point for this walk, the **Plaza de Mayo** is the focal point of the city, seat of the national government, and hub of political protests. The best time to do this walk may be in the morning, when all the attractions are open and the sidewalks are relatively empty.

PLAZA DE MAYO TO PLAZA DEL CONGRESO

1 Walk to the **Casa Rosada,** at the eastern end of the Plaza de Mayo. This building is best known for Juan and Evita Perón's appearances on its front balcony. The Casa Rosada faces the Pyramide de Mayo, a monument erected in 1811 to celebrate the country's independence.

the busy Avenida de Mayo with Casa Rosada in the background

2 Walk west along Avenida Rivadavia and you'll see the **Catedral Metropolitana,** Argentina's main Catholic cathedral. It's a peculiar mix of architectural styles, thanks to its having been rebuilt six different times. Peek inside for a glimpse at the German Walcker organ that has more than 3,500 pipes.

3 From the cathedral, turn south (left) onto Bolívar. Here is the **Cabildo,** one of Centro's few remaining colonial structures. Its bright white facade is a testament to Spanish architecture.

4 Jog north a few steps, then head west down Avenida de Mayo, a tree-lined avenue whose design was inspired by the boulevards of Paris and Barcelona. The Subte line (A) that runs underneath the street was the first underground line outside Europe and the United States. Admire the mixture of art nouveau and neoclassic architecture as you work your way down toward Plaza del Congreso. After three blocks (about 400 meters), **Café Tortoni,** the country's oldest café, will appear under a green awning on the right. Stop for a quick drink or snack in this historic and elegant space.

5 After you're suitably refreshed, head upstairs to the **Museo Mundial de Tango,** the city's only permanent museum about tango. Browse the small space that's full of historic tango memorabilia.

the Cabildo as seen from Plaza de Mayo

6 Continue west on Avenida de Mayo. In two blocks (just over 200 meters) you'll cross Avenida 9 de Julio, the widest avenue in the world. Another four blocks (500 meters) west is the **Palacio Barolo,** which was once the tallest building in all of South America, at 100 meters. Explore the ground floor or join a guided tour to see the higher floors.

7 After another 1.5 blocks (100 meters), the avenue veers northwest to skirt the elongated Plaza del Congreso, which stretches for over three blocks. Once you enter the plaza, keep your eyes peeled for Auguste Rodin's famous sculpture *El Pensador (The Thinker),* sitting pensively among the winding paths. Continuing west, cross Virrey Cevallos and confront the imposing Monumento a los Dos Congresos, carved from French stone to commemorate the centenary of Argentina's independence. Beyond the raised monument lies the Palacio del Congreso, home of the Argentine congress. From here, you can continue for another three kilometers (about 40 minutes' walk) or go back the way you came. To return to Plaza de Mayo, walk north one block on Avenida Entre Ríos, then turn west (left) onto Avenida Rivadavia and get on the eastbound Line A Subte until the Plaza de Mayo stop, and you'll be back where you started in about 15 minutes.

PLAZA DEL CONGRESO TO GALERÍAS PACÍFICO

8 The street that makes up the western border of the plaza, Avenida Entre Ríos, becomes Avenida Callao north of the plaza. Turn north (right) onto Avenida Callao and walk four blocks (about 500 meters) to Avenida Corrientes. As you walk east on Avenida Corrientes for five blocks, you'll be in the hub of the theater district. The facades of some of the theaters and cinemas hark back to decades of glory, but time has taken its toll on the district and it is now fairly run-down. At Talcahuano, turn north (left) and walk about a block to Plaza Lavalle and the **Palacio de Justícia.** This neoclassical building with towering columns houses the Argentine supreme court.

9 At the intersection with Tucumán, turn east (right) and walk one block to the world-famous **Teatro Colón.** If you can, take one of the many daily guided tours of the theater in order to better glimpse its lavish interior and 700-bulb light fixture.

10 Back track to the corner of Libertad and Tucumán and turn south (left) onto Libertad. At the five-street intersection one block farther south, take Avenida Roque Saenz Peña southeast for a block. Cross Cerrito and half of Avenida 9 de Julio to reach the **Obelisco (Obelisk),** one of the city's most recognizable monuments.

The Obelisco is a perfect meeting point in the city center.

11 Stroll north on Avenida 9 de Julio one block (about 100 meters) then turn east (right) onto pedestrianized Lavalle. Lined with shops and cinemas, this used to be one of the city's major shopping streets, but it's always played second fiddle to Florida street, which you'll turn north (left) onto in four blocks. Watch as the endless rows of sparkling shops turn into beautiful old buildings—none more so than **Galerías Pacífico,** just before Avenida Córdoba. This shopping mall from the 1890s was designed to resemble the Galerie d'Orléans in Paris. Spend a while browsing the high-end international and Argentine shops.

Puerto Madero

Map 1

The newest and most **modern** area of the city, Puerto Madero houses the wealthiest residents while also being a **weekend respite** for families who take advantage of the wide, quiet streets, thriving **docklands,** open **parks,** relaxing coast, and the wild **Reserva Ecológica Costanera Sur.** This is a place to **relax** and **explore,** with few attractions beyond the odd museum or gallery. Prices for restaurants and hotels are much higher than the rest of the city.

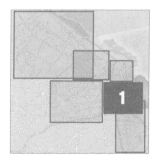

TOP SIGHTS
- Reserva Ecológica Costanera Sur (page 76)

TOP RESTAURANTS
- Cabaña Las Lilas (page 105)
- Costanera Sur Food Stalls (page 105)

TOP NIGHTLIFE
- Rojo Tango (page 133)

TOP ARTS AND CULTURE
- Colección de Arte Amalia Lacroze de Fortabat (page 154)

TOP SPORTS AND ACTIVITIES
- Costanera Sur (page 172)

GETTING THERE AND AROUND
- Major bus lines: 2, 111

PUERTO MADERO WALK

TOTAL DISTANCE: 4 kilometers
WALKING TIME: 1 hour

Puerto Madero attracts its visitors with vast open spaces, wide roads, and pedestrianized sections. The best time to do this walk is in the afternoon, or any time over the weekend.

Set off from the bridge that spans the north end of **Dique 4 (Dock 4)** on Cecilia Grierson. This is the first of five swing bridges that allow boats into the network of docks. Originally built by English engineers in 1895, it was replaced in 2011 and now only opens sporadically.

1 Head south along the water's edge on the city side, taking advantage of the pedestrian walkway that is lined by warehouses that used to store grain and other cargo. Nowadays they contain a wide variety of businesses, including restaurants, shops, offices, and even a university. Stop in at **Cabaña Las Lilas,** about 600 meters south of the bridge, for lunch at what's widely considered the best *parrilla* in the city.

Buque Museo Fragata *Sarmiento*

2 After lunch, continue south along the water (about 800 meters) to the first Argentine military training ship. Built in 1897, the Fragata *Sarmiento* made six complete circumnavigations of the world before being removed from service and becoming a floating museum, the **Buque Museo Fragata *Sarmiento.***

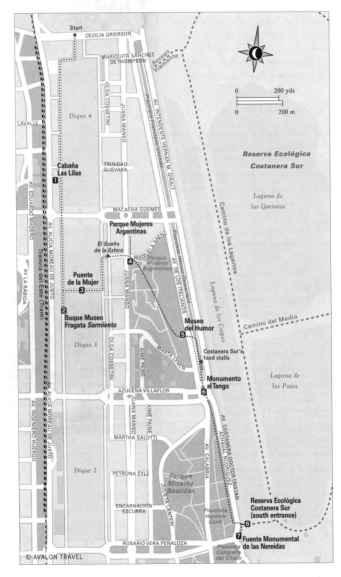

3 Double back a little to the north and cross over the **Puente de la Mujer.** 150 meters north along the opposite side of the dock, the sculpture *El Sueño de la Esfera (The Dream of the Sphere)* sits poised between two buildings as if it's about to roll down into the water. A large metal sphere three meters in diameter, it was built by local artist Eduardo Pla in 2002 and is covered by blue and white neon lighting at dusk in tribute to the Argentine flag.

Puerto Madero is a great area for a walk.

4 Head east along Manuela Sáenz for 100 meters to reach **Parque Mujeres Argentinas,** one of the largest parks in the city at over five hectares. Containing more than 1,000 trees and 200 rose plants, the park features an irregular amphitheater, with paths winding their way up to the raised walkway along the top. Its grass slopes fill with loungers.

5 Inside the park is the **Museo del Humor,** which overlooks the river. Walk through the museum and enjoy its collection dedicated to drawings and cartoons dating from the 19th century.

6 From the museum, walk south along Avenida de los Italianos for about 250 meters. At the intersection with Azucena Villaflor, you'll be able to see the impressive **Monumento al Tango,** which pays tribute to the renowned genre of music. Taking the form of a *bandoneon*, a key instrument in tango music similar to an accordion, the monument is the result of a joint effort by sculptor Estela Trebino and engineer Alejandro Coria. Reaching a height of 3.5 meters, it was the first public sculpture to

Monumento al Tango

pay homage to tango. A stone's throw to the east is the Costanera Sur, where you can get a bite to eat at one of the many food stalls.

7 Walking south down the Costanera Sur for 700 meters brings you to the **Fuente Monumental de las Nereidas** on Avenida Achaval Rodriguez. With its naked figures and erotic imagery, this dramatic

the edge of the Reserva Ecológica Costanera Sur

sculpture and fountain was swamped in controversy when Dolores Mora Vega (better known as Lola Mora) constructed it in 1900.

8 About 20 meters north of the fountain is the southern entrance to the **Reserva Ecológica Costanera Sur.** This vast area, previously wasteland, is now a protected nature reserve and home to a huge range of plants and animals. To end your tour of Puerto Madero, you can swing by the office at the entrance for a map and take any of the routes out to the far eastern point, where a rocky beach allows for views over the Río de la Plata.

San Telmo and La Boca   Map 2

Humble San Telmo and La Boca, to the south of the Centro, are **well-preserved** residential neighborhoods, where beautiful **Argentine architecture** contrasts against the evident lack of wealth.

With its **tango shows** and famed open-air market, the **Feria de San Pedro Telmo,** San Telmo is a major draw for tourists. La Boca is home to the colorful **Caminito** and a world-famous *fútbol* team, **Boca Juniors.**

TOP SIGHTS

- Caminito (page 78)
- El Zanjón de Granados (page 79)
- *Canto al Trabajo* (page 80)

TOP RESTAURANTS

- Untertürkheim (page 109)

TOP NIGHTLIFE

- La Milonga del Indio (page 134)
- El Viejo Almacén (page 134)

TOP ARTS AND CULTURE

- Fundación PROA (page 157)

TOP SPORTS AND ACTIVITIES

- Boca Juniors (page 174)

TOP SHOPS

- Cualquier Verdura (page 188)
- Feria de San Pedro Telmo (page 188)

TOP HOTELS

- Mansión Dandi Royal (page 209)

GETTING THERE AND AROUND

- Major bus lines: 8, 33, 64, 152

SAN TELMO WALK

TOTAL DISTANCE: 1.5 kilometers
WALKING TIME: 30 minutes

The street Defensa once played host to guerrilla battles between the Argentines and British invaders, but today it guides visitors through the heart of San Telmo. It remains the route into the heart of the city today, just as it was hundreds of years ago.

You may want to take this walk on a Sunday to visit the **Feria de San Pedro Telmo** in Plaza Dorrego, but keep in mind that the area will be very crowded.

1 Begin at **Parque Lezama,** at the intersection of Defensa and Avenida Brasil. When Buenos Aires was founded in 1536 by Pedro de Mendoza, an intrepid Spanish explorer, the settlement was based in what is today San Telmo—more specifically, Parque Lezama. A fascinating bronze and stone statue was erected in Mendoza's honor in this northwest corner of the park in 1937.

2 About 100 meters south of the Mendoza statue, along Defensa, is the **Museo Histórico Nacional.** Head up into the museum's tower for a view of San Telmo and, farther out, neighboring La Boca.

3 Head north along Defensa. In about five blocks, at the intersection with Humberto Primo, you'll pass the historic **Plaza Dorrego** on the left. This small square fills with stalls selling antiques on Sunday for the Feria de San Pedro Telmo; it's occupied by the tables of outdoor restaurants and bars the rest of the time. Note the low height of the buildings that line the streets—much of the old town has been protected from the encroachment of property developers.

4 Walk north one more block, then turn west (left) at Carlos Calvo and walk to the next street corner, Bolívar, to the entrance of the **Mercado de San Telmo,** a large indoor market that was built at the end of the 19th century. It retains its splendid metal and glass structure while selling everything from fresh fruit to antique toys.

5 Leave by any of the multiple exits and work your way to the intersection of Defensa and side street Estados Unidos. Go east along Estados Unidos for 200 meters before crossing to the island in the middle of Avenida Paseo Colón. Here among the passing waves of traffic sits the dramatic monument *Canto al Trabajo* (*Ode to Labor*) by

Argentine sculptor Rogelio Yrurtia. Its design speaks to the work ethic and hope for liberation evident in the struggle of working people. From here, you can continue north for one kilometer to Plaza de Mayo (see the Centro Walk on page 36).

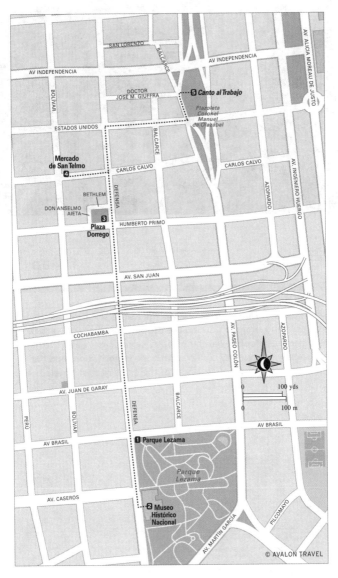

Retiro

Map 3

Based around the leafy **Plaza San Martín,** Retiro throbs with businesspeople and **shoppers** during the day before emptying as the evening arrives. **People-watching** spots abound, as it's also the main point of arrival in the city center, with huge **train stations** and **bus terminals.** Retiro also houses some of the city's **ritziest hotels.**

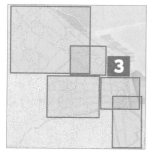

TOP RESTAURANTS
- Gran Bar Danzón (page 111)

TOP NIGHTLIFE
- Florería Atlántico (page 136)

TOP SPORTS AND ACTIVITIES
- Plaza San Martín (page 175)

TOP SHOPS
- Simonetta Orsini (page 189)
- Casa López (page 189)
- Playsport (page 190)

TOP HOTELS
- Four Seasons (page 210)
- Sheraton Buenos Aires (page 210)

GETTING THERE AND AROUND
- Subte lines: C
- Subte stations: General San Martín, Retiro
- Major bus lines: 5, 33, 92, 152

Recoleta

Map 4

Recoleta has always been home to the city's elite—evidenced by its **fine buildings** and the grand mausoleums at the **Cementerio de la Recoleta.** Important museums like the **Museo Nacional de Bellas Artes** can be found among its **grassy plazas,** while some of the city's most exclusive restaurants and hotels line the **elegant avenues.** Shopping is a pastime here, both in the high-end stores and weekend artisan markets.

TOP SIGHTS
- Cementerio de la Recoleta (page 86)
- Museo Nacional de Bellas Artes (page 87)
- Biblioteca Nacional (page 88)

TOP RESTAURANTS
- La Bourgogne (page 114)
- Rapa Nui (page 115)

TOP ARTS AND CULTURE
- Centro Cultural de Recoleta (page 160)

TOP SHOPS
- El Ateneo Grand Splendid (page 191)
- The Wine Gallery (page 193)

TOP HOTELS
- Alvear Palace Hotel (page 211)
- Palacio Duhau-Park Hyatt Buenos Aires (page 212)
- Poetry Building Recoleta (page 212)

GETTING THERE AND AROUND
- Subte lines: D, H
- Subte stations: Callao, Facultad de Medecina, Pueyrredón, Agüero (D); Santa Fe, Las Heras (H)

- Major bus lines: 64, 92, 111, 152

RECOLETA WALK

TOTAL DISTANCE: 3.5 kilometers
WALKING TIME: 1 hour

Best known for its cemetery, the neighborhood of Recoleta enthralls visitors with its elegant buildings lining sumptuous avenues.
Grassy squares line the northern side, while the southern regions
are filled with shopping and residential areas.

If you can, plan to take this walk on a Saturday or Sunday, to
coincide with the Feria Plaza Francia near the Cementerio de la
Recoleta.

1 On Avenida Las Heras, adjacent to Plaza Teniente General Emilio
Mitre, the **Facultad de Ingeniería** is a phenomenal Gothic structure
designed by Arturo Prins, with noticeable similarities to La Sagrada Fa-
milia in Barcelona, Antoni Gaudí's mega-project in Spain. The building
has remained in a perpetual state of incompletion since construction
began in 1912 and is missing the planned towers that would have more
than doubled its size. Today it houses the engineering faculty of the University of Buenos Aires as well as some fascinating engineering displays,
like a Foucault pendulum.

a mausoleum at Cementerio de la Recoleta

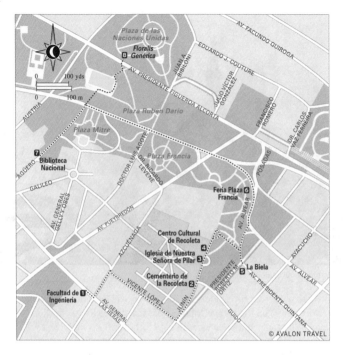

Iglesia de Nuestra Señora de Pilar

Centro Cultural de Recoleta

2 Head southeast for a block down Avenida Las Heras before turning north (left) up the hill on Uriburu. Pass the Village Recoleta shopping mall and turn right onto Vicente López, then left up Junín. This will take you to the entrance of **Cementerio de la Recoleta.** Spend some time wandering among the ornate mausoleums that honor the wealthy elite buried inside.

3 Adjacent to the cemetery to the north stands the **Iglesia de Nuestra Señora de Pilar,** completed in 1732. Though it's unobtrusive from the outside, the interior of this church is ornate. Peek inside for a look at the French tile walls.

4 One door farther north from the church is the **Centro Cultural de Recoleta,** the city's most prominent cultural center. Go inside to check out one of the many current exhibitions.

5 Backtrack south on Junín to the church, then cross the square to the southeast to get on Avenida Quintana. On the first

La Biela, *a bar notable* facing the Cementerio de la Recoleta

block is **La Biela,** one of the city's *bares notables* (historic cafés). Sip an iced coffee on their striking patio.

6 Walk north alongside the square to Avenida Alvear, where it becomes Plaza Alvear, site of the **Feria Plaza Francia.** On Saturday and Sunday, artisans sell their wares here; browse for souvenirs, toys, or even produce. In this plaza you can also spot a monument honoring Torcuato de Alvear, the first mayor of Buenos Aires. The marble bust of Alvear sits one-third of the way up a column that's topped by a bronze winged figure.

7 Continue west across the plaza. Cross Avenida Pueyrredón, then wander across Plazas Francia and Mitre, which are adjacent to each other. Make a left turn onto Agüero, and with a few steps you'll be in front of the **Biblioteca Nacional.** Head up to the library's fifth-floor reading room for a breathtaking view of the city.

8 Next, head north up Agüero, then cross Avenida del Libertador and Avenida Figueroa Alcorta until you reach the Plaza de los Naciones Unidas. Here you'll see *Floralis Genérica,* a 23-meter steel and aluminum sculpture of a flower. The petals of the flower move, closing at dusk and reopening again at dawn.

Palermo

Map 5

The favored neighborhood for many expatriates in the city, Palermo is split into **lush parklands** and **trendy shopping districts.** Clusters of **restaurants, bars, boutiques,** and **nightclubs** draw crowds of people in the evenings and over the weekends, as do the vast parks that offer endless activities and exploration. Some of the city's most popular **museums** can also be found here.

TOP SIGHTS

- Museo de Arte Latinoamericano de Buenos Aires (MALBA) (page 90)

TOP RESTAURANTS

- Museo Evita (page 115)
- 1810 (page 116)
- Las Cabras (page 117)
- El Muelle (page 120)
- Artemisia (page 121)

TOP NIGHTLIFE

- Del Colorado (page 138)
- Thelonious (page 140)
- Niceto Club (page 140)

TOP SPORTS AND ACTIVITIES

- Graffitimundo (page 175)
- Parque Tres de Febrero (page 175)
- Buenos Aires Fútbol Amigos (BAFA) (page 176)

TOP SHOPS

- Mar Dulce (page 194)
- Alto Palermo (page 196)
- Mercado de las Pulgas (page 198)

TOP HOTELS

- Mine Hotel (page 214)

GETTING THERE AND AROUND

- Subte lines: D
- Subte stations: Bulnes, Scalabrini Ortiz, Plaza Italia, Palermo, Ministro Carranza
- Major bus lines: 64, 92, 111, 152

PALERMO WALK

TOTAL DISTANCE: 3.6 kilometers
WALKING TIME: 1 hour

Exploring the contrasting areas of Palermo is great fun, especially on weekends, when crowds fill the streets, browse the markets, and stroll through the adjoining parklands. It's easy to extend this walk into a whole day by exploring the areas surrounding each of these stops, like the Jardín Botánico, Parque Tres de Febrero, and the Rosedal.

Begin the walk at Plaza Italia, in 1870 the site of Buenos Aires's first tram station, which has since been replaced with a Subte station.

1 Head southeast down Avenida Santa Fe about 250 meters to the entrance of the **Jardín Botánico,** a haven of tranquility and nature. Originally the pet project of the city's designer and landscape artist, Carlos Thays, the botanical garden provides an excellent opportunity to view many of Argentina's indigenous plants and trees, some wonderful art nouveau greenhouses, a butterfly garden, and over 30 statues, monuments, and busts dotted among the vegetation.

the Jardín Botánico

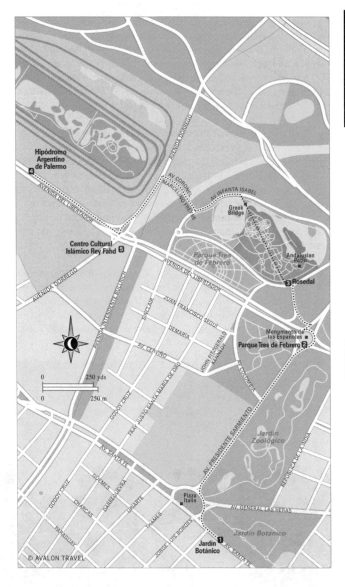

Hipódromo
Argentino
de Palermo 4

AVENIDA DORREGO

AV CORONEL MARCELINO TRES DE FE

AV. INFANTA ISABEL

Greek
Bridge

AVENIDA DEL LIBERTADOR

Centro Cultural
Islámico Rey Fahd 5

Parque Tres
de Febrero

Andalusian
Patio

AVENIDA DORREGO

AVENIDA DEL LIBERTADOR

Rosedal 3

AVENIDA INTENDENTE BULLRICH

SINCLAIR

JUAN FRANCISCO SEGUI

DEMARIA

AV. CERVIÑO

JOHN FITZGERALD KENNEDY

Monumento de
los Españoles
Parque Tres de Febrero 2

AV. COLOMBIA

0   250 yds

0   250 m

GODOY CRUZ

FRAY JUSTO SANTA MARÍA DE ORO

AV. PRESIDENTE SARMIENTO

Jardín
Zoológico

REPÚBLICA DE LA INDIA

AV. SANTA FE

GÜEMES

DARREGUEYRA

URIARTE

THAMES

Plaza
Italia

AV. GENERAL LAS HERAS

GODOY CRUZ

CHARCAS

PARAGUAY

JORGE LUIS BORGES

Jardín Botánico

Jardín
Botánico 1

AV. SANTA FE

© AVALON TRAVEL

2 Exit the garden the way you came and retrace your steps to Plaza Italia, but keep right to join Avenida Sarmiento as it heads north. This imposing tree-lined avenue carves its way through **Parque Tres de Febrero,** a vast parkland also known as the Bosques de Palermo. After 800 meters, Sarmiento intersects with Avenida del Libertador, made more impressive by the towering Monumento de los Españoles, which was carved by a collective of Spanish and Catalan artists.

3 Continue north through the park and, after 200 meters, carefully cross the running track to find the entrance to the **Rosedal.** Designed and built in 1914, this garden contains tens of thousands of roses, as well as busts of many of the world's greatest writers, such as William Shakespeare and Jorge Luis Borges. On the right side immediately after entering, look for the wonderful Andalusian patio, with its original architecture. Continue walking northwest along the central path through the sea of roses until you reach the Greek Bridge that will deposit you on the other side of the lake that rolls through the park.

4 Turn left onto Avenida Infanta Isabel and follow it for 200 meters to Avenida Coronel Marcelino Freyre, which shoots off to the right under a viaduct that now functions as elevated train tracks. Continue on this small street until it tees into Avenida Dorrego, where you'll catch a glimpse of the racetrack inside the **Hipódromo Argentino de Palermo.**

Rosedal

sculpture at the Hipódromo Argentino de Palermo

If there are horse races going on, swing over to the entrance on Avenida del Libertador and drop in to watch a few—entry is free.

5 From Avenida Dorrego, turn east (left) onto Avenida del Libertador, then make a quick right onto Avenida Bullrich. Just 200 meters along this road is the mammoth **Centro Cultural Islámico Rey Fahd,** which houses the largest mosque in Latin America. The elegant architecture of the building contrasts against the neighboring mall and apartments, making it one of the most interesting structures in the city.

Almagro and Balvanera   Map 6

Humble Almagro is a **residential** neighborhood, steeped in the history of tango and religion, while run-down Balvanera has important political and **heritage sites.** Both offer insight into life in Buenos Aires. People-watching in Balvanera and strolling around the **up-and-coming nightlife scene** in Almagro are two of the most underrated activities available for visitors.

TOP NIGHTLIFE
- La Catedral (page 142)
- DNI Tango (page 143)
- Lo de Roberto (page 143)
- Amerika (page 143)
- Konex (page 146)

TOP ARTS AND CULTURE
- Museo de la Deuda Externa (page 162)
- Teatro Ciego (Blind Theater) (page 163)

TOP SHOPS
- Calzados Correas (page 199)

TOP HOTELS
- La Taba (page 216)

GETTING THERE AND AROUND
- Subte lines: A, B, H
- Subte stations: Río de Janeiro, Castro Barros, Loria, Plaza Miserere, Alberti, Pasco, Congreso (A); Angel Gallardo, Medrano, Carlos Gardel, Pueyrredón, Pasteur, Callao (B); Córdoba, Corrientes, Once, Venezuela (H)
- Major bus lines: 2, 5, 8, 64, 92

SIGHTS

Spend time walking around the different neighborhoods of Buenos Aires, as each *barrio* (neighborhood) is strikingly different from the next. The city's eclectic mix of architectural styles was influenced by the presence of various European groups over the centuries. While there is little remaining from the Spanish colonial era, later themes have centered around art nouveau, neo-Gothic, and Bourbon styles, which were introduced by French, Italian, British, and other European immigrants during the last 200 years.

Casa Rosada in Plaza de Mayo

The Plaza de Mayo is a good starting point to explore the historic city center, with its cobbled streets and crumbling houses sitting alongside sweeping avenues and glass skyscrapers. Discover the city's roots in the underground tunnels of El Zanjón de Granados or cast your eye over the cityscape from the panoramic reading room in the Biblioteca Nacional.

The MALBA and Museo de Bellas Artes, two of the city's finest art museums, are conveniently located within a few hundred meters of each other. The historic wealth of Buenos Aires is epitomized at the mausoleums at the Cementerio de la Recoleta, while the Caminito in La Boca, a street packed with brightly painted buildings, artists selling their work, and impromptu tango dancing, shows the city's more colorful side—but also its more down-to-earth aspects. To learn about the darkest periods of *porteño* history, a visit to ESMA, the site of a former military detention center, is essential.

HIGHLIGHTS

✪ **MOST SIGNIFICANT PLAZA:** Historic **Plaza de Mayo** gives an instant impression of the city (page 68).

✪ **MOST DRAMATIC THEATER IN SOUTH AMERICA:** Discover the plush decorations, extravagant architecture, and volatile history of the **Teatro Colón** by taking a tour (page 69).

✪ **OLDEST CAFÉ: Café Tortoni** gives a taste of what high society life was like 100 years ago (page 70).

✪ **MOST SOOTHING ANTIDOTE TO URBAN MAYHEM:** At the **Reserva Ecológica Costanera Sur,** it's easy to forget that the city lies just beyond the trees (page 76).

✪ **MOST COLORFUL STREET:** The explosion of color known as the **Caminito** is like nowhere else in the city (page 78).

✪ **BEST UNDERGROUND EXPERIENCE:** Delving into the tunnels of **El Zanjón de Granados** brings the city's fascinating past to life (page 79).

✪ **BEST PIECE OF STREET ART:** Stranded in the middle of a busy avenue, *Canto al Trabajo* is a dramatic homage to laborers (page 80).

✪ **BEST PLACE TO PONDER THE AFTERLIFE:** Perusing the mausoleums in **Cementerio de la Recoleta** provides insight into the wealth and splendor that once reigned in Argentina (page 86).

✪ **MOST IMPRESSIVE ART COLLECTION:** The **Museo Nacional de Bellas Artes** is a bastion of Argentine art—and faces the cemetery where many of its featured painters are buried (page 87).

✪ **BEST CITY VIEW:** Surveying Buenos Aires from the **Biblioteca Nacional** provides a wonderful panorama of the city and the Río de la Plata (page 88).

✪ **MOST POPULAR MUSEUM:** The beloved **Museo de Arte Latinoamericano de Buenos Aires (MALBA)** showcases pieces by Frida Kahlo, Roberto Matta, and Antonio Berni (page 90).

✪ **BEST EDUCATION ON ARGENTINA'S DARKEST HOUR:** A guided tour around **ESMA** presents a vivid picture of the horrors that occurred during the military dictatorship from 1976 to 1983 (page 96).

CENTRO

✪ Plaza de Mayo

Plaza de Mayo has been the center of Buenos Aires since the city was first founded by Juan de Garay in 1580, although it has been transformed and renamed numerous times over the centuries. The current plaza is the amalgamation of two former squares, Plaza de la Victoria and Plaza del Fuerte, which were separated by a market building. It has been the scene of notorious protests and demonstrations as well as jubilant celebrations.

The eastern side is taken up by the Casa Rosada, the seat of Argentina's government and the main reason crowds draw to political demonstrations in the square. The sprawling Ministry of Economy lies to the south, while the cavernous national bank opposes it to the north. Next to the bank is the city's cathedral, Catedral Metropolitana.

The western end of the plaza is sliced in two by Avenida de Mayo. To the south of Avenida de Mayo, the Cabildo, a relic of the colonial era, stares across the plaza at the Casa Rosada.

A barrier was erected across the square during the violent protests that resulted from the country's economic collapse in 2001, and it remains to this day. The plaza also played witness to weekly peaceful demonstrations by the Madres de Plaza de Mayo, a group of mothers whose children were "disappeared" by the dictatorship during

The benches in Plaza de Mayo are great spots for contemplation.

the Dirty War. From 1977 until 2006, they brandished photos of their children and attracted hundreds of participants. Today, protesters include a group of war vets.

Palm trees provide ample shade to sit and take in the view, although visitors are required to use benches—the grassy areas are off limits. Children buy bags of corn to feed the many pigeons in the square. Don't be put off by the barrier dividing the square, as police officers stationed at the pass points let people through without question.

MAP 1: Bordered by Av. Rivadavia and Av. Hipólito Yrigoyen, where Av. de Mayo intersects with Av. Roque Sáenz Peña and Av. Julio A. Roca

NEARBY:

- Visit the Cabildo, the last remaining colonial building in the area (page 71).
- Check out the Casa Rosada, where Juan and Evita Perón made their famous balcony appearances (page 71).
- View the art and varied architectural styles at the Catedral Metropolitana (page 72).
- Sample traditional Japanese food at FuraiBo (page 102).
- Get a crash course on the city's evolution at the Museo de la Ciudad de Buenos Aires (page 151).

✪ Teatro Colón

Widely regarded as one of the greatest performance venues in the world, Teatro Colón is a source of pride to Argentines. Originally situated on the northeast corner of Plaza de Mayo, the city government decided to build a new theater with the same name at the current location in 1914. The multiple lanes of traffic just outside have no impact on the phenomenal acoustics, of which Luciano Pavarotti was an admirer. Occupying a city block, Teatro Colón was designed by Francesco Tamburini. Due to Tamburini's death, the murder of his apprentice, Vittorio Meano (who also designed the Palacio del Congreso), financial problems, and political battles, the construction lasted for decades. The original lavish interior remains, with scarlet and gold the predominant colors. Busts of famous composers are on display, while the concert hall itself is crafted from marble, gold, and ivory, among other materials, all lit by a massive light fixture holding 700 bulbs.

The theater's season runs from May to November, although there are concerts year-round with tickets selling out long in advance. Free concerts are often held on Sunday mornings (queue

the auditorium in the Teatro Colón

at the ticket office on the Friday morning before to get tickets), although these showings, unfortunately, attract a crowd that is more interested in taking photos than enjoying the show.

Excellent guided tours (US$14, free under age 7) are offered from 9am until 5pm daily, departing from the ticket office at Tucumán 1171 every 15 minutes. The language of the tours varies, so check beforehand for an English-speaking guide. The tour lasts around 50 minutes and includes the various levels of the theater and the costume and scenery workshops. The ticket office is open 10am-8pm Monday-Saturday and 10am-5pm Sunday.

MAP 1: Cerrito 628, tel. 011/4378-7100, www.teatrocolon.org.ar

NEARBY:

- Admire the grandeur of the Palacio de Justícia, home to the Argentine supreme court (page 75).
- For a special occasion, dine at sophisticated Tomo 1 (page 101).

- Before seeing a show at the theater, have a coffee or cocktail at Petit Colón (page 103).
- For more theater, catch a play or musical at the iconic Teatro Nacional Cervantes (page 159).
- Explore the area on one of the tours offered by Buenos Aires Free Walks (page 171).

✪ Café Tortoni

Café Tortoni's title of oldest café in Argentina is somewhat misleading, as it was not in its current location until Torcuato de Alvear decided to carve Avenida de Mayo through existing city blocks at the end of the 19th century. The current iteration of the café opened in 1893 and became the first to place tables and chairs on the pavement (a novelty that no longer occurs). The elegant exterior is merely a preview of the luxurious rooms inside. The café's tables and chairs are carved from oak and marble, while the paneled walls speak of a long lost style.

Curtains hide the view from

passersby, while a dapper host has visitors wait outside briefly before ushering them to a table. Drop by for a quick refreshment, perhaps during one of the daily live shows (usually tango), which are held at 8pm and 10pm. Due to high prices, poor attention from servers, and ordinary food, locals tend to steer clear.

MAP 1: Av. de Mayo 825, tel. 011/4342-4328, www.cafetortoni.com.ar; 8am-3:30am Mon.-Sat., 8am-1am Sun.

Basílica de Nuestra Señora del Rosario

This Dominican temple was built between 1751 and 1784 on land that used to look out over the Río de la Plata. The adjoining Convento de Santo Domingo was built slightly later, with construction terminating around 1805. The church was used for refuge by British troops during their ill-fated 1807 invasion, from which damage is still visible to the tower. The body of Manuel Belgrano (a national hero who designed the Argentine flag) is buried in a mausoleum in the front courtyard. The church was upgraded to the status of basilica by Pope Pius X in 1910. In 1955, the basilica was part of a rash of church burnings instigated by Juan Domingo Perón; it suffered serious structural damage as well as the destruction of the altar and the organ. Masses occur weekdays at 12:30pm, Saturdays at 6:30pm, and Sundays at 11am.

MAP 1: Defensa 422, tel. 011/4331-1668; 7am-6:30pm Mon.-Fri., 6am-7:30pm Sat., 10am-1pm and 3pm-6pm Sun.

Cabildo

Across Plaza de Mayo from the Casa Rosada, the Cabildo is the last remaining colonial building on the city's most historic square. Its bright white facade, a testament to Spanish architecture, has been maintained since the building was constructed in 1725. Originally much wider, with 11 arches instead of the current 5, it was progressively chopped into smaller pieces as Avenida de Mayo and Avenida Julio A. Roca were carved through the city blocks around the turn of the 20th century.

The Cabildo now houses a museum within its small grounds, but the scant collection of photos, maps, and paintings of the surrounding area aren't all that enthralling. Concerts and other cultural events are regularly held in the courtyard and in front of the building.

MAP 1: Bolívar 65, tel. 011/4334-1782, www.cultura.gob.ar; 10:30am-5pm Tues.-Wed. and Fri., 10:30am-6pm Sat.-Sun.; free

the remaining section of the Cabildo

Casa Rosada

Despite its comparatively humble size, the Casa Rosada was the largest building in Buenos Aires until the end of the 19th century. Starting as a fort in 1594, when the bank of the Río de la Plata reached its back door, it underwent various reconstructions until it was finally completed and inaugurated as the government house in 1898. The pink color, exaggerated at night by fluorescent lights, was chosen by President Sarmiento in an attempt to bring harmony to the political battle between the red Federalistas and white Unitaristas. The building was immortalized in Argentine lore after Juan and Evita Perón made appearances on the front balcony, facing crowds of supporters in the plaza below. In 2001, these moments of national pride were contrasted by President De la Rúa fleeing the rooftop (and his presidency) via helicopter while mobs attacked the palace. Although it serves as the government house, the president tends to live in the official residence in Olivos.

The Museo del Bicentenario (Av. Paseo Colón and Av. Hipólito Yrigoyen, tel. 011/4344-3802, www.museobicentenario.gob.ar; 10am-6pm Wed.-Sun.; free) is located in the basement of the Casa Rosada, displaying personal items of former presidents. Visitors can also explore remains of previous buildings that existed on the site.

Casa Rosada

Free guided tours (Sat.-Sun.) of the Casa Rosada are offered in English (2:30pm), Spanish, and Portuguese and provide the opportunity to step out on the famous balcony that overlooks Plaza de Mayo. Tour reservations must be made online (http://

visitas.casarosada.gob.ar), no more than 15 days ahead of the desired date. MAP 1: Balcarce 50, tel. 011/4344-3600, www.casarosada.gob.ar; 10am-6pm Sat.-Sun.; free

José de San Martín's mausoleum in the Catedral Metropolitana

Catedral Metropolitana

The Catedral Metropolitana is the most important and prominent Roman Catholic church in Argentina. Situated in the northwest corner of Plaza de Mayo since 1580, when Juan de Garay founded Buenos Aires and designated this spot for the city's largest place of worship, it has been rebuilt six times. The result is an intriguing mixture of architectural styles, with Italian, Spanish, and Greek influences.

The remains of General José de San Martín, Argentina's great independence hero, lie in a mausoleum on the east side. Numerous works of art are displayed, and the cathedral itself could be considered a piece of art, given its elegant tiled floor and frescoes. The German Walcker organ, with over 3,500 pipes, is considered one of the finest of its kind; it can be heard at least once a month at free concerts.

Masses are held at 7:45am, 8:30am, 12:30pm, and 5:30pm Monday-Friday, at on 11:30am Saturday, and at 10am, 11:30am, 1pm, and 5:30pm on Sunday. The 11:30 mass on Sunday is a *missa solemnis,* a musical version of the traditional mass, which is sung by the cathedral's choir.

MAP 1: San Martín 27, tel. 011/4343-6272, www.catedralbuenosaires.org.ar; 7:30am-6:45pm Mon.-Fri., 9am-6:45pm Sat.-Sun.; free

El Pensador (The Thinker)

French sculptor Auguste Rodin produced eight bronze casts of a figure known as *The Thinker,* the third of which can be seen in Plaza del Congreso. Commissioned by museums director Eduardo Schiaffino in 1907, it was intended to be placed on the steps leading up to the Congress building, but was instead placed a few hundred yards away. The original casting is part of a larger piece, *The Gates of Hell,* depicting characters from Dante's *Divine Comedy.* The location of the statue is only a couple of blocks away from Palacio Barolo, a building whose design was influenced by the same poem.

MAP 1: East section of Plaza del Congreso

Galerías Pacífico

Originally designed as a replica of the Galerie d'Orléans in Paris, this decorative shopping mall was constructed in the 1890s, and included features such as electrical installations, heating systems, and elevators—advanced technology for the time. In the early 20th century, an English railroad company purchased the property, converted it into offices, and gave it its current name. From that point forward, the building went through several ups (murals contributed in the mid-1900s by renowned painters Antonio Berni, Lino Spilimbergo, and Juan Carlos Castagnino) and downs— the basement was used as a torture center and holding place for political prisoners during the military dictatorship of the 1980s.

The mall reopened in 1991 after extensive renovations, and today still retains its early glamour, housing many high-end stores. Short audio tours (20 min., free) can be picked up from the information desk on the ground floor at any time during the opening hours. The tour is offered in English, Spanish, French, and Portuguese.

MAP 1: Florida and Av. Córdoba, tel. 011/5555-5420, www.galeriaspacifico.com. ar; 10am-9pm Mon.-Sat., noon-9pm Sun.

Manzana de las Luces (Illuminated Block)

The Manzana de las Luces is one of the oldest pieces of architecture remaining in Buenos Aires. This collection of buildings began with the Iglesia de San Ignacio in 1686. At the time it was owned by the Jesuits, who added a school, a library, offices, and

Iglesia de San Ignacio in Manzana de las Luces

laboratories before they were ousted in 1767. From then on the church was used by multiple organizations and government departments until 1972, when it was turned into a museum, a process that involved the demolition of many buildings that were not part of the original design. A network of underground tunnels was discovered in 1912. Alongside the church, there also remain some Jesuit buildings that were originally used for living and storage.

Guided tours (4pm Mon.-Fri., 3pm, 4:30pm, and 6pm Sat.-Sun.; US$4) of the property are offered, although these are less exciting and educational than similar tours offered in the nearby Zanjón de Granados. Opting for a drink on the patio café is a more enjoyable option.

MAP 1: Perú 272, tel. 011/4343-3260, www.manzanadelasluces.gov.ar; 10am-8pm Mon.-Fri., 2pm-8pm Sat.-Sun.

Monumento a Don Quijote

Given to Argentina by Spain on the 400-year celebration of the 1580 founding of Buenos Aires, this statue of Cervantes's renowned antihero was created by Spanish sculptor Aurelio Teno. Teno crafted the 15-meter statue in Uruguay with a 100-person team before transporting it across the river and placing it on one of the islands in the middle of Avenida 9 de Julio.

The statue's design and placement have provoked criticism since its unveiling. Argentine artists have described its appearance as that of a scarecrow and a sugar cube. Nicolás García Uriburu, an Argentine painter, branded it "the ugliest thing in the city." There have been repeated calls for the statue to be moved to Plaza España, but the government has held firm on its location. It has, however, ceased replacing the statue's plaque after successive acts of vandalism and theft. Indeed, the statue can now be identified by the graffiti across its base as much as the figure of Don Quixote himself.

MAP 1: Av. Hipólito Yrigoyen and Lima

Obelisco (Obelisk)

Built in a mere 31 days in 1936, the Obelisco (Obelisk) has become one of the most recognizable monuments in Buenos Aires. Standing 67 meters tall, it was built to celebrate the 400th anniversary of the city's founding. The destruction of the Church of Saint Nicolás to make way for the Obelisco upset many, and three years later it was almost torn down by the city government.

At the top are four small windows. Although the monument is not open to the public, it is the focal point for celebrations after any international *fútbol* victories, as well a favored location for protests.

MAP 1: Plaza de la República, Av. Corrientes and Av. 9 de Julio

Palacio Barolo

Once the tallest building in South America, Palacio Barolo is a magnificent piece of architecture whose design was influenced by Dante's *Divine Comedy*. It stands 100 meters tall (one meter for each of Dante's cantos); Italian architect Mario Palanti divided the structure into three sections, with the lower floors representing hell, the middle floors purgatory, and the top floors heaven. Inaugurated in 1923, the building is graced with a lighthouse in the tower, whose beam sweeps across the city on important occasions. Palacio Barolo can be

the Obelisco

viewed from the top of a similar building in Montevideo, Uruguay, which was designed and constructed as its smaller sibling.

Although the ground floor can be accessed by the public while the building is open, it's required that visitors join a guided tour (www.palacio-barolotours.com.ar; from US$20) to explore the higher echelons. A small booth in the lobby takes reservations and provides information on the different tour options available, some of which include wine-tasting, tango, or even nighttime trips up the tower. One of the best is the photography tour, held on the second Saturday of each month, which offers access to the roof terrace and a commanding view of the surrounding area.

MAP 1: Av. de Mayo 1370, tel.
011/4381-2425, www.palaciobarolo.com.ar;
8am-8pm Mon.-Sat.

Palacio de Justícia

The Palacio de Justícia, more commonly referred to simply as Tribunales, is an impressive neoclassical building that houses the Argentine supreme court as well as some smaller courts. Originally operating out of the Cabildo, the courts transitioned here beginning in 1910; construction was completed in 1942.

The building features towering columns and large dimensions. The interior is equally grand, with long balconied corridors supported by numerous columns and adorned by statues. The courtrooms themselves are ornate yet somber.

Although the building is generally closed to the public, the city provides free guided tours (tel. 011/4114-5791, visitasguiadas_entur@buenosaires. gob.ar, 2:30pm Fri.), for which there are limited spaces that must be booked in advance by telephone or email.

MAP 1: Talcahuano 490

✪ Reserva Ecológica Costanera Sur

Covering over 350 hectares, this ecological reserve contains over 250 species of birds and a huge range of local and imported trees. During the 1970s, the military dictatorship undertook a campaign of public works, which included the construction of many expressways. The debris accrued from the demolition of hundreds of city blocks was deposited in the Río de la Plata with the intention of extending the city into the river. For various reasons, including the outbreak of the Malvinas war and the general risk of flooding, the project was abandoned. In the years that followed, nature took over, resulting in an area populated with woods, lakes, and many wild animals. It is a favorite place for residents, who use the area for walking, jogging, and bird-watching.

guided tour at the Reserva Ecológica Costanera Sur

There are two entrances to the Reserva: the main entrance is at the southern end of the Costanera Sur, and a smaller entrance is at the north end. The information offices are located at the main entrance.

A number of guided tours are available, all of which are free. Day tours (9:30am and 4pm Sat.-Sun. Nov.-Mar., 10:30am and 3:30pm Sat.-Sun. Apr.-Oct.) depart from the main office. To reserve a space on the full moon tour (held on the Friday closest to full moon), send an email the preceding Monday to reserva_cs@ buenosaires.gov.ar, including your name, passport number, and a contact number.

MAP 1: Costanera Sur, tel. 011/4893-1853, 8am-7pm Tues.-Sun. summer, 8am-6pm Tues.-Sun. fall-spring; free

NEARBY:

- Admire the beautiful figures in the controversial Fuente Monumental de las Nereidas (page 77).
- Take in the massive Monumento al Tango, an homage to the beloved musical genre (page 77).
- Order a grilled meat sandwich from one of the many food stalls along the Costanera Sur (page 105).
- Visit the Colección de Arte Amalia Lacroze de Fortabat, with its eclectic range of art (page 154).
- Enjoy a chuckle at the Museo del Humor (page 155).
- Take to the water in a kayak or stand-up paddleboard with Puro Remo (page 172).

Fuente Monumental de las Nereidas

Dolores Mora de Hernández, a rebellious Argentine sculptor, carved this spectacular fountain, which depicts the mythical birth of Venus amid a sea of nude nymphs and men wrestling winged horses. The entire piece is carved from white Carrara marble originating from the north of Italy.

Mora designed and carved the fountain and statues in Rome. The pieces were sent to Buenos Aires in 1900, where they were due to be installed in the Plaza de Mayo. The fountain's arrival was greeted with outrage over the naked figures and erotic depictions, prompting its location to be changed to Parque Colón, a few blocks away. People continued to call for the fountain's removal; the government finally moved it to the Costanera Sur in 1918.

MAP 1: Av. Padre M. L. Migone and Av. Dr. Tristán A. Rodríguez

Monumento al Tango

It's rare for a type of music to be associated as strongly with one city as tango is with Buenos Aires. In 2007, a monument was erected to the musical genre in a ceremony that progressed through the city, settling in the center of a small plaza. Designed and built by Estela Trebino and her son, Alejandro Coria, this sculpture depicts a bandoneon, an instrument similar to an accordion that is integral to tango music. Officially named *Virulazo*, it is 3.5 meters tall and made from two tons of stainless steel. Various versions of the sculpture have since been installed around the world in cities where tango is prevalent, including Tarbes, France; Medellin, Colombia; and São Paulo, Brazil.

MAP 1: Azucena Villaflor and Av. de los Italianos

the Monumento al Tango

Puente de la Mujer

Inaugurated during the chaos of the 2001 economic crisis, this controversial US$6 million bridge was designed by Spanish architect Santiago Calatrava, who intended it to represent a couple dancing tango. It has become a striking architectural feature of Puerto Madero

that contrasts with the converted dock-land buildings and towering skyscrapers that surround it. Its wooden planks can only be crossed by pedestrians, bicycles, and skaters. Slicing across Dock 3 directly behind the Casa Rosada, the bridge swings open occasionally to allow ships to drift through. The bridge's name, Women's Bridge, refers to Puerto Madero's streets, which are named after renowned Latin American women.
MAP 1: Spanning Dique 3

Puente de la Mujer

San Telmo and La Boca   Map 2

✪ Caminito

One of the city's most photographed sights, Caminito is a quaint, single-block backstreet that winds between brightly painted buildings—an open-air museum of sorts. It began as a stream; after the water dried up, the route was used for rail lines, some of which still exist just past the north end of the street. As part of a locally run project involving Argentine artist Benito Quinquela Martín, the street and its surrounding buildings were eventually transformed into the Caminito. The pastel colors that Quinquela Martín used in the renovation of the buildings became popular across the neighborhood and now extend beyond the Caminito area.

The street is lined with painters who sell their work, most of which feature tango or scenes of Buenos Aires. Don't take unsolicited photos of the artists' colorful displays; the same goes for the tango dancers, who ask for a small "donation" to have their photo

taken, often inviting visitors to dress up and join the photo.

It only takes a few minutes to wander up and down the Caminito. At the southern end of the street, Magallanes branches off to the west and contains a concentration of shops, restaurants, and outdoor tango shows. It's not a good idea to wander much farther than a couple of blocks beyond Caminito (with the exception of the bank of the Riachuelo) as the neighborhood is known for petty thieves. Public bus lines 20, 29, 64, 86, and 152 connect the Centro to Caminito, as

artists selling paintings along the Caminito

do taxis. On foot, the best route is via Avenida Almirante Brown.

MAP 2: Magallanes and Dr. del Valle Iberlucea

NEARBY:

- Lounge around the colorful **Plazoleta Bomberos Voluntarios de la Boca** (page 83).
- Check out the modern art at **Fundación PROA** (page 157).

TOP EXPERIENCE

✪ El Zanjón de Granados

El Zanjón de Granados is unlike any other attraction in Buenos Aires. The building that houses this archaeological site was once buried a few meters deep in rubble until it was bought in 1986 to be converted into a cultural center. The renovation process uncovered astounding artifacts and a network of tunnels that burrowed under the surrounding neighborhood and encased the Tercero del Sur (originally named the Zanjón de Granados), a stream that ran from Plaza Constitución to the Río de la Plata.

After a long renovation process, the space was opened to the public, allowing visitors the chance to admire architecture and technology from the past five centuries, as far back as the origins of Buenos Aires. The beautifully presented archaeological site is dramatically lit. The systems used to direct the flow of the river are shown alongside the colonial patios and residences of the time, including the

Explore the city's origins at El Zanjón de Granados.

casa mínima, the narrowest house in Buenos Aires.

It is only possible to visit El Zanjón on a guided tour (noon, 2pm, and 3pm Mon.-Fri., every 20 minutes 11am-6pm Sun.), which are run in Spanish and English. It's best to attend the hour-long weekday tour (US$17), when there are fewer people. Sunday tours (US$13) leave every 20 minutes and last half an hour. This is generally regarded as the most important archaeological project in the city and is run as a private initiative.

MAP 2: Defensa 755, tel. 011/4361-3002, www.elzanjon.com.ar; tours noon, 2pm, and 3pm Mon.-Fri., every 20 minutes 11am-6pm Sun.; US$17 Mon.-Fri., US$13 Sun.

NEARBY:

- Try one of the unusual meat dishes at El Baqueano (page 107).
- Experience a traditional steak dinner at Desnivel (page 108).
- Enjoy a homemade burrito from the food stall run by Don Esculapio (page 110).
- Go for a snack or refreshment at the quaint La Poesía (page 110).
- Explore the city on two wheels by renting a bike from La Bicicleta Naranja (page 173).
- Browse the wide range of books for sale at La Libre (page 187).

✪ *Canto al Trabajo*

Rogelio Yrurtia, one of Argentina's most renowned sculptors, created *Canto al Trabajo* (*Ode to Labor*) in 1907. Depicting 14 figures in front of a giant stone, the sculpture, cast from bronze, represents work as a creative activity as opposed to a chore. One group of figures drags the stone, conveying their hatred of the work and their perception of it as punishment. The other group, led by a man with outstretched arms, conveys strength and unity. The boys in front stand with their arms stretched forward, a joyous expression on their faces.

The sculpture was originally placed

outside Yrurtia's workshop on Plaza Dorrego, but it was eventually moved to its current location, nearly hidden by trees in the middle of Avenida Paseo Colón. Cars pass especially quickly along this avenue, so be careful crossing over to the plaza that contains the sculpture. To see more of Yrurtia's work, visit the Museo Casa de Yrurtia in Belgrano.

MAP 2: Av. Paseo Colón 850

Canto al Trabajo, a sculpture by Rogelio Yrurtia

Iglesia de la Santísima Trinidad (Cathedral of the Most Holy Trinity)

This cathedral is a Russian Orthodox church facing Parque Lezama. Notable for its vivid blue onion domes decorated with gold stars—as well as the building's general lack of cohesion with its neighbors—the church is the seat of the South American diocese. Designed by Mihail Preobrazensky in St. Petersburg, it was adapted and constructed between 1898 and 1901 by Alejandro Christopherson, a Norwegian architect based in Buenos Aires. Materials and funds were provided by Russia, and the crosses on top of the domes point east, as does the altar within the church. Visitors are welcome, although opening hours are irregular.

MAP 2: Av. Brasil 315, tel. 011/4361-4274, www.iglesiarusa.org.ar

Pasaje de la Defensa

Built in the 1870s by the wealthy Ezeiza family, this home was abandoned when the Ezeizas fled the area after the yellow fever epidemic. Visitors can admire the original floor and structure of the building, which is divided into three patios, interconnected with passages and balconies. The layout is typical of traditional Buenos Aires houses, with the first patio surrounded by the dining room, living room, and study; the second patio enclosed by the bedrooms; and the final patio, where the house workers toiled away. The beautifully tiled second floor is reached via the original staircases, allowing visitors to wander around the columned balconies.

Over the years, the building has served as a school and an institute for deaf-mute children, and was at one point occupied by 36 families. In 1980, local architects renovated the building, converting it into a shopping gallery. Today it still houses some intriguing stores and draws large crowds, especially on the weekends.

MAP 2: Defensa 1179; 10am-6pm daily

Plaza Dorrego

This small but popular plaza takes up less than a quarter of a city block. Established in 1586 as a place for horse-drawn carriages to stop before crossing into the city center, in 1900 it was turned into a public square. The plaza's Sunday market, known as the

PAINTING THE TOWN RED
(AND WHITE, AND BLUE, AND GREEN)

mural by local artist collectives

An abiding feature of Buenos Aires is the vast murals that decorate the city's streets and buildings. Sides of buildings, shop shutters, and even house fronts are adorned with art of genuine quality. While the majority of locals loathe the city's incessant political graffiti, which involves whitewashing walls before daubing the names of candidates in two-meter-high letters, they generally approve of the murals. The government also acknowledges that street art should be encouraged, tacitly allowing amateurs to paint away while overtly funding many.

Unlike in many countries, in Argentina a person can paint their house however they like, without the need to obtain planning permission. This in part explains why the city is so laden with murals. Many hopeful artists approach homeowners to ask for permission to paint the facade, which is often given, especially if there is graffiti already there to be covered. They artist may or may not ask the homeowner to pay for the paints, although simply being given urban canvasses is usually enough recompense.

Certain areas, such as the **Mercado de las Pulgas,** have become hot spots for smaller artworks, but you are just as likely to come across a two-story painting in the middle of a residential zone. **Subte stations** are a traditional location to paint, and fine examples can be found on all the lines. A **tribute painting to Benito Quinquela Martín,** a renowned Argentine street artist who oversaw the renovation of Caminito in La Boca, was commissioned by the city government in 2013 and turned out to be the largest in the world painted by one person, at 2,000 square meters. It can be seen at the intersection of San Antonio and Lavadero in Barracas.

Travelers can take street art tours with groups who both paint and show visitors around. **Buenos Aires Street Art** (www.buenosairesstreetart.com) offers guided tours (about 3 hours; US$20) on Tuesday, Thursday, and Saturday afternoons. **Graffitimundo** (www.graffitimundo.com) offer a selection of tours (about 3 hours; US$25) on Wednesday to Monday afternoons, as well as a tour on bicycles (US$45). Both offer private tours as well as classes and workshops, with Graffitimundo also hosting a form of gallery-shop at **Hollywood in Cambodia** (page 194).

Feria de San Pedro Telmo, was established in 1970. It has since grown, extending beyond Plaza Dorrego's borders for hundreds of meters to the north, and is the place to shop for antiques, curios, and artisanal produce. In Plaza Dorrego, the focus is on antiques. Throughout the rest of the week, the plaza is a romantic and peaceful place to enjoy a drink at one of the surrounding restaurants.

MAP 2: Defensa and Humberto Primo

Plazoleta Bomberos Voluntarios de la Boca

This plaza, whose name translates to "Small Square for the Voluntary Firemen of La Boca," boasts large murals and an amphitheater. Located at the end of Caminito, it is a continuation of the open-air museum. The colors on the plaza's murals seem to explode in this open space, which fills with people lounging on the amphitheater steps.

The plaza was named in honor of the first firefighting organization of Argentina, which formed in La Boca in 1884. To this day, firefighters in Argentina are volunteers. Those stationed in La Boca have a special engine that is painted in the blue and yellow colors of the local *fútbol* team, Boca Juniors.

MAP 2: Garibaldi and General Gregorio Aráoz de Lamadrid

Puente Transbordador Nicolás Avellaneda

This iron bridge spans the Riachuelo and was designed to carry pedestrians, cars, carts, and trams. Constructed between 1908 and 1914, it was the first link connecting Buenos Aires to the city's outskirts on the opposite bank, and it was operational until 1960. Its platform, which measures 8 meters by 12 meters, would be raised and lowered to accommodate both vehicular and shipping traffic.

The bridge has been given protected status by both the city and the national government. Since 2012 there have been discussions on rehabilitating the structure and returning it to use. For now, it attracts sightseers for its architectural beauty and photogenic surroundings.

MAP 2: Av. Don Pedro de Mendoza and Av. Almirante Brown

Retiro   Map 3

Basílica del Santísimo Sacramento

This basilica was built at the behest of Mercedes Castellano de Anchorena, the owner of Palacio San Martín, who said that if she lived in a palace, so should God. Inspired by Angoulême Cathedral in France, the basilica combines an eclectic mix of styles to create a harmonious aesthetic. The towers are topped by rounded turrets, while the interior remains traditional, despite being laden with statues, carvings, and artwork. Inaugurated in 1916, the church is a popular location for high-society weddings. The organ at the head of the church, purchased in Paris by Castellano de Anchorena, is an impressive sight.

Legend has it that Castellano de Anchorena disapproved of her son's relationship with Corina Kavanagh, which she succeeded in putting an end to. Kavanagh arranged to have the Edificio Kavanagh erected directly between the basilica and Palacio de San Martín, thereby preventing Castellano de Anchorena from gazing at her pride and joy. Masses occur four times on weekdays (7am, 8am, 1pm, and 7pm), twice on Saturdays (8am and 7pm), and five times on Sunday (9am, 11am, noon, 7:30pm, and 9pm). MAP 3: San Martín 1039, tel. 011/4312-2314; 7am-8pm Mon.-Fri., 8am-8pm Sat., 9am-10pm Sun.

Edificio Kavanagh

This art deco skyscraper, which becomes smaller the higher it reaches, is characterized by its austerity and lack of ornamentation; it contrasts with the surrounding buildings, which adopt classic French styles. Upon completion in 1936, it was the only reinforced concrete skyscraper in the world, and also the tallest building in Latin America, reaching 120 meters. Considered a significant building by UNESCO and the American Institute of Architects, it was built to house wealthy residents and included the most modern technology, such as central air conditioning, Otis elevators, and sliding doors. The rigid exterior and austere appearance are rumored to have been a ploy to detract from the beauty of the neighboring Basílica del Santísimo

Edificio Kavanagh

Sacramento. The interior is not open to the public.
MAP 3: Florida 1065

Monumento a los Caídos en las Malvinas

This somber memorial, designed by Andrés Morán, is dedicated to those who were killed in the war against Britain in 1982, when the Argentine military dictatorship occupied the Islas de Malvinas (also known as the Falkland Islands). The memorial consists of 25 marble plaques with the names of the 649 Argentine victims of the war (with no mention of rank, to ensure that they all remain equal). A flag is raised daily at 8am, then lowered again at 6pm, while an eternal flame burns above a map of the islands.
MAP 3: North side of Plaza San Martín

Palacio de San Martín

Designed by Alejandro Christophersen in 1905, this Beaux-Arts palace was commissioned by Mercedes Castellano de Anchorena, a member of one of Argentina's most powerful families. The palace consists of three separate mansions, which Castellano de Anchorena built to share with her three sons, connected by a patio and sharing one facade. The incredible detail on the exterior along with the elegant interior is typical of the high quality construction of this era in Buenos Aires.

In 1936, the national government purchased the property and converted it into the foreign ministry, although this department later moved to a separate building in 1993. The building remains the foreign ministry's ceremonial base; official functions are regularly held here. The palace contains works of art by many 19th-century

Latin American painters, such as Antonio Berni and Lino Spilimbergo, as well as a piece of the Berlin Wall (other segments are dotted around the city). When it is not being used for diplomatic purposes, free guided tours (3pm Tues. and Thurs.) are offered in English. Otherwise the building is not open to the public.

MAP 3: Arenales 761, tel. 011/4819-7297; tours 3pm Tues. and Thurs.; free

Palacio Paz

Once home to the family of José Camilo Paz, the founder of *La Prensa* newspaper, this palace was designed by French architects. It's the clearest example of French influence in Buenos Aires, imitating the Louvre and Chantilly Palace. With 140 bedrooms and 40 baths, the property required a staff of 80 to clean and maintain it. The interior is notable for its ornate doorways, fireplaces, and windows.

In 1938 the palace was purchased by Círculo Militar, a military club, who have kept it mainly for their own use to this day. It is also the location of Argentina's most important military museum, the Museo de Armas de la Nación, which houses artifacts from the last 1,000 years of warfare.

Guided tours in English (3pm Thurs.) and Spanish (3pm Tues., 11am and 3pm Wed.-Fri., 11am Sat.) offer visitors the only way to explore the building.

MAP 3: Av. Santa Fe 750, tel. 011/4311-1071, www.palaciopaz.com.ar; English tours 3pm Thurs., Spanish tours 3pm Tues., 11am and 3pm Wed.-Fri., 11am Sat.; US$5

Torre Monumental

Originally named Torre de los Ingleses (Tower of the English), this 75-meter structure was a gift from the British to honor the centenary of the May 1810 revolution that led to Argentina's independence. Built with materials shipped over from England, the tower is adorned with symbols of the British Empire and contains bells imitating those in Westminster Abbey, which play every hour. The 1984 Malvinas conflict spurred vandalism to the tower, including an attempt to blow it up with dynamite; it was eventually renamed Torre Monumental to soothe public angst. Although the tower consists of eight floors, only the ground floor is open to the public. Here, a small museum contains a few interesting photos from throughout the neighborhood's history.

MAP 3: Plaza Fuerza Aérea Argentina, tel. 011/4311-0186; noon-6pm Mon.-Fri.; free

Torre Monumental

Totem Canadiense

When the city government decided to name a square Plaza Canadá in 1961, the delighted Canadian ambassador, Richard Plant Bower, arranged for a traditional totem pole to be erected in its center. Standing 20 meters tall and weighing four tons, the totem was carved by indigenous people in

Vancouver before being installed in Plaza Canadá in 1964. The totem deteriorated badly and was taken down in 2008 and, during repair attempts, cut into pieces. Canada donated another totem pole in 2012, this one carved by the son of the original pole's creator. At a more modest 12.9 meters, the second pole is brightly colored and a welcome contrast to the surrounding chaos of Retiro.

MAP 3: Plaza Canadá

Recoleta   Map 4

✪ Cementerio de la Recoleta

Standing on the edge of Recoleta's sprawling parks and plazas, this cemetery houses the tombs of Argentina's wealthy elite. There are no simple gravestones in this small village of the dead; instead, its residents display their prestige with ornate mausoleums. There's a high cost associated with maintaining these extravagant tombs, resulting in many dilapidated vaults. The broken doors and dusty coffins within can be unsettling, but this is somewhat lightened by the cats that live here, sunning themselves on the mausoleums' roofs. Like the rest of Buenos Aires, the Cementerio de la Recoleta has tree-lined avenues with smaller streets and passages leading off them—it's easy to get lost here.

The resting places of many former presidents can be found here, alongside renowned writers, Nobel Prize winners, and important military figures. Most visitors, however, head straight for the tomb of Eva Perón.

Burial ceremonies occur regularly, and visitors are asked to steer clear of such gatherings. Maps are available at the entrance, which is also the departure point for free guided tours (11am Tues.-Fri., 11am and 3pm Sat.-Sun.).

At the time of writing, tours are only offered in Spanish, but plans are afoot to add English tours. Entry has always been free, but authorities are attempting to implement a fee of around US$6 to cover maintenance costs.

MAP 4: Junín 1760, tel. 011/4803-1594; 7am-5:45pm daily; free

NEARBY:

- Take a peek at the surprisingly colorful interior of the Iglesia de Nuestra Señora de Pilar (page 89).
- Sip a coffee in the pretty patio at La Biela (page 115).
- Check out one of the many exhibitions at the sprawling Centro Cultural de Recoleta (page 160).
- Take in a movie at the underground Village Recoleta (page 161).
- If it's the weekend, stop by the bustling Feria Plaza Francia (page 193).

Cementerio de la Recoleta

✪ Museo Nacional de Bellas Artes

The national fine arts museum has been in its current location, a former drainage pumping station, since 1933. Home to over 12,000 pieces of art, it is the largest public collection in Latin America, noted especially for its 19th-century European art as well as the most valuable collection of Argentine pieces in the world. Two dozen exhibition halls are spread out across the ground floor and include the work of diverse European artists such as Rodin, El Greco, Rembrandt, Manet, and Van Gogh alongside local greats such as Berni, de la Carcóva, and Pueyrredón. The influence of colonial culture on Argentina can be seen in many of the pieces, including large portraits of former dictator Juan Manuel de Rosas and stirring images of gauchos. The set of paintings by Cándido López depicting battles in meticulous detail should not be missed.

The second floor is home to a stunning collection of 20th-century Argentine art in 10 exhibition halls. A particular highlight is Ernesto de la Carcóva's emotive *Sin Pan y Sin Trabajo* (*Without Bread and Without Work*), a perspective of the world's plight at the end of the 19th century. A collection of over 150,000 publications can be found in the second-floor library that overlooks a sculpture garden.

The interesting guided tour (in English, 1 hour, 1pm Tues.-Wed. and Fri.; free) explains the history of many of the works and provides great context for visitors to browse through the museum afterward. The museum also hosts tours in Spanish (including a monthly tour for blind and partially sighted visitors) and a diverse selection of cultural activities, as well as activities and tours for children. Behind the museum is Mercedes Haus (Av. Figueroa Alcorta 2270, 8am-2am

87

daily), a novel café and restaurant that offers a view of the sculpture garden.
MAP 4: Av. del Libertador 1473, tel. 011/5288-9900, www.bellasartes.gob.ar; 11am-8pm Tues.-Fri., 10am-8pm Sat.-Sun.; free

NEARBY:

- Watch the blossoming metal petals of the *Floralis Genérica* (page 89).
- Check out one of the many exhibitions or cultural events at the Palais de Glace (page 160).
- Lounge on the wide-open grassy spaces of Plaza Rubén Darío (page 175).
- Purchase trendy household items from Buenos Aires Design (page 193).

✪ Biblioteca Nacional

The national library stands on the grounds of the former presidential palace, which was demolished soon after the death of Juan Domingo Perón. Housing the largest library collection in Argentina, the building took over 20 years to build and is elevated by vast columns, giving it the appearance of hovering over the surrounding parks. The main book depository is underground, which reduced the weight of the upper floors, allowing the building to reach such an altitude. The brutalist structure contrasts with its surroundings and draws as much scorn as it does praise for its exposed concrete design.

The reading room on the fifth floor provides panoramic views of the northern section of Recoleta and the Río de la Plata. (Get permission to take photos at the entrance.) The sixth floor offers a relaxed reading room, where visitors are even allowed to eat and drink, but silence is still expected. Access to the catalogue is available to the public, but the procedure to obtain books is complicated (get instructions at the fifth floor's information desk). During periods of heavy study for students, the library is packed.

Entry to the library is free, but requires presenting identification, such as a passport. Free guided tours (4pm Mon. and Thurs.) are offered in English, departing from the entrance hall.
MAP 4: Agüero 2502, tel. 011/4808-6000, www.bn.gov.ar; 7am-midnight Mon.-Fri., noon-7pm Sat.-Sun.; free

Facultad de Ingeniería

This building is the only major non-religious neo-Gothic structure in the city. Designed by Arturo Prins in 1909, construction began in 1912 but was beset by an interminable series of setbacks that led to the building never being completed. The main part of the unfinished work was the towers and roof; the building as it stands is a stunning piece of architecture and is now occupied by the Universidad de Buenos Aires's engineering faculty. Imposing staircases, stained-glass windows, and looming arches can be found among exposed girders and modern renovations that create a unique mixture of styles. An eclectic display of items from the various schools of engineering, including transportation, construction, and industry, can be viewed behind the main staircase, while a Foucault pendulum swings from the towering roof to demonstrate the Earth's rotation. Visitors are free to explore the building (provided they don't interrupt lectures) and admire architecture that is normally reserved for churches.

MAP 4: Av. Las Heras 2214, tel. 011/4514-3000; 7am-11pm Mon.-Fri.; free

The *Floralis Genérica* opens its petals to the sun.

Floralis Genérica

One of the most iconic monuments in Buenos Aires, this 23-meter sculpture of a flower sits in the Plaza de las Naciones Unidas. Designed by Argentine architect Eduardo Catalano in 2002, the steel and aluminum structure was given to the city as a gift. It was originally designed to close its petals at night and open them again in the morning, but mechanical problems left it permanently open. Due to structural damage, the flower began to wilt, with some petals threatening to drop off. All kinds of remedies and treatments were used to resurrect the dying sculpture. Today the structure is functioning as intended. A large pool surrounds the base.

MAP 4: Av. Figueroa Alcorta 2351

Iglesia de Nuestra Señora de Pilar

This Jesuit-built church, whose construction was completed in 1732, was home to Franciscan Recollects until they were ousted in 1821 by the government. Despite being closed for years, the grounds were later taken over for the creation of the Cementerio de la Recoleta and the Centro Cultural de Recoleta. The friars live on in the neighborhood to this day. Despite the church's humble size and unobtrusive exterior, the inside is surprisingly decorative and colorful. An ornate, baroque reredos reaches up to the ceiling behind the altar, which is itself an item of beauty (an Inca design from Peru, elegantly produced from silver). The walls are decorated with tiles brought over from northern France.

There are masses at 8am, 11am, and 7:30pm Monday to Friday; 8:30am, 11am, and 7pm Saturday; and 8:30am, 10am, 11am, noon, 7pm, 8pm, and 9pm Sunday.

MAP 4: Junín 1904, tel. 011/4806-2209

Map 5

SIGHTS

PALERMO

✪ Museo de Arte Latinoamericano de Buenos Aires (MALBA)

MALBA is perhaps the most popular and famous museum in the city. Opened in 2001, the building was designed to complement the works it contains, of which there are over 200 examples from across the 20th century. Unlike the national fine arts museum a few hundred meters up the road, MALBA does not receive donations of art and so has a more limited permanent collection. Of particular note are the pieces by Antonio Berni, one of Argentina's most revered artists from the last century. His development can be followed from his early days painting murals of the Nuevo Realismo movement—including the famed *Manifestación* (*Manifestation*) and *Desocupados* (*Unemployed*)—through a period of political paintings, terminating in the collages of Juanito Laguna. Other Argentine artists, including Xul Solar, can be found alongside continental greats such as Chilean Roberto Matta and Mexicans Frida Kahlo and Diego Rivera.

As impressive as the permanent collection is, locals are drawn (often in droves that form queues stretching for hundreds of meters) by the temporary exhibitions that fill the top floors. Rotating on a monthly basis, the exhibits cast a wider net, with artists from North America and Europe attracting the greatest numbers.

The gallery spaces all lead off from an airy hall that basks in natural light thanks to its glass walls and ceilings. A cinema on the ground floor shows independent films and hosts educational and cultural events. A decent (yet pricey) café offers a patio on which to eat and drink. Guided tours (included in admission) are offered for the permanent collection (4pm Wed. and Sat.) and for the temporary exhibitions (5pm Thurs.-Fri. and Sun.).

MAP 5: Av. Figueroa Alcorta 3415, tel. 011/4808-6500, www.malba.org.ar; noon-9pm Wed., noon-8pm Thurs.-Mon.; US$6, Wed. US$3

NEARBY:

- Stroll through the exquisite Jardín Japonés, then stop for a bite of sushi at the garden's restaurant of the same name (pages 91 and 119).
- Bask in the smells of fresh-baked bread and pastries at Le Pain Quotidien (page 121).
- Learn about Argentina's gaucho tradition at Museo de Arte Popular José Hernandez (page 159).
- Browse through high-end shops at Casa Cavia (page 197).

Centro Cultural Islámico Rey Fahd

When former President Carlos Menem made an official visit to Saudi Arabia in the 1990s, nobody expected him to return to Argentina and donate over 30,000 square meters of public land to King Fahd for the building of what would become South America's largest mosque. With the hippodrome horse racing track on one side and a bulky shopping mall on the other, the oddly located Centro Cultural Islámico is evidence of the 700,000 Muslims who reside in Argentina.

With an elegant and modern design, the vast property offers solitude, with only a few hundred worshippers attending prayers, despite a capacity of 1,400. The rest of the time, few people can be seen in the manicured gardens or courtyards. Free guided tours (in Spanish, noon Tues., Thurs., and Sat.) are available, although they're less interesting than the building itself. Visitors, particularly women, should take care to dress appropriately.

MAP 5: Av. Bullrich 55, tel. 011/4899-1144, www.ccislamicoreyfahd.org.ar

Jardín Botánico

These botanical gardens were designed by French landscaper Charles Thays, who lived in the house that sits in the middle of the gardens until they were opened to the public in 1898. Notable for its impressive collection of trees, the Jardín Botánico offers plenty of shade. The park can be divided into three main styles: the Roman garden, based on Pliny the Younger's garden; the French garden, with symmetrical designs that date from the 17th and 18th centuries; and the Oriental Garden, including plants from diverse regions of the world. Five ornamental greenhouses—one of which is in art nouveau style, thought to be the only version of its kind in the world—contain thousands of plants. There is also a gardening school and a library available to visitors, as well as a small museum that holds delightful paintings of early Buenos Aires. Cats roam freely among the greenery and sculptures. Guided tours (in Spanish, 10:30am and 3pm Sat.-Sun.) are given, with a tour of the ornamental greenhouse offered at 4:30pm.

MAP 5: Av. Santa Fe 3951, tel. 011/4831-4527; 8am-8pm daily summer, 9am-6pm daily winter; free

a statue of Mercury in the Jardín Botánico

Jardín Japonés

Inaugurated in 1967 by then-Crown Prince Akihito and Princess Michiko, the Japanese Gardens are nestled behind hedges in the woods of Palermo. They are meticulously cared for and are thought to be the largest of their kind outside Japan. The park, set around a small carp-filled lake and spanned by a number of traditional bridges, is full of Japanese flora, as well as some species particular to Argentina. Towers, sculptures, temples, a tea house, and a monument to the Japanese immigrant population are also present.

A building housing a restaurant

and reading room overlooks the lake. The park is particularly attractive when illuminated at night, although this can only be enjoyed from the restaurant, as the gardens themselves are not open into the evening. A nursery offers a reasonably priced selection of Japanese plants and seeds; there is also a gift shop. Free guided tours (hours vary; email visitas@jardinjapones.org.ar to make a reservation) are offered to visitors on the weekend.

MAP 5: Av. Casares 3401, tel. 011/4804-9141, www.jardinjapones.org.ar; 10am-6pm daily; US$5

festivities at the Jardín Japonés

Rosedal

Within the Parque Tres de Febrero is a haven of nearly 20,000 roses. In 2014, the Rosedal celebrated its centenary by receiving the Garden of Excellence award, the highest international recognition for rose gardens. Surrounded on three sides by a lake, the Rosedal is situated in grounds that once belonged to Juan Manuel de Rosas, a dictator from the first half of the 19th century. The garden also includes an amphitheater, pergolas, an Andalusian patio, a poet's garden containing busts of Argentine and international poets and writers, and a Greek bridge. October through April is the best time to visit, when the explosion of color is overwhelming, although there are species in bloom throughout the year.

MAP 5: Parque Tres de Febrero, main entrance at intersection of Av. Pedro Montt and Av. Iraola; 8am-8pm Tues.-Sun. summer, 9am-6pm Tues.-Sun. winter; free

Almagro

Map 6

Basilica de San Carlos y María Auxiliadora

One of the most intriguing churches in Buenos Aires sits on a humble backstreet in Almagro. Built by the Roman Catholic Salesians of Don Busco between 1901 and 1910, it became such an icon that it was included in the neighborhood's official emblem. An eclectic mix of architectural styles includes Romanesque arches and floor, Byzantine ornamentation, a Baroque interior, and Gothic columns and windows. The crypt contains 16 altars, while the main hall is incredibly ornate and seems to drip gold. The upper level contains a *camarín* (chapel) for María Auxiliadora (who also appears in a five-meter illuminated image in the main cupola) that is a point of pilgrimage for many Catholics. One of the finest organs in Buenos Aires, designed by Carlo Vegezzi Bossi, can be viewed in the church, where Pope Francis was baptized in 1936. Mass is held at 8am and

7:30pm Monday-Friday, 8am and 7pm Saturday, and 8am, noon, and 7:30pm Sunday.

MAP 6: Av. Hipólito Yrigoyen 4000, tel. 011/4981-7752

Monumento a Osvaldo Pugliese

Although statues and tributes abound in Buenos Aires for Carlos Gardel, the most internationally known star of tango, there are far fewer for the more humble exponents of the genre. Osvaldo Pugliese was a pianist and composer, whose music heralded the introduction of large-scale orchestras to tango. His outspoken communist beliefs won him no favors with the government of the time, and Juan Domingo Perón is rumored to have had him locked in a sinking boat before being saved as a form of threat. He was the first tango musician to perform in the Teatro Colón, a monumental achievement that he accomplished in 1985 at the age of 80.

This monument, which depicts Pugliese playing the piano with his orchestra, was sculpted by Paula Franzi and inaugurated on what would have been the maestro's 100th birthday, in 2005. Two years later the figure of Pugliese was stolen, while the rest of the figures were vandalized, but the monument was restored to its original state.

MAP 6: Av. Corrientes 5190

Museo Casa Carlos Gardel

This museum is a tribute to tango's most renowned and popular singer, Carlos Gardel. Housed in his mother's former residence, the small museum contains a wealth of information about the life of the artist and the progression of his career, including photos, articles, and musical instruments, with each room devoted to different themes. Concerts are held regularly, while tango classes are also sometimes given.

MAP 6: Jean Jaurés 735, tel. 011/4964-2015; 11am-6pm Mon. and Wed.-Fri., 10am-7pm Sat.-Sun.; US$0.50

Balvanera   Map 6

Casa de los Lirios (House of Lilies)

This urban house was designed by Rodríguez Ortega, a great admirer of Antoni Gaudí's structures in Barcelona. It stands out from neighboring buildings due to its ornate botany-themed facade, upon which carved lilies and trees wind their way around the brickwork and balconies. The cornice is decorated with the face of an old man, which many associate with the Greek god Poseidon, whose beard and hair stretches across the width of the building. It has received protected status from the city government, which explains why it stands alone among a dreary collection of more modern structures. The house is not open to the public.

MAP 6: Av. Rivadavia 2031

Confitería del Molino

This legendary café, opened in 1916, is located on a corner facing the Palacio del Congreso. Italian architect

Francisco Gianotti designed the iconic turret that is adorned with windmill sails and stained-glass windows. Materials were imported from Italy for the construction. The building was one of the tallest in the city at the time, quickly becoming a favorite meeting point for politicians, businessmen, and locals. It closed in 1997 and fell into disrepair, with unregistered tenants occupying the building. The government expropriated the building in 2014 and the *confitería* (Argentine term for a café) was scheduled to reopen on July 9, 2016, the bicentenary celebration of Argentine independence. The opening was delayed, with the expected date moving out a year. The ground floor and basement will return to their original function and serve as a café and pastry shop, with the upper floors holding a museum that tells the story of the iconic building's history.

MAP 6: Av. Rivadavia 1801

Iglesia de Nuestra Señora de Balvanera

This church is one of the city's most visited, revered by Catholics because of its status as the principal sanctuary of Saint Expeditus (San Expedito in Spanish). Tens of thousands of followers converge on the church on April 19, his saint's day, queuing for hours for the opportunity to pray in front of his image and ask for help. The saint is known for solving urgent problems, protecting young people, healing the sick, and mediating disputes.

The church itself was inaugurated in 1842 by the dictatorial governor of Buenos Aires, Juan Manuel de Rosas, although Franciscan monks had been living on the territory since the late 1700s. The church's name was originally Nuestra Señora de Valvanera,

but colloquial Argentine Spanish converted this to Balvanera. The importance of the church is evidenced by the fact that the neighborhood later adopted Balvanera as its name.

Mass is held at 8am, 12:30pm, and 7:30pm Monday-Friday; 8am, 6pm, and 7:30pm Saturday; and 9am, 10:30am, noon, 6:30pm, and 8pm Sunday. Special heavily attended masses for San Expedito are held at 8am, 10:30am, noon, 3pm, 5pm, 7:30pm, and 9pm on the 19th of every month.

MAP 6: Bartolomé Mitre 2411, tel. 011/4951-2218; 7:30am-8pm Mon.-Sat., 8:30am-9pm Sun.

Palacio de las Aguas Corrientes

Buenos Aires began growing at a ferocious rate in the second half of the 19th century, leading to overcrowding and insufficient public services. Faced by outbreaks of cholera and typhoid in the 1860s and yellow fever in 1871, the authorities installed underground pipes and pumping stations. As part of this process, the Palacio de las Aguas Corrientes was constructed to house 12 massive tanks that hold 72 million liters of water.

As was customary at the time for public buildings, the exterior of this pumping station was designed to look beautiful despite the building's mundane function and mechanical interior. The result was one of the most outstanding buildings in the city. With over 300,000 multicolored terracotta tiles imported from Europe, the French Renaissance palace also boasts a tin mansard roof with two caryatids.

Ownership of the building changed as the water service was nationalized, then reprivatized before once again being returned to State control. The building has been declared a

the Palacio de las Aguas Corrientes, perhaps the most attractive pumping station in the world

National Historic Monument; it now houses water company offices and a small museum, while the 135,000-ton tanks contain city archives, not water. The museum offers an intriguing glimpse into 19th-century plumbing techniques and equipment, as well as excellent guided tours in Spanish. The main entrance is on Avenida Córdoba.

MAP 6: Riobamba 750, tel. 011/6319-1104; 9am-1pm Mon.-Fri.; free

Palacio del Congreso

One of the last public buildings constructed before the introduction of French architectural styles to the city, the Palacio del Congreso, which houses Argentina's national legislature, was designed in 1898 by Italian architect Vittorio Meano, who was murdered before construction was completed. This imposing building, exaggerated by the large open plaza in front of it, is made largely of white marble.

Despite being used by the Senate since 1906, the intricate carvings and decorations were not finished for another 40 years. The green cupola, standing 85 meters tall and 65 meters above the Blue Room below it, is the largest in Buenos Aires and was the crowning achievement of Meano's

Palacio del Congreso

design. The interior is elaborately furnished, with sculptures, wood finish, and frescoes lining the hallways and chambers.

Free guided tours of the upper house are offered in Spanish (12:30pm Mon.-Tues. and Thurs.-Fri.) and in Spanish and English (5pm Mon.-Tues. and Thurs.-Fri.) and provide the only way for the general public to explore the interior of the building. Enter via the entrance at Avenida Hipólito Yrigoyen 1849.

MAP 6: Av. Rivadavia and Av. Callao; tours 12:30pm and 5pm Mon.-Tues. and Thurs.-Fri. (Spanish), 5pm Mon.-Tues. and Thurs.-Fri. (English); free

✪ Espacio para la Memoria— Escuela de Mecánica de la Armada (ESMA)

This former military compound on the northern limits of the city was the most notorious torture center used by the military dictatorship during 1976-1983. Around 5,000 people were held here and tortured before the majority of them were killed, either by shooting squad or by being thrown out of planes over the Río de la Plata and the Atlantic Ocean. Only 150 survived.

Originally a naval training base, ESMA is a sprawling woodland with dozens of buildings, most of which are standard Argentine military constructions. It was turned into a detention center on the day of the military coup d'état in 1976 and quickly descended into more nefarious activities. The national government tried to raze it in 1999, but protests from human rights organizations and the public prevented this. Eventually it was opened to the public as a museum, which aims to educate its visitors about the facility's disturbing past.

The harrowing, three-hour guided tours (Tues.-Sun.; free) are excellent, although they can be emotionally draining. Tours visit the buildings where prisoners were interned and tortured, while revealing how the military carried out their clandestine activities. Tours must be reserved beforehand, either by telephone (011/4704-7538) or email (visitasguiadas@espaciomemoria.ar). Various museums are located within the grounds, as is a cultural center that holds regular events.

Visitors should expect to spend half a day here to take in the full scope of everything on offer.

MAP 7: Av. del Libertador 8151, tel. 011/4702-9920, www.espaciomemoria.ar; general hours 9am-5pm Mon.-Sun., individual museum and center hours vary; free

Cementerio de Chacarita

One of the largest necropolises in the world, this cemetery was built to accommodate the sudden influx of bodies as a result of the cholera and yellow fever epidemics of the 1870s. When the traditional city cemetery for the wealthy (Cementerio de la Recoleta) started refusing to accept cadavers that had perished as a result of these plagues, the government was forced to claim land in the Chacarita neighborhood to start the unpleasant task of burning the disease-ridden corpses.

The record number of bodies cremated on a single day was 564. The resulting smell and poor hygiene appalled the surrounding neighbors and led to a temporary closure.

Upon passing through the grand entrance, exaggerated mausoleums abound, housing the remains of many famous writers, composers, actors, and public figures. The most visited grave is that of Carlos Gardel, whose tomb is plastered with small plaques. Fans traditionally leave lit cigarettes in the tango singer's hand. Juan Domingo Perón was also buried here, but his remains were moved to a different location in 2006. A section on the west side, managed independently and entered by separate gateways, houses the British and German cemeteries, which were created to house the bodies of the great number of English and German people that lived in Argentina in the 19th century.

MAP 7: Guzmán 680, tel. 011/4553-9338, www.cementeriochacarita.com.ar; 7am-6pm daily; free

Parque de la Memoria

Located on the Costanera Norte, a mere 300 meters from a military airport from which "death flights" took off during the military dictatorship (with the goal of dropping disappeared people into the open water), the Parque de la Memoria is a contemplative memorial to the victims of the regime. The open layout of the park and view out over the water can feel emotionally overwhelming, as can the many sculptures and art displays. The park includes 30,000 plaques naming those who died in the Dirty War, although the engraving of these is a work in progress.

Guided tours (11am and 4pm Sat.-Sun.; free) are available in Spanish or English, offering a chance to learn more about the disappearance of people during the dictatorship as well as the art on display.

MAP 7: Av. Costanera Norte Rafael Obligado 6745, tel. 011/4787-0999, www.parquedelamemoria.org.ar; 10am-6pm Mon.-Fri., 10am-7pm Sat.-Sun.; free

RESTAURANTS

Argentine cuisine is a blend of all the different cultures that have reached the

Grilled meats are a large part of the city's cuisine.

country's shores over the centuries, and this is most apparent in Buenos Aires. The city and the country are also unequivocally tied to beef. Indeed, the most renowned Argentine dish is the *asado,* a version of barbecue in which meat, usually beef, is cooked slowly over coals. The atmosphere is hard to recreate in a restaurant setting, so if you're invited to an *asado* while in Buenos Aires, accept the offer.

Dishes that can be considered indigenous or authentically Argentine, such as tamales or *locro* (hearty stew), can be hard to find in Buenos Aires. Instead, the city has developed an eclectic fusion of cuisine from its many immigrants over the years, all of whom blended their native recipes with the others around them, creating a *porteño* cuisine that is hard to define.

Traditional restaurants in Buenos Aires, known as *bodegones,* serve grilled beef and pasta in rustic, unpretentious environments. *Parrillas* are basically steak houses, which can range from a counter in front of a grill to a huge salon with servers lofting trays laden with meat.

A distinct type of café in the city, *bares notables* (bars of note) have been granted special status by the government to acknowledge historical or architectural importance.

While Palermo is generally regarded as the restaurant mecca, it tends to be pricier and less traditional. Centro, San Telmo, La Boca, and Recoleta offer a

HIGHLIGHTS

✪ **MOST TRADITIONAL STAND-UP PIZZA JOINT:** Drop by for a quick slice or sit down for a meal at **Güerrin,** where you'll find an award-winning quantity of cheese on the pizzas (page 101).

✪ **BEST BEEF:** It's widely accepted that **Cabaña Las Lilas** is a cut above the rest of the city's *parrillas* (page 105).

✪ **BEST PLACE TO EAT LIKE A LOCAL:** Join *porteños* in enjoying a meat sandwich from the **Costanera Sur food stalls** (page 105).

✪ **BEST IMITATION OF A GERMAN BEER HALL:** Order one of the 70-plus beers at **Untertürkheim** to accompany the delicious sausage and sauerkraut (page 109).

✪ **BEST SPLURGE:** Splash out for a meal at **Gran Bar Danzón,** and don't forget to choose a glass of wine from their first-class list (page 111).

✪ **FINEST FRENCH CUISINE:** Spend an evening at **La Bourgogne** to experience the best of France in Buenos Aires (page 114).

✪ **MOST INTENSE ICE CREAM:** Rarely are chocolate and ice cream combined to such levels of excellence and richness as the offerings from **Rapa Nui** (page 115).

✪ **BEST OUTDOOR RESTAURANT:** The terrace at **Museo Evita** offers sun, shade, plants, and sumptuous food—a rare combination in Buenos Aires (page 115).

✪ **BEST REGIONAL FOOD:** Wholesome dishes that are more typical in other regions of the country are offered at **1810** in an ambience reminiscent of Argentina's colonial past (page 116).

✪ **BEST-VALUE *PARRILLA*:** Expect a long wait at **Las Cabras,** as the portions and prices are the best in the city (page 117).

✪ **BEST SEAFOOD WITH A VIEW:** An intriguing structure poised halfway down a lengthy wooden pier, **El Muelle** offers a uniquely panoramic view of the Río de la Plata while serving up the catch of the day (page 120).

✪ **BEST VEGETARIAN FOOD:** With innovative and often eccentric dishes, **Artemisia** uses plants to create an organic atmosphere that goes beyond their food (page 121).

PRICE KEY

$	Entrées less than US$10
$ $	Entrées US$10-20
$ $ $	Entrées more than US$20

Maté is the national drink.

wide variety of cuisines, while Puerto Madero's restaurants are at the top of the price spectrum. Balvanera and Almagro are generally the cheapest areas to eat, offering authentic and simple options.

MEALS

It can be hard to find a decent *desayuno* (breakfast) in Buenos Aires, where the continental style prevails. *Medialunas* (similar to croissants) and *facturas* (pastries) are the most common option. *Pan tostado* (toast) is also common, sometimes with ham and cheese.

Often considered the main meal of the day, *almuerzo* (lunch) kicks off around 1pm or 2pm. Many restaurants offer a midday fixed menu, which can involve anything from a starter, main course, dessert, and drinks to just the *plato del día* (dish of the day).

A brief *merienda* (afternoon snack) is sometimes taken toward the end of the afternoon. This usually consists of maté served with *facturas* (pastries) or light sandwiches.

Argentines tend to have *cena* (dinner) late, from 9pm onward; eating after 11pm is not unusual. Restaurants tend to have two rushes in the evening, the first building up to 9pm and then a second one around 10:30pm. Turning up to a popular eatery during these hours will often lead to a lengthy wait, sometimes up to a couple of hours.

RESERVATIONS

Porteños are obsessed with eating out, and despite sharply increasing prices over recent years, many restaurants have queues in the evenings, even on weekdays. Some places are even completely booked and turn away walk-ins. While this is not as widespread at midday, restaurants can fill up then as well.

The city's restaurants are fairly evenly split when it comes to their reservation policy. Some restaurants do not take reservations on the same day, while others don't accept bookings at all. Some will say that reservations can only be made on the day; if this is the case, call in the morning before reservation slots are fully taken. If you're hoping to eat at a particular place, call or email two or three days in advance to inquire about their reservation policy.

DIETARY RESTRICTIONS

Despite the Argentine obsession with meat, there is a decent selection of vegetarian, vegan, organic, and macrobiotic restaurants, although their prices tend to be high. Organic food is increasingly common and easy to find, especially in *dietéticas* (health food stores) or specialty markets and restaurants.

CENTRO

PORTEÑO
Tomo 1 $$$

A sophisticated and stylish restaurant in the Panamericano Hotel, Tomo 1 was founded by the family of its head chef, Federico Fialayre, who likes to come out and converse with diners. His specialty is the lamb gigot, one of the best lamb dishes around. Prices may dissuade many; indeed, locals consider it an option for special occasions, but the food is exquisite.

MAP 1: Carlos Pellegrini 521, tel. 011/4326-6698, www.tomo1.com.ar; noon-3pm and 7:30pm-midnight Mon.-Fri., 7:30pm-midnight Sat.

gourmet desserts at Tomo 1

PERUVIAN
Chan Chan $$

Offering what is easily some of the best Peruvian food in the city, Chan Chan is located on a run-down street a few blocks from Congreso. The brightly colored tiling goes well with the dishes expertly prepared by chef Angel Ubillus García, who makes an excellent ceviche. As with many quality Peruvian restaurants, Chan Chan requires some patience, but

the pisco sours go down easily in the meantime.

MAP 1: Hipólito Yrigoyen 1390, tel. 011/4382-8492; noon-4pm and 8pm-midnight daily

ITALIAN AND PIZZA
✪ Güerrin $

Güerrin makes use of so much cheese each day that they produce their own mozzarella. Situated in the heart of the theater district, this crowded pizzeria is a fine example of the traditional way of eating pizza in Buenos Aires: buying by the slice and eating standing at the counter (free ice water is available). The *muzzarella* is a simple specialty here, but the *verdura con salsa blanca* (vegetables with white sauce) is a delightful surprise.

MAP 1: Av. Corrientes 1368, tel. 011/4371-8184, www.pizzeriaguerrin.com; 11am-late daily

FRENCH
Brasserie Petanque $$

Closer in feeling to nearby San Telmo than the Centro, sophisticated Brasserie Petanque brings the French concept of a brasserie to Buenos Aires, meaning that noise and heat are to be

Brasserie Petanque

expected. A fairly simple yet traditional French menu is served. *Conejo a la mostaza de dijón* (rabbit and Dijon mustard) is an excellent choice, as are the *caracoles* (snails), for those who dare.

MAP 1: Defensa 596, tel. 011/4342-7930, www.brasseriepetanque.com;
12:30pm-3:30pm and 8pm-midnight Tues.-Sun.

GERMAN
Zirkel $$$

Although the food in Zirkel is perhaps overpriced and unreliable in quality, the view is simply unbeatable. Set on the 21st floor of a tower in the center of town, there are no other places that the public can enjoy such a panoramic view of Buenos Aires. The menu is relatively uninspired, despite the influence of the restaurant being part of the city's German club, and the starters and desserts generally outshine the mains.

MAP 1: Av. Corrientes 327, 21st fl.,
tel. 011/4311-3313, www.zirkel.com.ar;
9am-6pm Mon., 9am-midnight Tues.-Fri.,
6pm-1am Sat.

JAPANESE
FuraiBo $$

A beautifully decorated restaurant, FuraiBo goes to great lengths to immerse its clients in Japanese traditions and culture. A converted second-floor apartment, the oriental salon is based on a Buddhist temple and offers seating on the floor to enjoy sushi and other traditional Japanese dishes. Reservations are advised for this room in particular, as it is by far the most popular.

MAP 1: Adolfo Alsina 429, 2nd fl., tel.
011/4334-3440, www.furaiboba.com.ar;
noon-11pm daily

CAFÉS AND *BARES NOTABLES*
El Gato Negro $

Nestled among the theaters and cinemas of Avenida Corrientes, El Gato Negro serves as a favorite meeting point before heading to a show, as well as a cup of one of the many different international coffees and teas on offer. The walls are lined with towering oak cabinets filled with spices from around the world, available for purchase, while a discreet bar on the second floor is favored by those looking for a stronger drink.

MAP 1: Av. Corrientes 1669, tel.
011/4374-1730; 9am-10pm Mon., 9am-11pm Tues., 9am-midnight Wed.-Thurs., 9am-2am Fri.-Sat., 3pm-11pm Sun.

El Gato Negro is both a café and a spice store.

Los 36 Billares $

Los 36 Billares is one of the oldest cafés in Buenos Aires, occupying the ground floor and basement of the Hotel Marbella. The house specialty is pizza. The ornate decoration, felt-topped card tables, checkered floor, and bow-tied waiters populate a space above an underground salon filled with billiard tables. A theater at the back offers regular tango shows (dance and music) and classes.

a pool table in Los 36 Billares

Av. de Mayo 1271, tel.
011/4122-1500, www.los36billares.com.ar;
7am-2am Mon.-Thurs., 7am-4am Fri.-Sat.,
7am-1am Sun.

Petit Colón $

Sitting across Plaza Lavalle from the imposing courts and judicial buildings, Petit Colón is habitually filled with lawyers during the day and dressed-up folk in the buildup to evening shows at neighboring Teatro Colón. Romantic and quaint, the café's lavish wallpaper and wooden interior are a throwback to old Parisian styles. The coffee is perhaps not the best and the tables are a bit squashed together, but sitting outside while sipping a cold drink in the sun is hard to beat.

MAP 1: Libertad 505, tel. 011/4382-7306, www.elblogdelpetitcolon.com.ar; 8am-1am daily

DELIS AND SANDWICHES
Latino Sandwich $

It's easy to pass this relatively nondescript sandwich shop without noticing, and this isn't a place to come for a sit-down meal. Latino Sandwich offers an impressive range of sandwiches and salads, as well as a few extra daily dishes, all listed on a giant chalkboard. The chicken, pancetta, and cheddar sandwich is hard to resist and often sells out quickly, as do other popular options. Long queues form at lunchtime.

MAP 1: Tacuarí 185, tel. 011/4342-2809, www.latinosandwich.com; 8am-5pm Mon.-Fri.

BARES NOTABLES

A favored gathering place for *porteños*, Buenos Aires's ornate bars and cafés are so important to local culture that in 1998 the government granted special status to those holding historical or architectural importance. In addition to receiving subsidies for conservation, these designated establishments, known as *bares notables* (bars of note), are also protected from the ever-hovering hand of property development. Over the years, thousands of bars and cafés have been granted this prestigious status, but it's currently held by around 70.

Stepping through the glassed wooden doors of one of these *bares* is like passing through a time warp. Waiters glide across marble floors in bow ties and suits while huge coffee contraptions spout steam from behind elegant, beautifully stocked bars. Many sell food and produce, harking back to their early days as general stores. Sit and read for hours or grab a seat next to a sliding window and take in the movement on the street outside.

La Biela, a *bar notable* facing the Cementerio de la Recoleta

While the official list is constantly evolving, most of the city's oldest and finest *bares* have already been recognized. The majority are in the center of town, although there are some delightful ones hidden away in residential neighborhoods farther afield. All of them proudly have a sticker on the door declaring their status as one of the city's renowned drinking holes. For a full list of current *bares notables*, check the city government website (www.turismo.buenosaires.gob.ar).

Puerto Madero   Map 1

ARGENTINE

Chila $$$

Maria Soledad Nardelli opened Chila after perfecting her culinary skills in Spain and France, creating a lovingly prepared menu that focuses on regional ingredients, such as boga fish from the Río Paraná. There are two menus to choose from, three courses or seven courses, which offer exquisite dishes, although the prices may be imposing at US$90 and US$120, not including drinks. Modern and simplistic decor beckon to the upmarket clientele that frequent the restaurant.

MAP 1: Av. Alicia Moreau de Justo 1160, tel. 011/4343-6067, www.chilaweb.com.ar; 8pm-midnight Tues.-Sun.

Gourmet Porteño $$$

Come to Gourmet Porteño, an upscale all-you-can-eat restaurant, if you fancy eating until you burst. There is a huge range of food: cold meats, cheeses, salad, *parrilla*, sushi, pasta, seafood, and pizza, to name a few. At around US$20 per person, drinks and dessert not included, it is good value, although doggy bags are not allowed. Sit outside if tables are available.

MAP 1: Av. Alicia Moreau de Justo 1942, tel. 011/4312-3021, www.gourmetporteno.com.ar; noon-4pm and 8pm-late daily

PARRILLAS
☼ Cabaña Las Lilas $$$

Often touted as the highest quality *parrilla* in Buenos Aires, Cabaña Las Lilas has been voted one of the world's top 10 restaurants. The succulent meat, sourced from a private stock of cattle, will leave you swooning. *Ojo de bife* (rib eye) is the specialty, but the menu offers great variety. The decor of traditional items from the countryside seems somewhat forced and is perhaps one of the reasons, along with the hefty prices, that most Argentines choose more authentic alternatives, but this remains a popular

draw for visitors to the city. Expect to pay US$100 overall and hear fellow diners speaking a wide variety of languages.

MAP 1: Av. Alicia Moreau de Justo 550, tel. 011/4315-1010, www.restaurantlaslilas.com; noon-midnight daily, noon-1am Fri.-Sat.

☼ Costanera Sur Food Stalls $

Lining the Costanera Sur are small shacks that offer snack food such as sandwiches and hamburgers. Though the food isn't comparable to the nearby exclusive gourmet restaurants that line the docks, the stalls are a popular destination for *porteños* to eat a *bondiola* (grilled pork) or *lomito* (grilled beef) sandwich on the folding chairs alongside the Reserva Ecológica Costanera Sur. The main difference between each of the shacks is the variety of salad and sauces they offer to flesh out the sandwiches.

MAP 1: Costanera Sur; 24 hours daily

The meat dishes at Cabaña Las Lilas are succulent and flavorful.

STREET FOOD

Food trucks offer some of the best meals in the city.

Street food in Buenos Aires is cheap, delicious, and easy to find.

PIZZA

When eaten as a snack, pizza is consumed standing at the pizzeria's bar, although tables are available for slightly higher costs. The traditional style is thick crust with a deep layer of cheese; one slice is often sufficient for a meal. An interesting variety is *fugaza,* which comes with sliced onions instead of cheese (to include cheese, ask for *fugazetta*).

EMPANADAS

Empanadas are small filled pastries that can be bought from any pizzeria or general food store. The most traditional fillings are *carne* (ground beef) and *jamon y queso* (ham and cheese), but other flavors include *pollo* (chicken), *humita* (sweet corn in white sauce), and *caprese* (tomato, cheese, and basil). They come in two forms: *al horno* (oven-cooked) or *frito* (fried).

CHORIPANES

Choripanes (chorizo sandwiches) are often sold from rustic grills, particularly on the Costanera Sur and outside *fútbol* stadiums. Ensure that the sausage is cooked through by asking for it to be *un poco mas cocido* (cooked a little longer) or *estilo mariposa* (butterflied). A *morcipan* is exactly the same but with a *morcilla* (blood sausage).

PANCHOS

Panchos are hot dogs, sold on the street and at *kioscos* (newsstands). The sausages are made from beef and pork; they are boiled in water rather than grilled. In addition to ketchup and mayonnaise, some stalls offer other toppings, such as a *lluvia de papas* (sprinkling of crispy potatoes). They are sometimes called Super Panchos.

SANDWICHES DE MIGA

Miga refers to a type of thin-sliced bread without crust. These sandwiches are sold in all *panaderías* (bakeries), containing combinations of ham, cheese, salad, tuna, olives, and so on. A "triple" contains an extra slice of bread between two separate ingredients.

SANDWICHES DE VACIO

Also known as *vaciopan,* this is a sandwich with a hunk of meat in the middle. These can be bought at any *parrilla.* Alternatives are *sandwich de bondiola* (pork shoulder sandwich), *lomito* (a leaner steak sandwich), and *sandwich de milanesa* (breaded beef or chicken sandwich).

GARRAPIÑADAS

Commonly found in *fútbol* stadiums, *garrapiñadas* (caramelized peanuts) are also sold on the street, often by old men stirring copper woks of peanuts bubbling in water and sugar. These very sweet snacks are sold in plastic tubes and cost less than US$1.

ITALIAN AND PIZZA
Marcelo $$$

Prepared by the hands of chef Marcelo Piegari, the pastas in this restaurant are naturally the highlight. Plates are large enough to share between two, as pointed out by the waiters and the menus, although two hungry souls should throw in a starter as well. The simple, modern decor is designed not to detract from the dishes, while plenty of space between tables allows for privacy.

MAP 1: Av. Alicia Moreau de Justo 1140, tel. 011/4342-8243, www.marcelorestaurante.com.ar; noon-4pm and 8pm-late daily

Cucina d'Onore $$

This Italian restaurant prides itself on pasta and seafood, but the prices are relatively inflated. Promotional menus provide a more affordable spread at around US$10, although these are only available between noon and 4pm. The *gamberi impanati* (a form of breaded langoustine) are a tasty example of the chef's imagination. The glitzy, red-ceilinged interior is a contrast to the brick-arched patio overlooking the water, where it is especially enjoyable to take in the view during dinner.

MAP 1: Av. Alicia Moreau de Justo 1768, tel. 011/4315-9260, www.cucinadonore.com; noon-4pm and 8pm-late daily

San Telmo and La Boca   Map 2

ARGENTINE
El Baqueano $$$

A notable exception to the beef-filled menus of the city, El Baqueano offers a surprising selection of native meats such as llama, wild boar, and alligator. The waiters are excellent at explaining the menu and suggesting how to share dishes, while the popular seven-course tasting menu allows eaters to try a range of exotic well-prepared meats. A wood-themed interior tries to create a traditional atmosphere but misses the mark a bit.

MAP 2: Chile 495, tel. 011/4342-0802, www.restoelbaqueano.com; 5pm-midnight Tues.-Sat.

the elegant wooden bar at El Federal

El Federal $

The 30-page menu can seem quite daunting at first, but the *picadas* and *sandwiches de lomito* are both excellent choices here. El Federal is an icon of the city and is as popular with locals as it is with visitors. The service is not particularly fast but the beautifully carved bar makes up for any shortcomings. Prices are reasonable, especially considering that many plates can be shared between two people.

MAP 2: Carlos Calvo 599, tel. 011/4300-4313, www.barelfederal.com.ar; 8am-late daily

El Obrero $$

Lovingly attended by its owners, El Obrero has been pleasing locals with its dishes since 1910. It is a traditional *bodegón* that fortunately couldn't care less about renovating, with the same furniture being used since the 1950s. Hugely popular and prone to queues in the evening, it can also be tricky to find. A varied menu is on offer, but the *corvina a la vasca* (a Basque fish dish) is one of the best.

MAP 2: Agustín R. Caffarena 64, tel. 011/4362-9912, www.bodegonelobrero. com.ar; noon-4pm and 8pm-late Mon.-Sat.

PARRILLAS
Desnivel $$

Traditionally an obligatory stop for visitors to Buenos Aires, Desnivel offers reasonable prices and an enjoyable atmosphere. Make sure to ask for the meat to be rarer, if desired; otherwise it will almost certainly be well-cooked, if not overcooked. The *bife de chorizo* is a solid bet, as are the dense fried empanadas. There is a more spacious patio toward the back if the noise and crowds are daunting.

MAP 2: Defensa 855, tel. 011/4300-9081; 5pm-1am Mon., noon-1am Tues.-Sun.

1880 $$

A traditional *parrilla* that sits a few blocks away from the hustle of San Telmo, 1880 typically fills with locals rather than tourists, which is always a good sign. The *chinchulines* (intestines) and *pechito de cerdo* (pork ribs) are especially tasty, although all beef cuts are cooked to perfection. With

tango music playing in the background and walls covered in framed pictures and old advertisements, this compact restaurant couldn't feel more Argentine.

MAP 2: Defensa 1665, tel. 011/4307-2746, www.parrilla1880.com.ar; noon-3:30pm and 8pm-late Mon.-Sat., noon-late Sun.

SOUTH AMERICAN
Mercadito Latino $

This small and colorful restaurant offers a diverse Latin American menu including food from Peru, Bolivia, Colombia, the Caribbean, and Mexico. The dishes, while not overly complex, are interesting and varied, produced by chefs who have traveled all around the continent. Cocktails are also available, as well as desserts, even though they are not listed on the menu.

MAP 2: Carlos Calvo 488, tel. 015/5046-7775; 10am-midnight daily

ITALIAN AND PIZZA
Il Matterello $$

Il Matterello specializes in pasta—stuffed pasta, specifically. Close to the Boca Juniors stadium, it can be slightly hectic around match times, but the matches are always displayed on a television, creating a lively atmosphere. The prices are not particularly cheap, even in this casual space. Although a second restaurant (Thames 1490, 6pm-late Mon., noon-late Tues.-Sun.) has opened in Palermo, it does not have the same charm as this original location.

MAP 2: Martín Rodríguez 517, tel. 011/4307-0529; noon-4pm and 8pm-late Mon.-Sat., noon-4pm Sun.

Banchero $

One of the first pizzerias in Buenos Aires, Banchero opened in 1893 when La Boca was home to many Italian immigrants. It was here that one of

PARRILLAS (STEAK HOUSES)

Argentine beef is widely regarded as some of the best in the world, with cows having the luxury of vast grasslands out in the pampas to graze on. Averaging almost 200 kilograms of meat consumption per year during the 19th century, residents now consume a more modest yet still impressive 60 kilograms annually. The majority of this is eaten at home, where the favored method is to throw it on the *parrilla* (grill) and cook it over slow-burning coals until the flavors have reached their peak—different cuts are brought out progressively. Eating in a *parrilla* (steak house, which goes by the same name as the grill itself) is an essential experience to any trip to Buenos Aires.

steak at La Cabrera

Every local has their favorite *parrilla*, and the neighborhood joints often have longer queues than the fancy ones in the city center; this has as much to do with cost and authenticity as it does quality. There are very few that are overly formal, and these can generally be recognized by their significantly higher prices. Dining at a *parrilla* can roll on for hours, with *sobremesa* (chatting after eating) often lasting longer than the meal itself. All *parrillas* serve vegetarian dishes (mainly pastas and salads).

Below are some of the best *parrillas* in Buenos Aires, although if you spot any no-frills neighborhood spot with a queue forming, it is also guaranteed to be delicious.

the city's most famous pizzas, the *fugazzeta*, was invented, and this is definitely worth a try. Prices are high, as is the quantity of fat. There is often a bit of a wait for a table, but this is a popular and traditional pizzeria in a romantic part of the city.

MAP 2: Suárez 396, tel. 011/4301-1406, www.bancheropizzerias.com.ar; noon-4pm and 8pm-late Tues.-Sun.

MEDITERRANEAN
Nacional $$

Set back from the hustle of the street, Nacional offers a shady patio, which is something that's hard to find in Buenos Aires. With an intriguing mixture of Mediterranean dishes, ranging from tapas to *focaccia*, they provide an alternative to many of the more

standard restaurants in the city. The art nouveau furniture adds charm to the warm and inviting salon, while a room in the basement offers art exhibitions and live music shows.

MAP 2: Perú 858, tel. 011/4300-2887, www.espacionacional.com; 8am-late daily

GERMAN
✪ Untertürkheim $$

Aiming to imitate a traditional German beer hall, Untertürkheim offers more than 70 beers to drink from its attractive wooden tables. Although a great place for just a drink, the food is delicious, with sausages a rare and welcome inclusion, alongside their usual accompaniments such as sauerkraut. Despite the slightly remote location, the reasonable prices and rowdy atmosphere mean that the place is often full, meaning larger groups should make reservations.

MAP 2: Humberto Primo 899, tel. 011/4307-3265; 5pm-late Mon.-Sat.

INDIAN
Mash $$

The only curry house in Buenos Aires that specializes in British curries, Mash offers a small yet delicious menu. Especially popular with locals, the restaurant recently moved to a large modern venue in the heart of San Telmo. Run by an eccentric Englishman, whose specialty is Thai green curry, Mash includes rice with their curries, unlike most of their competitors, and the depth of flavors is impressive.

MAP 2: Defensa 1338, tel. 011/6829-6829; 7:30pm-midnight Tues.-Sat., 1:30pm-5pm Sun.

MEXICAN
Don Esculapio $

The ever enthusiastic and smiling Don Esculapio has been selling homemade burritos from a food stall on the side of the road in the Feria de San Pedro Telmo for years. With only three options (meat, chicken and pancetta, or vegetarian), the menu is simple, although his special hot sauce is an advisable addition. A popular option is to eat on the move while perusing the market stalls.

MAP 2: Defensa 678; 11am until sold out Sun.

VEGETARIAN
Naturaleza Sabia $$

Slightly hidden on a cobbled backstreet, Naturaleza Sabia has achieved widespread acclaim for its colorful and tasty vegetarian dishes. Although the menu is not extensive, it offers a good variety, including vegan and gluten-free options, such as lentil hamburgers, spinach cannelloni, and quinoa steaks. The portions are well sized and reasonably priced, and there is a room that offers yoga classes most afternoons of the week.

MAP 2: Balcarce 958, tel. 011/4300-6454, www.naturalezasabia.com.ar; noon-3:30pm and 8pm-midnight Tues.-Sat.

CAFÉS AND *BARES NOTABLES*
Bar Británico $

Named in honor of the World War I veterans who once frequented the establishment, Bar Británico gazes out over the tranquil Parque Lezama. It's a favorite of locals, many of whom come for the *minutas* (snack-like meals), such as *milanesas* or burgers, which are served in an old-school bar atmosphere. Tables next to the huge windows are ideal not only in sunshine but also when the cobblestones outside are being pelted by rain.

MAP 2: Av. Brasil 399, tel. 011/4361-2107; 6am-late daily

El Estaño 1880 $

The history of El Estaño 1880 is a testament to La Boca's resilience and pride. The beauty of the interior, with its carved wooden cabinets, tin bar, and antique ornaments has led to multiple films, such as *Evita*, using it as a set. It also draws famous soccer players from the Boca Juniors. *Picadas* and *sorrentinos* (an Argentine filled pasta) are the house specialties.

MAP 2: Aristóbulo del Valle 1100, tel. 011/3535-1015; 10am-7pm Sun.-Wed., 10am-midnight Thurs.-Sat.

La Poesía $

During the 1980s, La Poesía was a general store that also functioned as a meeting place for poets and other bohemians. Today it retains much of its original splendor, with the shelves still stocked with goods and cured hams hanging from the ceiling. It's a small, cramped spot, with a tiny mezzanine perched above the main salon, while the tables outside sit along the cobbled streets. An extensive menu covers everything from sandwiches, *picadas*, steaks, burgers, and pastas. Live shows of various musical genres are held on Thursday and Friday evenings.

MAP 2: Chile 502, tel. 011/4300-7340, www.cafelapoesia.com.ar; 8am-2am Sun.-Thurs., 8am-4am Fri.-Sat.

DELIS AND SANDWICHES
El Banco Rojo $

One of the few places in Buenos Aires where lamb is predominant on the menu, El Banco Rojo offers a decent range of easy-to-eat items, although they don't offer much space to eat, making this more of a place to drop by on a whim. It is run by the same people as La Puerta Roja (Chacabuco 733, tel. 011/4362-5649) and they don't hold back on the music here. The Philly cheesesteak, inspired by the North American version, is a favorite here.

MAP 2: Bolívar 914, tel. 011/4362-3177; noon-12:30am Tues.-Sun.

ICE CREAM
Nonna Bianca $

This ice cream parlor is more notable for its entertaining and eccentric flavors, such as *cerveza* (beer), maté, and *fernet* (a spice-based liquor). Just a few meters off Defensa street, it's an ideal place to drop by when exploring San Telmo. Chunky wooden picnic tables are available to use inside, but the best spot is on the bench out front.

MAP 2: Estados Unidos 425, tel. 011/4362-0604; 9am-2am daily

Retiro   Map 3

ARGENTINE
BASA $$$

A sophisticated and modern restaurant in the center of town, BASA offers a wide variety of dishes, although the meat cooked on the *parrilla* is the most popular. An interesting item is *arañita a la parrilla*, a rare and delicious flank cut. The intimate atmosphere of the simple modern venue is enhanced by the ceiling-mounted spotlights. BASA also has an excellent cocktail menu.

MAP 3: Basavilbaso 1328, tel. 011/4893-9444, www.basabar.com. ar; noon-3pm and 7pm-2am Mon.-Fri., 8pm-2am Sat.

✪ Gran Bar Danzón $$$

A restaurant that doubles as a wine bar, Gran Bar Danzón is always full and bustling with noise. The bare brick walls and music, often provided by a live DJ, add to the sophisticated ambience. Elevated food prices are accompanied by a first-class wine list, with over 400 choices. A fairly short menu offers extravagant dishes such as salmon and squid ceviche or grilled lamb with a velvety eggplant and mushroom mash. The apple and goat cheese tarte tatin is a perfect end to any meal.

MAP 3: Libertad 1161, tel. 011/4811-1108, www.granbardanzon.com.ar; 7pm-late daily

ITALIAN AND PIZZA
Filo $$

Although the menu at Filo includes an impressive range of regional Italian dishes, the pastas and pizzas are the specialties. Cooked in a wood oven, the pizzas are thin-crust rather than the locally predominant deep-pan style. The Filo pizza comes with different toppings on each slice, according to the whims of the chef. Colorful decoration, artwork (including a basement gallery), and a live DJ provide a vibrant atmosphere.

MAP 3: San Martín 975, tel. 011/4311-0312, www.filo-ristorante.com; noon-late daily

El Cuartito $

This raucous traditional pizzeria has been serving pizza, by the slice or by the oozing platter, since 1934. Loudly decorated with sports photos and a noise level to match, it is renowned for its *fugazzetta* (type of pizza with cheese and onions). The waiters feel no need to write down orders, no matter how complicated, although they can be notoriously hard to flag down when at full throttle. One person taking on

El Cuartito is famed for its pizza with cheese and onions.

a whole pizza in this place would be practically impossible.

MAP 3: Talcahuano 937, tel. 011/4816-1758; 12:30pm-1am Tues.-Sun.

FRENCH
Le Sud $$$

An elegant restaurant found in the Hotel Sofitel, Le Sud combines traditional French dishes with regional produce. Chef Olivier Falchi is well known in the city, and has come up with one of the more interesting French menus in Buenos Aires. Of particular note, the *cordero Patagónico* (Patagonian lamb) is cooked twice to bring out its sublime tenderness. Diners are expected to be well dressed to fit in with the ambience of the upmarket hotel.

MAP 3: Arroyo 841, tel. 011/4131-0130; noon-3pm and 8pm-late daily

SPANISH
Tancat $$$

Jorge Cavaliere founded Tancat after falling in love with tapas bars during a trip to Spain. It's an original and striking restaurant; vivid red decoration accompanies a specially designed bar that seats up to 38 people. As with most tapas bars, portions are on the small side and noise is constant, but the Spanish tortilla is one of the best in the city.

MAP 3: Paraguay 645, tel. 011/4312-5442, www.tancatrestaurante.com; noon-late Mon.-Sat.

CAFÉS AND *BARES NOTABLES*
Florida Garden $

An attractive and elegant café for coffee or mid-afternoon snacks, Florida Garden sits in the center of busy Retiro. The waiters do not feel the need to rush, however, and sometimes require heavy prompting. The

Florida Garden

cakes and pastries are excellent here, as are the original 1960s-era decorations.

MAP 3: Florida 899, tel. 011/4312-7902; 6am-late Mon.-Fri., 6am-11pm Sat., 8am-11pm Sun.

Recoleta   Map 4

PARRILLAS
El Estrebe $$

This *parrilla* is popular with locals for the quality of its meat and its focus on providing special attention to customers. The waiters offer sound advice for those who are overwhelmed by the extensive menu, which includes over 250 wines. Many of the steaks are so large that they can be easily shared between two people. Decorated with traditional items from the Argentine countryside, this restaurant never fails to please its customers, especially with the lamb.

MAP 4: Peña 2475, tel. 011/4803-0282, www.elestrebe.com.ar; noon-4pm and 8pm-late daily

PERUVIAN
La Causa Nikkei $$

Located in a low, modern building away from the busy Avenida Callao, La Causa Nikkei offers a blend of Japanese and Peruvian food, a popular concept in Buenos Aires. The decor is colorful and fun, as are the dishes. The ceviche is delicious, and small individual portions are sometimes served for free upon seating. The noise level becomes high at peak hours, with surprisingly loud music, but then quiets down later in the evening.

MAP 4: Av. Callao 1290, tel. 011/5218-0900, www.lacausanikkei.com; noon-3pm and 8pm-midnight Mon.-Sat., noon-3pm Sun.

FRENCH

✪ La Bourgogne $$$

Guided by the hands of chef Jean Paul Bondoux, La Bourgogne is in the Alvear Palace Hotel and arguably serves the city's best French food. The *merluza negra* (Chilean sea bass) melts in the mouth, but the menu is so varied that there are choices for all tastes. Service is exemplary and some of the tables even allow diners to watch the chefs bustle around the kitchen through a glass wall. Prices are very high and the dress code is formal, so it's an not an ideal place to just drop by.

MAP 4: Ayacucho 2027, tel. 011/4808-2100; 7:30pm-midnight Mon.-Sat.

Restó $$$

Because it's located within the Socíedad Central de Arquitectos (Central Society of Architects), it's no surprise that the building that houses Restó is beautiful. The restaurant itself is simple, with sparse decorations and a brief but sublime menu, which includes their famed *codorniz asada* (stuffed quail). The chefs are also open to alterations to their dishes made by guests. Despite the cheaper prices at lunchtime, it can be difficult to find a table on the only two evenings that Restó is open, making reservations strongly advised.

MAP 4: Montevideo 938, tel. 011/4816-6711; noon-3pm Mon.-Wed., noon-3pm and 8pm-11pm Thurs.-Fri.

Croque Madame $$

Located in the gatehouse and surrounding patio of the beautiful Museo Nacional de Arte Decorativo, Croque Madame is favored more for its stunning ambience than its food, which is pricey and of average quality. Bustling Avenida del Libertador is on the other side of a gold-embellished iron fence but doesn't intrude on the peaceful atmosphere. This is an ideal location to drink an afternoon tea or coffee while munching on a smoked salmon and brie sandwich or, of course, a *croque madame*. There's no obligation to visit the museum (or pay the admission fee) in order to dine here.

MAP 4: Av. del Libertador 1902, tel. 011/4806-8639, www.croquemadame.com.ar; 10am-midnight daily

SPANISH

José Luis $$$

At this Spanish restaurant, popular for its seafood, a delicious option is the *parrillada de mariscos* (mixed platter of grilled seafood), although it may be slightly small if shared. The desserts, on the other hand, are of ample sharing size. Reserve a table on the patio, as the dimly lit interior can be noisy. Not as elegant as some of its neighboring competitors, José Luis is down-to-earth and welcoming.

MAP 4: Av. Quintana 456, tel. 011/4807-0606; noon-4pm and 8pm-midnight Mon.-Sat.

INDIAN

Tandoor $$

One of the oldest and most reliable curry houses in Buenos Aires, Tandoor is located in a residential area of Recoleta. The decor is elegant and clean, while prices are also significantly higher than other Indian restaurants. The chefs are devoted to their dishes and regularly come up with innovative and seasonal curries. The variety of starters is particularly enticing.

MAP 4: Laprida 1293, tel. 011/4821-3676, www.tandoor.com.ar; noon-3pm and 8pm-11:30pm daily

CAFÉS AND *BARES NOTABLES*
La Biela $$

With one of the most attractive patios in the city, overlooking plazas, churches, and the Cementerio de la Recoleta, La Biela charms guests looking for afternoon drinks. Local residents, especially car enthusiasts, have long favored La Biela for its location and automobile-related decor. Iced coffee is served, unlike in most cafés. Prices are at the top end of the range for cafés and *bares notables*, although it is cheaper to drink and eat inside (La Biela charges higher prices for the privilege of sitting on their lovely patio).

MAP 4: Av. Quintana 600, tel. 011/4804-0449, www.labiela.com; 8am-late daily

BURGERS
Be Frika $$

Named after a Danish meatball dish, this restaurant specializes in homemade gourmet hamburgers. Made from minced *lomo* (tenderloin), the burgers are unsurprisingly succulent and come with imaginative sauces. You'll need to eat at least two of the Tini-Minis, alongside fries or some other accompaniment, to satisfy a hungry stomach. Its American diner ambience comes with noise and bright, yet tasteful, decoration.

MAP 4: Junín 1350, tel. 011/4821-0010, www.frika.be; 9am-1am daily

ICE CREAM
✪ Rapa Nui $

More than just an *heladería* (ice cream parlor), Rapa Nui is a proponent of the Argentine chocolate tradition. Originating from Bariloche, where their chocolate is still made, Rapa Nui's ice creams are among the richest and most chocolaty around. The Fra Nui (white chocolate, blueberry sauce, and chocolate flakes) and 80% Cacao flavors are perhaps the best. Enticing chocolate sweets are also available in their modern storefront, as are seats on which to devour your purchases.

MAP 4: Arenales 2302, tel. 011/4827-1431, www.chocolatesrapanui.com.ar; 11am-1am daily

Palermo   Map 5

PORTEÑO
✪ Museo Evita $$

Tucked in among the plush buildings of one of Palermo's more exclusive areas, a museum on Eva Perón offers one of the city's largest and most attractive outdoor eating spaces, filled with plants and decorated in an elegant colonial style. The set menu provides great options, including *brotola* (cod) and *cuadril* (rump steak), both of which melt in the mouth, as do the crepes for dessert. Service is excellent and efficient, although menu items are often out of stock in the later lunch and dinner hours. Visitors are allowed to bring pets.

MAP 5: Juan María Gutiérrez 3926, tel. 011/4800-1599, www.museoevitaresto.com.ar; 9am-midnight Mon.-Sat., 9am-7pm Sun.

diners in the shady patio at Museo Evita

ARGENTINE
✪ 1810 $$

Part of a franchise around Buenos Aires, the best location of 1810 lies in the quiet Palermo Viejo, serving up traditional regional Argentine food in an intimate and cozy space with stone walls and solid wood tables. The small menu contains some of the city's best tamales and *locro*, an Argentine stew made of beans and various meats. It's practically impossible to get a seat here on national holidays.

MAP 5: Julián Álvarez 1998, tel. 011/4865-0030, www.1810cocinaregional. com; 11am-4pm and 7pm-late daily

Paraje Arévalo $$$

The simple layout of this small and intimate restaurant, run by budding chefs Estefania de Benedetto and Matias Kyriazis, emphasizes the attention and care given to each plate. Grouped in taster menus of 6 to 10 courses (with only 2 or 3 at midday), dishes here feature minimal ingredients yet combine flavors in novel ways, such as salmon cooked in beet juice.

MAP 5: Arévalo 1502, tel. 011/4775-7759, www.parajearevalo.com; 8pm-late Tues.-Fri., 1pm-3pm and 8pm-late Sat., 1pm-3pm Sun.

Tegui $$$

Easy to miss from the street at its location behind a graffitied wall, Tegui is a hidden gem run by acclaimed chef Germán Martitegui, who adjusts the small menu according to his whims and the season's produce. He is perhaps best known for his methods of cooking beef and seafood. An open kitchen allows guests to view the cooking process, while tables in the main salon offer views of the garden through looming windows. This sophisticated restaurant is small, and reservations are strongly advised.

MAP 5: Costa Rica 5852, tel. 011/4770-9500, www.tegui.com.ar; 8:30pm-late Tues.-Sat.

Perón Perón $$

The decor and atmosphere at this restaurant are themed on former President Juan Domingo Perón, with photos and banners of the man everywhere. The food is traditional, reasonably priced, and often wittily named after him or Evita Perón. The osso buco is the favored cut of meat, either in empanadas or as a steak. The music is patriotic, one of the reasons—along with the artisanal beer served in pitchers—that the restaurant fills up most nights.

MAP 5: Angel Carranza 2225, tel. 011/4777-6194; 7pm-2am Mon.-Sat.

Club Eros $

Set in the grounds of a local sports club, this restaurant is as down-to-earth as you will find in Palermo. Offering a family vibe, with no

La Cabrera

pretensions in its decor, Club Eros offers just a few pastas and meat from the *parrilla*. Their *bife de chorizo* is particularly juicy, while the *milanesa* (thin breaded steak) struggles to fit on the plate. With outstanding prices for the area, this is an authentic neighborhood restaurant.

MAP 5: Uriarte 1609, tel. 011/4832-1313; noon-4pm and 8pm-late daily

PARRILLAS
✪ Las Cabras $$

The queues outside Las Cabras pay testament to its popularity as an affordable *parrilla* offering quality meat from a mammoth grill. Offering a wide menu of beef, pork, and chicken cuts, Las Cabras offers starters like *chinchulines* (small intestine) which are cooked till crispy. All steaks come with a large Caesar salad. Pastel reds and greens adorn the walls, and diners are given crayons to doodle on the disposable tablecloths. With only two designated group tables, groups of more than four should arrive early or expect a wait.

MAP 5: Fitz Roy 1795, tel. 011/5197-5301; noon-midnight daily

La Cabrera $$$

Attention is given to style and presentation in La Cabrera, a gourmet *parrilla* if ever there was one. Consisting of four confusingly separate restaurants within 100 meters of one other, queuing is a necessity (although complimentary drinks and snacks are provided while you wait). The rustic stone walls are laden with pictures and bottles of wine. Rather than order side dishes, wait for the waiter to bring a tray laden with an exotic range of extras; taking all of them is encouraged. Everything is 40 percent cheaper when dining before 8:30pm.

MAP 5: Cabrera 5099, tel. 011/4831-7002, www.parrillalacabrera.com.ar; 12:30pm-4:30pm and 7pm-1am daily

Club El Don Steak House $$

A loose homage to the *Godfather* films, Club El Don offers some of the best steaks in Buenos Aires in a modern black-and-white setting. Careful selection ensures that all the meat comes from grass-fed animals, while some unusual dishes are also available, such as wild boar sausages, lamb sweetbreads, and bull testicles. Unlike most *parrillas*, it's worth mentioning if you would like the meat well-done, as they tend to cook on the rarer side.

MAP 5: Carranza 1859, tel. 011/4774-7389, www.clubeldon.com; 8pm-late Mon., noon-3pm and 8pm-late Tues.-Sun.

El Trapiche $$

This traditional *parrilla,* among the shiny modern restaurants that abound in Palermo Hollywood, serves portions that can easily be shared. The menu is large as well, but the *cordero* (lamb) or *matambre* (side flank) are perhaps the best picks. The atmosphere can become quite rowdy in the later hours, especially as the tables are crammed in fairly close to one another; the window seats offer some space and a quieter setting.

MAP 5: Paraguay 5099, tel. 011/4772-7343; noon-4pm and 8pm-late daily

PERUVIAN
Osaka $$$

The first franchise of this Peruvian chain to appear outside Peru, Osaka serves up the traditional combination of Japanese and Peruvian dishes in typical Palermo Soho style, with the ceviche being almost obligatory. The building is fronted by large bamboo, while the acoustics inside are loud. With a cocktail bar on the ground floor and the restaurant upstairs, a whole evening can nonetheless be spent here.

MAP 5: Soler 5608, tel. 011/4775-6964, www.osaka.com.pe; 12:30pm-4pm and 8pm-late Mon.-Sat.

ITALIAN AND PIZZA
Guido's Bar $$

Plenty of small restaurants and *bodegones* in Buenos Aires don't have menus, but the interesting thing about Guido's is that he just starts placing dishes in front of you as soon as you sit down. The antipasto dishes are more popular than the pastas, which may be drier than some like. The only way to stop the flow of food is to ask for the bill, a reasonable US$15 per head. Traditional Italian checkered tablecloths go hand-in-hand with the standard Argentine decoration of pictures and photos covering every inch of wall space.

MAP 5: República de la India 2843, tel. 011/4802-2391; 8am-4pm and 8pm-late Mon.-Fri., 8am-4pm Sat.

SCANDINAVIAN
Olsen $$$

Famed for their Sunday brunch, Olsen offers a garden terrace that fills up even in winter, despite the heaters failing to have much impact. The decoration inside is modern and minimalist, as is the menu, with only eight options. The Nordic canapés are possibly the most interesting item on the menu and are well accompanied by the selection of over 50 different vodkas.

MAP 5: Gorriti 5870, tel. 011/4776-7677; noon-1am Tues.-Thurs., noon-2am Fri.-Sat., 10:30am-1am Sun.

MIDDLE EASTERN AND ARMENIAN
El Manto $$$

An ideal place for romantic dinners, with low lighting and private spaces, El Manto also offers outdoor tables. The staff and owner ensure that guests are content and well-fed throughout their visit. Taster menus offer the chance to try a good variety of traditional Armenian dishes, such as *mousaka* (a type of eggplant lasagna) and shish kebabs. Despite usually being full, service is efficient.

MAP 5: Costa Rica 5801, tel. 011/4774-2409, www.elmanto.com; 8pm-late daily

Sarkis $$

Widely regarded as the best non-Argentine restaurant in Buenos Aires, Sarkis offer Armenian food at very reasonable prices. The result is a long queue, so arrive early or make a reservation. The menu can be a little confusing, as many of the items may be unfamiliar, but the opinions and advice of the excellent waiters are generally accurate. Notable for its lack of decoration, it is the food and enthusiastic diners that ensure the reputation of the restaurant remains so high.

MAP 5: Thames 1101, tel. 011/4772-4911; noon-3pm and 8pm-1am daily

Al-Zein $

This simple restaurant serves up cheap, delicious Middle Eastern food, including *shawarma*, falafel, *kebe*, and hummus, all freshly cooked and prepared. A pleasant area out front allows for eating outdoors, even in the rain, while the inside offers very little in the way of decor. A large proportion of customers are served from a separate take-out counter. Alcohol is not served.

MAP 5: Arce 488, tel. 011/4775-1402; noon-midnight Tues.-Sun.

JAPANESE
Jardín Japonés $$$

The spectacular view of the Japanese gardens propels this sushi restaurant above others, although the food itself is relatively mediocre and not particularly original. Romantic and relaxed, the elegant lighting and option of sitting on lowered tables increases the enjoyment of meals. During the day, visitors must pay the US$1 entrance fee to the gardens, although this is not necessary at night, when the gardens themselves are closed.

MAP 5: Av. Casares 2966, tel. 011/4800-1322, www.jardinjapones.org. ar/restaurant; 10am-6pm and 7:30pm-late Wed.-Mon.

INDIAN
Taj Mahal $$

As is traditional in India (yet rare in Argentina), no beef is served at this restaurant, but the lamb is tender and flavorful. Options are limited, but the quality of the food is high and cooked in a traditional tandoor oven. Behind the decorative exterior, the decor is simple, and there is plenty of space between tables. The *tabla de degustación* (a variety of small tasters) is a little underwhelming, so it's wiser to share a few full dishes, which the waiters are happy to explain and give sound advice on.

MAP 5: Nicaragua 4353, tel. 011/4831-5716, www.tajmahalresto.com; 8pm-late Mon.-Sat.

THAI
Phuket $$

A small modern restaurant with excellent service, Phuket offers some of the best Thai food in Buenos Aires, and it's cooked by a Thai chef. An ample menu has excellent dishes, notably the house dessert: chocolate mousse with grapefruit and orange ice cream. A small deck allows diners to enjoy the open air in this attractive part of town.

MAP 5: Honduras 4169, tel. 011/4861-1679, www.phuketwok.com.ar; 8:30pm-late Mon.-Sat.

El Muelle stands over the Río de la Plata.

Sudestada $$

Although the ambience of Sudestada is fairly basic, with a minimalist interior, the food is excellent and the lunch menu is a great value. The dishes, including curries and stir-fries, are all from Southeast Asia and are among the spiciest in Buenos Aires. In the evening, the plates are large enough to be shared by couples, and diners are welcome to bring their own wine, although there is a small corkage fee.
MAP 5: Guatemala 5602, tel.
011/4776-3777; noon-3pm and 8pm-late Mon.-Thurs., 8pm-late Fri.-Sat.

MEXICAN
María Felix $$

Unlike many of its competitors in Buenos Aires, María Felix is decorated to recreate an authentic Mexican restaurant. A rooftop terrace provides space to eat during the summer evenings, as mariachi groups stroll among the tables and cactuses. Complimentary chips and salsa perhaps reduce the need for starters, although the mains are not overly large, and ordering extra tortillas is advisable. The jugs of margarita are spectacular. Groups of women receive a 30 percent discount on Wednesday.
MAP 5: Guatemala 5200, tel.
011/4775-0380, www.mariafelix.com.ar; noon-4pm and 8pm-late daily

SEAFOOD
☺ El Muelle $$$

Located in the beautiful Club de Pescadores (Fishermen Club), a wooden Tudoresque mansion on the Costanera Norte, El Muelle is one of the city's few restaurants offering a river view, sitting on a wooden jetty on the Río de la Plata. The Mediterranean-inspired menu is filled with produce from elsewhere, such as the *atún rojo a las brasas* (grilled red tuna), which comes from Ecuador. Only recently opened to the public, the restaurant has a relaxed atmosphere at lunch and is decidedly more formal in the evening. Try and get a table on the outdoor terrace if it's a nice day. If you're taking a taxi here, ask for the *club de pescadores,* rather than El Muelle.

MAP 5: Av. Rafael Obligado and Av. Sarmiento, tel. 011/4773-2216, www. elmuellerestaurante.com.ar; 8am-midnight Tues.-Thurs., 8am-1am Fri.-Sat., 8am-8pm Sun.

Nemo $$

The site of a former oyster bar, Nemo is a popular place for seafood dishes, with little else on the menu. It is hard to pick a best dish from the many options, making the *tabla de pescados* (tastings of a variety of seafood) an attractive option. Tables are small and clustered, making it ideal for couples but less suitable for large groups.

MAP 5: Cabello 3672, tel. 011/4803-5878, www.nemoresto.com.ar; noon-4pm and 7:30pm-midnight daily

VEGETARIAN
✪ Artemisia $$

With vines creeping around the inside and outside of this restaurant, guests are meant to feel at one with nature. Every dish is prepared to order, which can lead to long waits during busy periods. Taking great pride in their organic ingredients, the options are far more interesting than the usual vegetarian fare, with dishes such as barley risotto or polenta lasagna alongside the odd fish entrée, such as pollock and prawn curry. Prices may seem high but are reasonable given the adventurousness of the chefs.

MAP 5: Costa Rica 5893, tel. 011/4773-2641; 10am-late Tues.-Sat., 10am-5pm Sun.

Buenos Aires Verde $$

With an extensive menu and an established kitchen led by renowned chef Mauro Massimino, the food at Buenos Aires Verde is reliably delicious. Portions are large enough to share between two, which is advisable so as to leave space for the excellent desserts. Cannelloni, rice burgers, and stir-fries are well paired with the homemade lemonades and smoothies. The restaurant is somewhat cluttered and usually full, but retains a relaxed atmosphere. A small store sells organic produce.

MAP 5: Gorriti 5657, tel. 011/4775-9594; 9am-12:30am Mon.-Sat.

BURGERS
Burger Joint $

The walls inside Burger Joint are covered in graffiti by customers, often praising the quality of the food. With a small menu—burgers, fries, fizzy drinks, and beer—that includes only four different burgers, ordering doesn't take very long. Despite the high quality meat in Argentina, decent burgers can be hard to find, but this is definitely one of the best options.

MAP 5: Borges 1766, tel. 011/4833-5151; noon-midnight daily

BAKERIES
Le Pain Quotidien $$

A French bakery with locations all around the world, Le Pain Quotidien is wildly popular in Buenos Aires for its baked goods, such as croissants, muffins, and bread, although they also offer meals. Their set breakfasts, or brunch, may seem overpriced at US$30, but buying a croissant and coffee à la carte will come to less than a quarter of this. Large tables are intended to be shared with strangers. The sumptuous smells and French café atmosphere attract a hip crowd of all ages.

MAP 5: Jeronimo Salguero 3075, tel. 011/4807-2098, www.lepainquotidien. ar; 8am-9pm Mon.-Fri., 9am-9pm Sun.-Sat.

ICE CREAM
Jauja $
Handily located near the sprawling parks of Palermo, Jauja is a favorite for locals on hot summer days. Renowned for being particularly sweet, the artisanal ice creams come from El Bolsón, in the south of Argentina, and some of the fruits are native to that region.

Worth trying are flavors such as boysenberry or *chocolate arabé* (chocolate, almonds, walnuts, peanut pralines, raisins, and rum).

MAP 5: Cerviño 3901, tel. 011/4801-8126, www.heladosjauja.com.ar; 8:30am-1am Mon.-Thurs., 8:30am-2am Fri., 10am-2:30am Sat., 11am-1am Sun.

Almagro   Map 6

ARGENTINE
Doña Cocina Tipo Casa $
A traditional Argentine *bodegón* that has been run for generations of the same family (of whom there are many photos on the wall), Doña is small and homey. They specialize in fresh pasta, although the *albondigas* (meatballs) are also excellent, though the dishes are not overly complex. Show up early at lunch, as the whole neighborhood seems to converge here to eat—which is unsurprising given that the dish of the day costs a mere US$7.

MAP 6: Bulnes 802, tel. 011/4862-9278; noon-3:30pm Mon., noon-3:30pm and 8pm-late Tues.-Sun.

PARRILLAS
Don Ignacio $
A relatively nondescript *parrilla* from the outside, Don Ignacio is regarded as the best place in Buenos Aires to eat *milanesas* (a breaded slice of meat found on practically every menu in Argentina). Specializing in this dish, the best here is the *milanesa napolitana Don Ignacio,* which comes laden with ham, tomato, and melted cheese. Decoration is rock music-themed. Prices are kept low. Service, while

somewhat lackadaisical, is friendly and welcoming.

MAP 6: Av. Rivadavia 3439, tel. 011/4861-3133; noon-3pm and 8pm-midnight Tues.-Sun.

Lo de Mary $$
A typical neighborhood *parrilla*, Lo de Mary is lined with shelves holding dusty bottles of wine and antique wooden fridges, and features a nightly queue. Lo de Mary is wildly popular with locals, most of whom opt for the *bife de chorizo* and *vacio* steaks. A few tables line the pavement—but watch out for the adjacent bike lane. Order one of the pastas, or ask your waiter what's best that night.

MAP 6: Humahuaca 4099, tel. 011/4864-8033; 8:30pm-late Tues.-Thurs., 12:30pm-3:30pm and 8:30pm-late Fri.-Sat., 12:30pm-3:30pm Sun.

PERUVIAN
Lucuma $$
This delightful restaurant is as family run as it feels. The tables are few, yet the waiting time for orders is long, as the kitchen is small and great attention is given to each exquisite plate. Although the prices

may seem high, most mains can be shared between two. You can't go wrong with *papas a la Huancaina* (potatoes in a spicy sauce) followed by ceviche. Trust any suggestions given by the servers.

MAP 6: Humahuaca 4101, tel. 011/4861-2838, 8pm-late Mon.-Sat.

VENEZUELAN
Arepera $

As its name indicates, this restaurant specializes in *arepas* (a traditional flatbread from Venezuela and Colombia), with over 15 different fillings available. Although there is no mention of it on the menu, the kitchen will prepare half-and-half *arepas*, allowing you to try various options. The starters, mainly fried, are another interesting alternative to the standard food in Buenos Aires. The plain restaurant offers simple decoration and lack of pretension.

MAP 6: Av. Estado de Israel 4316, tel. 011/2076-7607; 7pm-late Tues.-Sun.

ITALIAN AND PIZZA
Pierino $$

This traditional Italian cantina, one of the few remaining of its style in Buenos Aires, has been serving pastas and casseroles since 1909. The peculiar collection of paraphernalia hanging from the ceiling does nothing to stop locals from coming back. Indeed, it is common to arrive only to discover that all the tables are reserved until the next day, so booking in advance is essential. Try the lamb ravioli or any of the *sorrentinos* (large, round raviolis) to discover how pasta should really be made.

MAP 6: Lavalle 3499, tel. 011/4864-5715, www.lacantinadepierino.com.ar; 8:30pm-late Tues.-Sun.

INDIAN
La Reina Kunti $

A menu based on a Hindu diet (involving no meat) is unusual in Buenos Aires, yet La Reina Kunti is regularly packed, especially on weekends. Unassuming and easy to miss from the outside, the restaurant features an interior decorated with intriguing colors and furniture. Greater attention than in other Indian restaurants is given to items that are not curries, such as *koftas* and *pakoras*. Good prices also contribute to its popularity, so booking in advance is advised.

MAP 6: Humahuaca 3461, tel. 011/4863-3071; 12:30pm-4pm and 8pm-late Tues., 10:30am-4pm and 8pm-late Wed.-Sat.

CUBAN
Melão $

With only six tables, Melão, best described as a kitchen with a few tables, is not looking to attract crowds, but those who discover the restaurant regularly return. Diners can watch as their food is prepared beside them. While most of the menu contains Cuban dishes, there are also items from countries as diverse as Turkey, Pakistan, and Madagascar. Friendly service, including from the chefs, ensures that you get exactly what you want from a visit here.

MAP 6: Castillo 52, tel. 011/4854-5920; 6pm-midnight Tues.-Sat.

CAFÉS AND *BARES NOTABLES*
Las Violetas $$

Opened in 1884, Las Violetas is a renowned *confitería* (a type of café that also sells baked goods) on an Almagro street corner. With curved glass doors and marble tabletops, it's a throwback

Las Violetas is a tearoom as well as a pastry shop.

to the times when cafés were something to be marveled at. Most of the café's many regulars come to eat platters of sandwiches and pastries mid-morning or mid-afternoon, although it is also a popular spot for breakfast. A section includes a store that sells pastries and sweets.

MAP 6: Av. Rivadavia 3899, tel. 011/4958-7387, www.lasvioletas.com; 8am-late Sun.-Fri.

Balvanera   Map 6

ARGENTINE
La Americana $

Long considered one of the best places to eat empanadas in Buenos Aires, La Americana serves up these small pastries in a nonstop stream. A typical pizzeria, brightly lit and full of chatter at all hours, it's large and popular, but service is quick. Pay attention to the waiter's indication of the different fillings when the empanadas are brought over, as it's hard to distinguish them afterward. The *carne salteña* (mincemeat with raisins) is their specialty.

MAP 6: Av. Callao 83, tel. 011/4371-0202, www.pizzerialaamericana.com.ar; 8am-late daily

La Viña del Abasto $

A humble restaurant frequented by locals, La Viña del Abasto offers a small variety of plates, but they make up for it in portion size. The *ravioles mixtos a la principe de Nápoli* (mixed ravioli in white sauce with ham) won't fail to please, nor will the *chivito* (steak sandwich). Cheap prices, friendly atmosphere, and a propensity toward lots of garlic in the sauces are key ingredients to this local favorite.

MAP 6: San Luis 3007, tel. 011/4963-4890; 8pm-late Tues.-Fri., noon-3pm and 8pm-late Sat., noon-3pm Sun.

PERUVIAN
La Conga $$

The droves of Peruvians that fill this large restaurant are testament to the authenticity and quality of the food. Tables are close together in canteen style, so privacy is limited, and reservations are advised. Portions are large and can be shared, while family-size portions are also offered. Unlike at most Buenos Aires restaurants, the spicy dishes served here are genuinely spicy.

MAP 6: La Rioja 39, tel. 011/4865-5084; noon-midnight Thurs.-Tues.

Carlitos $

Although standard Peruvian fare is available in abundant portions, Carlitos is wildly popular for its spit-roasted rotisserie chicken. A whole chicken, a mountain of fries, and a bucket of salad will set you back less than US$10 each when shared between four people. Cheap beer and fluorescent Inca Kola (a Peruvian soft drink) add to the draw. The plastic tablecloths, boisterous atmosphere, and generally run-down appearance may not appeal to everyone.

MAP 6: Av. Corrientes 3070, tel. 011/4861-6440; noon-2am Sun.-Thurs., noon-4am Fri.-Sat.

SEAFOOD
Damblee $$

Ostensibly offering food from the Basque region of France and Spain, Damblee is favored for its seafood. The *mejillones provenzal* (garlic and parsley mussels) are excellent as are the salmon or *lenguado* (sole) in garlic sauce. The wine cellar is particularly noteworthy, and the waiters can help you pick out unusual yet delicious bottles. Try to grab a table by one of the large windows to enjoy the action outside while eating, as the restaurant sits on a busy street corner.

MAP 6: Av. Rivadavia 3401, tel. 011/4861-1629, www.damblee.com; noon-3pm and 8pm-1am daily

CAFÉS AND *BARES NOTABLES*
Café de los Angelitos $$

A café decorated in a beautifully ornate style, this historic venue sits outside the center of town. Although the café is intriguing, the magic here occurs in the nightly tango shows that are held in a specially designed salon complete with balconies and tables where you can dine on sumptuous *bife de chorizo* or *lomo* steaks and complimentary wine while enjoying a nightly performance (dinner 8:30pm, show 10:10pm, from US$130) at cheaper prices than many of its competitors. Most famous singers in the genre have performed here at some point during their careers.

MAP 6: Av. Rivadavia and Rincón, tel. 011/4952-2320, www.cafedelosangelitos. com; 10am-11:30pm daily

PORTEÑO
Café de García $$

Lying a little outside the city center, Café de García is easily reached by the San Martín train line. A vast collection of objects, ranging from old hair-gel pots to sewing machines, cover the walls, and are testament to the eccentric yet down-to-earth charm of so many *bodegones* in Buenos Aires. The real draw, however, is the famous *picada*, a platter of cheeses and cold meats, which includes almost 30 separate items and is served only in the evening Thursday to Saturday.

MAP 7: Sanabria 3302, tel. 011/4501-5912; 7:30am-1pm Mon.-Wed., 7:30am-1pm and 8:30pm-1am Thurs.-Sat., noon-4pm Sun.

Odisea $$

Hidden behind a mass of climbing plants and trees, this ancient house has been converted into a beautiful and little-known restaurant that cooks up gourmet dishes for reasonable prices. The *sorrentinos de salmon* (oversized ravioli filled with salmon) are popular. Odisea is romantic and atmospheric, with very friendly (although somewhat slow) service.

MAP 7: Olazábal 1767, tel. 011/4780-1725; 8pm-late Mon.-Sat.

ARGENTINE
Pan y Arte $$

Part of the burgeoning cultural scene in Boedo, Pan y Arte strives to deliver exactly what its name suggests—bread and art. The food is based on regional recipes and ingredients from Mendoza, a western Argentine province, and is served in an attractive and warmly lit salon. Art is displayed around the restaurant, while there is a theater on the second floor and a patio where events are hosted. A small store allows visitors to purchase regional food products.

MAP 7: Av. Boedo 878, tel. 011/4957-6702, www.panyarte.com.ar; 8am-late daily

Pan y Arte mixes food with art.

PARRILLAS
El Ferroviario $$

Formerly a canteen for train workers, El Ferroviario now opens its doors to the public. The result is a queue of two hours, so don't consider the long trek without a reservation. Mammoth portions, delicious meat, and excellent prices (including the wine) make the wait worthwhile. The starters should be shared, while the *asado ancho* (a large cut of meat, fat, and bone) and the *cochinillo* (half a suckling pig) are out of this world. The canteen-style *bodegón* (essentially, a traditional *parrilla*, as opposed to a modern one) features curing hams hanging from huge wooden beams.

MAP 7: Av. Reservistas Argentinos 219, tel. 011/4644-2360; noon-4pm and 8pm-midnight Tues.-Sun.

WE ALL SCREAM FOR ICE CREAM

The wave of Italian immigration around the turn of the 20th century influenced the local population in many ways, including language, architecture, and food. One of the most visible features that can be attributed to these Mediterranean roots is the prolific number of *heladerías* (ice cream parlors) around the city.

The style of ice cream is similar to Italian gelato and is either *a la crema* (cream-based) or *al agua* (water-based). A vast array of flavors are available, with most parlors offering a dozen chocolate-based options and almost as many varieties based on *dulce de leche* (caramelized milk). *Tramontana,* a mix of *crema americana* (similar to vanilla) ice cream, *dulce de leche,* and small chocolate-covered cookies, is especially popular with children and adults with a sweet tooth.

Porteños love to eat ice cream at all times of the day.

Most places will let you try a small amount on a spoon if asked nicely. Ice cream can be bought in *vasitos* (small wafer cups) or *cucuruchos* (cones) which come with one, two, or three *bochas* (scoops). A quarter kilo is the ideal size to share between two as a snack and usually allows for three different flavors. Buying one kilo often entails receiving a second for free.

Three of the largest chains around today were originally started by the same family. The dominance of such franchise-based parlors has led to the slow decline and eventual disappearance of some of the city's most emblematic independent parlors. The higher quality chains, which all have numerous outlets, are **Freddo, Persicco,** and **Munchi's.** Cheaper alternatives, such as **Grido,** tend to blend their flavors from powder-based compounds.

El Tano $$

Despite lying outside the city limits, El Tano is not difficult to reach and is well worth the trip. At this traditional *parrilla libre* (an all-you-can-eat *parrilla*), the friendly waiters bring plate after plate until asked to stop, making it an ideal moment to try all the extras, such as *chinculines* (intestines) and *molleja* (gizzards). Tables are close together and the noise level can be excessive. Booking in advance is a necessity; set aside plenty of time to get here.

MAP 7: Av. Güemes 567, tel. 011/4265-2079; 5pm-late Tues.-Fri., noon-late Sat., noon-5pm Sun.

CAFÉS AND *BARES NOTABLES*

Café Margot $

A historic presence on the main street of Boedo, Café Margot was so well-known for its chicken sandwiches that President Juan Perón is said to have halted his motorcade when passing one day so that he could try one himself. Its extensive menu provides many other treats, such as *picada* (platter of cold meats and cheeses) and *lomitos* (steak sandwiches), as well as craft beer. The walls around the bar display local artwork.

MAP 7: Av. Boedo 857, tel. 011/4957-0001, www.cafemargot.com.ar; 8am-late daily

ICE CREAM

Furchi $

For low-fat ice cream, head to Furchi in Belgrano, a long-standing spot offering over 60 flavors, including some unique options such as *manzana con perejíl* (apple and parsley) or *higo con roquefort* (fig and Roquefort cheese). Despite opening in 1959, the parlor is airy and an enjoyable place to sit inside or outside and enjoy your selection. Alternatively, lick away while strolling the leafy blocks to the north.

MAP 7: Av. Cabildo 1508; 9:30am-2am daily

NIGHTLIFE

For many, nighttime in Buenos Aires is more exciting than the day. After the sun sets, bars and restaurants open their doors and people of all ages take to the streets. Buenos Aires offers a huge range of evening activities, from rooftop bars to dance clubs on the coast and one of the most relaxed gay and lesbian scenes in Latin America.

The *porteño* drinking culture is relaxed and lasts all night.

Palermo has long been the heart of the action, with a high density of bars and clubs, although the Centro, San Telmo, and Almagro also draw crowds with their more varied offerings. Bars start filling up after 10pm and clubs rarely open before 1am.

Tango is the most traditional form of entertainment, and can be experienced in several ways: *milongas* (tango dance events), **tango shows,** and **dance classes.** Classical music has always been of great importance to *porteños,* as has rock. The ethnic complexity of the city has brought music from all over the world, including salsa, flamenco, and *candombe.*

While buses run throughout the night, their frequency decreases, and the Subte stops running between 10pm and 11pm, depending on the line. Taxi fares increase by 20 percent, and extra precaution should be taken, especially by women traveling alone.

HIGHLIGHTS

✪ **MOST GLAMOROUS TANGO SHOW:** For the luxurious side of tango, look no further than **Rojo Tango** (page 133).

✪ **MOST AFFORDABLE WAY TO WATCH TANGO:** Every Sunday sees **La Milonga del Indio,** where it's possible to watch a cluster of dancers in Plaza Dorrego (page 134).

✪ **BEST HISTORIC TANGO VENUE:** **El Viejo Almacén** has been entertaining guests with its shows since the 1930s (page 134).

✪ **MOST CREATIVE COCKTAILS:** The bartenders at the underground **Florería Atlántico** are waiting to mix you a range of concoctions (page 136).

✪ **MOST TRADITIONAL NIGHT OUT:** The food, folk music, and traditional dancing at **Del Colorado** allows you to experience culture from far-flung regions of Argentina (page 138).

✪ **SMOOTHEST VIBE:** Sipping a drink while soaking in the dulcet tones of jazz at **Thelonious** is romantic and relaxing (page 140).

✪ **MOST FRENETIC DANCE PARTY:** Late-night DJ parties induce serious adrenaline rushes at **Niceto Club,** one of the hottest nightspots in Buenos Aires (page 140).

✪ **BEST *MILONGA* FOR BEGINNERS:** Relaxed and informal **La Catedral** opens tango up to the uninitiated (page 142).

✪ **BEST PLACE TO LEARN SOME TANGO MOVES:** With its young, fun-loving crowd, **DNI Tango** is one of the freshest tango schools for beginners to tread the dance floor (page 143).

✪ **BEST TANGO MUSIC:** Sit back, close your eyes, and listen to the magic of a couple of old-timers singing and strumming guitars at **Lo de Roberto** (page 143).

✪ **HOTTEST GAY AND LESBIAN HANGOUT:** Offering free drinks two nights a week and scintillating entertainment, **Amerika** often fills to capacity (page 143).

✪ **BEST PLACE TO CATCH LOCAL ACTS:** Keeping a finger on the pulse of the local scene, **Konex** showcases the best local acts, including those who have gone on to international acclaim (page 146).

✪ **BEST BAR FOR DRINKING GAMES:** The doors at **Café San Bernardo** remain open 24-7 for late-night pool players, early morning table tennis fanatics, and midday pizza fans (page 148).

Centro

Map 1

TANGO SHOWS

El Querandí

Named after the indigenous community that previously ruled the Buenos Aires region, El Querandí is an atmospheric restaurant taking up a large street corner a few blocks south of Plaza de Mayo that hosts tango shows in the evening. Less flamboyant than others but with excellent food, the history of tango is taught through the dance and music, which includes costumed dancers performing daring waltzes along the beautiful wooden bar.

MAP 1: Perú 322, tel. 011/5199-1770, www.querandi.com.ar; dinner 8:30pm, show 10:10pm-11:40pm daily; from US$60 show only, US$140 show and dinner

tango dancers holding a traditional pose

Piazzolla Tango

The stunning Galería Güemes shopping center plays host to this tango show, which is situated in a lavishly decorated salon of cream and scarlet. Tables are crammed onto the main floor while two levels of spacious *palcos* (balconies) circle the room above. The music revolves around the work of Ástor Piazzolla, a revolutionary *bandoneón* player who fused classical music into tango. The food is excellent and prices are reasonable compared to similar tango shows.

MAP 1: Florida 165, tel. 011/4344-8200, www.piazzollatango.com; dinner 8:45pm, show 9:45pm-11:15pm daily; from US$30 show only, US$100 show and dinner

Tango Porteño

A glitzy and star-studded affair, Tango Porteño has gathered together some of the genre's greatest dancers to act out an homage to the golden age of tango, the 1940s. Impressive costume and set design, alongside superb choreography and production, lend great authenticity to this act, which can be enjoyed with or without a meal on tables that fill the salon in sweeping lines. Dinner includes a free tango class.

MAP 1: Cerrito 570, tel. 011/4124-9400, www.tangoporteno.com.ar; dinner 8:30pm, show 10:15pm-midnight daily; from US$45 show only, US$127 show and dinner

DANCE CLASSES

Escuela Argentina de Tango

The Escuela Argentina de Tango (Argentine Tango School) operates within the Centro Cultural Borges in Galerías Pacífico, an elegant shopping center in Centro. Classes of all levels are held throughout the day. The roster of teachers constantly changes, attracting some of the most well-known dancers, teachers, and musicians.

TANGO

Tango belongs to Buenos Aires. There are several ways to enjoy tango: *milongas* (tango dance events), shows, and classes. It's also common, especially in neighborhoods such as Almagro, for tango musicians to drop into small bars to perform short sets. Additionally, the annual **Tango Buenos Aires Festival y Mundial** is devoted to tango in all its forms.

MILONGAS

Milongas occur in bars, cultural centers, sports clubs, or even on the street. While *milongas* are steeped in etiquette and tradition, visitors are always welcome, and there is never an obligation to dance. The regular dancers don't really show up until after midnight, so it's best to arrive later in the night.

Traditionally, men invite women onto the dance floor. This may be done with a suggestive raise of the eyebrows, an indication of the head called a *cabaceo,* or a verbal invitation. Dancers may invite women who already have partners. Age differences are ignored. Couples move to the dance floor for each *tanda,* a group of three or four songs.

It's generally not appropriate to dance without previous experience. There are *milongas* specifically oriented toward beginners. Many venues also host *prácticas* (practices), a relaxed version of a *milonga.* Most venues maintain a dependable weekly schedule.

TANGO SHOWS

For visitors, shows are perhaps the preferred form of experiencing tango. Often held in venues known as *tanguerías,* they generally consist of flamboyant, choreographed dancing on a stage accompanied by a live orchestra. While these events cater to the tourist market, they can be a pleasing and exciting spectacle. Most tickets include a taxi transfer to and from the venue.

DANCE CLASSES

There are a huge variety of tango classes, starting from *principiantes* (beginners), or Tango 1 through to *acanzados* (experts), or Tango 5. Classes are always available in groups, where it is common to dance with strangers, but private classes can be arranged.

All of the schools listed in this guide accept drop-in students. Many *milongas* offer classes before the dance starts, which generally include free entry to the event itself.

Inquire beforehand to get a sense of which class you're most suited for.

MAP 1: Viamonte 525, 2nd fl., tel. 011/4893-0718, www.eatangoge.com; 11:15am-5pm daily; from US$8

BARS
Absinth

An old-school bar located on a corner a few blocks from Palacio de Congreso, Absinth offers three floors of activities. The ground floor is a standard bar, while the second floor is more suited to group gatherings. The basement is the real star, however, where some of the funniest Buenos Aires comics present their latest stand-up shows (in Spanish) and where bands sometimes play. Absinthe is, unsurprisingly, the drink of choice.

MAP 1: Bartolomé Mitre 1699, tel. 011/4372-4358, www.absinthrestobar.com.ar; 9am-late Mon.-Fri., 7pm-late Sat.-Sun.; no cover

La Cigale

This dim, high-ceilinged bar occupies a stunning building in the center of the city. Functioning as a restaurant at lunchtime, in the evenings it turns into a nonstop party, with live music, dancing, and cocktails being the main draws. La Cigale celebrates its French roots on Tuesday, Wednesday is dub night, while Friday and Saturday, the most popular, are dedicated to electronic music. Although there is music and dancing, people mainly visit it as a bar.

MAP 1: 25 de Mayo 597, tel. 011/4893-2332; noon-3pm and 6pm-3am Mon.-Fri., 9:30pm-4am Sat.; no cover

Puerto Madero   Map 1

TANGO SHOWS
✪ Rojo Tango

Unlike the traditional *milongas* and tango bars of Buenos Aires, Rojo Tango is one of the plushest and most luxurious places to watch professional dancers on stage. Located in the five-star Faena Hotel, the show includes a delicious steak dinner during which dancers swirl among the tables. With some of the top dancers in the world, extravagant costumes, renowned orchestras, and glitzy decoration, Rojo Tango is of the most expensive options, but it is also one of the most popular: Reservations are essential.

MAP 1: Martha Salotti 445, tel. 011/4952-4111, www.rojotango.com; dinner 8:30pm, show 10pm-midnight daily; from US$190 show only, US$250 show and dinner

dancers performing at Rojo Tango

DANCE CLUBS
Asia de Cuba

Serving pricey meals by day, Asia de Cuba turns into a lavish upmarket club later in the night, attracting wealthy *porteños* and visitors. The music is fairly generic, covering electronic, Latin, and pop, but the view over the docks of Puerto Madero adds charm to this Eastern-themed club. Wednesday is the big night, but smart dress and hefty wallets are necessary every night. Reservations are strongly advised.

MAP 1: Pierina Dialessi 750, tel. 011/4894-1328, www.asiadecuba.com.ar; 1pm-midnight Sun.-Wed., 1pm-6am Thurs.-Sat.; cover US$15, free before 2am

San Telmo and La Boca   Map 2

MILONGAS
✪ La Milonga del Indio

When the market stalls are cleared away from Plaza Dorrego on Sunday evening, a cluster of dancers takes over the western side of the square, where local dancers mingle with tourists under the trees and romantic lighting on an improvised dance floor. It's an ideal place to watch tango dancers, as there is no fee—tables in surrounding bars offer great views.

MAP 2: Plaza Dorrego, Defensa 1100; 7pm-10pm Sun.; no cover

TANGO SHOWS
Bar Sur

With only a handful of tables dotted around an ancient drinking salon with a beautifully tiled floor and wooden interior, Bar Sur offers the most intimate tango shows in the city, where dancers pass within inches of the tables. Open during the day as a typical bar-café where customers can come and go as they please, by night it transforms into a cozy affair and you'll need to pay a cover to enter. Although the show lasts two hours, a fair portion of this is taken by performances from the orchestra and the singer. Drinks are not included in the price.

MAP 2: Estados Unidos 299, tel. 011/4362-6086, www.bar-sur.com.ar; 8am-late daily, show 8pm-10pm daily; US$50 show only

✪ El Viejo Almacén

One of the oldest tango shows in Buenos Aires, El Viejo Almacén has been a venue for tango since the early 1930s. Guests are offered dinner in the five-floor restaurant before the show starts, with the notable addition of a folklore section, providing an even wider presentation of Argentine music. An introductory film is also shown in the intimate theater before the dancers take to the stage.

MAP 2: Av. Independencia 313, tel. 011/4307-7388, www.viejoalmacen.com.ar; dinner 8pm, show 10pm daily; from US$90 show only, US$140 show and dinner

DANCE CLASSES
Escuela Mariposita

Mariposita, a boutique hotel, tango school, and cultural center set in an old San Telmo mansion, is the result of Carolina Bonaventura's passion for tango. With group classes throughout the week, mainly in the evenings, the space is dedicated to art and the expression of tango. Specific plans can

For pints and curry, swing by Gibraltar.

be drawn up for students looking for a short period of intensive classes.
MAP 2: Carlos Calvo 950, tel. 011/4300-3247, www.mariposita.com.ar; US$6

LIVE MUSIC
El Samovar de Rasputín
This small and intimate bar in La Boca offers some of the best live blues music in Buenos Aires. Brightly colored on the outside but dark and dingy on the inside, blues music is played at all hours via a projection screen, only stopping when a band is playing. Although food is served throughout the day, El Samovar is most enjoyable for sipping on a beer and listening to music during the evenings alongside the loyal regulars.
MAP 2: Del Valle Iberlucea 1251, tel. 011/4302-3190; 8am-late Fri.-Sun.; no cover

BARS
Gibraltar
One of the first English-style pubs in the city, Gibraltar is known for its rowdy nights and international crowd. Beer, served in English pint glasses, is unsurprisingly the most common tipple. The pub grub here is notable, with curries, roasts, and fish-and-chips among the options. A pool table lies just before a small patio out back. Late at night it gets crowded inside, so it's worth arriving early.
MAP 2: Perú 895, tel. 011/4362-5310, www. thegibraltarbar.com; noon-4am daily

La Puerta Roja
A little farther from San Telmo's tourist attractions, La Puerta Roja (The Red Door) is nonetheless consistently full of locals and foreigners alike. True to its name, the bar is found behind a bouncer-protected red door. A flight of stairs leads to a bar with three rooms, including a pool table. The music is decidedly international, and the party rolls on to dawn.
MAP 2: Chacabuco 733, tel. 011/4362-5649, http://lapuertaroja.com.ar; noon-late daily; no cover

GAY AND LESBIAN BARS

Flux

One of the newer and more relaxed gay bars in Buenos Aires, Flux also draws a heterosexual crowd. A stylishly decorated basement bar, it also offers a patio space. It's a little cheaper than alternatives and also has earlier opening and closing times. Occasional events (advertised on the website) are held, such as DJs, drag shows, and even tango classes.

MAP 3: Marcelo T. de Alvear 980, tel. 011/5252-0258, www.fluxbarbuenosaires. blogspot.com; 7pm-3am Sun.-Thurs., 7pm-4am Fri.-Sat.; cover up to US$5

BARS

✪ Florería Atlántico

Since opening in 2013, this speakeasy-themed bar has been voted the best bar in Latin America by various publications. A fridge door in the back of an innocuous flower shop leads down to a long, rustic basement, where the city's finest mixologists prepare innovative and delicious cocktails. The exhaustive wine list (also available in bottles in the flower shop upstairs) is also prepared by top sommeliers, while a *parrilla* in the kitchen ensures nobody goes cold or hungry. The crowd is mixed, with some coming for food and others for the cocktails, but the bar invariably fills with people soon after opening, so come early or make reservations.

MAP 3: Arroyo 872, tel. 011/4313-6093, www.floreriaatlantico.com.ar; 7pm-2am Mon.-Thurs., 7pm-4am Fri., 8pm-4am Sat., 8pm-2am Sun.; no cover

Sky Bar

The aptly named Sky Bar is on the 13th floor terrace of the Hotel Pulitzer and offers stunning views of the city during the evening. Live music, ranging from jazz to electronic, is played most nights, producing a serenade to the sunset. Bartenders whip up original cocktails, while tapas are laid out for bar-goers to munch on while listening to the relaxing music in the swanky surroundings. Sky Bar is only open between October and April. Check their website for upcoming performers.

MAP 3: Maipú 907, tel. 011/4316-0800, www.hotelpulitzer.com.ar; 5pm-midnight Sun.-Wed., 5pm-2am Thurs.-Sat. Oct.-Apr.; no cover

Sky Bar

LIVE MUSIC
Notorious

Access this modern and upscale jazz club by passing through a CD/DVD store into a room where many tables are crammed into a small space. The food menu is limited but popular, and there is an interesting selection of cocktails. Food and drink prices are high, as are the tickets, but this is where the cream of international performers come to play in Buenos Aires. Saturday nights generally feature artists performing bossa nova. You can buy a ticket in advance or just pay at the door.

MAP 4: Av. Callao 966, tel. 011/4813-6888, www.notorious.com.ar; noon-4pm and 9pm-1am Mon.-Thurs., noon-4pm and 9pm-2am Fri.-Sat., 9pm-midnight Sun.; cover from US$18

DANCE CLUBS
Club Shampoo

This former cabaret is one of the city's most popular clubs. Decorated with endless disco balls, chandeliers, and draped curtains, it oozes style. Queuing for entry can be quite a wait, especially on Halloween, when fancy dress is obligatory and droves head to this club. The dress code on most other nights is formal and the music is electronic, varying from Latin American artists to international commercial hits.

MAP 4: Av. Quintana 362, tel. 011/4816-4200, www.clubshampoo.com.ar; 12:30am-6am Thurs.-Sat.; cover US$10-20

GAY AND LESBIAN
KM Zero

This smallish basement venue in a central location offers electro-house music and exotic dancers, and is open every night of the week. Leather sofas and tables provide views of the stage, while a divey atmosphere surrounds the dimly lit bar. Men are predominant, although women are equally welcome. A variety of shows (cabarets, burlesque) are held during the week.

MAP 4: Av. Santa Fe 2516, tel. 011/4822-7530, www.kmzero.com.ar; midnight-late daily; cover from US$5

BARS
El Alamo

On a quiet side street in Recoleta, this rowdy bar is always bursting at the seams. Bars on three floors offer customers a choice of where to drink or eat. Women drink beer for free until midnight, while many beverages can be bought in four-liter pitchers for great prices. Beer pong is common, as is dancing on the tables, while U.S. sports matches are always screened. This is not a place for a quiet night.

MAP 4: Uruguay 1175, tel. 011/4813-7324, www.elalamobar.com; 4pm-4am Mon.-Wed., 10am-4am Thurs.-Sat., noon-4am Sun.; cover US$10

Jobs

Archery, darts, Jenga, dominoes, dice, table tennis, air hockey, and pool are just some of the activities you can partake in while drinking or eating pizza at this bar. Prices are reasonable and many games are free, although the slightly dingy interior

bartender at El Alamo

MAP 4: Arenales 2932, tel. 011/4822-9391, www.jobsbar.com.ar; 7pm-4am Tues., 7pm-3am Wed.-Thurs., 7pm-5am Fri., 9pm-5am Sat., 9pm-3am Sun.; no cover, board games free, other games from US$3

Milión

One of the most attractive bars in Buenos Aires, Milión occupies a beautifully restored three-floor French building that boasts a splendid garden where customers can sit. The eccentric clientele makes it an excellent place for people-watching. Although there is a food menu, it is not as good as the prices suggest, and people generally come here for the cocktails, which feature adventurous ingredients and are known for being strong.

MAP 4: Paraná 1048, tel. 011/4815-9925, www.milion.com.ar; noon-2am Mon.-Wed., noon-3am Thurs., noon-4am Fri., 7:30pm-4am Sat., 8pm-2am Sun.

can become raucous as the drinks start flowing. This is an ideal place to come with a group. Check the website for promotions on different activities each day.

Palermo   Map 5

PEÑAS FOLKLÓRICAS

Peñas folklóricas, generally referred to simply as *peñas,* originated in the Andean regions of Argentina, becoming popular in Buenos Aires when people from these communities looked to replicate the relaxed party atmosphere from back home. *Peñas* generally involve traditional food, live music, and dancing. Later in the evening, anyone can pick up a guitar and join in, although the traditional dancing is difficult for the uninitiated. Sporadic *peñas* pop up across the city, but the two in this guide are the best permanent offerings.

✪ Del Colorado

A rustic bodega in a quiet part of Palermo, Del Colorado fills in the evenings to the sounds of live *folklórica* music. The most popular *peña folklórica* in Buenos Aires, Del Colorado's starts with a show, during which delicious regional food is served, but the night really kicks off afterward, when anyone can pick up one of the instruments lying around and play.

MAP 5: Guemes 3657, tel. 011/4822-1038, www.lapeniadelcolorado.com; 8pm-4am daily; cover from US$5

milonga at Salon Canning

Los Cardones

Decorated in a traditional style, Los Cardones recreates the *peñas* of the northern province of Salta, from where *peñas folklóricas* originated. This includes regional food, such as tamales and empanadas, as well as traditional music and dancing. All ages congregate here in a family-oriented atmosphere. Shows are only from Wednesday to Saturday and draw up to 500 people, making reservations advisable.

MAP 5: Borges 2180, tel. 011/4777-1112, www.cardones.com.ar; 9pm-5am Wed.-Sat.; cover from US$6

MILONGAS
La Viruta

This late-night *milonga* kicks the evening off with dance classes (tango, salsa, and rock) before turning into a free-for-all event that is one of the largest and rowdiest in the city. You can watch from the tables and chairs that surround the basement dance floor, but these fill up quickly as the live orchestras, dancing, and shows start. This is one of the less formal *milongas* and one of the best for beginner dancers.

MAP 5: Armenia 1366, tel. 011/4832-4105, www.lavirutatango.com; 6:30pm-late Wed.-Thurs., 7pm-late Fri.-Sat., 8pm-late Sun.; cover US$8

Salon Canning

Many professional tango dancers consider Salon Canning to have the highest quality floor of all, which means that it draws some of the city's best. Various *milongas* are held by different organizations during the week, but Parakultural (www.parakultural. com.ar, 7pm-11pm Mon.-Tues. and Fri., US$7) hosts the biggest ones, with tango orchestras giving live accompaniment to the dancers and classes beforehand.

MAP 5: Scalabrini Ortiz 1331, tel. 011/4832-6753; 11pm-5am Mon.-Fri.; cover US$7

Villa Malcolm

A sports club by day, *milonga* by night, Villa Malcolm offers nightly dances that are much more relaxed and informal than many others, with less attention paid to traditional rules and dress. As a result, the crowd is much younger and the atmosphere less tense, which makes it ideal for beginners and visitors. Classes beforehand include free entry to the *milonga* or *práctica* (a less formal *milonga*).

MAP 5: Av. Córdoba 5064, tel. 011/4772-5993; 10pm-late Mon., 11pm-2:30am Wed., 10:30pm-2am Thurs., 11:30pm-3:30am Fri., 11:30pm-3am Sat.; cover from US$6

DANCE CLASSES
La Viruta

Home to a boisterous *milonga*, La Viruta also offers group dance classes on Tuesday and Saturday. Classes include all levels, from beginner to expert, with individual teachers for each level, all of whom speak English and Spanish. Choose from tango, *bachata*, salsa, folk, or rock. Saturday lessons even include entry to the *milonga*.

MAP 5: Armenia 1366, tel. 011/5263-2255, www.lavirutadesolanas.com; 6:30pm-midnight Tues., 5pm-6am Sat.; US$6 Tues., US$8 Sat.

LIVE MUSIC
✪ Thelonious

Inspired by the jazz clubs of New York, Thelonious is a beautifully lit atmospheric bar that stretches around a first floor corner. Offering international acts as well as local ones, the club has a limited capacity (70-80 people), which means that early arrival is advisable, especially if you're hoping for a spot on a leather sofa at the front. The bar mixes decent cocktails and also serves up delicious pizzas and basic *picadas*. The first show is at 9:30pm (reservations accepted); the second show is at 12:30am (no reservations).

MAP 5: Jeronimo Salguero 1884, tel. 011/4829-1562, www.thelonious.com.ar; 9pm-late Wed.-Sat.; cover from US$10

jazz musicians at Thelonious

Boris Jazz Club

Despite being the newest of the main players on the Buenos Aires jazz scene, Boris has quickly become one of the most important, hosting some of the finest international acts visiting the city. It's decidedly more modern that its contemporaries, and patrons are expected to be well dressed and willing to open their wallets a little further. The main room is spacious, with tabled balconies above and atmospheric lighting.

MAP 5: Gorriti 5568, tel. 011/4777-0012, www.borisclub.com; 10am-5pm and 6pm-3am Tues.-Sun.; cover from US$10

Café Vinilo

At first, Café Vinilo appears to be a tiny bar with a small patio, but this is in fact just the space where people wait before entering the music hall at the back. Some of the city's most admired artists play here, representing a wide range of genres, including tango, rock, jazz, and salsa. Spectators sit at tables, which enables eating before and during the show. Tempting dishes are on offer, as is beer brewed on-site.

MAP 5: Gorriti 3780, tel. 011/4866-6520, www.cafevinilo.com.ar; 7pm-late daily; cover from US$8

DANCE CLUBS
✪ Niceto Club

Although most nights feature live performances in Niceto Club, the real party starts after the shows, when DJs take to the stage and pound out music until the early morning. Mainly featuring electronic music, they also play *cumbia*, rock, and other eclectic genres to a young crowd. The raucous Invasion party on Friday is the highlight. It's a compact venue, but people squeeze in, with balconies providing a bit of breathing space. Check the website for a schedule and to get on the guest list, as this is one of the hottest clubs in the city.

MAP 5: Niceto Vega 5510, tel. 011/4779-9396, www.nicetoclub.com; 9pm-7am Thurs.-Sat.; cover from US$10, drink included

Club Aráoz

Quick to fill up due to free entry before 2:30am, Club Aráoz is a frenzied party all weekend, with a wide range of mostly mainstream music, often played by some of the top local DJs. Thursday is the big night, however, when break dancing and hip-hop take over. The dress code is relaxed, and the crowd is a real mix. A decent food menu is also available.

MAP 5: Aráoz 2424, tel. 011/4832-9751, www.clubaraoz.com.ar; 11pm-7am Thurs.-Sat.; cover US$5, free before 2:30am

Crobar

Found under the railroad bridges on the edge of the parks in Palermo, Crobar is one of the largest and most popular clubs in Buenos Aires. It's also one of the priciest. Drawing top local and international DJs, the music is mainly house and electronica and the visual effects, such as light displays and multimedia projector screens, are excellent. Friday is the big night, while Saturday is popular with gay and lesbian folk.

MAP 5: Av. Libertador 3886, tel. 011/4778-1500, www.crobar.com.ar; 10pm-late Thurs.-Sat.; cover from US$20

Pacha

On the north coast of the city, Pacha is part of the club chain that also has locations in Ibiza and New York. Drawing the biggest-name DJs, along with hordes of weekend revelers, the large dance floor bounces to techno, house, and trance music. An open-air terrace overlooking the Río de la Plata is a perfect spot to watch the sunrise after a long night. Taking a taxi will be necessary to get here.

MAP 5: Av. Costanera Rafael Obligado and La Pampa, tel. 011/4788-4280, www.pachabuenosaires.com; 1am-7am Fri.-Sat.; cover US$10

GAY AND LESBIAN BARS
Bach Bar

Bach Bar is the oldest gay bar in the city and one of the friendliest. It was originally strictly for women and still draws mainly lesbians. On the small side, it can become crowded, especially when there are live bands, drag performances, or cabaret shows. Wednesday is "Cupid Night," when visitors are urged to communicate with each other via special telephones, while Sunday has karaoke.

MAP 5: Cabrera 4390, tel. 015/5877-0919; 11pm-late Wed.-Sun.; no cover

Sitges

One of the oldest and proudest gay clubs in Buenos Aires, Sitges mainly attracts men, although women are also welcome. Music is electronic and an impressive range of cocktails are offered. Drag shows occur after midnight. Wednesday provides free pizza; on Friday it's free drinks. Thursday and Saturday have performers, while Sunday includes karaoke and a special telephone chat-up event. The spacious venue allows for relaxed drinks before the real party starts.

MAP 5: Av. Córdoba 4119, tel. 011/4861-3763; midnight-6am Thurs.-Mon.; no cover

BARS

Antares

Antares is a bar run by brewers of the same name. This sophisticated drinking hall is a haven for beer-lovers. The large open space is dominated by shiny towering kegs along one wall. There is plenty of space between tables, although the noise still inhibits conversation later in the evening. A small food menu is available, but everyone comes here to drink, often opting for the sample tray of every beer available.

MAP 5: Armenia 1447, tel. 011/4833-9611; 7pm-late daily

Frank's

A traditional, sophisticated speakeasy, Frank's has been named the best bar in South America in multiple contests. Chandeliers hang over the bar, which is manned by barmen in waistcoats and bow ties. Low chairs and tables are surrounded by patterned walls. Prices are high but the drinks are excellent and the atmosphere buzzes with a 1920s theme. To enter, you must whisper the password (listed daily on the website) to the doorman, who will give a code to type into a phone box, granting access to the bar itself (which also, strangely, includes a sex shop).

MAP 5: Arevalo 1445, tel. 011/4777-6541; 9pm-3am Tues.-Sat.; no cover

Oliver's Club

A concept bar purportedly based on 19th-century Paris, Oliver's specializes in cocktails served in an open space that offers sporadic live music and events. On Friday night they embrace the international side of Buenos Aires with a language exchange night: Small flag badges are handed out to customers that indicate the languages that they speak; you're then urged to mingle and practice speaking in Spanish, English, Italian, or whatever tickles your fancy.

MAP 5: Guatemala 4462, tel. 011/4832-5858; 9pm-2am Thurs., 10pm-3:30am Fri-Sat.

Almagro   Map 6

MILONGAS

✪ La Catedral

Looking industrial and worn down from the outside, La Catedral is full of color and quirks on the inside, with framed pictures crammed together on the walls and strange sculptures hanging from the ceiling. One of the city's best-known *milongas*, it's notable for the relaxed and informal atmosphere, making it perfect for unsure foreigners and beginner dancers, especially on Tuesday, when the focus is entirely on beginners.

La Catedral

Classes (US$7) are held every evening and include free entry to the *milonga* afterward, which usually includes live music and shows. This is one of the most popular choices for visitors, as the teachers speak English and encourage beginners.

MAP 6: Sarmiento 4006, tel. 0115325-1630, www.lacatedralclub.com; 6pm-4am daily; cover US$7, free before 10pm

DANCE CLASSES
✪ DNI Tango
One of the freshest tango schools in Buenos Aires, with a youthful and airy vibe, DNI Tango is spread over multiple floors of a house in Almagro. Private and group classes for all levels are available. Some classes focus on specifics such as a closed embrace, women's technique, or musicality. Classes are held Monday through Saturday, and there is also a tango store and café. The first class is free.

MAP 6: Bulnes 1011, tel. 011/4866-6553, www.dni-tango.com; 2pm-9:30pm Mon.-Sat.; US$5

Tango Escuela Carlos Copello
The Copello family has included a number of top dancers over the years, including the revered Carlos and his son Maxi. As teachers, the Copellos' passion fills their students with confidence and determination. Class schedules vary.

MAP 6: Guardia Vieja 3530, tel. 011/4864-6229, www.carloscopello.com; 7:30pm-9pm Mon.-Fri.; from US$5

LIVE MUSIC
✪ Lo de Roberto
Located on the corner of Plaza Almagro, Lo de Roberto, also known as El Boliche de Roberto, is a *bar notable* as well as a meeting point for tango musicians who wander around the neighborhood in the evening, playing wherever they can. Most hope to play here, as there is always a vibrant, mystical atmosphere. Formerly a general store, Lo de Roberto has a tiny bar and can be crammed with customers of all ages into the night. Silence is expected during music sets, which tend to go onstage from 10pm onward.

MAP 6: Bulnes 331, tel. 011/4862-0415; 6pm-3am Tues.-Fri., 10pm-3am Sat.; no cover

Club Atlético Fernández Fierro
This former auto mechanic shop has been converted into a live music space that's home to the Orquesta Típica Fernández Fierro, a tango collective that plays here every Wednesday. Although it was originally intended for just the tango orchestra, this venue quickly started hosting other acts, as well as dances, classes, and other social events. The musical style tends toward modern tango, often with influences from other genres such as rock and reggae. The informal atmosphere and simple decoration attracts a fun-loving crowd.

MAP 6: Sánchez de Bustamante 764, www.caff.com.ar; hours vary by event; cover from US$10

GAY AND LESBIAN BARS
✪ Amerika
The rowdiest and largest gay disco in Buenos Aires, Amerika has male and female exotic dancers, large screens, and various bars. The main dance floor plays electronica, while a smaller, darker room plays Latin music. On Friday and Saturday, drinks

are free, which ensures that it fills to the 2,000-person capacity, with plenty of straight people joining in the fun. Queues can be very long, meaning that it is worth arriving before 2am.

MAP 6: Gascón 1040, tel. 011/4865-4416, www.ameri-k.com.ar; 12:30am-7am Fri.-Sun.; cover from US$12

Casa Brandon

A little off the beaten track, Casa Brandon explodes with activities, music, art, and socializing. The venue hosts film events, displays sexually themed artwork, and presents live acts. It's aimed toward lesbians, although gay men and people of any sexual orientation are more than welcome. Karaoke nights and lively parties all support the goal of promoting a queer cultural scene.

MAP 6: Luis Maria Drago 236, tel. 011/4858-0610, www.brandon.org.ar; 8pm-late Wed.-Sat.; no cover

BARS

Casona Humahuaca

A bar that doubles as a cultural center run by neighbors and members, Casona is a cooperative running out of a converted house. Casona offers a wide range of free events, from film nights to theater performances and spontaneous jam sessions with professional musicians. A huge wooden carving of the neighborhood hangs from the ceiling inside, while a patio offers a leafy outdoor space to drink. Simple in its concept, it nonetheless offers culture and friendliness on warm summer evenings. They also serve simple drinks, such as beer, wine, and fernet (as well as a few other spirits and nonalcoholic drinks). The inside of the bar is cozy and warm.

MAP 6: Humahuaca 3508, tel. 011/4862-5369, www.casonahumahuaca. com.ar; 4pm-late Mon.-Fri., 3pm-late Sat., 7pm-late Sun.

Club Cultural Matienzo

Originally located in a small house, Club Matienzo moved to a larger space when their eclectic and varied offerings began drawing large crowds. Film screenings, book readings and workshops, musical performances, and drawing sessions are just a small selection of the activities available in this sprawling club. (These activities often cross over with one another, such as a drawing session of a jazz band performing.) A rooftop bar sits above everything, while freshly cooked food is also served. Check the website for upcoming activities and events. Drawing a varied but young crowd, Matienzo has an atmosphere that is cultured yet fun.

MAP 6: Pringles 1249, tel. 011/6610-1520, www.ccmatienzo.com.ar; 7pm-2am Tues.-Thurs., 7pm-5am Fri., 8pm-5am Sat., 8pm-2am Sun.; donation requested for activities

El Banderín

One of the first *bares notables* in Buenos Aires, El Banderín takes its name from the hundreds of *fútbol* pennants and flags that adorn the walls. While it's a delightful spot to drop by for an afternoon drink, alcoholic or not, the evenings are filled with tango music (sometimes live), *fútbol* on the television, and relaxed drinkers. Drinks come with free nibbles; the owner, Mario, greets all his guests with a smile and a few words.

MAP 6: Guardia Vieja 3601, tel. 011/4862-7757, www.elbanderin.com.ar; 8:30am-11pm Mon.-Thurs., 8:30am-3am Fri.

La Tribu

A bar that hosts regular events, such as films on Friday night and concerts performed from the street balcony, La Tribu can be easily spotted by the colorful murals that cover the front of the building. Armchairs and sofas provide comfy seating, and the prices for the drinks and simple bar food are excellent. The atmosphere tends to be relaxed, though it gets really lively on nights when parties are held. A community radio station by the same name is broadcast from a studio at the back of the building.

MAP 6: Lambare 873, tel. 011/4866-1095, www.fmlatribu.com; noon-late Mon.-Fri., 4pm-late Sat.; no cover

Señor Duncan

A beautiful mansion on a dreary avenue, Señor Duncan shines from inside, with stained glass, wood decor, and looming ceilings. A cultural center that offers theater, live music, open mic, dance classes, and more, this bar is wildly popular among locals. A piano is available for guests to play, and there are daily live music performances of all genres. Their Facebook page lists upcoming events.

Señor Duncan also offers tango dance classes on Tuesday night. Classes are catered to all levels and include a *práctica* (informal *milonga*) with a live orchestra. There's no set cost for the classes; dancers are asked to pay what they feel is appropriate.

MAP 6: Av. Rivadavia 3832, tel. 011/4958-3633; 7pm-late daily; no cover

WINE BARS
La Cava de Jufré

A wine bar that doubles as a wine store, La Cava de Jufré is a must-stop for vino enthusiasts. The owner, Lito, personally attends to his guests, offering informed opinions and advice as well as tasting sessions. Situated on an attractive corner, the bar is beautifully decorated with bare brick and wood, while the cellar is a joy to behold: Looming racks of wine line the walls and the dim lighting around a sole wooden table creates a magical atmosphere. Generous *picadas* (platters of cold meats and cheeses) go down well with the wine.

MAP 6: Jufré 201, tel. 011/4775-7501, www.lacavajufre.com.ar; 11am-2pm and 6:30pm-late Tues.-Sat.

Balvanera

Map 6

MILONGAS

El Beso

A favorite place of professional dancers, El Beso is a traditional *milonga* that hosts high-quality dancing. Traditional rules are enforced, such as the *cabaceo* (a technique used by men to invite women to dance with movements of the head) as well as men and women sitting on opposite sides of the room. It is a small, intimate venue up a flight of stairs. On Friday they host a gay and lesbian *milonga*.

MAP 6: Riobamba 416, tel. 011/4953-2794; 6pm-1am Mon., 9pm-3am Tues., 10:30pm-3am Wed., 6pm-12:30am Thurs., 10:30pm-3am Fri., 10:30pm-5am Sat., 10pm-3am Sun.; cover from US$5

TANGO SHOWS

Complejo Tango

The show put on at Complejo Tango is dramatic and entertaining, educating its audience on the history and traditions of tango. Located in an old neighborhood house, the large salon seems to appear from nowhere, with sweeping balconies above the oak floor. The evening kicks off with free tango classes, followed by dinner and the show. Discounts are available online.

MAP 6: Av. Belgrano 2608, tel. 011/4941-1119, www.complejotango.com. ar; class 7:30pm, dinner 8:30pm, show 10:00pm-11:15pm daily; show and drinks from US$85, show and dinner US$120

Esquina Carlos Gardel

Once a favorite haunting ground for Carlos Gardel, the legendary tango singer, this venue in the heart of the Abasto neighborhood in Balvanera is one of the most authentic tango shows around. The elegant cream-and-black decorations become a vivid red under the lights when up to 25 dancers twirl onstage after dinner has been served. A taxi to transport guests to the venue is included in the price.

MAP 6: Carlos Gardel 3200, tel. 011/4867-6363, www.esquinacarlosgardel. com.ar; dinner 8:30pm, show 10:30pm-midnight daily; show only from US$100, show and dinner US$140

LIVE MUSIC

✪ Konex

Home to La Bomba de Tiempo, a 16-piece drumming trance group who kick up a rave every Monday night, Konex consistently hosts the most popular musicians of Buenos Aires. The outdoor stage moves into a large warehouse when it rains, but the party always rocks on well into the night. Beer and fernet are pretty much the only drinks on offer and are available by the liter. Queues stretching a few blocks are common, so arrive early.

MAP 6: Sarmiento 3131, tel. 011/4863-3200, www.ciudadculturalkonex. org; hours vary by event; cover from US$8

FERNET FRENZY

Fernet is the most popular liquor in Argentina. More of it is consumed here than anywhere else in the world, with an estimated average of 740 drinks knocked back every minute. Initially brought over by Italian immigrants around the turn of the 20th century, it is now considered one of the national drinks of Argentina. A bitter, spiced liquor, its oily appearance and medicinal taste come with an alcohol content of around 45 percent, all of which means that it can be an acquired taste.

Numerous health benefits have been attributed to fernet over the years. Due to its digestive properties, it was traditionally drunk neat after a meal. Today, it's almost always consumed with cola (*fernet con cola*), and it is generally agreed that this *must* be Coca-Cola.

The most common brand of fernet is **Fernet Branca,** which originates from Italy. The main alternative is **1882,** which comes from Córdoba province in Argentina, the real heart of fernet appreciation. Cheaper alternatives, such as **Vittone** or **Lusera,** are drinkable but harsher and less refined in flavor. Pre-mixed versions of *fernet con cola* can be bought in most supermarkets and *kioscos*, often costing less than cola alone, but these are poor imitations.

It's not uncommon for bars to sell little else besides beer and *fernet con cola,* often served in generously sized pitchers to share. A standard mix is around one-third fernet and two-thirds cola, with plenty of ice.

Greater Buenos Aires   Map 7

MILONGAS

La Glorieta

Open-air *milongas* are held in the park overlooking Plaza Barrancas de Belgrano and its accompanying train station throughout the year, although they are most enjoyable during the warmer months. Locals and visitors mix in this relaxed and informal venue, for which a "suggested donation" of US$1.50 is required. The charm of this *milonga* is the surrounding park and feeling of freedom when dancing. It's also a great place to watch the dancers without having to pay an entrance fee.

MAP 7: 11 de Septiembre, between Sucre and Echeverría; 7pm-11:30pm Mon. and Wed., 7:30pm-11:30pm Fri., 6pm-11pm Sat.-Sun.; minimum donation US$1.50

Los Laureles

More than 100 years old, Los Laureles is a *bar notable* that retains the charm and traditions of old times. Away from the center, there are few visitors in the Barracas neighborhood, but there is no need to feel out of place. In the evening, the tables are pushed aside to reveal a stone dance floor and live bands and orchestras perform. Weekends are the best time to come, and the *milongas* are gay-friendly.

MAP 7: Av. General Iriarte 2290, tel. 011/4303-3393, www.barloslaureles.com.ar; 8pm-2am Wed.-Thurs., 8pm-4am Fri.-Sat., 8pm-2am Sun.; no cover

Sin Rumbo

Declaring itself the "tango cathedral," Sin Rumbo is indeed one of the most traditional and revered *milongas* in Buenos Aires. Close to where the city borders Buenos Aires province, in the neighborhood of Villa Urquiza, the ceramic floors of Sin Rumbo have been graced by many tango aficionados. The formal dress code, sparse decor, and garish lighting are all a throwback to what a *milonga* used to be.

MAP 7: Tamborini 6157, tel. 011/4574-0972, www.elsinrumbo.com.ar; 10pm-4am Fri.; cover US$5

TANGO SHOWS
Esquina Homero Manzi

On one of the city's most historic street corners in the southern neighborhood of Boedo, Esquina Homero Manzi is a large café and restaurant by day that hosts tango shows in the evening. The dancers and musicians recapture the magic of tango's golden era with costumes, orchestras, and wild choreography. The show and setting aren't as glamorous as most others, but that's the point, with this being one of the more authentic tango shows around, as well as one of the best values.

MAP 7: Av. San Juan 3601, tel. 011/4957-8488, www.esquinahomeromanzi.com.ar; 6am-1am daily, dinner 9pm, show 10pm-11:30pm daily; show only from US$25, show and dinner US$90

BARS
✪ Café San Bernardo

Pool and Ping-Pong tables from the 1930s are the main attraction at Café San Bernardo, one of the oldest and largest bars in the neighborhood. Its age is evident, with sparse decor and simple furnishings, but this doesn't stop the crowds from enjoying the cheap games, beer, pizza, and free peanuts. Patrons are a mix of all ages, with the older generations playing dominoes and cards, while eccentric youngsters smash their way around the table-tennis room. An extra bonus: It's open 24 hours daily.

MAP 7: Av. Corrientes 5436, tel. 011/4855-3956; 24 hours daily; no cover

ARTS AND CULTURE

Although European influences have historically dominated the essence of Buenos Aires, *porteños* have developed an authentic cultural scene that's all their own. It's one of the reasons that young people from across the globe are drawn to the city.

Buenos Aires boasts the highest number of weekly live theater performances of any city in the world—even more than London and New York. The city is home to hundreds of theaters, large and small, traditional and modern, mainstream and independent.

Cinema was traditionally popular in the city, and although most of the fine old establishments have been demolished or converted into mega-churches, screenings regularly sell out at those that remain.

The quantity of museums and galleries across the city is extensive; their quality is unsurpassed. Many of the best are free to visit. Others offer free or discounted entry one day a week, most often on Wednesday.

Centro Cultural Kirchner

Coupons that offer discounts are very popular with locals for cultural activities and can result in huge savings. The main sources are Cuponstar (www.cuponstar.com) and Groupon (www.groupon.com.ar).

HIGHLIGHTS

✪ **BEST NIGHT OUT AT THE OPERA:** The glitz of **Teatro Colón** draws thousands to its ballet, opera, and classical music performances (page 151).

✪ **BEST MUSEUM ON A RAINY DAY:** With views overlooking Puerto Madero, the **Colección de Arte Amalia Lacroze de Fortabat** is at its most contemplative with rain splashing onto the large windows (page 154).

✪ **MOST ECCENTRIC GALLERY:** Hugely varied in its offerings, the **Fundación PROA** often surprises with unusual and magnificent pieces (page 157).

✪ **BEST CULTURAL CENTER:** The **Centro Cultural de Recoleta** offers huge variety, both in its exhibitions and its seemingly endless festivals (page 160).

✪ **MOST EDUCATIONAL MUSEUM:** The **Museo de la Deuda Externa** sheds light on the fascinating story of Argentina's foreign debt (page 162).

✪ **MOST UNUSUAL ENTERTAINMENT:** At the **Teatro Ciego (Blind Theater),** dinner is served and theater and musical performances are staged under the cover of darkness (page 163).

✪ **MOST _PORTEÑO_ FESTIVAL:** The **Tango Buenos Aires Festival y Mundial** offers an excellent chance to watch, listen, dance, and learn about the local traditions behind tango (page 166).

MUSEUMS

Museo de la Ciudad de Buenos Aires

A small, unassuming place on the second floor of a corner building, the Museo de la Ciudad documents the history of Buenos Aires and its inhabitants, including architecture and daily life. Alongside over 8,000 photos, there are a wealth of objects, mainly donated by the general public, such as toys, tiles, and radios, as well as a special exhibition on *filete,* an elegant style of drawing and painting signs.

MAP 1: Defensa 219, tel. 011/4343-2123, www.buenosaires.gob.ar/ museodelaciudad; 10am-7pm daily; US$0.50, free Mon. and Wed.

Museo del Bicentenario

Located under the Casa Rosada, in the brick foundations of a customs house and fort that previously sat here, the Museo del Bicentenario showcases the development of Argentina over the past two centuries. Housing historic artifacts, an impressive mural by Mexican artist David Alfaro Siqueiros, and other art pieces on a temporary basis, the museum spreads out from an airy glass-covered patio.

MAP 1: Av. Paseo Colón 100, tel. 011/4344-3802, www.museobicentenario. gob.ar; 10am-6pm Wed.-Sun.; free

Museo Etnográfico Juan B. Ambrosetti

Founded by the University of Buenos Aires in 1905, this museum, which serves as a research project alongside its educational objectives, contains some excellent archaeological and anthropological exhibits, most of which come from Patagonia and northeast Argentina. Highlights include over 10,000 individual bones, mummified bodies, and pre-Colombian ceramics and tapestries. A smaller collection of ethnographic items from North America, Africa, and Asia can also be found in separate rooms.

MAP 1: Moreno 350, tel. 011/4345-8196, www.museoetnografico.filo.uba.ar; 1pm-7pm Tues.-Fri., 3pm-7pm Sat.-Sun.; US$2

Museo Mundial de Tango

Given the passion for tango in Buenos Aires, it is surprising that this is the only permanent museum in the city dedicated to it. Found above Café Tortoni, it comprises three rooms stuffed with information and memorabilia from tango's history, such as Carlos Gardel's fedoras or dancing shoes from the 1920s. Occasional performances are held, while classes are given in the on-site National Academy of Tango, which is the sponsor and host of the museum.

MAP 1: Av. de Mayo 833, 2nd fl., tel. 011/4345-6967; 2:30pm-7:30pm Mon.-Fri.; US$1

THEATERS

✪ Teatro Colón

The best way to enjoy the majesty of Teatro Colón is by attending one of the many concerts, operas, or ballets performed here. Locals dress up for shows, adding to the sense of occasion, and congregate beforehand in the surrounding bars, such as Petit Colón. The most expensive seats can cost as much as US$200, but prices drop the higher up and farther from the stage, with the *paraíso* (paradise) level, which is standing room only, never costing more than US$10. Occasionally, free concerts are given on Sunday morning. The theater's ticket office (10am-8pm Mon.-Sat., 10am-5pm Sun.) is at Tucumán 1171.

MAP 1: Cerrito 628, tel. 011/4378-7100, www.teatrocolon.org.ar

Paseo La Plaza

An open-air theater complex on the Broadway of Buenos Aires, Paseo La Plaza is an enclosed plaza in the middle of a block that houses five auditoriums, bars, shops, and restaurants. The theaters, with capacities ranging from 30 to over 500, offer a wide range of plays, dance, and comedy acts. Another surprise feature is the Cavern, a Beatles-themed bar and venue. Take heed of the many fliers handed out at the entrance—some include discounts.

MAP 1: Av. Corrientes 1660, tel. 011/6320-5300, www.paseolaplaza.com.ar

Teatro San Martín

After extensive renovations in 2015, the auditoriums in San Martín are among the best in the city, despite the fact that the rest of the building fails to inspire. The largest auditorium holds more than 1,000 spectators and is renowned for presenting high-quality productions while refusing to fit into the mold of a traditional theater. The entrance hall is also often home to photo exhibitions and live concerts. Check the website for listings.

MAP 1: Av. Corrientes 1530, tel. 011/4371-1251, www.complejoteatral.gob.ar

CONCERT VENUES
Luna Park

The *porteño* answer to Madison Square Garden, Luna Park serves as a multiuse arena in the heart of the city center. Originally intended for boxing bouts, it has hosted a wide range of events, including Diego Maradona's wedding party, Carlos Gardel's funeral, the 1950 FIBA World Basketball Championship, and World War II Nazi rallies. It is most revered for its role in the development of tango, rock, ballet, opera, and classical music in Buenos Aires, hosting acts as diverse as Frank Sinatra and Luciano Pavarotti.

MAP 1: Av. Madero 420, tel. 011/5279-5279, www.lunapark.com.ar; ticket office 10am-7pm Mon.-Fri., noon-7pm Sat., 2pm-7pm Sun.

La Trastienda

An intimate venue that only holds 700 people, La Trastienda is renowned for drawing larger acts than its size would suggest, including local greats such as Charly García and Divididos, as well as international acts such as George Clinton, Pavement, and the Kooks. Hosted in an antique building on a San Telmo backstreet, La Trastienda also serves food and a large variety of drinks at various bars dotted around the building. Shows are generally followed by club nights that play a wide variety of music.

MAP 1: Balcarce 460, tel. 011/4342-7650, www.latrastienda.com

CULTURAL CENTERS
Centro Cultural Borges

Housed in the upper realms of a shopping center that has been historically linked to the arts, the Centro Cultural Borges offers an eclectic and varied selection of exhibitions that range from experimental videos to the World Press Photo competition. Dedicated to culture and its many strands, many projects combine different forms, such as a recent photography exhibition of musicians from Manchester, England. All this is held under some of the most stunning frescoes in Argentina.

MAP 1: Viamonte 525, tel. 011/5555-5358, www.ccborges.org.ar; 10am-9pm Mon.-Sat., noon-9pm Sun.; US$3

Centro Cultural Kirchner

Buenos Aires's former central post office has been converted into Latin America's largest cultural center, named after the president's late husband. The building's grand architecture, including the central cupola, has been admirably preserved, and the cultural offerings within—including many free concerts—are of the highest quality. An interesting basement museum details the history of the building, while a viewing terrace up above provides a panoramic view of the city.

MAP 1: Sarmiento 151, tel. 0800/333-9300, www.cck.gob.ar; noon-8pm Tues.-Sun.; free

Centro Cultural Kirchner

CINEMA

Cine Gaumont

Located on one side of Plaza Congreso, with the governmental palace occupying the head of the square, Cine Gaumont shows mainly Argentine films, although smaller foreign films are also shown. The upper floors consist of two smaller screens above the large old-school main theater. This movie theater is the figurehead of a national scheme of subsidized cinemas, offering very cheap tickets. With tickets costing less than 10 percent of other cinemas, many films sell out, especially in the evenings. Tickets should be bought ahead of time, though the same day will suffice; arrive early for the showing, as there are no seat assignments.

MAP 1: Av. Rivadavia 1635, tel. 011/4371-3050; US$0.50

Lorca

The only surviving example of the collection of arthouse cinemas that crowded along Avenida Corrientes during the 1970s, the Lorca's once modern style now has a decidedly retro feel. With wooden furnishings and high ceilings, along with the original illuminations outside and inside, it is a cinema for aficionados of the old scene. Two screens allow for a decent mix of around four films on rotation.

MAP 1: Av. Corrientes 1428, tel. 011/4371-5017; US$5

Sala Leopoldo Lugones

Perched on the 10th floor above Avenida Corrientes, Sala Leopoldo Lugones is an intimate one-screen cinema that attracts an eccentric crowd of cine fanatics, some of whom brazenly flout the norms of cinema etiquette. Arthouse films are shown in cycles generally lasting around a couple of weeks, with two or three showings per day. Films in all languages (subtitled at least in Spanish, but often in English as well) are shown.

Puerto Madero

Map 1

MUSEUMS
✪ Colección de Arte Amalia Lacroze de Fortabat

Built mainly out of concrete, much like the patron Amalia Lacroze de Fortabat's vast fortune (she was the richest woman in Argentina, thanks in large part to her cement company, until her death in 2012), this museum houses her personal collection of art. An eccentric mix of artists, such as Andy Warhol, Salvador Dalí, and Auguste Rodin, are represented, while one of William Turner's few privately owned oil paintings is perhaps the pride of the bunch. The building itself is peculiar, with a curved glass roof dropping down to face the docks, offering great views of the yacht club and surrounding neighborhood.

MAP 1: Olga Cossettini 141, tel. 011/4310-6600, www.coleccionfortabat.org. ar; noon-8pm Tues.-Sun.; US$5, half price on Wed.

Buque Museo Fragata *Sarmiento*

Standing proudly across the dock from the shiny modern boats of the Buenos Aires elite, the wooden Fragata *Sarmiento* was the first training ship for the Argentine navy, circumnavigating the world seven times between 1898 and 1938. Once retired from service it became a museum, documenting its intrepid voyages around the world as well as giving insight into life aboard a 19th-century military ship. Obscure items, such as a piece of the Great Wall of China and a taxidermy dog, ensure that visitors' interest remains piqued.

MAP 1: Juana Manuela Gorriti 600, tel. 011/4334-9386; 10am-7pm daily; US$1

Faena Arts Center

Originally one of the city's first flour mills, the Faena Arts Center was inaugurated in 2011 as the cultural section of the Faena complex in Puerto Madero, which also includes the acclaimed Faena Hotel. Soaring ceilings, windows, and open spaces allow for the exhibition of large-scale multimedia projects, which tend toward the colorful, participatory, and experimental.

The Census at Bethlehem by Pieter Brueghel can be seen at the Colección de Arte Amalia Lacroze de Fortabat.

Faena Arts Center

MAP 1: Aime Paine 1169, tel. 011/4010-9233, www.faena.com/faena-art-center; noon-7pm Wed.-Sun.; US$4

Museo del Humor

Set in an exquisite building that originally served as a *cervecería* (beer house) overlooking the river, the Museo del Humor is a tribute to Argentine humor. For now, this is limited to the graphic form, with drawings and cartoons dating as far back as 1810, many of which non-Spanish speakers can appreciate. The museum offers an enjoyable introduction to the singular Argentine humor.

MAP 1: Av. de los Italianos 851, tel. 011/4516/4079, www.buenosaires.gob.ar/museodelhumor; 11am-6pm Mon.-Fri., 10am-8pm Sat.-Sun.; adults US$1, under age 14 free, free Mon.-Fri.

San Telmo and La Boca   Map 2

MUSEUMS

Museo Argentino del Títere

This museum, located on a secluded street corner of a San Telmo backstreet, displays more than 300 puppets from around the world. With one room devoted to European and Asian specimens, another on Latin America, and a third with only Argentine models, a huge variety of designs can be viewed. Puppet shows are held at 4:30pm on Saturday and Sunday (US$5, free under age 3), making this a popular draw for families visiting the San Telmo *feria* on Sunday.

MAP 2: Estados Unidos 802, tel. 011/4304-4376, www.museodeltiterebsas.wix.com; 12:30pm-6pm Tues.-Fri., noon-6pm Sat., 3pm-6pm Sun.; free

live performance by Liu Bolin at the Museo de Arte Contemporáneo de Buenos Aires

Museo de Arte Contemporáneo de Buenos Aires (MACBA)

One of the newer art museums in Buenos Aires, the MACBA opened in 2012 and is dedicated to the exhibition and promotion of contemporary art, both national and international. Although the mediums and styles are varied, emphasis is placed on geometric abstraction. The constantly

The Museo de Arte Moderno de Buenos Aires sits next to the Museo de Arte Contemporáneo de Buenos Aires.

expanding permanent archive is bolstered by temporary exhibitions.
MAP 2: Av. San Juan 328, tel. 011/5299-2010, www.macba.com.ar; 11am-7pm Wed.-Mon.; US$4, US$2 on Wed.

Museo de Arte Moderno de Buenos Aires (MAMBA)

Sitting next to the MACBA, the MAMBA reopened in 2010 after a five-year multimillion-dollar refurbishment. Formerly a cigarette factory, the museum houses over 7,000 pieces of art, including photography, paintings, collages, and audiovisual productions by Argentina's most renowned artists from the last few decades. International artists are also routinely exhibited. It also contains a vast library and documentation center.
MAP 2: Av. San Juan 350, tel. 011/4361-6919, www.buenosaires.gob.ar/ museoartemoderno; 11am-7pm Tues.-Fri., 11am-8pm Sat.-Sun.; US$1, free on Tues.

Museo Histórico Nacional

The Museo Histórico Nacional, strangely perched at the top of Parque Lezama, houses some of the nation's oldest artifacts. Items such as sabers and flags as well as the odd reconstructed bedroom mainly relate to the 1810 revolution. A viewing tower offers views of the surrounding neighborhood and out toward La Boca.
MAP 2: Defensa 1600, tel. 011/4307-1182, www.cultura.gob.ar; 11am-6pm Wed.-Sun.; free

Museo Penitenciario Argentino

Dating back to 1760, this is one of the oldest buildings still standing in Buenos Aires. Serving since the 1970s as a museum of the Argentine penitentiary system, some of its rooms (cells) are still intact, preserving an idea of how prisons changed throughout the centuries. Information focuses on the local prison system, including the harsh Patagonian camps that housed the country's most notorious criminals in the early 20th century. The museum doesn't delve into the issues of military dictatorships and police brutality, which are covered by other museums.

MAP 2: Humberto Primo 378, tel. 011/4361-0917; 2pm-6pm Thurs.-Sun.; free

Fundación PROA is just off the Caminito.

GALLERIES
✪ Fundación PROA

More sophisticated than the brightly colored Caminito lying alongside, the PROA is one of the leading contemporary and modern art galleries in the city, presenting an unlimited range of mediums. Renowned national and international artists are exhibited in a traditional white-walled gallery on a temporary basis. A café overlooks the old port of La Boca, while interactive events are regularly held in specially designed rooms. Guided tours in English are available; check the website.

MAP 2: Av. Don Pedro de Mendoza 1929, tel. 011/4104-1000, www.proa. org; 11am-7pm Tues.-Sun.; US$2, free for students on Tues.

CULTURAL CENTERS
Centro Cultural Usina del Arte

This stunning building was constructed as an electricity power plant between 1912 and 1916. Privatization of electricity toward the end of the 20th century saw it fall into a period of abandonment until the city government converted it into a cultural center in 2000. An impressive selection of music (tango, folk. and classical) and art exhibitions are hosted here, with its concert hall widely praised by musicians for its superb atmosphere and acoustics. The most popular events are held on weekends, as are free 40-minute guided tours (2pm-6pm Sat.-Sun.). Event tickets are distributed on a first-come, first-served basis.

MAP 2: Agustin R. Caffarena 1, www. usinadelarte.org; hours vary based on program; free

Centro Cultural Usina del Arte

RETIRO

MUSEUMS

Museo de Arte Hispanoamericano Isaac Fernández Blanco

Originally located in the family home of its founder, Isaac Fernández Blanco, this museum showcases one of the most extensive collections of Spanish American art, the majority of which is silverware and paintings from Peru. Other eclectic yet equally admired items on display are musical instruments, combs, and hand fans. In 1943 the city government provided the stunning neocolonial building in which the museum now resides, although the original site (Hipólito Irigoyen 1420, noon-6pm Tues.-Fri., 11am-5pm Sat.-Sun.) in Congreso can still be visited and contains exhibits with toys, clothing, silverware, paintings, and photos.

MAP 3: Suipacha 1422, tel. 011/4327-0228, www.buenosaires.gob. ar/museofernandezblanco; 1pm-6pm Tues.-Fri., 11am-5pm Sat.-Sun.; US$1

Museo de la Inmigración

This museum celebrates the city's diverse roots by exploring the historic, cultural, social, and economic importance of immigration to Argentina. It's located in a section of the former Hotel de Inmigrantes, where newly arrived immigrants were sent directly from the port in the 19th century while their arrivals were recorded. The museum gathers photos, luggage, beds, and much more to form a fascinating view of that crucial moment in the city's history.

MAP 3: Av. Antártida Argentina 1355, tel. 011/4317-0285; 11am-7pm Tues.-Sun. winter, noon-8pm Tues.-Sun. summer; donation suggested

Museo Ferroviario

Now condemned to one of the world's worst train systems, Argentina once boasted one of the world's best: There was a time when one could cross the country in stylish wooden carriages pulled by magnificent steam engines. Visit this train museum to learn how dramatic the fall from grace has been. Photos, informative displays, memorabilia, clocks, and an obscure Morse transmitter offer interest to anyone fascinated by trains.

MAP 3: Av. del Libertador 405, tel. 011/4318-3343, www.adifse.com.ar/museo. php; 10am-6pm daily; free

GALLERIES

Galería Vermeer

A gallery of great importance historically in Buenos Aires, Vermeer has been showcasing emerging talent in Argentina since the 1970s. Focusing mainly on Argentine and other South American artists, they have also exhibited some of the regions great names, such as Antonio Berni, Joaquin Torres García, and Lino Spilimbergo, many of whom can be found for sale in the impressive shop.

MAP 3: Suipacha 1168, tel. 011/4394-3462, www.galeriavermeer.com.ar; 11am-3pm and 5pm-7:30pm Mon.-Fri.; free

THEATERS
Teatro Nacional Cervantes

Despite suffering an extensive fire in 1961, the Teatro Nacional Cervantes remains the most iconic theater in the city after Teatro Colón, from which it is separated by a mere 150 meters. The decorative facade is reminiscent of Spanish architecture, while the extravagant interior makes the main auditorium seem smaller than it actually is. The state-run theater offers plays, musicals, and dance at reasonable prices. It also houses the national theater museum. Check the website for listings.

MAP 3: Av. Córdoba 1155, tel. 011/4816-4224, www.teatrocervantes.gov.ar

CULTURAL CENTERS
British Arts Centre

Tucked in among the grand buildings of northern Recoleta, the BAC is committed to deepening the cultural ties between Argentina and Great Britain. For those struggling to find some entertainment in English, this place can provide some light relief, offering a regular smattering of theater and films, as well as art exhibitions and concerts, all of which are free.

MAP 3: Suipacha 1333, tel. 011/4393-6941, www.britishartscentre.org.ar; 2pm-8pm Mon.-Fri.; free

Recoleta

Map 4

MUSEUMS
Museo de Arte Popular José Hernandez

Named after the writer of *Martín Fierro,* an epic gaucho poem, this museum showcases folk art—predominantly textiles and silver work. Somewhat out of place in a neighborhood rooted in wealth and land ownership, it nevertheless provides an interesting opportunity for those who are not able to visit the surrounding gaucho territory to learn about the country's rural history and traditions. A wide range of workshops is available.

MAP 4: Av. del Libertador 2373, tel. 011/4803-2384, www.buenosaires.gob. ar; 1pm-6:30pm Tues.-Fri., 10am-7:30pm Sat.-Sun.; US$1, free on Sun.

Museo Nacional de Arte Decorativo

This ornate neoclassic structure on the edge of Recoleta's parks was designed and built for Matías Errarúiz and Josefina de Alvear, two prominent members of Argentine high society, between 1911 and 1916. Over the next 20 years, they decorated the mansion with art and antiques. Upon the death of de Alvear in 1936, the building and its contents were donated to the government and immediately became the Museo Nacional de Arte Decorativo. The combination of architectural styles is arguably as fascinating as the 4,000 pieces on display. Pre-19th-century East Asian art is rife, and you'll find impressive El Greco paintings and sculptures by Auguste Rodin.

English-language tours (2:30pm Tues.-Fri., US$3) are offered. Croque Madame (10am-midnight daily) is the museum's delightful café and restaurant in the gardens.

MAP 4: Av. del Libertador 1902, tel. 011/4801-8248, www.mnad.org; 2pm-7pm Tues.-Sun.; US$2, free on Tues.

GALLERIES
Palais de Glace

Modeled after the Paris building with the same name, this belle epoque structure originally opened in 1911, serving as an ice rink, social club, and tango venue until finally establishing itself as an art gallery. Temporary exhibitions, including the annual national exhibition of fine arts, present the work of award-winning photographers and artists over the two floors. Kino Palais, a cinema showing free cult films, is housed in back of the building; seating is first-come, first-served, with functions at 7pm on most weekend days.

MAP 4: Posadas 1725, tel. 011/4804-1163, www.palaisdeglace.gob.ar; noon-8pm Tues.-Fri., 10am-8pm Sat.-Sun.; free

Rubbers

A contemporary art gallery that was founded in 1957 by Natalio Jorge Povarché, Rubbers is now directed by his daughter, Mariana Elena Povarché. Over the years it has exhibited artists such as Xul Solar, Pedro Figari, Andy Warhol, Antonio Berni, and Fernando Botero. In the heart of Recoleta, this museum offers some fresh, more modern displays than Recoleta's other more austere galleries.

MAP 4: Av. Alvear 1595, tel. 011/4816-1864, www.rubbers.com.ar; 11am-8pm Mon.-Fri., 11am-1:30pm Sat.; free

CULTURAL CENTERS
✪ Centro Cultural de Recoleta

Located on the grounds of a former Franciscan convent, this is arguably

murals in the Centro Cultural de Recoleta

Buenos Aires's most important cultural center. A sprawling layout of exhibition halls and theater and cinema space, the center is based around a large open plaza that overlooks Plaza Alvear and the surrounding parks. The most impressive auditorium is housed in El Aleph, a former chapel. Numerous exhibitions are held throughout the year, but its most lively time is mid-June, when it hosts Ciudad Emergente, an explosive festival of Argentine music, art, dance, and film. MAP 4: Junín 1930, tel. 011/4803-1040, www.centroculturalrecoleta.org; 1:30pm-8:30pm Tues., 1:30pm-10pm Wed.-Sun.; free

CINEMA
Village Recoleta

Below the modern Village shopping mall lies an underground cinema that refuses to progress from the mid-20th century, with its carpeted curved walls. The seats, however, are definitely of more modern comfort. The traditional home of the Buenos Aires International Independent Film Festival (BAFICI), an explosion of independent films in April, the cinema sticks to mainstream international films throughout the rest of the year. MAP 4: Vicente López 2050, tel. 011/4802-0990, www.villagecines.com; 11am-late daily; from US$8

Palermo   Map 5

MUSEUMS
Museo Evita

Devoted to former first lady Eva Duarte, this museum covers her life from childhood through becoming a political activist, then an actor, before finally becoming the wife of Juan Domingo Perón. With a host of personal items on display alongside thousands of photos and other items, it is a chance to discover a little more about this fascinating woman than the image portrayed by Madonna in the 1996 musical film *Evita*. Have a drink or a bite to eat on the patio after your visit. MAP 5: Lafinur 2988, tel. 011/4807-0306, www.museoevita.org; 11am-7pm Tues.-Sun.; US$2

Planetario Galileo Galilei

This planetarium dates back to the 1960s. Located in the middle of the vast parklands of Palermo, it's a point of reference to *porteños*. Over 9,000 stars flash across the inside of the dome, and the outside illuminates the otherwise dark surroundings at night in a blaze of bulbs. Many cultural events, including live concerts, are hosted both inside and outside the venue, and special facilities are offered for visitors with visual and hearing impairments. MAP 5: Av. Sarmiento and Av. Belisario Roldán, tel. 011/4772-9265, www.planetario.gob.ar; 9:30am-5pm Tues.-Fri., 11:30am-7pm Sat.-Sun.; US$3

Almagro

Map 6

MUSEUMS

Museo Argentino de Ciencias Naturales

This institution, the country's largest natural science museum, has been educating and preserving for over 200 years. Given the high number and quality of dinosaur skeletons unearthed in Argentina, it is unsurprising to find many replicas on display here, alongside space rocks, stuffed animals, and informative displays about environmental development within Argentina and the region. Nestled on the side of Parque Centenario, it is especially popular on weekends, with many school groups visiting during the week.

MAP 6: Av. Angel Gallardo 490, tel. 011/4982-6595, www.macn.secyt.gov.ar; 2pm-7pm daily; US$2

THEATERS

El Camarín de las Musas

Emerging from the wreckage of the 2001 economic crisis, El Camarín is a passionate house of theater and dance that presents over 750 productions per year. A bare, stripped-down space that focuses all the attention on the performance, it's one of the highest-rated venues in the independent scene. An excellent bar and restaurant serves preshow drinks and food, but the focus at El Camarín is on art and its many forms.

MAP 6: Mario Bravo 960, tel. 011/4862-0655, www.elcamarindelasmusas.com; from US$7

The Actors Studio

Although it's in no way connected to the identically named New York school, The Actors Studio is a learning place for budding thespians in Buenos Aires. Many (though not all) of the productions performed here are done so by in-house actors, and quality is assured. It is an ideal place to come and see budding confident young actors. Check the website for performance dates.

MAP 6: Av. Díaz Vélez 3842, tel. 011/4983-9883, www.actors-studio.org

Balvanera

Map 6

MUSEUMS

✪ Museo de la Deuda Externa

The entire history of Argentina's foreign debt is covered in this informative and unique museum, starting with the unabashed extractions of colonial times and leading up to the more modern economic crises, most notably around 2001. Most of the displays are text-based and written in Spanish, although there are accompanying images and charts. Located in the economics faculty of the University of Buenos Aires, the museum is staffed by enthusiastic docents who will answer any questions.

MAP 6: José E. Uruburu 781, 1st fl., tel. 011/4370-6105, www.museodeladuda.econ.uba.ar; 9am-9pm Mon.-Fri.; free

THEATERS
✪ Teatro Ciego (Blind Theater)

Claiming to be the first of its kind in the world, Teatro Ciego presents theater and live music performances in complete darkness. Most of the employees and performers have visual impairments. The most interesting shows are on Thursday, Friday, and Saturday evenings, when dinners are served in a pitch-black environment. Workshops and classes are also given.

MAP 6: Zelaya 3006, tel. 011/6379-8596, www.teatrociego.org; showtimes vary by performance; from US$15

Teatro Ciego (Blind Theater)

Greater Buenos Aires   Map 7

MUSEUMS
Museo Casa de Yrurtia

Formerly the home of Rogelio Yrurtia, an Argentine sculptor best known for his work *Canto al Trabajo,* this delightful building and gardens now form a museum to present Yrurtia's work. It also includes works by other artists, many of which Yrurtia and his wife collected on their travels around the world. Yrurtia's interesting furniture collection is also on display, making the house a trove of international treasures.

MAP 7: O'Higgins 2390, tel. 011/4781-0385, www.cultura.gob.ar; 10:30am-5pm Wed.-Fri., 10:30am-6pm Sat.-Sun.; US$2, free on Wed.

Museo de Arte Español Enrique Larreta

Steeped in the history of the *porteño* aristocracy, this neocolonial residence was a wedding gift to Argentine writer Enrique Larreta by his mother-in-law, Mercedes Castellanos de Anchorena. Now housing his extensive art collection, which includes pieces ranging from the middle ages, a rarity in Argentina, the property also includes a meticulously maintained Andalusian garden, where open-air concerts are occasionally held.

MAP 7: Juramento 2291, tel. 011/4784-4040, www.buenosaires.gob.ar/museolarreta; 1pm-7pm Mon.-Tues. and Thurs.-Fri., 10am-8pm Sat.-Sun.; US$1, free on Thurs.

Festivals and Events

Second only to Edinburgh as the city with the most festivals in the world, Buenos Aires offers great diversity all year round. With some celebrations lasting up to three weeks, others are crammed into just one day. Many have free admission, including most of those organized by the city or the national government, although these tend to operate on a first-come, first-served basis, which can mean long queues, especially for the festival's main event. Dates and venues can vary year to year, so refer to each event's website for up-to-date information.

FEBRUARY
Carnaval
While the main Argentine carnival is held in Gualeguaychu, a city 240 kilometers northwest of Buenos Aires, *porteño* neighborhoods erupt with drumming and dancing every weekend throughout February. Processions are held long into the night across the city, with dozens of sections of main avenues closed down to allow room for the colorful costumes and foam-spraying children.

Citywide: www.carnavalargentina.com.ar; Sat.-Sun. throughout Feb.

Argentina Open
The annual tennis championship usually draws a few big names, with Rafael Nadal and David Ferrer making recent appearances. Played at the pleasantly located Buenos Aires Lawn Tennis Club in Palermo, tickets are sold through Ticketek.

Palermo: Buenos Aires Lawn Tennis Club, Olleros 1510, tel. 011/4772-0983, www.argentinaopenatp.com; late Feb.

MARCH
Buenos Aires Fashion Week
Held in one of the swankier hotels of Buenos Aires, such as the Hilton in Puerto Madero or the Sheraton in Retiro, this is part of the global World Fashion Week. As if one opportunity to dress up and mix with the wealthy trendsetters wasn't enough, there are actually two fashion weeks per year—one in March for the autumn-winter collections and another in September for the spring-summer outfits.

Various locations: www.argentinafashionweek.com; 2nd week of Mar.

Ciudanza
Part of the global "Dancing Cities" movement, Ciudanza brings contemporary dance onto the streets of Buenos Aires, improvising stages out of the most unexpected places in a bid to reflect on the interchange between architecture and choreographic art. Held over four days, the venues change each year.

Various locations: www.buenosaires.gob.ar; 2nd weekend of Mar.

MatBaires
One of the more peculiar and enlightening festivals on offer in Buenos Aires is this math extravaganza, during which a few days are given over to the appreciation and learning of lesser known aspects of mathematics. Thousands descend on the Centro Cultural de Recoleta for talks, competitions, games, debates, and films, while some of the world's greatest minds appear to share their thoughts.

Recoleta: Centro Cultural de Recoleta, Junín 1930, tel. 011/4803-1040, www.buenosaires.gob.ar; 3rd weekend of Mar.

APRIL
Buenos Aires International Independent Film Festival

Known simply as BAFICI, its Spanish acronym, this independent film festival has become one of the most important in Latin America. Showcasing local talent, as well as international films that often lack attention, the festival draws over a million viewers during its three-week run in March-April. The main venue is the Village Recoleta cinema, and tickets can be bought online or in the participating theaters.

Recoleta: Village Recoleta, Vicente López 2050, tel. 011/4802-0990, www.buenosaires.gob.ar; late Mar.-mid-Apr.

Buenos Aires Book Fair

Arguably the most important annual literary event in the Spanish-speaking world, the Feria Internacional del Libro offers three weeks of events, including workshops, book sales, authors' talks, and debates. The cavernous *La Rural* is converted into a huge bookstore, although a wide range of free events are held across the city. Tickets for entry to the fair itself are sold on the door.

Palermo: La Rural, Av. Sarmiento 2704, tel. 011/4777-5500, www.el-libro.org.ar; late Apr.-mid-May

MAY
Polo Circo

Parque Patricios is the unlikely neighborhood for this annual avant-garde circus festival, where trapeze artists have been known to ride down high wires on bicycles from the surrounding buildings. Based in the large open park at Avenida Juan de Garay 2200, Argentine acts are free to watch while international shows require tickets, sold at the gate or in advance.

Greater Buenos Aires: Av. Juan de Garay 2200, www.polocirco.org; 2nd week of May

ArteBA

One of the largest contemporary art fairs in Latin America, ArteBA draws over 100,000 every year to its five-day exposition of mainly local artists. While there are a number of galleries dedicated to specific categories, one of the most popular is Barrio Joven (Young Neighborhood), which showcases young emerging artists. Held in La Rural, tickets can be booked in advance or at the venue.

Palermo: La Rural, Av. Sarmiento 2704, tel. 011/4777-5500, www.arteba.org; 3rd weekend of May

JUNE
Ciudad Emergente Cultural Festival

A joyful celebration of fresh new music and art, Ciudad Emergente is an annual opportunity for upcoming artists to present themselves. A few internationally established bands headline the main stage, but most of them are locally formed groups. It is not just music, however, with fashion, cinema, dance, street art, poetry, comedy, and theater all widely represented and enjoyed. The festival is held in the sprawling Centro Cultural de Recoleta and entry is free.

Recoleta: Centro Cultural de Recoleta, Junín 1930, tel. 011/4803-1040, www.buenosaires.gob.ar; mid-June

JULY
La Rural Agricultural Festival

Held in La Rural, a sprawling compound in the heart of Buenos Aires, farmers from across the country strut their pride animals around, the bulls provoking most interest, while gauchos compete and show off in daring contests and acts. Lasting a hefty three weeks in July-August, there is plenty of time to visit, although weekends can be unbearably busy. With so many people coming in from the country, the city is notoriously more lively during the festival.

Palermo: La Rural, Av. Sarmiento 2704, tel. 011/4777-5500, www.larural.com.ar; mid-July-early Aug.

AUGUST
✪ Tango Buenos Aires Festival y Mundial

Not just the largest and most important tango festival in the world, this event incorporates the world championships, a prestigious yet peculiar competition. With events held across the city, such as classes, *milongas,* and concerts, it is the time of the year when tango really comes out to play, drawing hundreds of thousands of people. Everything is free, although some events require prepurchased tickets. Everything else is run on a first-come, first-served basis.

Citywide: www.buenosaires.gob.ar; 2nd half of Aug.

SEPTEMBER
Vinos y Bodegas

Despite the far-flung wine regions of Argentina offering some of the most entertaining and interesting wine festivals, especially in Mendoza, this Buenos Aires offering is actually the largest in size. Held in La Rural, the *feria* gathers hundreds of the country's producers under one *porteño* roof for tasting and purchasing. Specialist talks are offered, while a gourmet food section is gaining traction each year.

Palermo: La Rural, Av. Sarmiento 2704, tel. 011/4777-5500, www.expovinosybodegas. com.ar; late Sept.

OCTOBER
Festival Internacional de Buenos Aires

Confusingly lacking any reference to theater in the name of the festival, FIBA is nonetheless a biannual celebration of performing arts, held in numerous venues across the city. Although the focus is on Argentine and international theater productions and improvisation, there are also concerts, dance, and other cultural events during the two weeks of festivities.

Various locations: www.buenosaires. gob.ar; 1st half of Oct.

Festival Buenos Aires Danza Contemporánea

Held over a few days in October every two years, the contemporary dance festival brings the newest and freshest interpretations to the streets and theaters of Buenos Aires. A constantly evolving concept and movement, the make-up and structure of the festival also throws up new surprises each time it is held.

Various locations: www.buenosaires. gob.ar; 1st week of Oct.

Buenos Aires Marathon

Held in October, before the heat really descends on Buenos Aires, the annual marathon sets off from the Obelisco and takes in many of the top sights around the city. Thousands of runners take part, with the Kenyan global dominance starting to take hold here as well. A half marathon, a quarter marathon, and even an eighth marathon are held in the weeks around the main event.

Citywide: www.maratondebuenosaires.org; 2nd weekend of Oct.

Casa Foa

Hosted in a different renovated venue sometime during October or November every year, Casa Foa is a design fair that expounds local and global trends in architecture, interior design, and landscaping. Thousands flock to the event for ideas on how to develop their home, while the fair itself aims to raise money for scientific research.

Various locations: www.casafoa.com; late Oct. or early Nov.

La Noche de los Museos

Drawing over a million people in its last edition, the Night of Museums is a one-night yearly event when practically all the museums in the city are open all night, with free admission. Spontaneous concerts and street theater appear from nowhere all across the city, while crowds crisscross the neighborhoods, taking advantage of the fact that public buses are free for the duration. Plan ahead, as queues can become horrendous, even at 3am.

Citywide: www.lanochedelosmuseos.gob.ar; Sat. in late Oct. or early Nov.

NOVEMBER

Argentine Polo Open Championship

Ever since 1893, the world's most important polo championship has been held in Palermo. The last decade has been dominated by Adolfo Cambiaso and his team, La Dolfina, but well-dressed crowds turn up every year nonetheless. Starting toward the end of November, the tournament lasts around three weeks, culminating in the grand final. Tickets are sold through Ticketek.

Palermo: Campo Argentino de Polo, Av. del Libertador 3902, www.aapolo.com; late Nov.-early Dec.

Creamfields

The first Creamfields festival to be held outside of Liverpool, England, since 2001 this electronic music festival has been drawing some of the world's top DJs for a night of laser-fueled dancing at iconic locations around the city. Held around mid-November, when the nights are beginning to warm up, a different venue is used each year. The lineup and ticket information are advertised on the website.

Various locations: www.creamfieldsba.com; mid-Nov.

Gran Premio Nacional

The main event in the Argentine horse-racing calendar, the annual Gran Premio Nacional takes place at the Palermo hippodrome on a weekend in early November. The day involves over 15 races, plenty of chances at betting, not to mention the underground casino, and the opportunity to rub shoulders with celebrities. The most remarkable part is that entry is free.

Palermo: Hipódromo Argentino de Palermo, Av. del Libertador 4101, tel. 011/4778-2800, www.palermo.com.ar; 1st or 2nd Sat. of Nov.

Día de la Tradición

Horse parades and general gaucho showmanship are the order of the day at celebrations across the country on the weekend nearest November 12, a date chosen to celebrate all things gaucho. While San Antonio de Areco, some 110 kilometers out of the city, is the heartland of festivities, the Feria de Mataderos offers the liveliest venue and events within the confines of Buenos Aires.

Various locations: Sat.-Sun. closest to Nov. 12

Gay Pride

Focused around the *marcha del orgullo* (pride parade), which gathers around Avenida de Mayo and Plaza de Mayo, increasingly large numbers of LGBT partygoers and their friends dance the day and night away on the first Saturday of November. Floats, fancy dress, and overt sexuality are widespread.

Centro: Av. de Mayo and Plaza de Mayo, marchadelorgullo.org.ar; 1st Sat. of Nov.

Festival Guitarras del Mundo

An initiative started by Juan Falú, a folk musician from Tucuman, this festival gathers together top guitar players from all over the world—some well-known, others barely heard of—for daily concerts. Most of them take place in Buenos Aires (check the website for dates and venues), and admission to all events is free.

Various locations: www.festivalguitarrasdelmundo.com; 1st half of Nov.

Buenos Aires Jazz

Usually lasting only a few days, the spring jazz festival brings an explosion of performances to many of the city's concert halls as well as the more renowned jazz venues. Jams, acoustic sets, and workshops, from classical through modern, are given by local acts as well as international musicians, of whom there are more every year. Outdoor concerts and free shows complete the bill in this festival, which is held sometime between October and December.

Citywide: www.buenosaires.gob.ar; mid-Nov.

DECEMBER

Festival Buen Día

Oriented toward young people, this festival of design, fashion, music, and journalism changes location each year, although it is always somewhere that allows a laid-back party atmosphere, such as the *bosques* of Palermo. Tens of thousands converge here in mid-December with the sole intention of having a *buen día* (good day).

Various locations: www.festivalbuendia.net; mid-Dec.

SPORTS AND ACTIVITIES

Respite from the urban chaos in Buenos Aires is both necessary and easy to find, thanks to the vast parks to the north of the city along with the bustling plazas sprinkled throughout. Especially on weekends, these spaces fill with young children playing, couples drinking maté, and old men playing chess.

A true *fútbol* mecca, Buenos Aires breathes "the beautiful game" all year round. Thousands of soccer fans pour into the stadiums over the weekend, while just as many play the game on countless fields in parks, under highways, and even on rooftops. Best of all, visitors are welcome to join in. Practically all neighborhoods contain soccer pitches, tennis courts, and swimming pools.

Despite being a coastal city, Buenos Aires offers little in the way of water sports or beaches. The murkiness of the Río de la Plata tends to put people off. Locals cope by taking a short train ride out to Tigre, in the river delta, where hobbies such as fishing and bird-watching are common. There are also sailing and boating opportunities to the north of the city.

Buenos Aires has many green spaces.

HIGHLIGHTS

✪ **MOST EFFICIENT CITY TOUR:** With its continuous flow of buses and multiple drop-off points, **Buenos Aires Bus** ensures you can explore the whole city easily (page 171).

✪ **BEST PLACE TO RELAX WITH THE LOCALS:** Head down to the **Costanera Sur,** a coastal park, to laze about with *porteños* (page 172).

✪ **MOST FAMOUS *FÚTBOL* TEAM:** Watch a soccer match at La Bombonera to see the legendary **Boca Juniors** play the game at its finest (page 174).

✪ **BEST PLAZA:** Stylish and centrally located, **Plaza San Martín** is a welcome touch of nature in the city center (page 175).

✪ **MOST ARTISTIC CITY TOUR:** Get to know Buenos Aires by exploring its street art on a tour with **Graffitimundo** (page 175).

✪ **BEST PARK:** Whether for jogging, sunbathing, cycling, picnicking, or simply relaxing, **Parque Tres de Febrero** accommodates your needs (page 175).

✪ **BEST PLACE TO PLAY *FÚTBOL*:** Join foreigners and locals alike with **Buenos Aires Fútbol Amigos (BAFA)** (page 176).

✪ **BEST PLACE TO WATCH *FÚTBOL*:** Watching a game at **River Plate** is unforgettable, especially if it is against Boca Juniors (page 180).

✪ **BEST SUMMERTIME DIVERSION:** Head out to **Parque Norte** to splash in gigantic swimming pools at this open-air water park (page 182).

Centro

Map 1

ACTIVITIES

CENTRO

CITY TOURS
✪ Buenos Aires Bus

Buenos Aires Bus is a hop-on, hop-off guided bus service that gives riders the opportunity to disembark at up to 32 locations around the city center. The three routes (blue, green, and red), with a 20-minute service frequency, last a total of three hours. An audio tour (Spanish or English) provides historical information along the route.

MAP 1: Av. Roque Sáenz Peña and Florida (1st stop), tel. 011/4018-0055, www. buenosairesbus.com; 9am-5pm daily; US$25, US$7 more for 2nd day

Buenos Aires Free Walks

Offering a daily afternoon tour of the city center, Buenos Aires Free Walks provides great historical context for any visit to Buenos Aires. Meeting at Palacio Congreso at 3pm, the walk zigzags past various points of interest up Avenida de Mayo to the Casa Rosada before heading on to the Obelisco. A similar tour of Recoleta and Retiro departs from Libertad 699 at 10:30am daily. Both tours last around three hours and are in English or Spanish. No reservation is necessary, just turn up—rain or shine.

MAP 1: Meeting point at Av. Entre Ríos 71, www.buenosairesfreewalks.com; 3pm daily; free, tip suggested

Explore the city with Buenos Aires Bus.

Puerto Madero Map 1

PARKS AND PLAZAS

✪ Costanera Sur

While the whole of Puerto Madero feels sleepy and relaxed compared to the rowdy city center, the Costanera Sur has long been locals' favored location to chill out, especially on the weekends. Stretching the length of the neighborhood, the *costanera* is the strip of land that used to run alongside the coast of the Río de la Plata until the Reserva Ecológica was formed. It consists of parks, a pleasant walkway overlooking the adjoining nature reserve's marshes, an endless stream of food stalls, an open-air theater, imposing statues, and a weekend street market.

MAP 1: south end of Av. Achával Rodriguez to north end of Av. Hernan Giralt

Parque Mujeres Argentinas

One of the city's largest parks, Parque Mujeres Argentinas was constructed in 2005; the fresh, youthful feeling of the park is distinctive from the others around the city. Situated on the latitude that runs from Palacio del Congreso, through the Casa Rosada, and over the Puente de la Mujer, the park, with its layered steps and panoramic views, was specifically designed to maintain the style of the buildings surrounding it. The whole space is focused around a large open-air theater.

MAP 1: Bordered by Juana Manso, Lynch Marta, Av. de los Italianos, and Manuela Sáenz; 24 hours daily

BOATING AND WATER SPORTS

Puro Remo

The passionate and professional team behind Puro Remo offers superb classes for rowing, kayaking, and stand-up paddleboarding. While the best place for these activities are in Tigre, in the Río de la Plata delta, Puro Remo provides the opportunity to take to the water right on the city's edge, which provides a unique vantage point of Buenos Aires. Classes are for all levels and can last for as long as you wish.

MAP 1: Olga Cossettini and Victoria Ocampo, tel. 015/4033-9061, www. puroremo.com.ar; 7am-7pm daily; from US$4 per hour

PARKS AND PLAZAS
Parque Lezama

Considered by some historians to be the location of the original founding of the city, Parque Lezama is one of the more interesting and enjoyable parks in Buenos Aires. Dropping down from a higher plain to the vast Avenida Paso Colón, it includes a viewpoint of the southern realms of the city, an amphitheater, important statues (notably that of Pedro de Mendoza, the city's founder), outdoor chess tables, a weekend market, and the Museo Histórico Nacional. Despite all this, the park is still large enough to afford ample space for visitors to spread out.

MAP 2: Av. Brasil between Defensa and Av. Paseo Colón

shady path in Parque Lezama

CITY TOURS
Biking Buenos Aires

Three different guided bicycle tours are offered by Biking Buenos Aires.
Parks and Plazas (5 hours, 13 kilometers, US$60) explores the green and open areas of Palermo and Recoleta; Heart of the City (5 hours, 19 kilometers, US$60) focuses on sights in Centro, San Telmo, Puerto Madero, and La Boca; and Ultimate City Tour (7 hours, 26 kilometers, US$90) covers most of the neighborhoods covered in this guide. All tours include a modest lunch and the chance to try some maté after setting off from the Biking Buenos Aires office in San Telmo. (The Parks and Plazas tour departs from Avenida Sante Fe 3951). Reservations are advised.

MAP 2: Perú 988, tel. 011/4300-5373, www.bikingbuenosaires.com; 8am-8pm daily; from US$60

BICYCLING
La Bicicleta Naranja

Cycling around Buenos Aires is the quickest and most pleasurable form of transportation—there's really no better way to explore the city. While the free Eco-bici bikes are great for short-term travel, it is necessary to rent a bike for long-term or long-distance plans. La Bicicleta Naranja offer bikes (including tandems) by the hour (US$4), half-day (US$10), day (US$17), or week (US$50). Discounts and guided tours are available. There's a second location in Palermo (Nicaragua 4817, 11am-5pm Mon.-Fri., 10am-6pm Sat.-Sun.).

MAP 2: Pasaje Giuffra 308, tel. 011/4362-1104, www.labicicletanaranja. com.ar; 9am-3pm Mon.-Fri., 9am-7pm Sat.-Sun.

SPECTATOR SPORTS
SOCCER
✪ Boca Juniors

Estadio Alberto J. Armando, also known as La Bombonera, is the stadium that hosts the neighborhood's world-famous soccer team, Boca Juniors. A towering yellow structure, the stadium forms a unique D shape, with three broadly curving sides of steeply tiered stands facing a vertical wall of VIP boxes. The Museo de la Pasión Boquense (www.museoboquense.com, 10am-6pm daily, US$12) allows visitors to learn about the club's history, and an extra US$3 includes a guided tour of the stadium.

MAP 2: Brandsen 805, tel. 011/5777-1200, www.bocajuniors.com.ar

La Bombonera, the stadium of Boca Juniors soccer team

Retiro

Map 3

PARKS AND PLAZAS
✪ Plaza San Martín

This delightfully wooded plaza is located the middle of bustling Retiro. It's easy to forget the drone of traffic when stretched out on the grass. The gentle downward slope allows for a surprisingly open view in such a restricted part of the city. The plaza contains various important monuments and is surrounded by dominating, luxurious buildings. Beware of pickpockets, as they are known to frequent the area.

MAP 3: Av. Santa Fe and Florida

Recoleta

Map 4

PARKS AND PLAZAS
Plaza Rubén Darío

Just one plaza among a collection of a dozen or so, Plaza Rubén Darío is nonetheless the area's hot spot for joggers, fitness enthusiasts, and strollers alike. A fenced-in lake in the middle, open-air gym equipment dotted around in various locations, the Museo Nacional de Bellas Artes, and wide-open grassy spaces all draw people to this square, especially in the evenings.

MAP 4: Av. del Libertador 1500

Palermo

Map 5

CITY TOURS
✪ Graffitimundo

The streets of Buenos Aires are an open canvas to artists who come from all over the world to paint here. Graffitimundo offer various tours of the north or south of the city that incorporate some of the most impressive examples. Tour options include private tours, bike tours, and a detailed tour on art and activism. Check the website for schedules and starting points.

MAP 5: Costa Rica 5829, tel. 015/3683-3219, www.graffitimundo.com; from US$25

PARKS AND PLAZAS
✪ Parque Tres de Febrero

An immense sprawling park also known as Bosques de Palermo (Palermo Woods), Parque Tres de Febrero is a collection of plazas, parks, and lakes that together come to some 40 hectares. Most loungers and joggers head to the area surrounding the Rosedal (rose gardens), where stands rent out large, four-person bicycles.

a four-person bike in Parque Tres de Febrero

Countless other sights and attractions, such as the planetarium, Japanese gardens, and hippodrome draw people to all corners of the park.

MAP 5: Av. Libertador 3600

SPECTATOR SPORTS
POLO
Campo Argentino de Polo

With the polo season restricted to March-May and September-December, you need to be in Buenos Aires at the right time to watch games in the city center. The emblematic Campo Argentino de Polo is a beautiful stadium and hosts the annual Open Championship, the most important polo tournament in the world, every December, for which day tickets range from US$8 to over US$500. Check the website for other tournaments throughout the season, many of which offer free entry.

MAP 5: Av. del Libertador 4500, tel. 011/4777-8005, www.aapolo.com; from US$8

HORSE RACING
Hipódromo Argentino de Palermo

Sweeping for almost a mile down the grand Avenida del Libertador, the city's hippodrome offers some delightful Beaux-Arts architecture alongside the sand horse-racing track. Horse races are held every Monday and alternate among Friday, Saturday, and Sunday. It's never full—except perhaps during the Gran Premio Nacional in November. There is also a sports bar, a casino, a restaurant, and art exhibitions. Access to the paddock and most stands is free, although the main stand costs US$5 and enforces a dress code that bans jeans and running shoes.

MAP 5: Av. del Libertador 4101, tel. 011/4778-2800, www.palermo.com.ar; free

Hipódromo Argentino de Palermo

SOCCER
✪ Buenos Aires Fútbol Amigos (BAFA)

Fútbol is ubiquitous in Buenos Aires. Most of the city's plazas or parks have some kind of pitch, be it a worn-out patch marked out by some kids or a professionally maintained enclosed field. BAFA draws people together from all over the world for competitive but friendly matches throughout the week in a number of locations across the city (mainly at El Salvador 5301 in

Locals and tourists alike play soccer with Buenos Aires Fútbol Amigos.

Palermo). Sign up on the website for upcoming men's, women's, and mixed-gender matches or other events.

MAP 5: El Salvador 5301; www.fcbafa.com; from US$5 per match

GOLF

Campo de Golf de la Ciudad

Somewhat hidden in a corner of Parque Tres de Febrero, the municipal golf course is the only 18-hole course in the city. Luckily, it's an excellent one, despite the fairways being slightly squeezed together. The major challenges are multiple holes with out-of-bounds and the notorious par-3 seventh hole, which requires a tee-off that floats over a clump of eucalyptus trees. Reservations must be made in advance via the website or telephone.

MAP 5: Av. Torquist 6397, tel. 011/4772-7261, www.golfpalermo.com; 8am-5pm Tues.-Sun.; 18 holes US$5 Tues.-Fri., US$7 Sat.-Sun.

GO-KARTS

Circuito 9

Overlooking a murky inlet from the Río de la Plata, Circuito 9 is a go-kart track that lies a terrifying few hundred meters short of the Aeroparque runway, in the Centro Costa Salguero. A bridge and trackside bar offer respite for those unwilling to get behind the wheel. On this largest track in Buenos Aires, 20 laps costs US$20, and 50 laps cost US$30.

MAP 5: Av. Costanera and Salguero, tel. 011/4803-0903, www.circuito9.com.ar; 4pm-midnight Tues.-Sun.; US$20-30

PARKS AND PLAZAS

Parque Centenario

A circular park in almost the exact center of the city, Parque Centenario was designed by Charles Thays and draws thousands of visitors, mostly locals, on the weekend. The main section, based around a lake, is controversially closed between 8pm and 8am, while the outskirts contain features such as an astronomical observatory, the city's natural history museum, an open-air amphitheater, a secondhand book market, and a weekend street fair. Families lounge around on the grass, as there are few benches, while musicians and acrobats practice their acts alongside folks selling *comida casera* (homemade food).

MAP 6: Between Av. Díaz Vélez 4800 and Av. Ángel Gallardo

CHESS CLUBS

Torre Blanca

While many of the city's parks and plazas (Parque Lezama and Plaza Almagro, for example) offer open-air *ajedrez* (chess) tables where players are free to walk up and set up their pieces or simply ask to join a game, Torre Blanca offers a more orthodox option. A small neighborhood chess club that has produced four grand masters, it holds weekly tournaments that visitors are welcome to join—although little English is spoken, there's no difficulty in participating. Food and drink is served. Check the website for upcoming events.

MAP 6: Sánchez de Bustamante 587, tel. 011/4862-3161, www.ajedreztorreblanca. com.ar; US$5

BIRD-WATCHING

Asociación Ornitológica del Plata

With over 10 percent of the world's bird species present in Argentina, tens of thousands of bird-lovers flock to the country every year. There are dozens of bird-watching organizations across Buenos Aires, and most of them are affiliated with Asociación Ornitológica del Plata. They can provide information on ideal places for bird-watching in the city or farther afield, and they also arrange regular events in plazas, parks, and open countryside. The most popular central location for bird-watching is the Reserva Ecológica in Puerto Madero.

MAP 6: Matheu 1246, tel. 011/4943-7216, www.avesargentinas.org.ar; 10:30am-1:30pm and 2:30pm-8:30pm Mon.-Fri.

SOCCER

Argentina's domestic *fútbol* (soccer) league is passionate and chaotic. Stadiums in Argentina draw thousands of fans each week. The love for the sport is strongest in Buenos Aires, where the stadiums are colorful and noisy, offering a spectacle that's unlike anything else.

TEAMS

The most popular teams are **River Plate** (www.cariverplate.com.ar) and **Boca Juniors** (www.bocajuniors.com.ar). Between them they have notched up over 60 national titles and more than 25 on the international stage. The next three largest teams, **San Lorenzo** (www.sanlorenzo.com.ar), **Racing** (www.racingclub.com.ar), and **Independiente** (www.clubaindependiente.com), are also from Buenos Aires. Other important teams, such as **Vélez Sarsfield** (www.velezsarsfield.com.ar), **Lanus** (www.clublanus.com), **Huracán** (www.clubhuracan.com.ar), and **Argentinos Juniors** (www.argentinosjuniors.com.ar) play in and around the city center. The best matches to attend are the *clasicos* (derby games), when fans are at their most passionate and colorful. Aside from the club websites, the Asociación del Fútbol Argentino (www.afa.org.ar) publishes all upcoming match schedules.

TICKETS

Getting tickets for most matches requires turning up at the stadium an hour or two before kickoff, but there are exceptions. Boca Juniors doesn't sell tickets to the general public—tickets are for club members only. River Plate tickets nearly always sell out, so you'll need to purchase them online far in advance. Derby games for any team also invariably sell out, so plan to buy tickets a few days in advance. All clubs publish ticket information on their websites (in Spanish) in the days leading up to the match.

There are two types of tickets. *Popular* (or *general*) is a standing-room only section, usually behind the goal. This is where the *barra brava* (unruly, often violent, fans) are found. It's wise to avoid this section. The other type of ticket, *platea*, is the assigned seating area along the side of the pitch and costs double the price of the *popular* section. Nonmembers must buy a specific type of the platea ticket, called *invitado* (or *no socio*). This ticket is more expensive than what a club member pays, because you aren't paying the monthly club fee.

TOUR PACKAGES

Tour packages are often your only option for attending a River Plate or Boca Juniors match. These generally include transportation to and from the stadium, an English-speaking guide, and the game ticket. Sometimes a drink and bite to eat are thrown in, too. Costing up to 10 times the price of a ticket, a tour package is an expensive option, but a good one for those uneasy about going to the match alone. **Tangol** (www.tangol.com) and **LandingPadBA** (www.landingpadba.com) are a couple of the more established companies selling tour packages.

GETTING TO THE STADIUM

Traveling to and from the stadium can be complicated, thanks to traffic congestion—taxi drivers may be reluctant to take fares and buses sometimes change their routes, both in an effort to avoid the traffic jams. Budget extra time for arriving and leaving the stadium.

SAFETY

All stadiums separate fans from the pitch with a razor-topped fence or even a moat. The *barra bravas* are notoriously violent groups that cause trouble inside and outside the stadiums. Visitors should not experience any trouble as long as they do not attract unnecessary attention. To avoid any safety issues, opt for the *platea* ticket.

SPECTATOR SPORTS
SOCCER
✪ River Plate

One of the city's most emblematic stadiums, in the northern part of the Belgrano neighborhood, the Monumental is home to the River Plate *fútbol* team. Two open-air tiers rise up surprisingly far from the pitch; the atmosphere when the stands are full is electric. The club museum (10am-7pm daily; US$9) displays trophies, photos, and memorabilia from throughout the club's history and, for an extra US$2, includes a guided tour of the stadium.

MAP 7: Av. Figueroa Alcorta 7597, tel. 011/4789-1200, www.cariverplate.com.ar; tickets from US$20

Independiente

The stadium that the Independiente *fútbol* team calls home was one of the world's first arenas constructed from reinforced concrete. The location is just a stone's throw from the team's rivals, Racing. Match tickets are sold from the stadium box office a few hours before kickoff (nonmembers can only buy *platea*, or assigned seating tickets). A match against Racing, in either stadium, is a brilliant spectacle. The stadium lies a few blocks from Avellaneda train station, which is a 10-minute train ride from the Constitución station outside San Telmo.

MAP 7: Bochini 751, tel. 011/4201-4234, www.clubaindependiente.com; tickets from US$30

Racing

Playing in an iconic circular stadium named after former-president Juan Domingo Perón, the *fútbol* team Racing are renowned for the unwavering support of their fans and are based in Avellaneda, just outside the southern limits of the city. Match tickets are sold from a box office at the stadium a few hours before kickoff and also in a club store (Lavalle 1650, 9am-7pm Mon.-Fri., 9am-1pm Sat.) in Centro. The stadium lies a few blocks from Avellaneda train station, which is a 10-minute train ride from the Constitución station outside San Telmo.

MAP 7: Colón and Italia, tel. 011/4229-1350, www.racingclub.com.ar; tickets from US$20

San Lorenzo

Originally from the Boedo neighborhood, the San Lorenzo *fútbol* team currently plays in Flores, at a complex with towering stands of a single tier. Some of the surrounding neighborhood is slightly unsavory and visitors are advised not to wander away from the crowds. Match tickets are sold from a box office at the stadium a few hours before kick-off, although nonmembers can only buy *platea* tickets (assigned seats, located at the side of the field). Buses routes serving the stadium are the 101 (Retiro, Recoleta, Balvanera), 143 (Puerto Madero, San Telmo), and 150 (Retiro, Centro).

MAP 7: Av. F.F. de la Cruz 2145, tel. 011/4016-2620, www.sanlorenzo.com.ar; tickets from US$25

AUTO RACING
Autódromo

Although neither a Formula 1 nor a motorcycle grand prix has been held

THE NATIONAL GARDENER

While *porteños* may grumble over Buenos Aires's lack of open spaces, they would have far more to complain about were it not for Jules Charles Thays, a French landscape architect born in Versailles during 1934. Thays, who idolized the work of Baron de Haussman, took to urban landscaping from an early age, eventually working under the acclaimed Édouard-François André.

Thays immigrated to Argentina in the late 19th century to work on park design. He was soon offered the prestigious job of Director of Parks of Buenos Aires. In his first year, Thays arranged the planting of more than 20,000 trees while planning for the design or redevelopment of numerous parks and plazas.

At Thays's urging, the **Jardín Botánico** was formed, and Thays moved into an old house in the middle of the grounds. In 1892

Jardín Botánico, the former home and creation of Carlos Thays

he married Cora Venturino of Uruguay. Together, they lived in the Jardín Botánico until it opened to the public in 1898.

Perhaps Thays's largest project was **Parque Tres de Febrero,** also known as the Bosques de Palermo (Palermo Woods). Formerly the grounds of Buenos Aires governor Juan Manuel de Rosas, the vast open space in the north of the city was reclaimed by the government upon his downfall. Earlier landscapers had already turned the grounds into parkland, but it wasn't until Thays arrived that the space adopted its present form. He added lakes, curved paths, and bridges—key features in all of his designs. Thays dreamed of transforming the Bosques into the Buenos Aires version of Paris's Bois de Boulogne.

In 1913, Thays's tenure as Director of Parks ended, but he continued to work in both the public and private sectors. The *estancias* of the aristocracy were playgrounds for refining his style, and he received many requests from abroad. Nonetheless, throughout his career, Thays remained as open to requests for public development as he was to more lucrative private initiatives. He incorporated play areas, bandstands, sports facilities, and public toilets in his designs whenever possible.

Today, many parks and plazas across Argentina bear Thays's hallmarks. Rosario, Córdoba, Mendoza, Salta, Tucumán, and Mar del Plata all owe a great deal to the visionary Frenchman's passion. Thays even designed the layout for Argentina's most popular national park, the **Parque Nacional de Iguazú,** which contains the waterfalls recently named one of the world's seven natural wonders.

In his downtime, Thays conducted scientific experiments and undertook voyages to study Argentina's native flora. This led to the rediscovery of the germination process of the yerba maté plant, which fostered the creation of a new industry in northern Argentina and allowed for the termination of the expensive import of yerba from Brazil and Paraguay.

Thays's life came to an end in 1934, when he died in Buenos Aires. **Parque Carlos Thays** (Av. del Libertador and Av. Callao) was named for him.

in Buenos Aires since the turn of the 21st century, for many decades these were both regular events on the circuit calendars. Many smaller races are still held here, however, and the racetrack looms large in the south of the city, with roaring engines heard for miles around. Check the website for information on driving the track yourself and for upcoming race schedules.

MAP 7: Av. General Paz and Av. General Roca, tel. 011/4605-3333, www.autodromo.com; tickets from US$10

WATER PARKS
✪ Parque Norte

This vast open-air complex at the western end of the city airport runway, wedged between a religious theme park and a somber memorial space, struggles to contain the thousands of people that descend on it daily during the warm months. Offering huge swimming pools, water slides, soccer competitions, and facilities for many other sports, a day can fly by here.

MAP 7: Av. Cantilo and Guiraldes, tel. 011/4787-1382, www.parquenorte.com; 8am-midnight daily; from US$8

THEME PARKS
Tierra Santa

The world's first religious theme park, Tierra Santa is dedicated to the life of Jesus according to the Bible. A reconstruction of Jerusalem, or at least parts of it, teaches and entertains visitors,

Tierra Santa

with the highlight being the hourly rising of a giant Christ. Don't expect roller coasters, although actors dressed up as characters from the Bible and biblical times wander around.

MAP 7: Av. Costanera Rafael Obligado 5790, tel. 011/4784-9551, www.tierrasanta.com.ar; 4pm-midnight Fri.-Sun.; adults and teens US$7, under age 11 US$3

Various Locations

CITY TOURS
Foto Ruta

Though it has now expanded to England and Spain, Foto Ruta's photography tours originated in Buenos Aires. Beginning with an introductory session during which different photography techniques are discussed, the tour leads participants out on the streets to take photos around the city for three or four hours, then returns to discuss the results. The meeting point is arranged when you confirm the tour. Check the website for tour schedules and to make reservations.

Various locations: tel. 015/6030-8881, www.foto-ruta.com; US$45-160

Foto Ruta helps visitors find the best photo ops.

SHOPS

Buenos Aires is regularly referred to as the "city of books." There is no other city in the world with a higher per-capita bookstore rate: approximately one bookstore for every 40,000 residents. The fashion industry is also booming in Argentina, and *porteños* love to keep up to date with the latest trends sold in the countless clothing stores. The best shops tend to reflect the diverse character of the city, with grand lavish boutiques often close to thrift stores. Certain areas, notably Palermo Soho, are shopping meccas and fill with crowds over the weekend, when there are sometimes queues just to enter a store.

The Feria de San Pedro Telmo occupies 12 blocks of Defensa.

Given the volatile economy in Argentina, as well as the protective import-export laws, the industry is in constant flux. Many major brands, such as Apple, do not have a presence in the country, given the heavy restrictions and high costs of importing goods. As a result, certain areas, such as electronics and renowned clothing labels, are sold at elevated prices, making them more expensive than elsewhere in the world. Limiting imported goods has been intended to promote the development and quality of local production and entrepreneurship, which, to a certain extent, has been successful. Independent stores have popped up everywhere, and there is a refreshingly adventurous feel to the scene.

HIGHLIGHTS

✪ **BEST FOR HOME DECOR:** It's easy to lose yourself in **Cualquier Verdura,** which is full of ideas and creativity for adding a piece of Buenos Aires to your home (page 188).

✪ **BEST OPEN-AIR MARKET:** The weekly **Feria de San Pedro Telmo** is the first port of call for most visitors, with countless stalls stretching outward from Plaza Dorrego (page 188).

✪ **BEST WATCHES:** At **Simonetta Orsini,** you can browse the impressive collection of elite timepieces (page 189).

✪ **MOST LUXURIOUS LEATHER: Casa López** offers high-end wallets, purses, and other accessories, all made from genuine Argentine leather (page 189).

✪ **MOST GENUINE JERSEYS:** Buy a *fútbol* jersey from **Playsport** and you're sure to get the real thing (page 190).

✪ **GRANDEST BOOKSTORE:** A former theater and cinema, **El Ateneo Grand Splendid** is a monument to culture and literature (page 191).

✪ **BEST WINE SHOP:** With its seemingly endless choices, **The Wine Gallery** always manages to select the perfect bottle for each customer (page 193).

✪ **HIPPEST ART VENDOR:** Small and quaint **Mar Dulce** exhibits and sells some of the freshest artwork from Argentina and Uruguay (page 194).

✪ **BEST WOMEN'S CLOTHING:** With a huge range of women's clothing shops, **Alto Palermo** is the favorite mall of *porteñas* (page 196).

✪ **BEST ANTIQUES:** Amid the labyrinthine **Mercado de las Pulgas** is a bevy of hidden gems (page 198).

✪ **BEST COBBLER:** For custom-designed shoes, look no further than **Calzados Correa** (page 199).

✪ **BEST PLACE TO BUY LOCAL ARTISAN GOODS:** The **Feria de Mataderos** has an excellent range of handicrafts, and it's generally cheaper than markets in the city center (page 201).

✪ **BEST LEATHER JACKETS:** In the middle of the leather district Villa Crespo, **Murillo 666** is one of the oldest and most popular stores for jackets (page 202).

SHOPPING DISTRICTS

Florida and Lavalle Streets

Florida and Lavalle streets have countless souvenir shops, but there are many others throughout the entirety of Centro.

MAP 1: Florida 1-1000 and Lavalle 600-1000

Avenida Corrientes

This street is lined on both sides by book shops and music stores.

MAP 1: Av. Corrientes between Av. 9 de Julio and Av. Callao

San Telmo

San Telmo is the place to go for antiques. The neighborhood is increasingly being taken over by small, trendy boutiques, but there are enough traditions and institutions to preserve the scene. Defensa is the main street for such items, especially between Avenida Independencia and Avenida San Juan, but darting down side roads and into markets can also prove fruitful.

MAP 2: Defensa 800-1200

Rue des Artisans

Constructed in 1887, this Retiro street is one of the oldest alleys in Buenos Aires, steeped in legends of feuding families that left it divided in two walled-off parts. Nowadays, its picturesque properties are filled with small boutiques, offering artwork, antiques, furniture, clothes, and more. French and Italian themes run throughout.

MAP 3: Arenales 1239 and Libertad 1240; 11am-7pm Mon.-Fri.

Avenida Santa Fe

Avenida Santa Fe is a major commercial avenue with over 30 blocks of shops lining each side, running from Retiro through Recoleta and into

patriotic paraphernalia for sale in Plaza de Mayo

Palermo before changing its name to Avenida Cabildo and racing off toward Belgrano. Although there is a wide variety of goods here, the general theme is upmarket clothing.

MAP 3: Av. Santa Fe 1100-4600

Palermo Soho

To the south of the Plaza Italia Subte station on Avenida Santa Fe lies Palermo Soho, where seemingly infinite boutiques and trendy stores sell clothing, art, furniture, and more, mostly at elevated costs.

MAP 5: Bordered by Godoy Cruz, Niceto Vega, Malabia, and Guatemala

Once

The largest shopping district in Buenos Aires, Once is a hive of merchandise and wholesale trade. Fabric and clothing are the most common items. Well-known brands are rare; instead, the focus is on variety and value. For those who like rifling through piles of clothes, toys, bags, or fabric—and can bear the thought of thousands of shops squeezed into a few blocks—this Balvanera district won't fail to please.

MAP 6: Bordered by Av. Pueyrredón, Av. Rivadavia, Junín, and Lavalle

Villa Crespo

Villa Crespo, which lies alongside Almagro and Palermo, is the "outlet" (the English word is used in Argentina) neighborhood and a popular destination for fashion. There are two sections, the main one to the north of Avenida Corrientes and a second to the south (Murillo 500-700), which is packed with leather stores.

MAP 6: Bordered by Av. Scalabrini Ortiz, Castillo, Av. Juan B. Justo, and Vera

Centro   Map 1

BOOKS AND MUSIC
Minton's

Even after moving from its original location in Belgrano to this nondescript space, Minton's remains the go-to shop for jazz records in Buenos Aires, especially mainstream and avant-garde albums. Hugely popular with both musicians and fans, Minton's draws many customers who come just to talk to owner Guillermo Hernández, who may offer a bottle of the store's personal wine brand. The space is tiny, but the variety and quality of the discs for sale don't suffer for it.

MAP 1: Av. Corrientes 1382, Local 26, tel. 011/4371-2216, www.minton-s.blogspot.com.ar; 1pm-8:30pm Mon.-Fri.

GIFTS AND HOME
El Boyero

Of the multiple tourist-oriented shops lining Florida, El Boyero offers the best selection and highest quality of goods. Leather jackets and silver knives sit alongside *mate* gourds and wine-bottle holders, while alpaca and wool products accompany wooden carvings and cowhide rugs, all of which are set off against the elegant wooden interior. The main store can be found on the second floor of Galerías Pacífico, but another location lies a few blocks up the street (Florida 953).

MAP 1: Florida 753, Local 306, tel. 011/4314-1260, www.elboyero.com; 10am-9pm Mon.-Sat., noon-9pm Sun.

DEPARTMENT STORES
Falabella

The department store concept only arrived in Argentina in 1993 when Falabella opened. To this day, it pretty much rules the market, selling clothes, perfume, furniture, household goods, electronics, wine, and books. This place spoils its customers with an abundance of choices. With a few outlets around the city, the Centro location is the most iconic and popular, with an open layout that encourages browsing and draws large crowds of families.

MAP 1: Florida 343, tel. 0810/555-3252, www.falabella.com.ar; 9am-9pm Mon.-Sat., noon-8pm Sun.

SHOPPING CENTERS
Galerías Pacífico

Taking up a whole city block in the heart of the central shopping district, Galerías Pacífico is a towering gallery whose design is based on its Italian and French contemporaries, with towering roofs, ornate decoration, and

Galerías Pacífico mixes art with shopping.

vast murals. Within, international outlets, such as Chanel, Nike, and Tommy Hilfiger, abound, although there is also a wide range of popular Argentine stores, such as Cuesta Blanca and Rapsodia, which sell the latest clothing fashions.

MAP 1: Florida and Av. Córdoba, tel. 011/5555-5420, www.galeriaspacifico.com. ar; 10am-9pm Mon.-Sat., noon-9pm Sun.

San Telmo and La Boca   Map 2

BOOKS AND MUSIC
La Libre

An outlet for an independent publisher, La Libre sells a wide range of books and is home to many cultural events, including concerts, theater, workshops and art exhibitions. On Wednesday night, the upstairs room is converted into a cinema where 16 mm films are projected to an avid crowd. A number of hard-to-find titles are available here, as well as a constantly changing selection of English books. As with most of the

city's bookstores, a thrift store ambience prevails.

MAP 2: Bolívar 646, tel. 011/4343-5328, www.lalibrearteylibros.wordpress.com; 1pm-10pm daily

Walrus Books

This cozy bookstore's tiny size belies the fact that it has over 4,000 new and used English-language books available—far more than any other local bookstore. All areas of fiction and nonfiction are represented. Walrus is run by Geoffrey Hickman and his wife, Josefina, both of whom will happily offer advice on South American writers. They also buy books from customers looking to exchange older titles.

MAP 2: Estados Unidos 617, tel. 011/4300-7135, www.walrus-books.com.ar; noon-8pm Tues.-Sun.

GIFT AND HOME
✪ Cualquier Verdura

Although it may look like any other house on a picturesque San Telmo street, Cualquier Verdura is far from it. The shop unfurls as you move around inside, each room piled high with displays and objects. Everything is for sale—including the ancient display cases themselves. From vintage toys to retro house accessories and obscure artwork, there are endless unique gift opportunities here. Or take something back for your own home that will serve as a reminder of Buenos Aires.

MAP 2: Humberto Primo 517, tel. 011/4300-2474, www.cualquierverdura.com. ar; noon-8pm Thurs.-Sun.

Cualquier Verdura

Artesanos de Argentina

Located inside a garish building wedged underneath an overpass, Artesanos de Argentina is a cooperative of artisans that formed to promote their wares. All items are handmade from a wide range of materials such as silver, alpaca hide, gems, bronze, and leather. The store is organized by type of handicraft, selling jewelry, clothing, and souvenirs alongside pieces of local art.

MAP 2: Defensa 1224, tel. 011/4300-5791, www.artesanosdeargentina.com; 10am-6pm daily

OPEN-AIR MARKETS
✪ Feria de San Pedro Telmo

Originally an antiques fair based in Plaza Dorrego, this open-air market has grown into the largest of its kind in the city. Every Sunday, thousands of shoppers flock to Defensa, which is lined with stalls selling handicrafts, food, clothing, accessories, and more. Plaza Dorrego remains the hub of the market, with the widest range of items for sale, ranging from the antique to the artisan. Prices also vary widely, but great bargains can be found. This is a great place to buy *fileteado*, the stylized drawings that adorn shop signs and buses across the city. Arrive early to beat the crowds.

MAP 2: Plaza Dorrego, Defensa and Humberto Primo; www.feriadesantelmo. com; 10am-5pm Sun.

VINTAGE AND ANTIQUES
Mercado de San Telmo

The Mercado de San Telmo is one of the city's best indoor markets, set in a historic building with a beautiful metal and glass roof tucked between

the Mercado de San Telmo

Defensa and Bolívar. The main attractions are antique goods, such as retro toys, old-fashioned home goods, and clothes from yesteryear, but it also houses grocers, butchers, and vendors of exotic goods. Although the market is open all week, many stalls only open on the weekend.

MAP 2: Bolívar and Carlos Calvo; no phone; 9am-8pm daily

Retiro

Map 3

ACCESSORIES AND JEWELRY
✪ Simonetta Orsini

Martin De Leeuw is understandably proud of the selection of elite watches that he sells from this beautiful old building. The modern interior holds timepieces of many styles, as well as jewelry, although everything is at the higher end of the price spectrum. Collectors come from all over South America to purchase watches here, as well as for repairs, since the expert watchmakers are trained to repair every single model that they sell.

MAP 3: Posadas 1101, tel. 011/4811-1409, www.simonettaorsini.com; 10am-8pm Mon.-Fri., 10am-2pm Sat.

LEATHER GOODS
✪ Casa López

High-end leather wallets, purses, and bags can be found here in huge variety. The original and delightful designs come in many different colors. All the products are built to last and withstand changing fashion trends, but they come with hefty price tags—from US$300 for a purse and US$80 for a wallet. Overlooking leafy Plaza

San Martín, the wooden and cream-colored interior attracts wealthy clients to this elegant store.

MAP 3: Marcelo T. Alvear 640, tel. 011/4311-3044, www.casalopez.com.ar; 9am-8pm Mon.-Fri., 10am-6:30pm Sat.-Sun.

Prüne

Although the selection isn't as varied or as high-quality as in Villa Crespo, Prüne draws crowds and is especially popular with Brazilian tourists for its leather goods. Quality products, including belts and jackets, are available, but their specialty is bags and purses. Other outlets can be found around the city, but this is the most popular one, given its central location and sophisticated feel. If you're looking to buy authentic leather products, make sure you don't accidentally wander into the synthetic leather section.

MAP 3: Florida 963, tel. 011/4011-4300, www.prune.com.ar; 10am-8pm daily

CLOTHING

La Martina

Brought over by the British in the 19th century, polo took hold of the Argentine elite and still garners much attention from *porteños*. Today, La Martina is perhaps the definitive polo clothing line, selling upscale clothing for both men and women. Within this location of the retailer, quality leather polo equipment is also on display.

MAP 3: Paraguay 661, tel. 011/4576-7999, www.lamartina.com; 10am-8pm Mon.-Sat.

✪ Playsport

Although few of the *fútbol* jerseys sold in the Centro are authentic, shoppers can rest assured that they are buying the genuine article at PlaySport. As well as selling the jerseys of all major clubs and the national team, there is also a wide selection of club-branded jackets, trousers, bags, and hats. The store is small but well laid out for easy browsing, and they will print any name or number on the back of jerseys.

MAP 3: Av. Córdoba 423, tel. 011/4928-1829, www.playsport.com.ar; 10:30am-7pm Mon.-Sat., 1pm-6pm Sun.

SHOES

Comme Il Faut

Run by Alicia Muñiz, who began her shoemaking career by crafting designs for her own personal use, Comme Il Faut specializes in tango shoes, although the high-heeled design need not be exclusively used for such activity. A tango aficionado, Alicia is always on hand to offer her opinion and knowledge on both the dance and the shoes, which come in all colors imaginable. Set inside a beautiful shopping gallery, the store is modern and minimalist.

MAP 3: Arenales 1239, tel. 011/4815-5690, www.commeilfaut.com.ar; 11am-7pm Mon.-Fri., 11am-3pm Sat.

ACCESSORIES AND JEWELRY

Fueguia 1833

A decidedly conceptual perfumery, Fueguia bottles and sells the exotic fragrances of South America in an atmospheric setting. The store is a beautiful combination of maps and glass bottles that evoke a sense of wanderlust that's only enhanced by the rich scents. Visitors are invited to participate in the creative process and alter fragrances as they like. The prices here are nothing to be sniffed at.

MAP 4: Av. Alvear 1680, tel. 011/4311-5360, www.fueguia.com; 11am-8pm daily

BOOKS AND MUSIC

✪ El Ateneo Grand Splendid

The Teatro Gran Splendid opened its doors in 1919, providing a stage for some of the world's greatest tango artists before becoming a cinema 10 years later. When this iconic cinema later closed down, it was converted into a bookstore that is now regarded as one of the finest in the world. The theater floor is filled with bookstands, while the curving balconies that reach up to the frescoed ceiling are lined with shelves. Although the stage has been converted into a café, many browsers choose to lounge in the private nooks that function as designated reading areas throughout the space. A large selection of English-language books are available, as well as an extended travel section.

MAP 4: Av. Santa Fe 1860, tel. 011/4813-6052, www.yenny-elateneo.com; 9am-10pm Mon.-Thurs., 9am-midnight Fri.-Sat., noon-10pm Sun.

Clásica y Moderna

Originally opening as a bookstore in 1938, Clásica y Moderna was converted into a cultural center half a century later. A restaurant and café host daily musical performances, such as jazz, tango, book readings, and theater productions. Books, including a decent selection of English-language titles, are still sold on two floors. As if all that wasn't enough, regular art exhibitions are displayed.

MAP 4: Av. Callao 892, tel. 011/4812-8707, www.clasicaymoderna.com; 9am-1am Mon.-Sat.

Librería Turística

Specializing in travel and tourism, Librería Turística offers a wealth of guides and maps for Argentina and Buenos Aires, as well as the rest of the world. It has an excellent selection of themed guidebooks (restaurants, cafés, archaeology, and so on),

El Ateneo Grand Splendid

Buenos Aires Design, Recoleta's home and design destination

many of which are in English. The staff's knowledge and willingness to help customers make up for the relatively obscure location and simple aesthetics.

MAP 4: Paraguay 2457, tel. 011/4962-5547, www.librosdeturismo.com.ar; 9am-7pm Mon.-Fri., 9am-1pm Sat.

CLOTHING AND SHOES
La Dolfina

If you can't find Adolfo Cambiaso, the world's best-known polo player, riding around Recoleta in his Jeep, rest assured that you will find photos of him modeling his own clothing line in this store. Cambiaso's menswear is top-notch—just expect to pay heftily for the privilege of taking it home. The store oozes the charm and sophistication expected from its location on an exclusive shopping street.

MAP 4: Av. Alvear 1751, tel. 011/4815-2698, www.ladolfina.com; 10am-8pm Mon.-Sat.

VINTAGE
Juan Pérez Vintage

The largest and best-known vintage store in Buenos Aires, Juan Pérez offers a huge amount of stock, including clothing, bags, shoes, jewelry, and accessories. It's easy to spend hours browsing through the unusual items—in fact, it's a popular activity with the neighborhood's elderly women. Prices are higher but generally reasonable. The decor is industrial and simple, with the sole focus being the colorful items crowded onto the shelves and racks.

MAP 4: Marcelo T. de Alvear 1441, tel. 011/4815-8442, www.vestitenjaunperez. blogspot.com.ar; 11am-7pm Mon.-Sat.

LEATHER GOODS
Silvia Eisele

An exclusive leatherwear store tucked in the rural heart of Recoleta, Silvia Eisele only accepts clients or customers by appointment. About as small a boutique as is possible and based in a private apartment building, the quality of product and attention to detail are second to none. While items are available for immediate purchase, the Eisele family specialize in custom-made designs. They are also happy to pick up prospective clients from their hotel if desired.

MAP 4: Arenales 2915, tel. 011/4829-9358, www.silviaeiselecueros.com.ar; by appointment only

GIFT AND HOME
Buenos Aires Design

Obscurely located underneath the Centro Cultural de Recoleta and the crematorium, Buenos Aires Design houses all the major players of the country's interior design industry under one roof. Furniture, appliances, and accessories are all here, as is an impressive open-air food court and the city's Hard Rock Café. The merchandise styles and inspiration come from all around the world. Spread over two floors, the iconic design of the mall itself is a testament to modern Argentine interior design.

MAP 4: Av. Pueyrredón 2501, tel. 011/5777-6000, www.designrecoleta.com.ar; 10am-9pm Mon.-Sat., noon-9pm Sun.

OPEN-AIR MARKETS
Feria Plaza Francia

Despite the fact that it's known as the Feria Plaza Francia, due to its original 1960s location, this market actually takes place in Plaza Alvear, on the opposite side of Avenida Pueyrredón. On weekends, the plaza's winding paths and slopes fill with artisans selling jewelry, souvenirs, and toys. Musicians and bands play in the open spaces, and empanadas are sold seemingly everywhere. Arrive as early as possible to beat the crowds and find the most produce.

MAP 4: Plaza Alvear, www.feriaplazafrancia.com; 11am-8pm Sat.-Sun.

SHOPPING CENTERS
Patio del Liceo

An alternative shopping mall, Patio del Liceo is situated in the middle of one of the classiest shopping districts in Buenos Aires. Spread over three floors connected with walkways, the gallery is centered around a courtyard that houses a few bars and cafés. There is ample diversity at this small spot, including independent bookstores, retro clothing, and glassware—but the main focus is local art. Parties are held on Friday night and include live music and art exhibitions.

MAP 4: Av. Santa Fe 2729, www.galeriapatiodelliceo.com; noon-late Mon.-Sat.

WINE
✪ The Wine Gallery

Martin Bushi, the owner of this fine establishment, knows his regular customers and their preferences and is always ready to suggest new vintages. He is also a good resource for those who want to start or develop their private collections. In a typical Recoleta building and stuffed with wine bottles in elegant wooden displays, the store encourages visitors to browse the merchandise by regions of the country. This is a great place to find exquisite Argentine wine, especially the country's most famed export, malbec.

MAP 4: Montevideo 1784, tel. 011/4815-4461, www.winegallery.com.ar; 10am-8pm Mon.-Sat.

ARTS AND CRAFTS
✪ Mar Dulce

Founded by Scotswoman Linda Neilson, Mar Dulce is a gallery of increasing importance, presenting work by Argentine and Uruguayan artists. Illustrators, photographers, painters, and artists of other mediums are offered space here alongside one main exhibition. The majority of the pieces are small- or medium-size, making them ideal purchases for travelers. The space is small but fills with natural light that comes through windows that overlook a leafy patio.

MAP 5: Uriarte 1490, tel. 015/5319-3597, www.galeriamardulce.blogspot.com.ar; 3pm-8pm Tues.-Sat.

Hollywood in Cambodia

Tucked into the back of Post Bar, a bohemian drinking hole in Palermo, lies Hollywood in Cambodia. More an exhibition space than a gallery, it displays constantly changing work (in mediums including paint, stencil, and graffiti) from important local street artists. Some of these original pieces are highly sought after and yet can be picked up for very low prices. There is always one of the founding artists sitting around to chat to about the works or the local street-art scene.

MAP 5: Thames 1885, no phone, www.hollywoodincambodia.com.ar; 5pm-9pm Tues.-Sun.

Palermo fills with shoppers over the weekends.

BOOKS AND MUSIC

Libros del Pasaje

A place to come and read as much as buy books, Libros del Pasaje is a cozy bookstore with a patio and a café. Shoppers scale towering bookshelves with ladders to reach the higher books, of which there are thousands. A decent selection of English-language books is available, and relaxing music accompanies browsers. Presentations by local authors are held weekly.

MAP 5: Thames 1762, tel. 011/4833-6637, www.librosdelpasaje.com.ar; 10am-10pm Mon.-Sat., 3pm-10pm Sun.

Miles Discos

Miles Discos, in business for more than 30 years, is an institution. It's the go-to place to discover new music for any aficionado, with tables, shelves, and boxes crammed full of albums. This record shop is run by Gustavo Broic, who can answer any music-related query. Check out the extensive variety of vinyl and CDs, covering everything from tango to rock, at the listening posts. A nearby second outlet (Gurruchaga 1580) offers film-related items.

MAP 5: Honduras 4969, tel. 011/4832-0466, www.milesdiscos.com.ar; 10am-midnight Mon.-Fri.

CLOTHING AND ACCESSORIES

Bensimon

A casual menswear label from Argentina, Bensimon specializes in fresh, comfy, and easy-on-the-eye clothing. The range of shirts, tops, and trousers is always at the cutting edge of fashion but maintain a low-key and unobtrusive look. With stores across the city, this location in the clothing haven of Palermo Viejo is one of the best, with much of the stock laid out on tables for easy browsing.

MAP 5: Honduras 4876, tel. 011/4833-6857, www.bensimon.com.ar; 11am-8:30pm Mon.-Sat., 2pm-8:30pm Sun.

Keak

Colorful and quirky, Keak sells men's and women's vintage and vintage-style clothing and accessories. Reasonable prices and an eccentric collection ensure that anyone seeking retro fashions will find something to their liking. From bracelets and bags to hats and dresses, the store has so much merchandise that there doesn't seem to be enough room to store everything. Rentals are also available. The colorful and quirky setup of the shop is typical of the Palermo neighborhood.

MAP 5: Costa Rica 5758, tel. 011/4772-2189; noon-8pm Mon.-Sat.

GIFT AND HOME

Monte Arte Étnico Argentino

Monte sells vividly colored blankets woven in Santiago del Estero. All the dyes used are natural—even the bright pink hues that dominate. Expect to pay up to a few hundred dollars for a decent blanket. There are also some decorative art pieces, as well as handcrafted furniture. The rustic ambience tries to recreate Argentine rural culture, which is possibly why locals shop here as much as travelers.

MAP 5: El Salvador 4656, tel. 011/4832-0516, www.monteargentino.com; 11am-7pm Mon.-Fri., 11am-2pm Sat.

OPEN-AIR MARKETS

Feria de Plaza Julio Cortázar

Formerly known as Plaza Serrano (and still widely referred to in this way), Plaza Julio Cortázar is the

BEST SOUVENIRS

Street fairs (especially those in San Telmo and Plaza Francia) are full of artisans and are ideal places to find souvenirs.

FOOD AND DRINKS

Put food and drinks in your checked luggage, as even packaged food items will be removed and confiscated from carry-on luggage.

- **Alfajores:** A sweet snack of cookies sandwiching a layer of *dulce de leche* or jam, encased in chocolate. The tastiest brands are **Havanna** and **Cachafaz,** available at any *kiosco* (newsstand) or in supermarkets.

- **Dulce de leche:** An intensely sweet caramel-like sauce made from milk and sugar that is sold at supermarkets. Artisanal *dulce de leche* can be found in open-air markets, but it's worth asking to taste first.

Mate gourds and **bombillas** are popular gifts to take home.

- **Beef:** Any beef packed into your suitcase will be confiscated at the border, but Argentine airports sell huge slabs of vacuum-packed beef once you're through passport control.

- **Fernet:** Although this liquor is available in other countries, it can be hard to find and up to four times as expensive. The best and most common brand, **Fernet Branca,** is available in supermarkets in Buenos Aires for around US$10 per liter.

very center of Palermo Soho. Artists and designers sell their creations at the market that takes place at this plaza Wednesday through Sunday, although the fair is at its biggest on the weekend. Local paintings are displayed on the roadside, while other artisanal products, such as jewelry and clothes, are sold from stalls. An intriguing feature of the fair is being able to talk to the artists themselves, many of whom sit and paint on the spot. Surrounded by bars and restaurants, this market is located at one of the few squares in the city with multiple open-air dining and drinking options.

MAP 5: Plaza Julio Cortázar (Honduras and Serrano), www.plazaserrano.8m.com; 3pm-8pm Wed.-Fri., 10am-8pm Sat.-Sun.

SHOPPING CENTERS
✪ Alto Palermo

The fact that this mall only opened in 1990 and is now one of the most important shopping centers in the city shows how the *porteño* obsession with North American culture has boomed. Alto Palermo contains three floors of stores in an intriguing wavy layout that fills with young and middle-age people. A diverse selection of shops, offering books, toys, gadgets, and jewelry, is strongly outnumbered by clothing stores, selling everything from formal evening wear to the latest casual trends. Popular menswear stores such as Original Penguin are also represented.

MAP 5: Av. Santa Fe 3253, tel. 011/5777-8000, www.altopalermo.com.ar; 10am-10pm daily

- **Maté:** This tea is one of the most popular souvenirs from Buenos Aires. Make sure to buy a few *bombillas* (metal straws) and a couple bags of *yerba* (leaves) along with the *mate* gourd itself. The best place to buy everything is at an open-air market, where the cheapest set will cost under US$10—but be prepared to spend at least twice that much.

- **Wine:** The best place to purchase a bottle of Argentina's beloved malbec is from a *vinoteca* (wine store), which offers greater quality and variety than a supermarket. Any bottle above US$10 should be an excellent vintage.

CRAFTS AND CLOTHING

- *Fileteado:* A colorful and fun style of signage, *fileteado* is most noticeable on city buses and store and restaurant fronts. Mass-produced versions (from US$7) are sold around San Telmo; for a higher price, artists at markets and street fairs, also in San Telmo, prepare better quality signs to order (from US$25).

- **Soccer Jerseys:** With dozens of teams in Buenos Aires, there are ample choices for *fútbol* gear, with **River Plate** and **Boca Juniors** the easiest to find. The smartest option is to buy from the clubs themselves (around US$60) to ensure authenticity, as fake versions are widespread.

- **Leather:** The prevalence of leather goods produced here should be no surprise, given the quantity of beef consumed. Avoid the tourist shops in the Centro and head to **Villa Crespo,** where a couple of blocks of Murillo (500-700) are packed with over 50 leather stores. Expect to pay at least US$200 for a decent leather jacket or US$50 for a bag.

- *Alpargatas:* While Toms have become a wildly popular shoe over the last few years, *alpargatas* (espadrilles, the shoe on which Toms based their design) have been worn in Argentina for centuries. They cost as little as US$5 and come as plain or as colorful as desired. Ask for them in shoe shops or track them down in street fairs.

Casa Cavia

A bohemian high-society concept in the heart of Palermo Chico, Casa Cavia is a renovated residence that houses an eclectic mix of high-end stores. Art, books, perfume, flower arrangements, and a patisserie all combine to forge an elegant and sophisticated setting. The building itself is a grand piece of architecture, with an inner patio that features an eclectic mix of antique and modern decor. Looming windows look out over a central patio that offers a great spot to sit and enjoy a refreshing drink or bite to eat.

MAP 5: Cavia 2985, tel. 011/4801-9693, www.casacavia.com; 9am-5pm Mon., 9am-midnight Tues.-Fri., 10am-midnight Sat., 10am-5pm Sun.

the patio at Casa Cavia

TOBACCO
La Covacha

While the standard selection of cigarettes are easily found in any *kiosco* (akin to a newsstand), it is necessary to hunt out a *tabaquería* (tobacconist)

SHOPS

PALERMO

for a greater choice of rolling and pipe tobacco or cigars. La Covacha stocks a wide selection of Cuban cigars, European and American tobacco, and smoking paraphernalia such as filters and rolling papers. If a brand is not stocked here, it's unlikely you'll find it anywhere else in the city. The staff are knowledgeable and helpful, while regular customers often stand around conversing amid the varied aromas that can be smelled upon entering.
MAP 5: Güemes 3996, tel. 011/4832-2209; 10am-8pm Mon.-Sat.

VINTAGE AND ANTIQUES
✪ Mercado de las Pulgas
Located on the edge of Palermo, the Mercado de las Pulgas is the largest flea market in Buenos Aires. Opened in 1988, it has recently been refurbished and is now busier than ever. Furniture and accessories are sold from over 150 stalls, or large cages, which are organized in a grid pattern that allows for easy and methodical exploration. Some stalls specialize in

It's easy to get lost hunting through the Mercado de las Pulgas.

198

specific items, such as chairs, suitcases, or hats, while others seem to contain the entire contents of a 19th-century house.
MAP 5: Av. Dorrego and Av. Niceto Vega, tel. 011/4779-2915; 10am-7pm Tues.-Sun.

WINE
Lo de Joaquín Alberdi
With an extensive knowledge of Argentine wines and vineyards, Joaquin and his helpers can help you choose the best wine to suit your tastes and your wallet. Samples are available before purchasing, making it hard to leave this climate-controlled space empty-handed. The striking yellow walls, both interior and exterior, contrast splendidly with the wooden floors, blue wine racks, and rows of deep-red bottles of wine. Wine-tasting sessions are offered Thursday and Friday evening, although private tastings can also be arranged.
MAP 5: Borges 1772, tel. 011/4832-5329, www.lodejoaquinalberdi.com; 11am-9:30pm Mon.-Sat., noon-9:30pm Sun.

Vinology
Run by María Mendizábal, an award-winning Argentina sommelier, Vinology offers wine from the classic Argentine *bodegas* (vineyards), but it's most notable for its selection of obscure and rare vintages, all of which are described in person by María. On a peaceful backstreet lined with trees, the light-filled store offers stools and tables for customers to sit and try wines before buying. Elegant glasses and decanters are sold, as well specially designed gift boxes for the bottles.
MAP 5: República de Eslovenia 1959, tel. 011/4776-4807, www.bin4vinology.com.ar; noon-8pm Mon.-Fri., 10am-1pm Sat.

Almagro

Map 6

SHOES

✪ Calzados Correa

A family-run shoemaker on a leafy cobbled street in Almagro, Calzados Correa offers some of the finest bespoke and handmade leather shoes available. The small store is crammed with shoes, bags, and clothing before opening up into the workshops out back. While premade shoes of all types are available, the ideal choice is buying a custom pair, a process that can take a few weeks. Traditionally specializing in men's shoes, they have now opened a vintage women's shoe store (Mario Bravo 735) right across the street.
MAP 6: Mario Bravo 750, tel. 011/4861-7344, www.calzadoscorrea.com. ar; 8am-1pm and 3pm-7pm Mon.-Fri., 8am-1pm Sat.

VINTAGE

La Percalina

Going by the motto "out-of-fashion fashion," La Percalina offers an eclectic yet carefully selected collection of women's clothing from 1940 to 1960. Entering through a sparsely decorated showroom, visitors descend into the basement, which contains a workshop and the main collection of clothing. Despite being secondhand, the clothes are all in perfect condition, lovingly restored and presented by the owner, although this ensures that prices are higher than most other secondhand stores. For personal attention and unique selection, it doesn't get much better than this.

shoes being fashioned by hand at Calzados Correa

MAP 6: Guardia Vieja 3566, www. lapercalina.blogspot.com.ar; 2pm-8pm Tues.-Sat.

vintage clothes for sale at La Percalina

OPEN-AIR MARKETS
Feria del Parque Rivadavia

It's a delight to wander through and browse this open-air market comprising permanent bookstalls. Tables and boxes of books sprawl all over the place in a labyrinthine layout. Given that few travelers head out here, there are some English-language gems stashed in dark corners for absurdly low prices. The market occurs every day of the week. Magazines and used records are also sold here.

MAP 6: Av. Rivadavia 4900; 9am-8pm daily

Balvanera   Map 6

SHOPPING CENTERS
Mercado del Abasto

When this looming art deco building was constructed in 1934, it housed a meat and vegetable market. Some 60 years later it was converted into a modern four-story shopping mall that is today one of the largest in Buenos Aires. It includes a multiscreen cinema, an indoor Ferris wheel, a food court, and a Subte station that deposits customers directly in the center, not to mention 200 stores connected by a complicated series of escalators. Everything can be found here, from clothes and electronics to furniture and artwork, as well as the Museo de los Niños (Children's Museum, 1pm-8pm Tues.-Sun., US$10), basically an oversized playground, with trains and other toys to distract bored children.

MAP 6: Av. Corrientes 3247, tel. 011/4959-3400, www.abasto-shopping. com.ar; 10am-10pm daily

OPEN-AIR MARKETS
✪ Feria de Mataderos

Formerly a meeting point for gauchos bringing their wares into the city, this is now the location of an open-air market that embraces traditional crafts, foods, and dances. Based around a cobbled square, the market features artisanal goods such as musical instruments, handmade toys, leather belts, and *mate* gourds, sold to the accompaniment of live traditional music. As the day wears on, tables are shoved aside and dancers take to the floor in a picturesque scene. Meanwhile, gauchos charge up and down the street on horses competing to pass a stick through a small ring. It is mainly locals here, thanks to its out-of-the-way location, but an hour's ride on any of the following buses will drop you off next to the market: 55 (Palermo); 92 (Retiro, Recoleta, Almagro); 126 (Puerto Madero, San Telmo); and 180 (confusingly signed as the 155, Centro, Balvanera, Almagro). A taxi ride will take about 40 minutes and cost around US$15. Confirm on the website that the market will be happening before heading out.

MAP 7: Av. Fernández de la Cruz and Av. Lisandro de la Torre, tel. 011/4342-9629, www.feriademataderos.com.ar; 6pm-1am Sat. Jan.-Mar., 11am-9pm Sun. Apr.-Dec.

the Mercado del Abasto

ARTS AND CRAFTS
SlyZmud

Slightly out of the center, although not hard to reach, SlyZmud is a thriving gallery in Villa Crespo. With contemporary Argentine work that is generally small in size, it is wildly popular with art collectors. The exhibitions last for a year, of which there are half a dozen in this gallery and another half dozen 50 meters up the street in a second space. Both galleries are airy and well lit, with attractive facades and floors befitting the work displayed within. All exhibitions are shown on the website, as are the items for sale. To get here, take the Subte Linea B to Dorrego station.

MAP 7: Bonpland 721, tel. 011/4857-0334, www.slyzmud.com; 2pm-7pm Mon.-Fri., by appointment only Sat.-Sun.

LEATHER GOODS
✪ Murillo 666

One of the most renowned leather stores in Argentina, Murillo 666 offers some of the highest-quality products available for both men and women. Specializing in jackets, of which there are endless choices of both formal and casual, they also offer a wide range of sizes. The showroom is stylish, with exquisite leather sofas to recline on. Prices are slightly higher than neighboring stores due to the high quality.

MAP 7: Murillo 666, tel. 011/4856-4501, www.murillo666.com.ar; 9:30am-8pm Mon.-Sat., 10am-7pm Sun.

SHOPPING CENTERS
Unicenter

You never actually leave the city to reach the Unicenter, the first and largest shopping mall in Argentina. Covering more than 10 city blocks, it includes over 300 stores, mainly international and Argentine chains, such as Armani, Levi's, and Christian Dior; a 16-screen cinema; a vast games arcade; and a seething gym. Take bus 60 or 130, but only the ones with a sign in the windshield saying "Panamericana."

MAP 7: Paraná 3745, tel. 011/4733-1111, www.unicenter.com.ar; 10am-10pm daily

WHERE TO STAY

Accommodations in Buenos Aires range from hostel dorms with 20 beds on top of each other to luxurious five-star hotels, although prices are not always indicative of quality. The last few years have seen a dramatic rise in the number of small boutique hotels and apartment-style hotels, especially in the Palermo and San Telmo neighborhoods. Most hotels and hostels are situated in refurbished old city houses, meaning that many are easy to slip into without too much fanfare, but a number of them are extravagant and highly visible, offering glitz at an often affordable cost.

restaurant in the Faena Hotel

Buenos Aires is one of the most popular destinations in South America, which means that accommodations, especially the smaller boutique hotels and more popular hostels, can be fully sold out in advance. Because of this, advance reservations are strongly advised.

Theft in hostels is a common problem. Lockers should be used, and many hostels are strict about not allowing nonpaying guests inside.

All neighborhoods are interconnected by public transportation options day and night. Bear in mind that the Subte only runs until around 10pm, after which you'll need to navigate the complicated bus system. It's worth inquiring at your hotel or hostel as to which buses serve the area.

Many hotels and hostels have *promociones* (offers) advertised on their websites and often give discounts to customers paying in cash. With the Argentine

HIGHLIGHTS

✪ **BEST SOCIAL SCENE:** With a raging club and constant events and activities, the **Milhouse Hostel Avenue** is the place for partiers (page 207).

✪ **BEST TANGO-THEMED ACCOMMODATION:** Doubling as a dance academy, the stunning **Mansión Dandi Royal** offers the perfect tango immersion (page 209).

✪ **BEST POOL:** Set in lush gardens, the outdoor pool at the **Four Seasons** is perfect for a quick dip (page 210).

✪ **BEST VIEWS:** With a commanding panorama of the Río de la Plata and city center, the **Sheraton Buenos Aires** is hard to beat (page 210).

✪ **GRANDEST HOTEL:** The timeless **Alvear Palace Hotel** has hosted innumerable dignitaries, and today has one of the city's best restaurants (page 211).

✪ **BEST PLACE TO SPLURGE:** With doubles starting at US$500, the **Palacio Duhau—Park Hyatt Buenos Aires** makes its guests feel like royalty (page 212).

✪ **MOST INTERESTING BUILDING:** Set in a restored mansion, the **Poetry Building Recoleta** is an architectural joy (page 212).

✪ **MOST RELAXED RESPITE:** In the vibrating Palermo neighborhood, **Mine Hotel** provides peace and quiet (page 214).

✪ **BEST VALUE:** Out-of-the-way and down-to-earth, **La Taba** offers great rates in the Almagro neighborhood (page 216).

PRICE KEY

$	Less than US$50 per night
$ $	US$50-150 per night
$ $ $	More than US$150 per night

economy particularly prone to fluctuations, the prices indicated are liable to change regularly. Wi-Fi is usually offered for free, although connections are often unreliable, even in larger hotels. A computer is almost always available for guests to use in both hotels and hostels.

Prices listed are for double rooms unless otherwise stated.

CHOOSING WHERE TO STAY

The architectural and cultural differences between Buenos Aires's neighborhoods are striking, with the atmosphere often changing noticeably from one block to the next.

CENTRO

All visitors are drawn to this neighborhood at some point during their stay due to its large number of sights. Most of the lodging options are hostels, although there are also some standard hotels.

PUERTO MADERO

This neighborhood caters to the wealthiest *porteños* and offers some of the city's most luxurious hotels. Less than half a dozen in number, none of these options are any less than five-star joints.

SAN TELMO AND LA BOCA

San Telmo is mainly a residential neighborhood and has long been the traditional choice for backpackers, although it now also offers an impressive choice of boutique hotels.

La Boca offers little in terms of accommodations. At night it can be uninviting and dangerous. It's also the only neighborhood without Subte connections.

RETIRO

Centrally located Retiro is home to some grand five-star hotels, most of which are based around Plaza San Martín. Evening entertainment in the area is scarce.

RECOLETA

When people talk about Buenos Aires being the Paris of South America, they are largely referring to Recoleta, with its architectural beauty and sophisticated air. The most famous and luxurious hotels in the city can be found in a small cluster in the heart of this neighborhood.

PALERMO

Palermo is the city's focal point for dining and nightlife, but this is a relatively recent trend. It offers a large number of smaller boutique hotels that can vary wildly in price.

ALMAGRO

Residential Almagro only recently exploded onto the popular nightlife, dining, and cultural scenes and therefore still offers little in the way of accommodations—but this also means that prices are respectable for the few options that do exist.

BALVANERA

Balvanera, although residential in parts, is more renowned for its shops, with little happening outside business hours. There are some cheap options, but many accommodations are residences that are more suited to lengthier stays of weeks or months.

ALTERNATIVE LODGING OPTIONS

With the global explosion of Airbnb (www.airbnb.com), more and more *porteños* are discovering the appeal

WHERE TO STAY . . .

IF YOU WANT TO BE IN THE THICK OF THINGS:
A little bit of everything can be found in **Centro.**

IF YOU WANT TO MEET OTHER BACKPACKERS:
San Telmo is the favored neighborhood for hostels and cheap accommodations.

IF YOU DESIRE RELAXED SURROUNDINGS (AND DON'T MIND PAYING FOR THEM):
The plush hotels of **Puerto Madero** offer a haven of tranquility.

IF YOU CRAVE NIGHTLIFE OR GASTRONOMIC DIVERSITY:
Palermo serves up a wealth of boutique hotels from which to explore.

IF YOU WANT TO EXPERIENCE LIFE AS A *PORTEÑO*:
Opt for the friendly and familial **Almagro** neighborhood.

IF YOU LIKE YOUR SURROUNDINGS GRAND AND LUXURIOUS:
Look no further than **Recoleta.**

IF YOU WANT TO SHOP:
Book a stay in **Palermo** or **Recoleta.**

IF YOU'RE ON A BUDGET:
Balvanera offers great-value accommodations—and food.

IF YOU'LL BE TRAVELING ONWARD IN ARGENTINA:
Stay in **Retiro** to avoid the stressful last-minute race to the bus station.

of short-term rentals, and a vast range of private accommodations are now available. Apartment options can easily be found throughout the city, especially at its outskirts. Rooms in shared houses can be found for less than US$10 on Airbnb, while whole apartments start from around US$30 per night.

Some rental websites list Centro as two neighborhoods: San Nicolás and Monserrat. To the south of Balvanera, Boedo is a historic neighborhood with plenty of bars and nightlife, while Caballito, to the west of Almagro, is the residential heart of the city center, with a large collection of shops.

North of here, Villa Crespo is a trendy and popular area akin to Palermo, although as it turns into Chacarita the area can become more run-down and of less interest to visitors. To the northwest of

Palermo, Belgrano is a buzzing neighborhood, with museums, entertainment, and lots of shops, as well as Chinatown. Constitución, although very central, is not a pleasant place to stay, especially at night, and should be avoided when looking for accommodations.

A number of established agencies, such as Buenos Aires Rent (www.rentba.com), Casa San Telmo (www.casasantelmo.com.ar), and Oasis Collections (www.oasiscollections.com) also offer apartments.

Couchsurfing (www.couchsurfing.com) is hugely popular in Buenos Aires. Of course, travelers, particularly women and those traveling alone, must use caution when opting for this form of lodging. The Couchsurfing community organizes regular events and activities geared toward visitors in and around the city.

✪ Milhouse Hostel Avenue $$

For those who like a party vibe and nonstop action, the Milhouse hostel will not disappoint. With a bar, club, terrace, free tango classes, and a prime central location, the intensity may prove to be too much for some. Staff can help arrange tours, get soccer tickets, and give Spanish classes. Rooms range from individuals to dorms with eight bunks, all with private baths.

MAP 1: Av. de Mayo 1245, tel. 011/4381-7191, www.milhousehostel.com

Claridge Hotel $$

The exuberant entrance of the Claridge, along with its pool and spa area, are the highlights of one of the city center's finest hotels. While doubles are available for as little as US$80,

it is worth looking at some of the pricier options, as the size and quality can improve dramatically. The hotel contains an exclusive restaurant and an English-style pub. Regular cultural events such as concerts and art exhibitions are hosted here.

MAP 1: Tucumán 535, tel. 011/4319-8000, www.claridge.com.ar

Hostel Estoril $$

Spread out over a few floors of a hundred-year-old building, Estoril is one of the most popular hostels in Buenos Aires. Colorful and relaxed, the pride and joy of the place is the roof terrace, where regular *asados* (Argentine barbecues) are held for guests. The rooms become cheaper as you move upward, with doubles from US$54 and six-bed

Employees at the Milhouse Hostel Avenue can offer advice on activities and events.

dorms from US$16 pp, both offering shared and private bath options.

MAP 1: Av. de Mayo 1385, tel. 011/4382-9073, www.hostelestoril3.com

Hostel Suites Florida $$

Situated on the busy shopping street Florida, Hostel Suites is one of the largest hostels in Buenos Aires and has received the stamp of approval of Hostelling International. A kitchen, laundry, free breakfast, a bar, computers, a pool table, a roof terrace, and a mini cinema are all available for guests. Free transportation from the airport when staying more than four nights can also provide a huge savings. Dorms housing 4-8 people all have individual baths, as do the private rooms.

MAP 1: Florida 328, tel. 011/4393-1397, www.florida.hostelsuites.com

Hotel Boca Juniors by Design $$

Claiming to be the first *fútbol*-themed hotel in the world, Hotel Boca Juniors by Design is a glitzy affair that is not actually in La Boca. While homages to Boca Juniors *fútbol* team abound, there is careful attention to detail with modern decor and stylish furnishing. The spa, luxurious swimming pool, sauna, and gym are of high quality, making it a favored place for soccer players to stay. Doubles start at US$108 with offers on the website.

MAP 1: Tacuarí 243, tel. 011/4590-8540, www.hotelbocajuniors.com

Hotel Castelar $$

This old-school hotel has been housing travelers for almost a century. A grand lobby draws guests in before dispersing them among its numerous floors and corridors to rooms that accommodate 1-3 people. Small meeting rooms dotted around add to the somewhat worn charm, while the front rooms, overlooking Avenida de Mayo, are the nicest. A tastefully refurbished spa can be found in the basement and is included in the rates.

MAP 1: Av. de Mayo 1152, tel. 011/4383-5000, www.castelarhotel.com.ar

common area in V&S Hostel Club

V&S Hostel Club $$

Nestled among the gray high-rises and five-star hotels that proliferate in Retiro, V&S Hostel Club is a more down-to-earth affair, offering private rooms and dorms, some of which contain the notorious triple-layered bunks, at a fraction of the cost. A roof terrace, patio, and kitchen are available to guests, while assistance is offered in finding events and activities. Dorms are US$14 per person (US$16 pp with air-conditioning); private rooms are US$50.

MAP 1: Viamonte 887, tel. 011/4322-0994, www.hostelclub.com

Art Factory $

A rambling colonial house in Centro and close to San Telmo, Art Factory serves as both a hostel and a canvas for international artists. It's hard to find anywhere here that hasn't been on the receiving end of a paintbrush. If you're a decent artist, they may let you stay for free as long as you paint a wall (materials provided). A terrace with hammocks is available for guests, as is a bar—not that there is a scarcity of those in the neighborhood.

Puerto Madero   Map 1

Hilton Hotel $$$
The Travelodge exterior may fool passersby, but on entering via a looming glass-roofed atrium, guests are welcomed to the Hilton with style and lavishness. There are glass elevators and a rooftop pool, and the hotel is a popular location for film shoots. A variety of offers are advertised on the website, with couples able to stay from around US$150.
MAP 1: Av. Macacha Güemes 351, tel. 011/4891-0000, www. hiltonbuenosaireshotel.com

Faena Hotel $$$
Belle epoque opulence and elegance abound in this conceptual hotel that is housed in a looming, recycled red-brick warehouse. Designed by Philippe Starck, the Faena offers acclaimed restaurants, bars, an outdoor swimming pool, a spa, and even a cabaret theater. A large portion of the building is portioned off as apartments for wealthy residents, but all the facilities are open to all. Many of the rooms offer a "third night free" policy.
MAP 1: Martha Salotti 445, tel. 011/4010-9000, www.faena.com

the Faena Hotel

MAP 1: Piedras 545, tel. 011/4343-1463, www.artfactoryba.com.ar

San Telmo and La Boca   Map 2

✪ Mansión Dandi Royal $$
A truly unique place to stay, the Mansión Dandi Royal is both a hotel and a tango academy. With the music and dance being a central theme, the elegant facade and lavish interior have been renovated lovingly and decorated with antique furniture, while walls are painted with murals of tango scenes and famous singers and musicians. With tango classes, a gym, a pool, a jetted tub, and a terrace, guests are spoiled for choice. Doubles start at US$70.
MAP 2: Piedras 922, tel. 011/4361-3537, www.mansiondandiroyal.com

America del Sur $$
Voted the best hostel in Latin America by Hostelworld in 2011, America del

Sur is airy and relaxed, set in a small modern tower. The rooms are simple; all have their own private baths and no more than four beds. Breakfast is included in the rate, which starts at just under US$50 for a double and US$14 for a bed in a dorm. Out back, there's a wooden deck where *asados* (Argentine barbecues) are held for guests.

MAP 2: Chacabuco 718, tel. 011/4300-5525, www.americahostel.com.ar

Telmotango $

Despite its name, Telmotango is not as tango-themed as some of its rivals, but it does offer tango tours. This calm, relaxing hostel has a beautiful glass ceiling and an enviable rooftop terrace where tango classes are held. Activities and outings are also put on for guests. The rooms are small, with no more than four beds, and a couple have balconies. At just US$24, they are an excellent value.

MAP 2: Chacabuco 679, tel. 011/4361-5808, www.hostelmotango.com

Bonito $

Located on a dingy avenue in the south of San Telmo, Bonito (formerly The Cocker Bed & Breakfast) is a boutique hostel set in a delightfully restored old building. Great attention has been paid to the architecture and design, with some stunning terraces overlooking the neighborhood. With only seven rooms, booking ahead is essential. A pricier yet equally attractive hotel with the same name and owner can be found at Chile 1507.

MAP 2: Av. Juan de Garay 458, tel. 011/4362-8451, www.bonitobuenosaires.com

Circus Hostel & Hotel $

Classier than a standard hostel, yet more bohemian than a hotel, Circus bridges the divide between the two. Simple private rooms with one to four beds are offered alongside dorms, with a tiled pool out back available to guests. A restaurant (with free breakfast) offers food, as there is no kitchen. Tango and Spanish classes are available as well as help getting *fútbol* tickets.

MAP 2: Chacabuco 1020, tel. 011/4300-4983, www.hostelcircus.com

Retiro   Map 3

✪ Four Seasons $$$

Jutting out in the middle of the chaotic Avenida 9 de Julio, Four Seasons is both a modern tower and a belle epoque mansion that regularly attracts visiting celebrities. Its exclusive gardens and pool, along with the luxurious interior decoration, come with a high price tag, with nothing available below US$400, although special offers on the website can bring the cost down.

MAP 3: Posadas 1086, tel. 011/4321-1200, www.fourseasons.com/buenosaires

✪ Sheraton Buenos Aires $$$

A bit of an eyesore from outside, the Sheraton is a 24-story tower that looms over Retiro and Puerto Madero, with spectacular views of the Río de la Plata and the city itself. The interior befits the hotel's five-star rating: Plush furnishings, indoor and outdoor pools, a spa center, two quality restaurants, and a fitness center are included, with doubles starting around US$150.

MAP 3: San Martin 1225, tel. 011/4318-9000, www.sheratonbuenosaires.com

Plaza Hotel $$

Proudly facing Plaza San Martín on the corner of Florida street, the Plaza Hotel was the first luxury hotel in Latin America, and remains one of the most iconic. Stunning city views, a sense of stepping back in time, and immaculate facilities are all part of the deal. The outdoor pool, Plaza Bar, and Plaza Grill are particular highlights. Salon services and Ping-Pong tables are also offered. Doubles start at US$130.

MAP 3: Florida 1005, tel. 011/4318-3000, www.plazahotelba.com

Recoleta   Map 4

✪ Alvear Palace Hotel $$$

Sitting snug on one of the most exclusive streets in Buenos Aires, the Alvear Palace is an exemplary bastion of the hotel industry. Doormen and butlers eagerly help guests to their rooms, which are soft, spacious, and delightfully decorated. Since opening in 1932, the Alvear has hosted countless dignitaries who have enjoyed the luxurious accommodations as well as the food at what is one of the city's

the luxurious Alvear Palace Hotel

top restaurants, La Bourgogne. Room rates range US$350-2,000.

MAP 4: Av. Alvear 1891, tel. 011/4805-2100, www.alvearpalace.com

✪ Palacio Duhau—Park Hyatt Buenos Aires $$$

The Park Hyatt consists of two buildings, one a renovated palace built in 1890, the other a modern addition. The rooms diverge from the grand eccentricities of the palace itself, adopting a more relaxed and unadorned feeling. Two restaurants, a tea room, an oak-themed bar, pool and spa facilities, and an art gallery are all available, although with rates starting at a hefty US$500, it's somewhat surprising that parking and breakfast are not included.

MAP 4: Av. Alvear 1661, tel. 011/5171-1234, www.buenosaires.park.hyatt.com

✪ Poetry Building Recoleta $$$

This beautiful historic mansion offers 18 apartments, some with private patios, for up to three or four people.

Poetry Building Recoleta

the sumptuous gardens at Palacio Duhau–Park Hyatt Buenos Aires

Despite its classical exterior, modernity reigns inside, with sleek furniture and smoothly polished floors. The building offers a large rooftop terrace with an open-air pool and an organic garden, which includes fresh fruit and vegetables that guests are invited to pick. High-season rates range US$145 to US$180 for two people, with a significant drop in prices during the rest of the year.

MAP 4: Junín 1280, tel. 011/4827-2772, www.poetrybuilding.com

CasaSur Art Hotel $$$

A small yet stylish hotel in the heart of Recoleta, CasaSur is notable for its wooden decor and modern design. Its restaurant specializes in Indian cuisine, and a gym, a spa, and a massage room are available to visitors. The staff are exceptionally helpful, although they enforce a strict policy of allowing only one nonpaying guest into rooms. With rates starting from around US$200, CasaSur is one of the more affordable luxury hotels in the area.

MAP 4: Av. Callao 1823, tel. 011/4515-0085, www.casasurhotel.com

Mio Buenos Aires $$$

The six-meter-high door of Mio is made of French oak from wine

Mio Buenos Aires offers an excellent breakfast spread.

barrels, a typical feature of this daring and pleasant wine-themed hotel. In each suite the bathtubs, also made of wood, are found in the middle of the main room instead of in the bathroom. The spacious rooms, at more than 50 square meters, start at US$200. A dimly lit pool allows a welcome break from the summer sun.

MAP 4: Av. Quintana 465, tel. 011/5295-8500, www.miobuenosaires.com

Etoile Hotel $$$

Although this hotel lacks the charm and beauty of its neighboring hotels, the views from the bedrooms facing the cemetery are stunning. Rooms that don't offer this view are somewhat dingy and less enticing, although all guests have access to the open-air pool and spa on the 14th floor. Standard rates start from US$110, with luxury suites at US$190.

MAP 4: Roberto M. Ortiz 1835, tel. 011/4805-2626, www.etoile.com.ar

Intersur Recoleta $$

The classical facade of this hotel blends delightfully with the stylishly decorated interiors. Even the standard rooms are of decent size, as is the breakfast. The hotel boasts Marcelo Restaurant, one of the most highly rated places to eat in Buenos Aires, serving exquisite Italian food and wine. Rates range from US$90 to US$150, making this a good value luxury hotel.

MAP 4: Av. Callao 1764, tel. 011/5533-4000, www.intersurrecoleta.com.ar

Reina Madre Hostel $

Located a few blocks from the heart of Recoleta, this is the cheapest option in the area. A roof terrace with reclining seats and a *parrilla* (grill) provides an ideal place to relax, although it can become lively in the evenings. A fully equipped kitchen is available for guests. Dorms are US$15, while privates are a reasonable US$40.

MAP 4: Anchorena 1118, tel. 011/4962-5553, www.rmhostel.com

✪ Mine Hotel $$$

A combination of natural materials are used in the interior decoration of Mine Hotel, creating a unique and intriguing aesthetic. The rooms are spacious and well-equipped: All come with jetted tubs, and some come with balconies. A garden and pool can be found out back, and the open lounge and buffet is also a pleasant area for relaxing. Doubles start at US$175, with a wide range of offers on the website.

MAP 5: Gorriti 4770, tel. 011/4832-1100, www.minehotel.com

Jardín Escondido $$$

Serving as Francis Ford Coppola's residence while in Buenos Aires, this luxurious property has now been converted into a small exclusive hotel. Built around a garden and pool, it offers a variety of seven suites and apartments, as well as a library with both literature and film, and a leafy terrace. Guests are welcome to cook on the *parrilla* (grill) while enjoying the furniture and decoration handpicked by the Coppolas.

MAP 5: Gorriti 4746, tel. 011/4834-6166, www.thefamilycoppolaresorts.com

Legado Mitico $$$

Themed on Argentine history, the refined Legado Mitico offers 11 rooms named after personalities from throughout the country's past. A library provides ample choice to brush up the subject, while the rooms themselves are luxurious and stylish, with mahogany, Chesterfield sofas, and fireplaces

garden patio at Jardín Escondido

commonplace. An outdoor pool is located on the terrace, and a bar is available for guests. Doubles start at US$250.

MAP 5: Gurruchaga 1848, tel. 011/4833-1300, www.legadomitico.com

Legado Mítico offers elegant spaces to unwind.

Purobaires $$$

As stylish as one would expect in the heart of Palermo Soho, Purobaires offers three different levels of rooms, ranging from US$168 to US$234. All rooms have a balcony, while a sauna, a gym, a massage parlor, and a rooftop terrace complete with an open-air pool offer great places to relax. Breakfast here is notably better than at most other hotels. Discounts are available if you pay in cash.

MAP 5: Niceto Vega 4788, tel. 011/4139-0100, www.purobaires.com.ar

Krista Hotel $$$

The old-fashioned furniture and elegant decor fit nicely with the early-19th-century home that houses this boutique hotel. Wooden or antique tiled floors, high ceilings, and intricate windows run throughout, while most of the rooms open onto patios. Massages and an outdoor jetted-tub spa are available. Rates start at US$150.

MAP 5: Bonpland 1665, tel. 011/4771-4697, www.kristahotel.com.ar

BoBo $$

Deriving its name from a cultural hybrid that combines bohemian and bourgeois concepts, BoBo is a small boutique hotel with just seven rooms. Artwork appears throughout the property, and each room is designed with its own unique aesthetics, with little price difference between the cheapest (US$84) and most expensive (US$120). While restaurants abound in the neighboring heartland of Palermo, BoBo offers its own high-class restaurant below the hotel that goes by the same name.

MAP 5: Guatemala 4870, tel. 011/4774-0505, www.bobohotel.com

The Glu $$

The Glu, with its odd name, is a modern boutique hotel that focuses on interior design. Floor-to-ceiling windows create well-lit rooms, all of which open out onto private balconies or patios. There is also a roof terrace complete with sun loungers and an open-air hot tub. Coffee is freely available to guests, as is a simple breakfast. Suite rates start at US$118.

MAP 5: Godoy Cruz 1733, tel. 011/4831-4646, www.thegluhotel.com

Play Hostel $$

Set in a traditional 19th-century *casa chorizo*, so named for the long row of rooms and apartments, rather like a string of *chorizo* sausages, Play is a music-themed hostel that offers rooms for 2-6 guests. Breakfast and use of a decent kitchen are included, while other services such as tango and Spanish classes or an *asado* (Argentine barbecue) cost extra. Doubles start at a reasonable US$58.

MAP 5: Guatemala 4636, tel. 011/4832-4257, www.playhostel.com

Almagro

Map 6

✪ La Taba $

A family-run hostel on the border between Almagro and Villa Crespo, La Taba offers a place to stay away from the chaotic city center while being close to the up-and-coming neighborhoods preferred by young locals. The rooms are basic, with balconies overlooking the street, while a rooftop terrace provides guests with the chance to try a genuine Argentine *asado* (barbecue) in the sunshine. For only US$16, the doubles are a bargain.

MAP 6: Av. Estado de Israel 4809, tel. 011/4854-3204, www.latabahostel.com.ar

Racó $$

One of the few decent accommodations in Almagro, Racó is a small boutique hotel with only 12 rooms. A leafy patio and bar are at the disposal of guests, while the rooms are elegant and maintain the original architecture and style of the building (although the Superior rooms are the least interesting). All rooms include private baths, and rates start at US$120.

MAP 6: Yapeyu 271, tel. 011/3530-6075, www.racodebuenosaires.com.ar

Lecer Apart $$

In the heart of the residential Almagro neighborhood and only a few steps from the splendid Parque Centenario, Lecer Apart offers 14 modern apartments equipped with kitchens and baths. Simple and refined, some suites are one-room affairs while others include a separate bedroom. Breakfast is included, as is access to the roof terrace. Apartments for two cost US$68 with a surcharge added for extra guests.

MAP 6: Juan Domingo Perón 4301, tel. 011/4862-2308, www.lecerapart.com

Balvanera

Map 6

Apart Hotel & Spa Congreso $$

Apart Hotel & Spa offers spacious apartments that contain small kitchens and baths right in the center of town. The four-star hotel includes a decent restaurant as well as spa facilities such as saunas and massages. Rooms hold one, two, three, or five guests, with doubles costing US$60. Discounts of up to 30 percent are available on the website. The Wi-Fi does not extend to the rooms themselves.

MAP 6: Bartolome Mitre 1824, tel. 011/4954-8410, www.apartcongreso.com.ar

ChillHouse $

A 20th-century family house that received a 21st-century conversion to a hostel, ChillHouse is a relaxed and classy place to stay on a low budget in the tango hub of Abasto. With only 10 rooms, two patios, a rooftop terrace, free bikes, a *parrilla* (grill), and cultural events, it has also become one of the city's most popular places to stay. Dormitories with bunks are US$13, while en suite doubles start at US$43.

MAP 6: Agüero 781, tel. 011/4861-6175, www.chillhouse.com.ar

ROOM FOR TWO?

Many a visitor to Buenos Aires has been confused when entering certain hotels and hearing rates quoted for the hour rather than the night. Such places, of course, are not standard hotels. They're pay-by-the-hour establishments known as *telos* (coming from an old *porteño* practice of rearranging the letters of a word) or *albergues transitorios*, and they exist solely for romantic purposes.

It's easy to understand why *telos* exist in Buenos Aires. It's common for young people in Argentina to live in their family home into their 30s, a situation that can present problems for those in amorous relationships. Naturally, *telos* also provide a convenient location for couples seeking a discreet place away from their habitual partners. While the concept may ruffle moral fibers, *telos* are widely accepted by the local populace, producing merely a smirk or wink from passersby.

There are dozens of *telos* in Buenos Aires. They generally call themselves hotels, albeit usually with some form of innuendo in the name. They are often identifiable by neon lighting or by the fact that it's not possible to see inside them from the street—although their garage entrances are usually prominent, to allow visitors to slip in inconspicuously. It's not uncommon for the curious—including tourists who want a giggle at the novelty—to take a room for an hour or two.

Greater Buenos Aires   Map 7

Buenos Aires Tango Hostel $

Situated in an early-20th-century building in the heart of the bohemian and hip Boedo neighborhood, Buenos Aires Tango Hostel is a great choice for those who would like to stay a little out of the city center. A kitchen, bar, and roof terrace with *parrilla* (grill) are available for guests. Laundry, tango and Spanish classes, event tickets, and tours can also be arranged. A bed in a 12-person dorm costs US$12, while a double room is only US$34.

MAP 7: Av. Boedo 847, tel. 011/4932-4178, www.buenosairestangohostel.com

Holiday Inn Ezeiza $$

On a good day, the Ezeiza international airport is a 40-minute taxi ride from the city center, so nervous travelers may want to take a bed in the Holiday Inn, the closest hotel. While nothing spectacular, it is a few minutes ride away and offers a pool and spa center, as well as a necessary restaurant that serves up some tasty meat. Doubles cost US$130 and include a free transfer to and from the airport.

MAP 7: M. M. de Güemes 4718, tel. 011/6380-2200, www.hinnezeiza.com.ar

DAY TRIPS

Heading to the outskirts of Buenos Aires or farther afield is as much about taking a break from this constantly moving city as it is about visiting new places. Indeed, *porteños* are known for fleeing the city on the weekend, many to second homes in the quiet suburbs and beyond, others to more novel locations.

Tigre, a simple hour's train ride from the city center, is the most accessible excursion, which also makes it the most popular with locals. Located on the delta of the Río de la Plata, with its hundreds of islands and rivers waiting to be explored, Tigre combines nature with history. Some of the oldest and most fascinating buildings in Argentina are on display here, and the city also boasts the largest artisanal and regional produce market in the country.

Iguazú Falls

Head to San Antonio de Areco to savor the traditional gaucho way of life. It is fiercely protected in this disarmingly peaceful and historic town. Museums and cultural activities are the largest draw. Getting here involves breaking out of the city limits and crossing 100 kilometers of sprawling plains.

Leaving Buenos Aires and visiting another country—Uruguay—is less complicated that one would imagine. Boats cross to Uruguay all day, every day, dropping passengers off in Colonia del Sacramento, Uruguay's oldest town. History and beauty are Colonia's main draws, although it also serves as a gateway to destinations deeper in Uruguay.

The largest waterfall system in the world lies in the northeastern tip of Argentina, set amid dense rainforest that teems with beasts, birds, and butterflies. Natural beauty and adventure combine for one of the world's greatest tourist attractions, although it's the priciest and most time-consuming of these trips.

HIGHLIGHTS

⭐ **BEST SHOPPING:** The **Puerto de Frutos** is the largest artisanal produce market in the country (page 221).

⭐ **BEST PLACE TO ENJOY THE DELTA FROM DRY LAND:** Strolling along **Paseo Victorica** or having a picnic on its banks is a great way to admire the water from a distance (page 221).

⭐ **MOST UNEXPECTED:** Explore the rivers and islands of the **Paraná Delta**, which feels like a different world from the city center (page 224).

⭐ **BEST PLACE TO LEARN ABOUT GAUCHO CULTURE:** The **Parque Criollo y Museo Gauchesco Ricardo Güiraldes** provides an education on the historic gaucho tradition (page 229).

⭐ **BEST PLACE TO SPOT GAUCHOS:** San Antonio de Areco fills with country folk, music, food, and parties during the **Fiesta de la Tradición** (page 232).

⭐ **MOST OUTSTANDING ATTRACTION:** Millions flock to **Parque Nacional Iguazú** every year to take in the beauty and majesty of the falls (page 247).

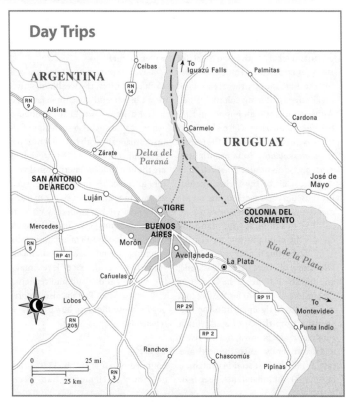

Day Trips

PLANNING YOUR TIME

While most of these destinations are feasible for day trips, it's worth staying at least one night, as most locals do, to recharge your batteries and soak in some of the wonderful alternatives to Buenos Aires. All provide ample choices of accommodations and dining, as well as excellent transportation connections. Iguazú Falls requires an overnight stay, although the cost and length of the journey make three or four days more worthwhile.

Bear in mind that such places are significantly busier on weekends, which can make it best to visit at quieter times (i.e. during the week)—although the flip side of this is that many restaurants, attractions, and shops offer reduced open hours outside the weekend, some even going so far as being closed from Monday to Thursday. In the end, it is a question of whether you would prefer to explore in a little more peace and quiet, or to do as much as you can regardless of the number of other people.

Tigre and the Paraná Delta

Around 30 kilometers north of the city, the Paraná delta opens up into the Río de la Plata at Tigre. Formerly a fruit, wicker, and wood port for the Spaniards and a smuggling base for the Portuguese, the area served great purpose during colonial times. Although it is still an important timber port, these days Tigre also functions as a city getaway, with the former fruit market now a mammoth artisanal and local produce market.

Almost all of the sights, including museums and markets, are on the mainland, or the *continente* as the locals like to call it. But for many, the delta is the main purpose for visiting Tigre. Consisting of over 13,000 square kilometers of rivers, streams, islands, and forests, it's one of the largest in the world, notable also for the fact that it doesn't strictly open into the sea. Starting from the Río Luján, which runs alongside the town, smaller rivers and streams branch off to the north and east. While the first section contains a fair number of inhabitants, deeper in the delta are fewer signs of human life. Indeed, it is quite easy to get lost in the labyrinth that awaits upstream without a map or guide.

Given its proximity and easy access to Buenos Aires, the wealth of activities it offers, and the simple fact that it is a different world from Buenos Aires, it's no surprise that Tigre fills up dramatically with *porteños* over the weekend. This means that weekdays are the best time for international visitors to come. Many attractions, such as museums and stalls in the market, will be closed, but a weekday visit ensures maximum peace and quiet, with fewer speedboats full of jeering youths zooming around. Heavy rainfall can severely affect the river level, making movement difficult and reducing visitors' options. Tigre is also notorious for mosquitoes, so be sure to take repellent.

TIGRE

Founded on an island in 1820, after previous settlements had been destroyed by floods, Tigre gets its name from the animals that were hunted in the region, although they were actually jaguars and not *tigres* (tigers). The buildings of Tigre are completely different from the center of Buenos Aires, with many belle epoque mansions looming alongside the river. A large number of the houses are Victorian and even Tudoresque, built from wood with sloped roofs, indicative of the times they were built and the nationality of the architects. There was a fair amount of wealth in the area, and the spectacular former clubhouse, now an art museum, pays testament to the grandeur and opulence of the 19th and 20th centuries.

SIGHTS
✪ Puerto de Frutos

A 10-minute stroll from the train station, the Puerto de Frutos (Sarmiento 160, www.wp.puertodefrutos-arg.com.ar; 10am-6pm Mon.-Fri., 10am-7pm Sat.-Sun.) market draws locals mainly for its wonderful furniture and housewares, but there is a lot more on offer, including the largest collection of regional products and handicrafts in the country. It's a bit of a labyrinth, with endless warehouses and walkways, and hours can be spent just wandering around. Only around 20 percent of the stores are open during the week, with most only operating over weekends, when the crowds arrive.

Museo del Mate

On the other side of the river from the *estación fluvial* (port), the Museo del Mate (Lavalle 289, tel. 011/4506-9594, www.elmuseodelmate.com; 11am-7pm Wed.-Sun. spring-fall, 11am-6pm Wed.-Sun. winter; US$2) is the country's homage to the national drink. Over 2,000 items are on display,

including gourds, *bombillas,* and every kind of paraphernalia that exists. The history of the drink and its origins are explained, and an outdoor maté bar serves up hot drinks.

✪ Paseo Victorica

Following the coast around to the north, the road splits into a kind of boulevard while a pedestrian walkway known as the Paseo Victorica rolls along the river edge, starting from where boats spurt out of the port into the Río Luján and finishing a little over one kilometer upriver at the Museo de Arte Tigre. Incorporating parks, restaurants, museums, and rowing clubs, the walkway is the favored spot in Tigre for locals to picnic and drink maté on the grass and benches, gazing over the river and its accompanying buildings, especially the stunning Club de Regatas La Marina, a historic rowing and social club on the other side of the river. On the weekend, hundreds of *porteños* join the locals from dawn until dusk. The walkway covers such a long stretch that you will always find a spot that's not too crowded.

Museo de Arte Tigre

A piece of art in itself, the Museo de Arte Tigre (Paseo Victorica 972, tel. 011/4512-4528, www.mat.gob.ar; 9am-7pm Wed.-Fri., noon-7pm Sat.-Sun.; US$2.50) was built in the heady days of the early 20th century as a social and sports club, serving as one of the finest locations for tango performances and dances during its golden period. The spired turrets and cavernous archways give a dreamlike feel to the building. Refurbished as an art museum in the 1990s, it may not contain as many gems as its inner-city contemporaries, but most major Argentine artists from

the magnificent Museo de Arte Tigre

the 19th and 20th centuries are represented, such as Antonio Berni and Lino Enea Spilimbergo. Browsing the grand halls of the ornate building and its grounds, which contain a sculpture garden, is a delightful experience.

Museo Naval de la Nación

About halfway up the Paseo Victorica, the Museo Naval de la Nación (Paseo Victorica 602, tel. 011/4749-0608, 8:30am-5:30pm Tues.-Fri., 10:30am-6:30pm Sat.-Sun.; US$2) contains an eclectic mix of displays on the Argentine navy and maritime history, including objects such as boats and airplanes. Those who aren't too enthused by warships may find it a little tedious, but anyone who is interested in such themes should definitely drop by.

Museo de la Reconquista

Tucked a few blocks inland from the Museo de Arte, the Museo de la Reconquista (Padre Castañeda 470, tel. 011/4512-4496; 10am-6:30pm Wed.-Fri., 2pm-6pm Sat.-Sun.; free) is housed in the former residence of Viceroy Liniers, the man who led the resistance against the 19th-century British invasions. Thoughtful exhibitions that often contain photos, alongside uniforms and other artifacts, give decent insight into these events and the independence struggle in general.

Parque de la Costa

A gentle theme park rolling along the river coast, Parque de la Costa (Vivanco 1509, tel. 011/4002-6000, www.parquedelacosta.com.ar; hours vary; from US$9) offers mainly low-key *montañas rusas* (roller coasters) and other rides mostly suitable for children. A separate water park, Aquafan, is joined on one side and includes slides, boats, hot tubs, and the like. A wide range of tickets and offers (such as a second day for only US$4 extra) are available, all of which are advertised on the website.

RESTAURANTS

Tucked in among the antiques stores and leafy streets to the south of the market, Almacén de Flores (Blv. Sáenz Peña 1336, tel. 011/5197-4009, www.elalmacendeflores.com.ar; 9am-7pm Tues.-Thurs. and Sun., 9am-midnight Fri.-Sat.; US$15) serves simple food with a flowery flourish, as it is located in a flower shop. Sandwiches and salads are the main thrust of the menu, although it is also a particularly popular spot for breakfast.

Held in a humble local sports and recreation club, Las Glorias (Av. Cazón 1011, tel. 011/5197-4863, noon-3pm and 8pm-midnight daily; US$8-18) is simple and unpretentious, yet it serves up some of the best-value food in Tigre in abundant portions. The menu is as Argentine as you will find, with meat fresh from the *parrilla* (grill) and pastas taking up most of the options. The friendly vibe is ideal for families and anyone wanting a relaxed feast.

If you're reluctant to head into the islands, Il Novo Maria del Luján (Paseo Victorica 611, tel. 011/4731-9613, www.ilnovomariadellujan.com; 8:30am-1am daily; US$12-25) is a decent option along the river edge, although prices are a little elevated, given its privileged location. The fish dishes are the most popular. A lovely patio fills quickly, making it worthwhile to phone (or send an email) in advance to book a table overlooking the water.

HOTELS

Although Tigre is only an hour's train ride from the center of Buenos Aires, it can be a lovely place to spend the night (although staying in the delta islands is even more enticing). A stone's throw from the train station and port, Posada de 1860 (Av. del Libertador San Martín 190, tel. 011/4749-4034, www.tigrehostel.com.ar; US$22 dorm, US$70 d) is a 140-year-old house set amid beautiful gardens. While the rooms and decoration are simple, the charm is overwhelming. Everything is provided for an enjoyable stay, including a sizable kitchen. Dorms are situated in a separate building across the street. Breakfast is included, and help is available for arranging activities.

INFORMATION AND SERVICES

The main tourist information center (9am-5pm daily) can be found at Juncal 1600, while the Estación Fluvial (port) contains another office at Mitre 354 (9am-5pm daily), as well as a small stand alongside the boat departure points. While the employees here are happy to assist in general inquiries and directions, specific information about boat excursions is best gleaned from the individual company stands alongside the port.

The modern, well-equipped Hospital Materno Infantil Dr. Florencio Escardó (Carlos de Alvear 1666; nonurgent services 8am-8pm Mon.-Fri.; emergency services 24

The Estación Fluvial is the departure point for delta excursions.

hours daily) receives patients, with 24-hour accident and emergency services.

Correo Argentino (Av. Cazón 1140; 10am-6pm Mon.-Fri.) provides postal services. Multiple ATMs line Avenida Cazón.

GETTING THERE

Train services run every 15 minutes or so from Retiro station (Av. Ramos Mejia 1358) to Tigre between 5am and 11pm. The trip takes about one hour and costs only US$0.40. If you are staying in Palermo, you can catch the same train farther down the line at Belgrano C station (Juramento 1708). At Maipu station, farther down the line, a second service branches off, offering a more scenic and expensive route. Despite being called the *tren de la costa* (coast train), it barely approaches the water's edge but is nonetheless an enjoyable experience. Tickets cost US$1.50, and you must cross a bridge on disembarking at Maipu. Note that the two train lines end at different stations in Tigre.

The number 60 bus runs 24-7 and costs about the same as the train (paid on board with a Sube) but the journey can last well over two hours.

A taxi from Buenos Aires's Centro costs around US$30, as the drivers charge for their own return journey back into the city. Ask the driver to take you to the *estación de trenes de Tigre* (Tigre train station) or *estación fluvial de Tigre* (Tigre port), a journey of around 30 kilometers from Buenos Aires city center that can last anywhere from 30 minutes to an hour, depending on traffic.

If driving by car, follow Ruta 9 (also known as the Panamericana) north of the city for about eight kilometers before forking off to the right on the Ramal Tigre for eight kilometers, following signs to "Tigre Centro."

The most pleasant way to reach Tigre is by boat, although such options are limited. There are two services run by the same company, although under different names, both of which depart from a small ferry terminal next to the city's major ferry port at the northern tip of Puerto Madero (Cecilia Grierson 400). One is provided by Sturla (www.sturlaviajes.tur.ar) and is intended for tourists. It includes free use of the company's tour bus around Tigre in the afternoon. The service departs at 10am with the return leaving Tigre at 4pm (US$26 one-way, US$36 round-trip). The second option, Proa Urbana (www.proa-urbana.com.ar) shuttles commuters in and out of the city center but can be used by anyone. Leaving Tigre at 7:45am, it returns from Puerto Madero at 6:30pm (US$5 each way). Both trips last a little over an hour.

GETTING AROUND

Most of the sights and attractions in the town of Tigre are within walking distance, although local buses operate (with the same coin or electronic Sube card as the city center) and taxis can be found everywhere. To reach locations on the islands within the delta, it is necessary to take a boat taxi from the Estación Fluvial (Mitre 319) in Tigre, although some hotels and restaurants offer private launches.

✪ PARANÁ DELTA

The delta is a sight in and of itself and should be considered the main purpose for visiting Tigre, although how it is approached (guided tour, circuit ride on the Interisleña, overnight stay on an island) depends on each visitor's desires and constraints. Although merely ambling alongside the rivers in Tigre without actually delving into the waterways and islands is enjoyable enough, this would mean missing an opportunity to explore a fascinating hidden world. Floating down the rivers and gazing at the houses passing by with their sloped lawns and private jetties cause even the most ardent city dweller to ponder moving out to the country. A sense of exploration results from the low-hanging trees and patchwork of islands and small rivers, with nature dictating the limits of human construction.

If you stay overnight in the delta, take plenty of water. The supply on the islands is often contaminated, and using tap water even for brushing your teeth can cause upset stomach and worse. Plenty of mosquito repellent is also essential, especially during summer and regardless of the length of your visit. Also be aware that it is practically impossible to buy anything once you are out in the islands. A floating supermarket bobs around, but it is not practical to depend on this, so bring food and drink supplies from the mainland.

The dense forest is within steps of most places in the delta.

BOATING IN THE DELTA

Heading out into the delta in a canoe or boat is one of the most magical activities available in Buenos Aires. It's best to take a guided tour due to the complex network of rivers, but some companies rent out canoes or boats for individual or group exploration. Many tour options can be found at the port in Tigre. A few are mentioned here, but it is worth heading to the stands alongside the port to check out the different and constantly changing alternatives.

Although crossing Río Luján, with its choppy waves and large boats, can seem like a daunting start when you depart, once you're across and into the delta itself, everything calms down.

One of the most popular and established companies, El Dorado Kayak (tel. 15/4039-5858, www.eldoradokayak.com) offers guided half-day (US$40) and full-day (US$60, including lunch) tours, as well as moonlight tours (US$40) when weather permits. You will be taken by boat to the Amarran Sancho nature reserve. From there, the group heads deeper into the delta; guides take care to not overestimate the abilities of participants.

Offering rowing boats to experienced rowers and kayaks for one, two, or three people, Puro Remo (Lavalle 235, www.puroremo.com.ar; 7am-7pm Tues.-Sun.) is one of the most reliable companies for personal rentals (from US$6 per hour). They also offer guided tours (from US$30 for 2 hours).

Operating from Stand 16 in the port, Bonanza Deltaventura (tel. 011/5245-9929, www.bonanza.com. ar) offers an array of activities based out of an ancient house out in the delta, including horseback riding, canoeing, and nature reserve walks. Transportation from Tigre to the delta house is included, as is lunch and free rein of the 60 hectares and facilities (hammocks, deck chairs, table tennis, and fishing rods). A day trip costs US$45-65, while an overnight stay is US$140 (30 percent cheaper Mar.-Nov.).

Selknam Canoas (Av. Victorica 50, tel. 011/4731-4325, www.selknam-canoas.com.ar) offers guided tours in beautifully handcrafted wooden Canadian canoes. Tours last two hours (US$35), but guides extend the length of the trip or the amount of time spent in the delta according to visitors' wishes. Occasional night tours (check the website for the schedule; US$35 for 2 hours) are conducted under the light of the full moon.

RESTAURANTS

If you make a reservation at a restaurant out in the delta, make sure to ask for the exact times that boats leave the port to ensure that you do not miss your table. Many of the farther-flung restaurants double as *hosterías* (inns), which means that you can sleep over if you miss the last boat back to Tigre. Some *hosterías* only accept diners who have made reservations.

One of the best ways to experience the delta on a day trip is to take the 50-minute ride on an Interisleña ferry to El Gato Blanco (Río Capitán 80,

El Gato Blanco restaurant

tel. 011/4728-0390, www.gato-blanco.com; noon-4pm daily; US$12-20) for lunch. Tables line the edge of the river in large grassy gardens, while a couple of wooden salons provide ample indoor space on cold or wet days. The seafood items are excellent, with *lenguado au citron vert* (sole with lime) perhaps the pick of the menu.

After floating through the islands for some 45 minutes on an Interisleña ferry, you will be deposited on the beach of Atelier Chez Lissie (Río Capitán 169, tel. 011/4728-0043, www.restaurantatelier.com.ar; noon-6pm daily, dinner by reservation only; US$13-26), the oldest restaurant in the delta, where the season and available fresh produce determine the menu and the price. If *dorado a la parrilla* (grilled dorado) is on offer, you're in luck. The dish should be shared among at least three people. Ample gardens are available to relax in all day, while cabins allow for overnight stays (from US$20 pp).

A little farther afield, Los Pecanes (Arroyo Felicaria, tel. 011/4728-1932 www.hosterialospecanes.com; daily by reservation only; US$20) is a birdwatchers' paradise, with over 120 species fluttering through its gardens. The menu is eclectic but always delicious, and the fresh produce comes straight from the garden. Sunday, when a set menu that includes multiple cuts of meat, salads, wine, and desserts is served, is the best day to visit. Canoes are available (free) to overnight guests (US$40 pp). Los Pecanes is about an hour from Tigre by Interisleña ferry.

A small paradise set up by María Teresa, Isla Margarita (Río Carabelas 300, tel. 011/4728-2495, www.islamargaritabue.com.ar; daily by reservation only; US$15-25), with nine hectares of lovingly grown flowers and plants spread across the island, is more than just a restaurant. A wide variety of European dishes, such as goulash and paella, are available, but many swing by merely for the pastries. If looking to dine somewhere completely isolated from civilization, this is the place. Líneas Delta boats get you there in around 90 minutes.

WHERE TO STAY

The islands can be a lovely place to spend the night. Here, the nighttime silence is interrupted only by the rocking boats sloshing in the water. It's possible to rent a cabaña through websites such as Cabañas.com (www. cabanias.com.ar). Many of the hotels in the delta offer private launches if booked in advance, which can make a huge difference in time, ease, and expense. If overnighting in the delta, don't forget to bring plenty of water and mosquito repellent.

For those who plan to spend a day or two in the delta, Recreo Abra Vieja 150 (Arroyo Abre Vieja 150, tel. 15/6376-4575, www.recreoabra-vieja150.wix.com; US$8 tents, US$20 pp dorm) is an ideal base and decidedly more relaxed than some of the larger alternatives. For US$15 per day, visitors have access to canoes, a swimming pool, *parrillas* (grills), and a few simple sporting facilities, including fishing. Dorms and tent rentals are extra. To get here, take an Interisleña boat.

Basically translated as "The House by the River," La Casona del Río (Río Carapachay 29, tel. 011/4728-0040, www.casonadelrio.com; US$20-28 s or d) is a bed-and-breakfast a mere 10-minute boat ride from the port. The owners are friendly and welcoming, and have succeeding in creating a homey atmosphere amid stunning scenery. Rooms are available for one to four people. Kayaks can be hired, while basic fishing equipment is freely available. There is no restaurant, but guests have free rein of a well-equipped kitchen as well as a *parrilla* (grill) outside. Reach La Casona by taking an Interisleña boat.

Located in a beautiful natural reserve five kilometers by boat from the port, Amarran Sancho (Arroyo Espera 288, tel. 011/4728-3143, www. amarransancho.com.ar; US$100-140 s or d) offers cabins and rooms in peaceful woodlands surrounded by rivers. Private beaches, an outdoor pool, a bar, a restaurant, sports facilities, *parrillas* (grills), and strolls through the reserve are all available to guests, as are massages (extra cost). Get here by taking an Interisleña boat. Check the website for special offers.

Out in the middle of the islands, La Becasina (Arroyo Las Cañas, tel. 011/4728-1253, www.labecasina.com; US$250-400 s or d) is one of the most exclusive hotels in Argentina, let alone the delta. Everything is made from wood, including the private bungalow suites on stilts and the interconnecting walkways. An open bar, gourmet restaurant, and outdoor pool are all available to guests, as is the free use of boats and canoes. A private launch picks up and drops off guests from Tigre.

GETTING THERE

To reach locations on the islands within the delta, it's necessary to take a boat taxi or ferry from the Estación Fluvial (port, Mitre 319) in Tigre, although some hotels and restaurants offer private launches. The most frequent and cheapest, Interisleña (www.lacolectivadeldelta.com.ar), is a fleet of delightful wooden long boats that slowly motor from jetty to jetty.

Connect with nature at Amarran Sancho.

Advise the crew of your destination beforehand; the price of a ride depends on the length of the journey (US$5-13 round-trip). Passengers must wait on the jetty when making the return journey (arriving earlier than the scheduled time is advised). You'll need to wave down the boat before it passes. Taking the Interisleña the full length of its journey can take up to two hours when there are large numbers of passengers. If you're heading into the islands, prepare to spend the whole day there.

Lineas Delta offers cruises throughout the delta, reaching as far as towns on the Uruguayan coast (3 hours each way, US$50 return) as well as dropping passengers off at requested stops along the way. Alternative companies offer private taxi services from the port and advertise from small wooden booths alongside the dock, although these prices vary wildly.

San Antonio de Areco

When the Spanish *conquistadores* arrived in South America and started thrashing their way across the continent, some of the first indigenous people that they came across in Argentina were the Querandí, an agile group of hunters that roamed the central region of the country. It's argued that the merging of these two cultures was the origin of the gaucho, a figure comparable to a North American cowboy or rancher. Nowhere in the country is this figure revered as much as in San Antonio de Areco.

Lying about 100 kilometers from the bustle of Buenos Aires, San Antonio de Areco is one of the country's oldest and most charming towns. Residents proudly guard the town's historic traditions and customs along with its iconic colonial architecture. Indeed, it was a writer from San Antonio de Areco, Ricardo Güiraldes, that wrote *Don Segundo Sombra,* which eulogizes the gaucho way of life and is one of Argentina's most acclaimed and emblematic novels. Music and dance are common expressions of gaucho tradition and culminate in the Fiesta de la Tradición. Held every November, the festival draws thousands of gauchos and city dwellers alike to the town.

San Antonio de Areco is also inundated with dozens of artisans' workshops, mainly of silver and leather. The high quality and professionalism of these labors are renowned across the country and are now arguably as great an attraction as the gaucho museums and historic buildings. The surrounding countryside is also awash with *estancias* (ranches), large rural properties similar to ranches, which offer immersion experiences and activities such as horseback riding and polo.

Favored by Buenos Aires residents as a weekend getaway, the town swells on Saturday and Sunday, when cars trundle up Ruta 8. Visiting during the week will help you avoid the crowds, but transportation connections are limited on weekdays, and many restaurants, sights, and shops are closed, especially on Monday and Tuesday. While the major sights can be visited in one day, it's worth staying at least one night to experience the calm when day-trippers depart. There are plenty of other activities and attractions that justify a stay of a few days.

However long you stay, getting around the town is simple and easy, with everything lying inside a radius of a kilometer or so. Cars don't hurry, and locals stroll down the middle of the road.

SIGHTS

There are a prolific number of museums around town, many of them claiming to be connected to gauchos in one way or another. The majority are small and eclectic and will not occupy much time. This is not to say that they are not worth visiting—on the contrary, some are quite charming. Additional information can be found at the town's tourism office.

The town's main square, Plaza Ruiz de Arellano is at the heart of what is known as the *casco histórico,* the oldest and most historic section of San Antonio de Areco. This plaza, shady and unobtrusive compared to the wide-open squares in Buenos Aires, is emblematic of the way of life and philosophy that San Antonio de Areco has always held so dear. A good way to approach the city is to visit Plaza Ruiz de Arellano and the sights around it before heading north, past the river and into the Parque Criollo y Museo Gauchesco Ricardo Güiraldes.

✪ PARQUE CRIOLLO Y MUSEO GAUCHESCO RICARDO GÜIRALDES

The Parque Criollo y Museo Gauchesco Ricardo Güiraldes (Camino Ricardo Güiraldes and Camino al Parque, tel. 2326/455-839; 11am-5pm Wed.-Mon.; US$1), on 90 hectares of sprawling open fields dotted with ancient trees at the northern tip of the town, is the most interesting of the museums in San Antonio de Areco. Visitors are first drawn through the Pulpería La Blanqueada, a former store and tavern that now

horses being led across the plains by a gaucho

plays host to a number of humorous wax statues depicting gauchos in a variety of acts. The adjacent courtyard includes an ancient adobe chapel and a flour mill.

As is common with many of the old *estancias* (ranches), a moat must be crossed to reach the main building, the location of Casa del Museo. This building is a replica, but it demonstrates well the architecture and style of the time. Rooms are dedicated to specific themes: Ricardo Güiraldes, gauchos, *estancias,* writers, and silversmiths, all of which present an educational and enjoyable coverage of gaucho life and culture.

You can reach Parque Criollo y Museo Gauchesco Ricardo Güiraldes by crossing Puente Viejo in Parque San Martín and proceeding 300 meters up the road that bears the museum's name. If, as is sometimes the case, the bridge is closed, walk east four blocks to the next bridge before working your way back along the other bank.

MUSEO LAS LILAS DE ARECO

In the *casco histórico,* the Museo Las Lilas de Areco (Moreno 279, tel. 2326/456-425, www.museolaslilas. org; 10am-8pm Thurs.-Sun. spring-fall, 10am-6pm Thurs.-Sun. winter; US$7) is an outstanding museum that displays the work of Florencio Molina Campos, a much loved Argentine artist who drew and painted *gauchesco* landscapes, scenes, and characters in a comedic cartoon style that attracted the attention of Walt Disney. Set in a wonderful old *casona* (residence) restored to great splendor, the museum also exhibits work from other artists and genres of the region. A separate carriage room, an outdoor patio, an atmospheric café, and a splendid gift shop help ensure that the surprisingly high price is a good value.

MUSEO Y TALLER DRAGHI

The north side of Plaza Ruiz de Arellano contains the Museo y Taller Draghi (Lavalle 387, tel. 2326/454-219,

The Museo Gauchesco Ricardo Güiraldes celebrates all things gaucho.

www.draghiplaterosorfebres.com; 9am-1pm and 4pm-7pm Mon.-Sat., 10am-1pm Sun.; US$2), a residence restored to its former glory by the influential Drago family. Flanked by the clan's silversmith workshop, where you can watch the craftspeople at work, and a bed-and-breakfast, it displays an eclectic collection of their silver products, ranging from maté paraphernalia to intricately carved bridles and jewelry, much of which is for sale.

Visit the Museo y Taller Draghi to see silversmiths at work.

PARROQUIA SAN ANTONIO DE PADUA

The southern side of Plaza Ruiz de Arellano is dominated by the Parroquia San Antonio de Padua, a delightful and beautifully maintained church that displays various architectural styles and is open to visitors. It's one of the oldest buildings in San Antonio de Areco and is woven into the history and development of the city perhaps more than any other building.

CENTRO CULTURAL USINA VIEJA

Lying half a block to the north of Plaza Ruiz de Arellano, the Centro Cultural Usina Vieja (Blvd. Alsina 66, tel. 2326/454-722; 11am-5pm Tues.-Sun.; free) is a museum that offers a ramshackle collection of odds and ends, including an intriguing biplane, ancient instruments, and some truly informative displays about the British follies of the early 19th century.

Housed in an excellently adapted former power plant that is more than 100 years old, it presents a basic introduction to the history and culture of the town and takes only a short time to peruse.

PARQUE SAN MARTÍN

A few blocks north of Plaza Ruiz de Arellano, Río Areco winds through the relaxing Parque San Martín, which fills with the laughter of families eating picnics and drinking maté in the afternoons. A small amphitheater can be found a couple of hundred meters downstream alongside an odd system of bridges and tunnels that once served as part of the structure of a water mill that burned down some 30 years ago. However, the unabashed highlight of the park is the Puente Viejo, a salmon-colored bridge that's a popular photo op for visitors.

FESTIVALS AND EVENTS
✪ FIESTA DE LA TRADICIÓN

The town reserves a special place in the nation's agenda in November, when it becomes the meeting point for gauchos and anyone else who wants to celebrate the embodiment of the historic ideal. Horse parades, craft fairs, folk concerts and dances, speeches, debates, culinary explosions, and gaucho showmanship all take place over the weekend closest to the Día de la Tradición, November 10. The main festivities occur on the closest Sunday, while smaller events occur the week before. Check the town's website (www.sanantonioareco.com) for information. If you want to stay overnight in San Antonio de Areco during the festival, make reservations well in advance for hotels and transportation, as well as restaurants, if you aren't

festivities on Día de la Tradición in San Antonio de Areco

planning on eating at the festival's culinary events.

RESTAURANTS

The vast majority of San Antonio de Areco's eateries are traditional in style and menu. The international cuisine that is so variable in Buenos Aires is limited pretty much to pizza, and even that can be hard to find. Meat is predominant, although the Italian heritage ensures that pasta is given a fair footing. Restaurants tend toward informal. It can be impossible to find a table in many places during the summer weekends, but throughout the rest of the year and during the week, there should be little problem. Many establishments don't accept credit cards, so check ahead of time if you don't have cash on hand.

Housed in a weathered building that shows its 200 years, Boliche Bessonart (Segundo Sombra and Zapiola, tel. 2325/1565-5600; 11am-3pm and 6pm-late Tues.-Sun.; US$7-18) is a local favorite. It's famed for its *picada criolla,* which includes locally prepared items such as cheese, salami, and ham. Young people and families alike munch around the table while drinking cold beer or fernet (staunchly served with Pepsi, for some reason). During the afternoon, it is an ideal place to drink *mate cocido* and chomp through a few *alfajores* (cookies).

La Esquina de Merti (Ruiz de Arellana 149, tel. 2326/456-705; 9am-midnight daily; US$5-19) is ideally situated on the corner of a plaza. If you can grab a seat on the pavement, you'll be set up for some decent people-watching, while the inside offers a splendid atmosphere of the past. Empanadas, *picadas,* steaks, and pastas are the specialties, with the traditional menu perhaps on the short side. Breakfast, lunch, and dinner are all served, as are drinks.

traditional form of cooking meat in the countryside

Almacén de Ramos Generales (Zapiola 143, tel. 2326/456-376, www.ramosgeneralesareco.com.ar; noon-4pm and 8pm-midnight daily; US$20-30) is one of the more refined places to eat in San Antonio de Areco and an excellent choice for local dishes in a beautifully traditional setting. Set in a refurbished house that is over 150 years old, the restaurant is decorated with gaucho paraphernalia. Old country dishes, such as their delicious *conejo al verdeo* (rabbit with spring

onions) are served, although meat from the *parrilla* (grill) is the most popular item.

Breaking with the local fervor to maintain tradition, Rossita (San Martín 326, tel. 2326/456-539; 8:30pm-2am Tues.-Sun.; US$14-25) is a fresh, modern restaurant, even if its ancient exterior suggests otherwise. Mood lighting adds ambience, while the elaborate dishes tend toward gourmet. Prices are slightly higher, but a visit includes a free welcome drink, and the attention to detail is excellent.

Overlooking the river that snakes through town, Puesto La Lechuza (Victor Althaparro 423, tel. 2326/1540-5745, noon-3pm and 8pm-late Sat., noon-3pm Sun.; US$10-18) is a simple, down-to-earth restaurant that serves up as much meat as you can eat. Pictures of gauchos and the like adorn the interior, but the charm here is eating outside. Unfortunately, its restrictive weekend hours limit its potential and generally deter locals, except during evening music sessions, when they come to dance.

Despite maintaining a traditional essence, Café de las Artes (Bolívar 70, tel. 2326/456-398, 8:30pm-late Fri., noon-3:30pm and 8:30pm-late Sat.-Sun.; US$15-24) branches out somewhat in decoration and ambience from its competitors. Pastas are the house specialty with some eccentric but tasty combinations. This is also one of the best places to try *carnes al disco,* which consists of meats cooked slowly in a wine-filled dish over a fire.

SPORTS AND ACTIVITIES
HORSEBACK RIDING
The main activity in and around San Antonio de Areco is horseback riding, and there are a fair number of stables

gauchos and their horses roaming around town

offering the opportunity. If you stroll along the north dirt track on the north side of the river to the east of Puente Viejo, you will come across a few. Guides will take you around the town and surrounding countryside for somewhere around US$5 per hour.

TOURS

Camino Pampa (tel. 15/4409-7002, www.caminopampa.com) offers historic tours around town as well as taking guests out to *estancias* (ranches). An all-inclusive excursion, including transportation from Buenos Aires, is US$180.

Areco Tradición (Alem 342, tel. 2326/454-900, www.arecotradicion. com) is a tourist agency that organizes trips to the nearby *estancias* (ranches) as well as activities in the surrounding countryside, including polo and horseback riding. They offer guides in English, French, and Portuguese, as well as private transportation to and from Buenos Aires. One day, including transportation, guided tour, and activities is US$160; two days (including lodging) is US$320.

BIKING

The town practically invites visitors to cycle around, given its empty streets and relaxed atmosphere. Many of the hotels, hostels, and B&Bs offer free use of a bike for their guests, but getting your hands on one otherwise can be difficult. The tourist information office (Zerboni and Arellano, tel. 2326/453-165, www.sanantoniodeareco.com; 8am-8pm daily) offers four bikes without charge until 7pm (requires leaving your passport as a security deposit). They can also advise on which B&Bs often let nonguests borrow their bikes.

SHOPS

Artisanal stores abound, with silver and leather being the main merchandise. Workshops are often attached to the stores and can be visited when dropping into the shop. The main streets for such places are Arellano and Alsina. Wander up and down these few blocks, perhaps exploring down the occasional side street, and you will come across a number of proud local artisans selling their wares from beautiful ancient buildings.

If you're in search of anything related to maté, be it the gourd itself, *bombillas,* or any other paraphernalia, El Fogón Matero (Alsina 36, tel. 2326/456-825; 9am-noon and 3pm-8pm Mon.-Fri., 10am-7pm Sat.-Sun.) can offer a range of options. A few steps away, Platería de Campo (Alsina 86, no phone, www.plateriadecampo.com.ar; 9am-noon and 4pm-8pm Mon.-Sat.) is one of the many silver specialists that produce their own stock, which includes jewelry, knives, maté paraphernalia, and much more.

For pottery, swing by the Paseo de las Tinajas (Belgrano 40, no phone, www.robertofalibene.com), where handmade bowls, jugs, and other items are produced, and you can chat with the artisans who mold and paint them.

For locally produced food products, including cheese, cured meats, bread, pastries, *alfajores,* and liqueurs, head to El Batará (Arellano 59, tel. 2326/1565-4983; 9am-7pm daily). Charito (Alem 334, tel. 2326/1540-5612; 9am-8pm Mon.-Sat.) is a similar place, although they specialize in preparing the ingredients for a *picada* (a spread of cold meats and cheeses), which can then be taken down to eat in the park beside the river.

A family-run business, La Olla de Cobre (Matheu 433, tel. 2326/453-105, www.laolladecobre.com.ar; 10am-1pm and 2:30pm-7:30pm Wed.-Mon.) fills the surrounding streets with rich aromas of blended chocolate and *alfajores.* Visitors are invited to sit and have a drink as well, but this can lead to temptation and ever more purchases.

Exquisite backpacks, handbags, and travel bags fashioned from high quality leather can be found at Arandú (Lavalle 391, tel. 2326/456-029, www.arandu.com.ar; 10am-6pm daily), but be prepared to pay anything from US$300 to US$800. Wallets, purses, bound diaries, and key rings are more affordable, but there's also a great selection of gaucho souvenirs, including silverware, *mates,* clothes, and shoes.

WHERE TO STAY

The number of accommodations options in San Antonio de Areco has increased dramatically over the last few years, with a large number of B&Bs opening around town. The tourist office also provides decent information on the different types of lodging. If you plan to visit during the Fiesta de la Tradición, when crowds flock to the town and prices rise, booking in advance is essential, and the only options may be in neighboring towns or *estancias* (ranches), depending how far in advance you reserve. The rather slender pickings on Airbnb tend to be expensive.

Found by strolling a few hundred meters up the river's south bank, Club Atlético River Plate de Areco (Camino de la Ribera, tel. 2326/454-998, www.riverplateareco.com; US$20 per site for up to 2 campers, US$28 for up to 4) is currently the only camping option, but it is a high-quality one, with a swimming pool, sports and fishing facilities, and *parrillas* (grills) for guests to use. Due to the campground's proximity to the river, it's best avoided during rainy periods.

A delightfully homey hostel right in the center of town, El Puesto (Belgrano 270, tel. 2326/1540-2159, www.hostelelpuesto.com.ar; US$15 pp dorm, US$30-60 s/d) is relaxing and enjoyable. A kitchen and simple garden with a pool and a *parrilla* (grill) are for guest use, while a small café-bar dispenses refreshments. Staff can help you find things to do around town, and bikes are available for rent. Towels are extra, and the lack of air-conditioning can be daunting in summer.

A perfect example of the town's Italian-influenced architectural style, **La Posada de la Plaza** (Alvear 480, tel. 2326/452-955, www.posadadelaplaza. com.ar; US$100-130) is a converted residence that overlooks Plaza Gómez. A lush garden and internal patio create a beautiful serenity that is enhanced by the antique furniture and decor throughout the property. Rooms accommodating two to four people all include air conditioning, and a simple breakfast is included in the rates.

A nine-room family-run hotel, **Paradores Draghi** (Matheu 380, tel. 2326/455-583, www.paradoresdraghi. com.ar; US$90 d, singles available Sun.-Thurs. for US$50) sits in the heart of the *casco histórico* alongside the family museum, Museo y Taller Draghi (free entry for guests). Antique furnishings abound. Rooms may lack in modern amenities but overflow with charm. A garden offers gurgling fountains and an outdoor pool. A decent breakfast is included in the price, as is the use of the house's bikes.

Formerly the home of Ricardo Güiraldes, writer of the acclaimed *Don Segundo Sombra,* **La Porteña** (Ruta 41 s/n, tel. 15/5626-7347, www.laporteniadeareco.com; US$300) is an *estancia* (ranch) a few kilometers outside San Antonio de Areco that sprawls among the woods and open fields. A range of ancient buildings and rooms are available, as is horseback riding

and the chance to eat an authentic countryside *asado* (barbecue). Call in advance to reserve and arrange transportation, or take a taxi from the center of town.

INFORMATION AND SERVICES

Found in a delightful little building in the park next to the crossroads of Zerboni and Arellano, the **tourist office** (Zerboni and Arellano, tel. 2326/453-165, www.sanantoniodeareco.com; 8am-8pm daily) provides good information on local businesses, restaurants, hotels, and artisans. They can provide tips on visiting *estancias* (ranches) surrounding the town, as well as other activities, such as horseback riding and renting bicycles.

Hospital Emilio Zerboni (Moreno and Lavalle, tel. 2326/452-759) attends to medical concerns.

For your postal needs, visit **Correo Argentino** (Alvear 201; 9am-5pm Mon.-Fri.). A string of banks with **ATMs** can be found on Alsina (100-200).

GETTING THERE

Trains no longer serve San Antonio de Areco, which means that the only form of public transportation that serves the town are buses, with three companies currently running from Retiro bus station: **Chevallier** (www.nuevachevallier.com), **San Juan** (www.atsj.com. ar), and **Pullman** (www.gralbelgrano. com.ar). Service is infrequent during the week and more extensive at the weekend. Tickets for all three companies are sold in Retiro bus station, and it is wise to book your return ticket at the same time, before seats sell out. The journey costs around US$8 each way and takes a couple of hours. San

Antonio de Areco's bus station (Av. Dr. Smith and General Paz) lies alongside the highway, a short five-block stroll east of the town center.

Those traveling by car should leave Buenos Aires on the northwest-bound Panamericana (Ruta 9) and then fork left onto Ruta 8 after about 20 kilometers. San Antonio de Areco lies alongside this highway, 76 kilometers farther, with ample parking all around town. The journey will take about 90 minutes each way.

GETTING AROUND

Most people walk around San Antonio de Areco. With most attractions lying in a concentrated radius of a few blocks, there's not much demand for transportation beyond connections with Buenos Aires.

There are a number of *remis* (private car, akin to a town car) companies in town, such as Centro (General Paz 412, tel. 2326/456-225), Avenida (Av. Vieytes 414, tel. 2326/453-288), and Sol (San Martín 344, tel. 2326/455-444).

Colonia, Uruguay

Colonia, which rarely goes by its full name of Colonia del Sacramento, is a small city on the Uruguayan coast approximately 50 kilometers across the Río de la Plata from Buenos Aires. Cited as the oldest city in modern Uruguay, it dates back to 1680, when a fleet of boats under the command of Portuguese Manuel de Lobo came traipsing around the coast from Brazil to set up shop across the water from the Spanish-controlled Buenos Aires. The provocative location irked the Spanish, who only a few months later invaded and conquered the town. Thus began almost 150 years of conflict for possession of Colonia. In 1830, Uruguay finally confirmed itself as a separate nation, upon which Montevideo rapidly became the country's most important city, and Colonia lost the inflated importance it had previously held.

Now recognized as a UNESCO World Heritage Site, Colonia's streets follow the terrain of the hilly peninsula. Although 27,000 people live in Colonia, few of them are based around the historic quarter, which is the main draw for visitors, with its crumbling old buildings and museums. The historic monuments are grouped fairly well together around Plaza Mayor.

While one day may be sufficient to stroll around the town, great pleasure can be found in soaking up the decidedly relaxed and unhurried atmosphere for a longer period. The whole town seems to breathe a sigh of relief when the day-trippers sail away. The sunsets over the Río de la Plata can be spectacular, especially when one isn't glancing at the clock every few minutes, fearful of missing the ferry back to Argentina.

SIGHTS

In Colonia, the best sightseeing is done by strolling the town and exploring the multiple small museums. The part of town that draws visitors is the *barrio histórico*, the old town, which rolls around the peninsula and is best entered through the Portón de Campo (Manuel Lobo and Henriquez de la Peña), a reconstructed gate that served as the original entrance to the town. Plaza Mayor (full name Plaza Mayor 25 de Mayo), a shady, elongated plaza surrounded by interesting buildings, is a good place to start exploring.

Although visitors are welcome to pay an entrance fee at each museum, the local municipality offers a US$2 ticket that's valid for the nine historic museums over a period of two days. The ticket can be bought in any of the museums, all of which share a website (www.museoscolonia.com.uy) and are open 11:15am-4:15pm daily, except for staggered off days. The museums are of varying size and interest. Some take a while to peruse, others a matter of minutes, although most people pass through them all in less than half a day.

MUSEO MUNICIPAL DR. BAUTISTA REBUFFO

The buildings surrounding Plaza Mayor include the Museo Municipal Dr. Bautista Rebuffo (Calle del Comercio 77, tel. 4522-7031; 11:15am-4:15pm Wed.-Mon.). With items ranging from dinosaur bones to colonial artifacts, Colonia's principal museum is a fairly jumbled and unorganized affair, and doesn't provide visitors with an overview of the town's history that it deserves or would be expected. Nonetheless, some interesting items, such as ancient weapons and furniture, are on display.

FARO DE COLONIA

On Plaza Mayor's southwest corner, the barely existing ruins of a 1683 Portuguese convent do their best to withstand the sea breezes and passing centuries. Stuck in the middle of

Colonia del Sacramento

Ferrocarril (Circunvación Plaza de Toros, tel. 4522-1496, www.recrearla-historia.com; 11am-4pm and 8pm-late Fri.-Sat., by reservation only evenings, 11am-4pm Sun.; US$16-28), the antique dining carriage of a former train that is held in the town's railroad museum. Upscale food, such as steak in a wine sauce, is served at reasonable prices. As an added bonus, diners have the opportunity to visit a crumbling former bullring next door.

WHERE TO STAY

The old town of Colonia is overflowing with small accommodations, such as posadas (similar to guesthouses or traditional inns) and boutique hotels. While the odd one may sell out, there will always be another one round the corner with space. Although prices tend to the more expensive side, there are a few decent budget options. A few luxury hotels and spa centers can be found outside the town itself, but such places are generally a trip in themselves.

A shaded campsite set in the woods above Colonia, Camping Los Nogales (Severino Ortiz and Ruta 1, tel. 9817-8; US$8 per tent plus US$2.50 pp) is a project set up by the local fútbol [tea]m, Peñarol de Colonia. With hot [wat]er, showers, and electricity, all [th]e amenities are covered, while par[rillas] (grills) are available for camp[ers a]nd a restaurant serves up food. [Pic]k up Avenida Buenos Aires from [the f]erry port for just over two kilo[mete]rs and turn right down Gregorio [Sever]ino Ortiz. The beach is a short [distan]ce south from the campsite.

[Hou]sed in an ancient colonial [hous]e, El Viajero (Washington [Barbo]t 164, tel. 4522-2683, www.el-[viajer]ohostels.com; US$15 dorms, [US$40]-60 s or d) is a Hostelling

International-affiliated hostel with small and compact rooms, the eight-bed mixed-dorm perhaps being the pick of the bunch. Guests can enjoy a rooftop terrace and patios or rent bikes, which enable exploration beyond the barrio histórico. Guests have access to a kitchen, but towels cost extra if you're staying in a dorm.

Posada Plaza Mayor (Calle del Comercio 111, tel. 4552-5812, www.posadaplazamayor.com; US$125-250 d) is one of Colonia's finest offerings, with around a dozen rooms spread throughout a restored mansion, all of which are at least double occupancy and include private baths and air conditioning. A delightful garden that overlooks the Río de la Plata becomes ecstatically peaceful when the day-trippers leave. Free breakfast is served in a canteen with a panoramic river view, but other meals must be eaten elsewhere.

An idyllic colonial mansion that contains 40 rooms spread over three floors, most of which look out over one of the patios, Don Antonia Posada (Ituzaingó 232, tel. 4522-5344, www.posadadonantonio.com; US$78-180 d) is surprisingly well priced. The pleasant classical exterior belies a simpler and more modern interior, although respect for the building's origins are clearly maintained. A decent-size open-air pool draws guests with its tiled galleries running alongside, while bedrooms include air-conditioning and private baths.

Perhaps the most charming feature of the Radisson Hotel & Casino (Washington Barbot 283, tel. 4523-0460, www.radissoncolonia.com; US$125-150 s or d) is the garden that allows guests to gaze out over the bay while lounging in or beside the pool. Hardly in keeping with the crumbling

them is the Faro de Colonia (daily 11am-sunset; US$0.80), a stout lighthouse that provides a splendid vista of the old town and Río de la Plata. Climbing the 118 steps may lead to the need for a contemplative sit-down at the top, which is especially enjoyable at sunset. On a clear day, you might just make out the ripple of Buenos Aires on the horizon.

MUSEO PORTUGUES

Halfway down the south side of the plaza, the Museo Portugues (Calle Enriquez de la Peña 180, tel. 4522-9240; 11:15am-4:15pm Sat.-Tues. and Thurs.) contains some of the most interesting museum exhibits. Copies of colonial discovery maps provided by the Portuguese government offer fascinating viewing and an intriguing approach to the events that surrounded Colonia's founding and development. The building itself is also an interesting example of early-18th-century Portuguese architecture, with walls made out of wood, stone, and adobe.

LA CALLE DE LOS SUSPIROS

The southeast corner of Plaza Mayor runs down to the coast via La Calle de los Suspiros (Street of Sighs). Shops, galleries, and restaurants line this quaint cobbled street, which is bathed in legends. Its name is variously attributed to the sounds emanating from its brothels, from prisoners awaiting execution, or the ghost of a murdered lover. On the coastal end to the eastern side, a few remains of one of the town's forts, Bastion de San Miguel, can be observed and walked around.

MUSEO DEL AZULEJO

It won't take too long to pass through the Museo del Azulejo (Misiones de

los Tapes 104, tel. 4522-1065; 11:15am-4:15pm Tues.-Sun.) on the western tip of the peninsula. This museum contains rooms that display an interesting array of tiles collected throughout the development of the region. Most are from France, but there are also examples from Spain, Catalonia, and Portugal. There is little explanation of historical information beyond the visual displays.

IGLESIA MATRIZ

In the center of the peninsula, Plaza de Armas (full name Plaza de Armas Manoel Lobo) sits in front of Iglesia Matriz, one of Colonia's many small churches, but more significantly the oldest one in Uruguay. Originally built in 1680, it was destroyed and rebuilt a number of times during the constant battles the town suffered. It now maintains a stubbornly simplistic and unadorned form of decoration, unlike most of the continent's lavish churches.

La Calle de los Suspiros

TEATRO BASTIÓN DE CARMEN

Directly north of Plaza de Armas on the coast is the Teatro Bastión de Carmen (Rivadavia 223; noon-8pm

the oldest church in Uruguay, Iglesia Matriz

daily; free), an arts complex that is located inside part of the city's ancient fortifications. Exhibitions are held on a regular basis, while permanent sculptures can be found in the grassy garden that looks out over the river. Concerts and theater productions are also put on occasionally.

MUSEO ESPAÑOL

Almost adjacent to the Teatro Bastión de Carmen, the recently renovated Museo Español (San José 152, tel. 4522-6055; 11:15am-4:15pm daily) contains a small collection of artifacts from colonial times, such as pottery and maps, as well as some of the little artwork on display in the town by local artist José Paéz Vilaró. All displays are in Spanish.

GRANJA COLONIA ARENAS

If you're willing to take a hike or a taxi, or even hitch a ride, head out to Granja Colonia Arenas (Km. 167, Ruta 1, tel. 4520-2025, www.granjacolonia.com.

uy; 8:30am-6pm daily; free), you will be rewarded with an eccentric collection of 16,000 pencils (no one has more), 35,000 key rings, 4,800 ash trays, 4,000 perfume bottles, and a whole range of other, equally seemingly arbitrary items en masse. The owner holds multiple world records and is, perhaps unsurprisingly, an interesting person to meet.

RESTAURANTS

Most restaurants accept Argentine pesos, which is great for those who are only over for the day and have no desire to start exchanging currencies. Bear in mind, however, that the exchange rate will never be particularly favorable, averse as the Uruguayans are to getting their hands on the weak Argentine currency. Card payments are rare in Colonia, so make sure to ask beforehand if this is how you want to pay. Many of the restaurants along the coast are overpriced because of the view they offer, and few of them live

up to expectations. On the other hand, they are ideal places to have a drink before or after a meal, especially at sunset. The local wine is tannat, a red wine traditionally produced in France but equally good here and sold in all restaurants and bars.

The self-proclaimed gastronomic artisans who run Buen Suspiro (Calle de los Suspiros 90, tel. 4522-6160, www.buensuspiro.com; 11:15am-midnight daily; US$15-24) certainly know a thing or two about whipping up wooden slabs piled high with cheeses and cold meats, intended to be picked at while sampling some of the many wines on offer. Such *picadas* are their specialty, although the soups are also delicious. A small patio with a handful of tables is the perfect spot, although sitting inside by the fire is a better bet during winter.

Distinctively unattractive, given the beauty of some of Colonia's other restaurants and buildings, Los Farolitos (General Flores 272; noon-1:30am daily; US$5-11) is nonetheless a local institution and the best place to try a *chivito*, a traditional Uruguayan steak sandwich filled with all kinds of salads and sauces. Other standard fast food such as hamburgers, fries, and the like are also on offer. Garish plastic chairs await on the roadside at this famed budget restaurant.

You'll find one of the finest menus in town at Charco (San Pedro 116, tel. 4523-5000, www.charcohotel.com; 8am-11pm daily; US$17-30), a decidedly modern restaurant with a great view looking out over the water, especially from the patio. The prices are high, but this is understandable once you try the food. The varied fish dishes are perhaps the highlight, but heed the waiter's knowledgeable suggestions, both on food and wine. It's

worth dropping by upon arriving i Colonia to make a reservation and e sure an outdoor table.

Delightfully light and tasty piz bases are topped with homema sauce and a wide array of toppi in Don Joaquín (18 de Julio 267, 4522-4388; 8pm-midnight Tues.-S US$7-14). A world away from the pan, cheese-laden Genoese sty pizza in Buenos Aires, the thin Neapolitan version served up comes with outlandish choices vors, such as carbonara. The ch also happy for customers to their own. You won't even le crust on these beauties.

Touted by many to be the *rilla* (grill) in Colonia, El (General Flores 333, tel. 45 noon-4pm and 8pm-midnig Sat., noon-4pm Sun.; US$ great value and serves up g portions of meat straight grill. Funky yellow paint well with all the wood on it's definitely best to sit out is space and the weather *vacio* (flank steak) is a gre the waiter that you wou too well-done.

An Argentine coup serves excellent gourm Florida (Odriozola 215, lunch only, open days v a converted residence into various eating sa a different atmosphe number of tables. All fully elaborated and quisite, especially g of such dishes on m open for lunch, the on the owners' whim swing by to check a

It's well worth t trek across town

aesthetics of the surrounding neighborhood, everything is spick-and-span here. With its 75 rooms, a restaurant, a casino, a gym, and an indoor pool available to guests, the Radisson is the only real luxury hotel in the city center.

INFORMATION AND SERVICES

The international telephone code for Uruguay is 598, whether calling from Argentina or anywhere else in the world.

The swish, modern ferry terminal that greets visitors to Colonia at the end of Avenida Roosevelt contrasts with the quaint local architecture. It contains a currency exchange office, an ATM (for Uruguayan pesos and U.S. dollars), and an information desk that hands out free maps. There are two tourist information offices; the largest sits just outside the ferry terminal's parking lot (Miguel Ordizola 434; 9am-6pm daily), while the other is in the old town, alongside the Portón de Campo (Manuel Lobo and Henriquez de la Peña; 9am-6pm daily).

For the last few years, many Argentines have hopped over to Colonia to take advantage of the less restrictive currency-exchange laws, although exchange houses there are reluctant to buy pesos and generally offer undervalued rates. A big difference in Colonia is that U.S. dollars can be withdrawn from the ATMs, a terribly exciting novelty for Argentines, although strict limits are in place (US$300, at time of writing), making it unsuitable for any meaningful transactions. There is an exchange house in the port, but banks in the old town will offer slightly better rates, as will an outlet in the town's shopping mall (Av. Roosevelt 458; 10am-10pm daily). Most restaurants and tourist

the patio inside Posada Plaza Mayor

shops will accept Argentine pesos and U.S. dollars, although be wary of the current exchange rate.

In the unlikely event of any problems, there is an Argentine consulate (General Flores 209) and an immigration office (18 de Julio 428). The old town is served by Hospital Colonia (18 de Julio 462), and there's also a post office (Lavalleja 226).

GETTING THERE
BOAT
Three major companies offer ferry services between Buenos Aires and Colonia, ranging between one and three hours, although the savings made by taking the slower option are often negligible. All three offer return day trips, which can work out cheaper and include a guided tour of Colonia.

Buquebus (tickets from Av. Córdoba 867, Retiro, www.buquebus.com; from US$80 round-trip) is the main player, with multiple crossings each day, offering a faster catamaran as well as the more traditional chugging ferry that also transport cars, with both types leaving from

an entrance to Colonia

the Terminal Fluvial (ferry port, Av. Antartida Argentina 821) smack in the center of town, between Retiro and Puerto Madero.

Seacat Colonia (tickets from Av. Córdoba 772, Retiro, www.seacatcolonia.com; from US$90 round-trip) also departs from the ferry port, offering smaller launches that bounce across the waves in a way that some find entertaining but others find somewhat nauseating.

The cheapest option is generally Colonia Express (tickets from Av. Córdoba 753, www.coloniaexpress.com; from US$50 round-trip), although this service departs from a more awkwardly located terminal (Pedro de Mendoza 330) in La Boca. While all three companies sell tickets from their respective ports of departure, it's worth visiting the ticket offices on Avenida Córdoba, as they are all within one block of each other and allow travelers to shop for the best deal.

An alternative route by boat, which often works out to be somewhat cheaper, is to take a Cacciola catamaran (tickets from Av. Córdoba 755, Retiro, www.cacciolaviajes.com.ar) from Tigre to Carmelo, a town farther up the Uruguayan coast, from where a connecting bus takes a couple of hours to trundle down to Colonia.

OVERLAND
The overland option is an inadvisable and lengthy adventure (500 kilometers instead of 50) that takes the best part of a day. Buses run from Retiro to Gualeguaychu, farther up the Río Uruguay, from where a connecting service can be taken to Colonia, a total journey time of around 11 hours costing from US$40. The terminal is to the right when leaving the ferry port's parking lot in Colonia, although

some bus services leave from the ferry terminal itself (especially services that are connections from the boat to Montevideo).

If traveling by car, the easiest way is to cross in the **Buquebus car ferry** (from US$240). Driving involves a 500-kilometer journey that takes about six hours. Head north out of the city on Ruta 9 for 56 kilometers and then fork right onto Ruta 12. After 80 kilometers, turn onto Ruta 14 and continue a further 72 kilometers until the turnoff to Ruta 136, which, after 40 kilometers, will take you to the Puente Libertador General San Martín and the border crossing. Follow Ruta 2 for 32 kilometers and then join Ruta 21, which will take you to Colonia after 200 kilometers. Given the complication of crossing the border with a rented car, it would be more economical, easier, and quicker to cross in the ferry and rent a car in Uruguay.

GETTING AROUND

Shortly after you arrive in Colonia, you'll see buggies and carts trundling past you. Although the old town is so small that transportation is superfluous, if you want to explore farther up the coast, renting one of these could be worthwhile. **Motorent** (Manuel Lobo 505, www.motorent.com.uy) is the most organized, offering cars, carts, motorcycles, and buggies.

Iguazú Falls

Iguazú Falls is the most famous natural landmark in Argentina, a huge cascade of water four times as wide as Niagara Falls, set in a protected reserve in the middle of the rainforest on the border with Brazil. Rather than one giant fall, Iguazú consists of almost 300 individual falls that sit alongside each other in a gorge cut deep into the Río Iguazú, which stretches for almost three kilometers, making it the largest waterfalls system in the world. Every year, over one million visitors explore the trails that wind along the falls' top edges and creep in toward their thundering bases.

Situated in the northeast corner of Argentina in Misiones province, 1,300 kilometers from Buenos Aires, visiting the falls is not as simple as the other day trips in this guide. Indeed, given the cost and time necessary for a visit, it's definitely worth staying at least one night, although two or three would be preferable, given that two days can easily be spent in the Parque Nacional, while Brazil, Paraguay, and the surrounding rainforest provide enticing side trips. A rainy day can mar a one-day visit to the Parque Nacional, although inclement weather doesn't prevent an outing here.

The subtropical climate of the region ensures that temperatures are fairly high throughout the year, but in January and February it can become unbearably hot and humid. This also coincides with Argentine and Brazilian holidays, making the high season, with resulting higher prices and larger crowds. Any point during the rest of the year is an ideal time to visit.

Most travelers who arrive from Buenos Aires base their trip from **Puerto Iguazú**, a small town 16

Iguazú Falls and Vicinity

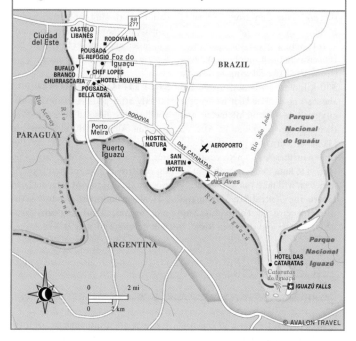

kilometers from the falls. Simple and unpretentious, the town caters to travelers, although hotels and restaurants are often overpriced.

While most visitors organize trips on their own, there are a huge variety of travel agencies that can assist travelers. These range from simple boat excursions in the Parque Nacional to complete packages (including transportation from Buenos Aires, lodging, and activities).

Below are agencies based in Puerto Iguazú:

- **Caracol** (Av. Aguirre 563, tel. 3757/420-064, www.caracolturismo.tur.ar)
- **Hunt & Fish** (Av. Misiones 161, tel. 3757/425-738, www.safarisinargentina.com)
- **Iguazeña** (Av. Aguirre 262, tel. 3757/420-317, www.iguazena.com.ar)
- **Sensitive Adventure** (Av. Misiones 257, tel. 3757/421-485, www.sensitiveadventure.com.ar)

The following agencies operate out of Buenos Aires and offer all-inclusive trips:

- **Say Hueque** (Thames 2062, Palermo; or Chile 557, San Telmo, tel. 011/5258-8740, www.sayhueque.com)
- **Tije** (Av. Santa Fe 898, tel. 011/5272-8450, www.tije.travel)
- **01 Argentina** (tel. 015/3673-3091, www.01argentina.com)

SIGHTS

There are few sights in the world greater than Iguazú Falls, so they should receive as much of your time as possible.

✪ PARQUE NACIONAL IGUAZÚ

The waterfalls within the Parque Nacional Iguazú (Km. 142, Ruta 101, tel. 3757/491-469, www.iguazuargentina.com; 8am-6pm daily; adults US$22, children under 12 US$5) are close to three kilometers wide and consist of almost 300 individual falls (depending on water levels) between 60 and 82 meters high. The park also provides a natural habitat for 450 species of birds, over 2,000 plant species, exotic animals such as crocodiles, monkeys, and coatis (raccoon-like creatures), and millions of butterflies.

Pass through the visitors center upon arrival for maps and background information. A free train shuttles visitors around the top section of the park, starting from close to the entrance and finishing by the Garganta del Diablo (Devil's Throat).

crowd in front of the Garganta del Diablo

Hiking

Five well-maintained and clearly marked trails traverse the distinct areas of the park, each with its own perks. The Circuito Superior (1.5 kilometers, 2 hours) winds easily along the rim of the waterfalls, offering dizzying views straight down over the edge, as well as including the best panoramic views of the park. The Circuito Inferior (1.5 kilometers, 2 hours), traverses the river's edge below the waterfalls, providing the deafening opportunity to get up close to the cascades. Free boats can be taken from a point along this route to Isla San Martín, an island that sits in the middle of the waterfalls.

The ominously named Garganta del Diablo (Devil's Throat) is the grandest and largest of all the waterfalls in the park, accessed by a series of walkways that zigzag out across the upper river and finally reach the top of a monumental drop.

The Sendero Macuco (7 kilometers, 3 hours) treks through the dense rainforest, ending up at, unsurprisingly, a waterfall, while the shorter Sendero Verde (800 meters, 30 minutes) winds through open woods. Both trails offer great chances to spot birds and monkeys.

Tours

A privately owned company, Iguazú Jungle (www.iguazujungle.com; tel. 3757/421-696) offers excursions and activities within the park, including truck rides through the rainforest, boat excursions into the faces of some of the waterfalls, and rafting through the quieter areas that are home to a rich variety of flora and fauna. Inquire at the visitors center for more information and tickets.

Practicalities

Inside the park, the Sheraton Iguazú Resort & Spa (Parque Nacional Iguazú, tel. 37/5749-1800, www.

sheratoniguazu.com; US$330 d) offers stunning views of the waterfalls only a few hundred meters away. Rooms are excellent and the spa center is top-notch. Guests are obliged to pay the national park entrance fee upon arrival (US$22), but they benefit from early entry and late exit. The hotel's bar, restaurants, patio, and observation deck all look straight out over the thundering falls. With only 176 rooms, all doubles, reservations are obligatory, especially in January and February.

Food and drink are available at various points throughout the park; it's expensive, so most visitors take their own supplies.

It's necessary to show ID, such as your passport, to gain entry to the park. If you're planning to return for a second day, make sure to get your ticket stamped upon leaving the park, so you receive a 50 percent discount the next day.

In the five-day period surrounding every full moon, visitors can opt to visit the park at night (from US$40), under strict supervision, and experience the waterfalls under moonlight—a truly mesmerizing sight.

HITO TRES FRONTERAS

Found at the convergence of the Río Paraná and Río Iguazú, the Hito Tres Fronteras (Triple Frontier, Av. Tres Fronteras and Av. Río Iguazú; free) is the point where the Argentina, Brazil, and Paraguay borders meet, a mere 15-minute stroll from the town center. A viewing point perched high above the water provides panoramic views along the wide rivers, the coasts of the adjoining countries, and the tall bridge that connects Argentina and Brazil. A small artisans market sells locally handcrafted wares, while well-designed gardens allow visitors space to relax, reflect, and lounge over a picnic.

rainbow crossing Iguazú Falls

Many species of birds call the falls home.

GÜIRA OGA

Wildlife rehabilitation center Güira Oga (Km. 1637, Ruta 12, www.guiraoga.com.ar; 9am-6pm daily) takes in sick animals from the surrounding area and revives them before releasing them back into the wild. Around 90 percent of the residents are birds, with the rest consisting of monkeys, crocodiles, and the occasional leopard. Visitors are taken on a guided tour (Spanish or English) and taught about the animals, local situations, and the environment. Far from being a zoo, the center receives visitors and their donations to remain independent of state funding.

ITAIPÚ DAM

Not content to merely boast one of the seven natural wonders of the world, this region also contains one of the seven modern wonders in the Itaipú Dam (Av. Tancredo Neves 6731, www.turismoitaipu.com.br; from US$3). Some 20 kilometers upriver from Puerto Iguazú in Brazil, the largest hydroelectric dam in the world was completed in 1984 to supply immense quantities of electricity. Its initiation displaced tens of thousands of people due to vast flooding. The dam is 4.5 kilometers long and almost 200 meters high, and welcomes visitors with a range of tours, including the fascinating Special Tour (2 hours; US$20), which explores the depths and summits of the structure.

Visiting the dam requires crossing the Brazilian border, meaning a passport is necessary, and travelers should check the ever-changing visa requirements beforehand. While local buses can be used to get here, it requires at least two transfers and payment in different currencies, as well as potential problems at the border. The simplest way to arrive is by taking a taxi or arranging a trip through an agency, such as Viator (www.viator.com; from US$20), which can pick you up from your lodgings.

RESTAURANTS

Dining is generally informal and reasonably priced in Puerto Iguazú, although there are a few upscale joints and gourmet offerings, as well as some along the river's edge with spectacular views. The food on offer is fairly generic, with few places offering much more than beef, pasta, and pizza.

The standout local cuisine is fresh fish from the surrounding rivers, which can be an absolute delicacy and is found in most restaurants, depending on availability.

Traditionally one of the restaurants most frequented by visitors, La Rueda 1975 (Av. Córdoba 28, tel. 3757/422-531, www.larueda1975.com.ar; noon-midnight daily; US$12-25) is renowned for its beef and river fish, such as *pacú* (akin to a piranha) and *surubí* (a local catfish). The traditional wooden building is home to dishes that have been cooked for generations.

The waiters and chefs can take a while to produce your food, but the wine cellar stores some wonderful regional vintages to enjoy in the meantime.

Ostensibly a wine bar, Vinosophie (Av. Brasil 136, tel. 3757/494-189; 5pm-1am daily; US$12-18) is a great place to enjoy tapas—especially the *patatas bravas* (sautéed potatoes). There are two daily meals (not listed on the menu) of fish and beef, which are always popular. The wine options are extensive, although also somewhat overpriced. The central location, modern decor, and outdoor tables make it a heavily frequented choice, especially in the early evening.

Six roads crunch together outside Puerto Bambu (Av. Brasil 96, tel. 3757/422-331; noon-late daily; US$6-18), but traffic is never too heavy. This bustling spot is popular with a young crowd, many of whom come to drink and pick at *picadas* (platters of cold meats and cheese) or the standard options of pizza, burgers, or steak, as well as a decent vegetarian selection. There is no indoor seating—tables curve around the pavement, immersing you in local life. This is not the place for a quiet, relaxed meal, but it's ideal for a good-value bite and a drink.

Overlooking the converging rivers and triple border of Argentina, Brazil, and Paraguay, Bocamora (Av. Costanera 20, tel. 3757/420-550, www.bocamora.com; noon-11:30pm daily; US$16-25) offers unrivaled views from its terrace. The locally caught and expertly cooked fish is the specialty. Grilled meat dishes are also available, and there is an excellent selection of wines. This is a perfect place to dine during sunset.

Lovingly constructed by the learned hand of international chef Matteo Lagostena, the delicately delicious plates at De la Fonte (1 de Mayo 611, tel. 3757/420-625, www.delafonterestaurant.com; 7:30pm-midnight Mon.-Sat.; US$14-26) all consist of fresh, local, organic produce. The menu is based on traditional Italian cuisine, including top-notch homemade pastas, but the fish and meat dishes melt in your mouth, especially the *tagliata* (grilled sliced steak) and El Poema del Costillar, a slow-cooked first-cut rib. Situated in a boutique hotel of the same name, De la Fonte allows for seating in the homey interior or on the spacious green patio.

WHERE TO STAY

There seem to be more hotels, hostels, B&Bs, and rental apartments than there are actual houses in Puerto Iguazú. The options are disproportionate for such a small town, ranging from budget to luxury, although many of them are overpriced. The most exclusive choice lies within the national park itself, while the road back into town is lined with options, although these can be awkward bases without a private car or willingness to use taxis. Most foreign travelers opt to stay in the center of Puerto Iguazú, where transportation is excellent and local amenities are at their best. Most accommodations have pools.

For those looking to immerse themselves in the fascinating nature of the region, Camping Costa Ramón (Irupé and Rosa Blanca, tel. 3757/461-188, www.campingcostaramon.com.ar; adults US$10, ages 7-10 US$5, under age 7 free) lies on the edge of town alongside the Río Paraná. Services include an outdoor natural pool, kitchen, *parrillas* (grills), showers, electricity, and Internet access.

They can assist in arranging transportation to the falls and Buenos Aires, as well as tours of the Parque Nacional.

Nestled away from the bustle of downtown Puerto Iguazú, Hostel Garden Stone (Av. Córdoba 441, tel. 3757/420-425, www.gardenstonehostel.com; US$12-43) offers simple dorms of four to eight beds (US$12-20 pp) or doubles (US$36) with shared baths. It's worth the extra cost for a double with a private bath (US$43). A charming garden with hammocks and a small pool provide excellent outdoor space with plenty of birds chirping all around. Guests have access to a kitchen and a decent free breakfast.

Just a couple of blocks from the bus station, Hostel Bambu Mini (Av. San Martín 4, tel. 3757/425-864, www.hostelbambu.com.ar; US$15-50) is a cozy, laid-back hostel with staff who are keen to help their guests. A small breakfast is included in the rates, while a kitchen and cooked meals are available. Dorms range in size from 4 beds (US$19 pp) to 16 beds (US$15 pp), while a double costs US$50. Although there is no pool, pleasant outdoor areas provide space to relax in the open air.

Just 50 meters from the Güira Oga wildlife sanctuary on the edge of town, Yaguareté Lodge (Km. 5, Ruta 12, tel. 3757/420-768, www.yaguaretelodge.com; US$55-100) offers wooden cabins set in the dense rainforest. One-bedroom cabins (US$55-75) sleep up to four while two-bedroom cabins (US$80-100) can sleep six. All cabins come with kitchens as well as access to the gardens, outdoor pool, and *parrillas* (grills), while trails allow you to explore the surrounding area.

Heading out of town toward the falls, La Aldea de la Selva (El Dorado and Ruta 12, tel. 3757/493-010, www.laaldealaselva.com; US$110-200) is a luxury lodge in the rainforest that enchants guests with its rustic yet refined atmosphere. An outdoor pool surrounded by palm trees and deck chairs provides the ultimate relaxation spot—although the private balconies with hammocks aren't bad either. There is a gourmet restaurant on-site.

Run by an architect whose hand is evident in all of the individually themed rooms, De la Fonte (1 de Mayo 611, tel. 3757/420-625, www.boutiquehoteldelafonte.com; US$110-160) is a boutique hotel that is an exception to the overpriced accommodations in Puerto Iguazú. Rooms are in a galleried villa around an outdoor pool, with spa facilities and an on-site masseuse available to guests. All the rooms are doubles with private baths. It's also home to one of the best restaurants in town, which goes by the same name.

For five-star luxury in the center of town, look no further than the Panoramic Hotel (Paraguay 372, tel. 3757/498-100, www.iguazugrand.com, US$140-200 d, US$260-330 t), with its lavish gardens, expansive pool, gourmet restaurant, buffet breakfast, private casino, and gym. Rooms offer splendid views over the adjoining Río Iguazú up toward the Tres Fronteras, especially at sunset. Rates increase according to the view and balcony space.

GETTING THERE
AIR
Daily two-hour flights with LATAM (www.latam.com) and Aerolíneas Argentinas (www.aerolineas.com.ar) connect Buenos Aires to Aeropuerto Internacional Cataratas de Iguazú (IGR), which lies 16 kilometers out of

town. If booked in advance, flights can actually be cheaper than bus tickets, starting from US$150 round-trip, but prices rise significantly closer to departure and during peak season, between December and February, with fares up to US$400.

There is no public transportation to or from the airport. A taxi to the center of Puerto Iguazú has a fixed fare of around US$25—but confirm with the driver before departing.

Four Tourist Travel (www.ftt.tur.ar) offers a minibus service from the airport to the town center (US$8 pp). Tickets are sold from the company's stand next to the departure gate; it's worth booking in advance online.

BUS

Being one of the most tourist-oriented destinations in the country, the buses connecting Puerto Iguazú with Buenos Aires are among the very best, although they need to be, given the lengthy 18-hour journey. The main bus companies that depart from Retiro are **Via Bariloche** (www.viabariloche.com.ar), **Expreso Tigre Iguazú** (www.tigreIguazú.com.ar), and **Expreso Singer** (www.expresosinger.com.ar); departures occur a few times per day. Most offer *semi-cama* (semi-reclinable seats, US$200 round-trip), *cama* (lay-flat seats, US$235 round-trip), and *super-cama* (US$270 round-trip) services. All prices are fixed, whether booking in advance or on the day of.

GETTING AROUND
BUS

The central **bus terminal** (Av. Córdoba and Av. Misiones) serves both long-distance and local buses. Puerto Iguazú is connected to the Parque Nacional by the yellow **Río Uruguay buses** that depart every 20 minutes between 7am and 9pm (20 minutes; US$5 one-way). Long queues can form in the morning during high season, so arrive early. Tickets can be bought in advance from many hotels and hostels or at the bus station, but don't buy the (often fake) tickets from touts on the street.

Other local buses connect the town to Foz do Iguaçu (Brazil) and Ciudad del Este (Paraguay).

TAXI

Unlike taxis in Buenos Aires, few drivers in Puerto Iguazú use meters, so make sure to establish the price before any journey begins. A taxi to the Parque Nacional costs around US$25 each way, as does the trip to or from the airport. Three local taxi companies are **Group 16** (Av. Córdoba 181, tel. 3757/420-973), **Wanda** (Paulino Amarante and Fray Luis Beltrán, tel. 3757/421-352, www.trasladoswanda.com), and **SOS Taxis** (tel. 3757/1557-3108, www.genesitios.com/sospaseossos). Hotels and restaurants will also call for a taxi if asked.

CAR

With excellent public transportation connecting the town and outlying accommodations with the Parque Nacional and nearby towns in Paraguay and Brazil—not to mention the questionable state of the roads and hassle of border-crossing, hiring a car can be more trouble than it's worth. Nonetheless, all the major rental companies have outlets in the city, such as **Alamo** (Jangadero 132, www.alamoargentina.com.ar), **Avis** (Av. Victoria Aguirre 1149, www.avis.com), or **Europcar** (Tareferos 111, www.europcar.com), as well as pickup points at the airport, from around US$60 per day.

INFORMATION AND SERVICES

The tourist information office (Av. Victoria Aguirre and Av. Brasil, tel. 3757/420-800, www.misiones-turismo.com.ar; 8am-8pm daily) assists with inquiries on visiting the waterfalls, other activities, and local accommodations.

Hospital Dra. Martha Schwartz (Av. Aguirre and Ushuaia, tel. 3757/420-288), named after a renowned local doctor, is the town's hospital.

Correo Argentino (Av. San Martín 384, tel. 3757/425-830; 10am-6pm Mon.-Fri.) will send your mail, while banks with ATMs can be found dotted across town (Bonpland 203; Av. Aguirre 179). There are also ATMs at the entrance to the Parque Nacional.

BACKGROUND

The Landscape

view of Buenos Aires

Buenos Aires sits on land that was originally joined to the west coast of Africa some 250 million years ago, meaning that it shares similar rock layers and fossils to its eastern counterpart. Located on the coastal edge of the vast plains of Argentina and near the country's border with Uruguay, the city is overwhelmingly flat. Buenos Aires sits at the mouth of the Río de la Plata, which empties into the Atlantic Ocean.

The Río de la Plata was named because its tributaries, the Río Paraná and Río Uruguay, headed toward the great silver mines of Bolivia—*plata* is Spanish for silver. In English it's often referred to as the River Plate, a corruption of the original meaning. Due to its brown color, largely due to silt being transported from upstream (as opposed to pollution), and cold temperature, the city has generally ignored the river, rather than building up around it, and there are no beaches in the vicinity. The city was built over a few significant rivers; the only one that survives aboveground to this day is the Riachuelo, a heavily polluted waterway that marks the southern limit of the city.

GEOGRAPHY

Ciudad Autónoma de Buenos Aires, as the city is officially named, is not actually in Buenos Aires province—nor is it the province's capital.

them is the Faro de Colonia (daily 11am-sunset; US$0.80), a stout lighthouse that provides a splendid vista of the old town and Río de la Plata. Climbing the 118 steps may lead to the need for a contemplative sit-down at the top, which is especially enjoyable at sunset. On a clear day, you might just make out the ripple of Buenos Aires on the horizon.

MUSEO PORTUGUES

Halfway down the south side of the plaza, the Museo Portugues (Calle Enriquez de la Peña 180, tel. 4522-9240; 11:15am-4:15pm Sat.-Tues. and Thurs.) contains some of the most interesting museum exhibits. Copies of colonial discovery maps provided by the Portuguese government offer fascinating viewing and an intriguing approach to the events that surrounded Colonia's founding and development. The building itself is also an interesting example of early-18th-century Portuguese architecture, with walls made out of wood, stone, and adobe.

LA CALLE DE LOS SUSPIROS

The southeast corner of Plaza Mayor runs down to the coast via La Calle de los Suspiros (Street of Sighs). Shops, galleries, and restaurants line this quaint cobbled street, which is bathed in legends. Its name is variously attributed to the sounds emanating from its brothels, from prisoners awaiting execution, or the ghost of a murdered lover. On the coastal end to the eastern side, a few remains of one of the town's forts, Bastion de San Miguel, can be observed and walked around.

MUSEO DEL AZULEJO

It won't take too long to pass through the Museo del Azulejo (Misiones de los Tapes 104, tel. 4522-1065; 11:15am-4:15pm Tues.-Sun.) on the western tip of the peninsula. This museum contains rooms that display an interesting array of tiles collected throughout the development of the region. Most are from France, but there are also examples from Spain, Catalonia, and Portugal. There is little explanation of historical information beyond the visual displays.

IGLESIA MATRIZ

In the center of the peninsula, Plaza de Armas (full name Plaza de Armas Manoel Lobo) sits in front of Iglesia Matriz, one of Colonia's many small churches, but more significantly the oldest one in Uruguay. Originally built in 1680, it was destroyed and rebuilt a number of times during the constant battles the town suffered. It now maintains a stubbornly simplistic and unadorned form of decoration, unlike most of the continent's lavish churches.

La Calle de los Suspiros

TEATRO BASTIÓN DE CARMEN

Directly north of Plaza de Armas on the coast is the Teatro Bastión de Carmen (Rivadavia 223; noon-8pm

the oldest church in Uruguay, Iglesia Matriz

daily; free), an arts complex that is located inside part of the city's ancient fortifications. Exhibitions are held on a regular basis, while permanent sculptures can be found in the grassy garden that looks out over the river. Concerts and theater productions are also put on occasionally.

MUSEO ESPAÑOL

Almost adjacent to the Teatro Bastión de Carmen, the recently renovated Museo Español (San José 152, tel. 4522-6055; 11:15am-4:15pm daily) contains a small collection of artifacts from colonial times, such as pottery and maps, as well as some of the little artwork on display in the town by local artist José Paéz Vilaró. All displays are in Spanish.

GRANJA COLONIA ARENAS

If you're willing to take a hike or a taxi, or even hitch a ride, head out to Granja Colonia Arenas (Km. 167, Ruta 1, tel. 4520-2025, www.granjacolonia.com.

uy; 8:30am-6pm daily; free), you will be rewarded with an eccentric collection of 16,000 pencils (no one has more), 35,000 key rings, 4,800 ash trays, 4,000 perfume bottles, and a whole range of other, equally seemingly arbitrary items en masse. The owner holds multiple world records and is, perhaps unsurprisingly, an interesting person to meet.

RESTAURANTS

Most restaurants accept Argentine pesos, which is great for those who are only over for the day and have no desire to start exchanging currencies. Bear in mind, however, that the exchange rate will never be particularly favorable, averse as the Uruguayans are to getting their hands on the weak Argentine currency. Card payments are rare in Colonia, so make sure to ask beforehand if this is how you want to pay. Many of the restaurants along the coast are overpriced because of the view they offer, and few of them live up to expectations. On the other hand, they are ideal places to have a drink before or after a meal, especially at sunset. The local wine is tannat, a red wine traditionally produced in France but equally good here and sold in all restaurants and bars.

The self-proclaimed gastronomic artisans who run **Buen Suspiro** (Calle de los Suspiros 90, tel. 4522-6160, www.buensuspiro.com; 11:15am-midnight daily; US$15-24) certainly know a thing or two about whipping up wooden slabs piled high with cheeses and cold meats, intended to be picked at while sampling some of the many wines on offer. Such *picadas* are their specialty, although the soups are also delicious. A small patio with a handful of tables is the perfect spot, although sitting inside by the fire is a better bet during winter.

Distinctively unattractive, given the beauty of some of Colonia's other restaurants and buildings, **Los Farolitos** (General Flores 272; noon-1:30am daily; US$5-11) is nonetheless a local institution and the best place to try a *chivito,* a traditional Uruguayan steak sandwich filled with all kinds of salads and sauces. Other standard fast food such as hamburgers, fries, and the like are also on offer. Garish plastic chairs await on the roadside at this famed budget restaurant.

You'll find one of the finest menus in town at **Charco** (San Pedro 116, tel. 4523-5000, www.charcohotel.com; 8am-11pm daily; US$17-30), a decidedly modern restaurant with a great view looking out over the water, especially from the patio. The prices are high, but this is understandable once you try the food. The varied fish dishes are perhaps the highlight, but heed the waiter's knowledgeable suggestions, both on food and wine. It's

worth dropping by upon arriving in Colonia to make a reservation and ensure an outdoor table.

Delightfully light and tasty pizza bases are topped with homemade sauce and a wide array of toppings in **Don Joaquín** (18 de Julio 267, tel. 4522-4388; 8pm-midnight Tues.-Sun.; US$7-14). A world away from the deep-pan, cheese-laden Genoese style of pizza in Buenos Aires, the thin-crust Neapolitan version served up here comes with outlandish choices of flavors, such as carbonara. The chefs are also happy for customers to invent their own. You won't even leave the crust on these beauties.

Touted by many to be the best *parrilla* (grill) in Colonia, **El Portón** (General Flores 333, tel. 4522-5318; noon-4pm and 8pm-midnight Tues.-Sat., noon-4pm Sun.; US$13-30) is great value and serves up good-sized portions of meat straight from the grill. Funky yellow paint inside goes well with all the wood on display, but it's definitely best to sit outside if there is space and the weather permits. The *vacio* (flank steak) is a great choice; tell the waiter that you would like it not too well-done.

An Argentine couple cooks and serves excellent gourmet food at **La Florida** (Odriozola 215, tel. 9429-3036; lunch only, open days vary; US$20-35), a converted residence that is divided into various eating salons, each with a different atmosphere and limited number of tables. All dishes are carefully elaborated and the lamb is exquisite, especially given the scarcity of such dishes on most menus. Only open for lunch, the exact days depend on the owners' whims, so you can only swing by to check at around midday.

It's well worth the four-kilometer trek across town to **Restaurant del**

Ferrocarril (Circunvación Plaza de Toros, tel. 4522-1496, www.recrearla-historia.com; 11am-4pm and 8pm-late Fri.-Sat., by reservation only evenings, 11am-4pm Sun.; US$16-28), the antique dining carriage of a former train that is held in the town's railroad museum. Upscale food, such as steak in a wine sauce, is served at reasonable prices. As an added bonus, diners have the opportunity to visit a crumbling former bullring next door.

WHERE TO STAY

The old town of Colonia is overflowing with small accommodations, such as *posadas* (similar to guesthouses or traditional inns) and boutique hotels. While the odd one may sell out, there will always be another one round the corner with space. Although prices trend to the more expensive side, there are a few decent budget options. A few luxury hotels and spa centers can be found outside the town itself, but such places are generally a trip in themselves.

A shaded campsite set in the woods above Colonia, Camping Los Nogales (Severino Ortiz and Ruta 1, tel. 9817-1008; US$8 per tent plus US$2.50 pp) is a project set up by the local *fútbol* team, Peñarol de Colonia. With hot water, showers, and electricity, all basic amenities are covered, while *parrillas* (grills) are available for campers, and a restaurant serves up food. Walk up Avenida Buenos Aires from the ferry port for just over two kilometers and turn right down Gregorio Severino Ortiz. The beach is a short hop due south from the campsite.

Housed in an ancient colonial house, El Viajero (Washington Barbot 164, tel. 4522-2683, www.el-viajerohostels.com; US$15 dorms, US$30-60 s or d) is a Hostelling International-affiliated hostel with small and compact rooms, the eight-bed mixed-dorm perhaps being the pick of the bunch. Guests can enjoy a rooftop terrace and patios or rent bikes, which enable exploration beyond the *barrio histórico*. Guests have access to a kitchen, but towels cost extra if you're staying in a dorm.

Posada Plaza Mayor (Calle del Comercio 111, tel. 4552-5812, www.posadaplazamayor.com; US$125-250 d) is one of Colonia's finest offerings, with around a dozen rooms spread throughout a restored mansion, all of which are at least double occupancy and include private baths and air conditioning. A delightful garden that overlooks the Río de la Plata becomes ecstatically peaceful when the day-trippers leave. Free breakfast is served in a canteen with a panoramic river view, but other meals must be eaten elsewhere.

An idyllic colonial mansion that contains 40 rooms spread over three floors, most of which look out over one of the patios, Don Antonia Posada (Ituzaingó 232, tel. 4522-5344, www.posadadonantonio.com; US$78-180 d) is surprisingly well priced. The pleasant classical exterior belies a simpler and more modern interior, although respect for the building's origins are clearly maintained. A decent-size open-air pool draws guests with its tiled galleries running alongside, while bedrooms include air-conditioning and private baths.

Perhaps the most charming feature of the Radisson Hotel & Casino (Washington Barbot 283, tel. 4523-0460, www.radissoncolonia.com; US$125-150 s or d) is the garden that allows guests to gaze out over the bay while lounging in or beside the pool. Hardly in keeping with the crumbling

A 200-square-kilometer area that is also known as Capital Federal, Buenos Aires is an autonomous district that sits surrounded by the nearly 3,000-square-kilometer Gran (Greater) Buenos Aires, which is itself divided into numerous districts that merge seamlessly into one another.

CLIMATE

The temperate climate of Buenos Aires follows four distinct seasons. Heavy thunderstorms are frequent throughout the hot and humid summers, with temperatures occasionally breaking over 40 degrees Celsius. Winters are largely dry and, although cooler, temperatures rarely drop below 0 degrees Celsius (thus there is no snow). Spring and fall are transition seasons, with variable weather and unpredictable rain patterns, although nights are cooler in spring than fall. Those who suffer in extreme heat are better off visiting outside December through February, when the city is at its hottest. When it rains, especially in summer, it's wise to stay indoors, as the storms tend toward downpours.

ENVIRONMENTAL ISSUES

The majority of Argentina's environmental concerns (deforestation, mining, oil production, pesticide use) are limited to the country's interior. Nonetheless, there are issues of pressing concern in Buenos Aires, as in any other great metropolis.

Air pollution is problematic, especially given the plethora of aged vehicles chugging out clouds of exhaust on the city's roads. Some relief has been found by pedestrianizing large zones and limiting buses to the avenues, but the benefits are small-scale and limited. Industry also pumps out toxic fumes across the city, as does the burning of plastic that occurs daily.

The heavy industrial action that the city has experienced over its lifetime has taken its toll on the waterways of Buenos Aires, with the Riachuelo at one point being claimed as one of the world's top 10 polluted rivers. Despite constant attempts to clean up the city's overland and underground rivers, they are undermined by the dumping of toxic industrial waste and sewage.

Buenos Aires struggles to cope with its huge quantities of waste, even with a daily garbage collection service. Recycling is not in the *porteño* mindset, and the government has historically done little to encourage it. Efforts are increasing, but the main source of recycling continues to come from *cartoneros,* people who sort through waste bins to collect paper, glass, plastic, and metals to then sell for woefully low rates (their carts hold between 100 and 120 kilograms of paper, for which they are typically paid around US$12).

ENERGY SHORTAGES

Great mineral riches and flowing rivers ensure that Argentina is self-sufficient in regard to fossil fuels and hydroelectric power, but despite this wealth in energy, large areas of the country suffer from extreme shortages, and in cities across the country there are regular power outages during periods of high use. In Buenos Aires this problem is exaggerated by the ubiquity of air-conditioning units, many of which double as heaters. Massive power surges during heat waves and cold periods lead to systemic collapses across the grid. The power companies are notoriously poor at fixing problems, let alone avoiding them. City blocks often find themselves without electricity for days or even weeks; without enough power to fill their water tanks, such a shortage means that they are also without water. Unsurprisingly, when this happens, residents tend to display their outrage at the situation by blocking off nearby streets with flaming tires.

PLANTS AND ANIMALS

Being one of the largest metropolitan areas in the world, Buenos Aires does not favor the survival of plants and animals. The only inner-city area that is specifically dedicated to conservation is the large Reserva Ecológica, a former landfill that was taken over by wildlife at the end of the 20th century. Outside of the city, Tigre is the best place to experience a vast variety of species and natural habitats in the river delta.

PLANTS

Buenos Aires has a splendid collection of trees, most of which were transplanted from northern Argentina or imported from around the world. The most beautiful and widespread is the jacaranda, with its vivid purple blossoms that come out in spring. The *palo borracho*, literally translated as "drunk stick," also blossoms in wonderful hues toward the end of summer, although it is covered with treacherous thorns. It's known in English as the silk floss tree. The *ombú* tree can be seen in many squares, with mazy root bases and long, low branches creating a canopy that almost touches the floor.

The city's parks suffer from prolonged periods of heavy rain and scorching sunshine, which means that they are hard to maintain and the grass itself is, unsurprisingly, of a hardier, more resistant nature than the pleasant equivalent in other parts of the world.

ANIMALS

Pigeons rule the city's skies; the network of aerial cables that line every street provide them with ample places to perch en masse. Although the Reserva Ecológica is home to an impressive 250 different species of birds, such variety is not common in the rest of the city, where tiny hummingbirds and the delightful green parakeets are the most enjoyable and widespread bird species.

Beyond the extensive range of shaggy-looking stray dogs, visitors are unlikely to come upon other wildlife on the streets of Buenos Aires. The Reserva Ecológica contains the most interesting mammals and reptiles, such as the coypu (river rat), the mouse-eared bat, and the tegu (a type of lizard).

a monarch butterfly in the Reserva Ecológica Costanera Sur

History

INDIGENOUS AND COLONIAL CLASHES

Indigenous people ruled South America for tens of thousands of years. In Argentina, the Querandí, a group of nomadic hunter-gatherers, lived in the Buenos Aires region. Sticking close to water supplies during winter, they would move inland for hunting during the summer. Precious little remains of these early people, except for their *bolas,* devices consisting of two weights on either end of interconnecting cords that were used to tangle in the legs of their prey, disabling them.

A monument marks the spot of the original founding of Buenos Aires.

When the Spaniard Pedro de Mendoza arrived in 1536 with thousands of soldiers and about 100 horses, he founded the Ciudad de Nuestra Señora Santa María del Buen Ayre in the area of San Telmo, which, at the time, sat right on the water's edge. There is some debate over whether this was the original location of the city, as there are no foundations or reliable sources to verify it, but the general consensus is that it was in the region of Parque Lezama.

At first, the Querandí were accommodating and willing to exchange their food for the goods that the Spanish had brought over with them, but after a few months they cut the explorers off from their precious food supply, a problem that was exaggerated by the colonizers arriving too late in the year to plant crops. A conflict ensued that culminated in a battle on the banks of the Río Luján. Despite inflicting heavy casualties on the Querandí, the Spaniards were driven back to the city, where they were forced to endure prolonged sieges and violent raids by the indigenous people. Within five years they had abandoned the city, destroying it on their departure, but leaving large numbers of cattle and horses roaming free, much to the benefit of the local hunters.

After this inauspicious first attempt at building a city, and given the general lack of resources in the region, attention shifted elsewhere: farther upstream of the Río de la Plata, where Asunción became the most important city in the region for the colonizers. It wasn't until 1580, when Juan de Garay returned from the north, that a second attempt was made to found Buenos Aires, this time around the area that today is Plaza de Mayo. Given the need to develop a strategic trade location at the mouth of the Río de la Plata, from which a constant of flow of Bolivian silver was arriving, great importance was placed on defeating the Querandí, which was achieved violently, even costing the life of Juan de Garay himself.

Despite freeing itself of conflict with the Querandí, the city

257

struggled to attract newcomers, as it was far from any other large city. Commodities and even much of the produce that Europeans were accustomed to eating were hard to come by. Spain gave little priority to Buenos Aires and left it to survive of its own accord, which it did by developing the gaucho tradition in the surrounding countryside, taking advantage of the flourishing cattle that had survived Pedro de Mendoza's original expedition. This led to widespread trade of contraband leather with the Portuguese in Brazil, a product that the Spanish deemed unworthy, or at least of insufficient value, to export back to Europe. This perceived sense of rejection by their homeland sowed the seeds of what would eventually become Buenos Aires's struggle for independence.

The population of Buenos Aires stagnated, reaching 10,000 only in the mid-18th century. The Spanish eventually began to appreciate the city's value, endowing it with the prestigious title of the Viceroyalty of the Río de la Plata. This was partially due to growing British influence and interest in the region, which became explicit in 1806 when Britain invaded Buenos Aires, driving the shocked Spanish rulers to the hills of Córdoba. It was reclaimed just a few months later, but a second British invasion came the following year. This time, the locals held off the invading forces without the help of the Spanish. When Spain was overrun by Napoleon in 1808, the Argentines realized that the time had come to break connections with their European motherland. Declaring itself independent in 1810, remembered to this day on May 25, Buenos Aires finally broke free of its colonial shackles.

INDEPENDENCE AND CIVIL WAR

With the Argentine independence struggle mainly being played out in other parts of the country, Buenos Aires suffered little material damage as a result. While Simón Bolívar was busy driving out the weary Europeans in the northern region of the continent, it was José de San Martín who took on the Spanish forces in northern Argentina, eventually overcoming them and leading to the 1816 formal declaration of independence in the city of San Miguel de Tucumán.

Internal struggles surfaced immediately, however, with Federalists seeking almost complete autonomy for the provinces and Unitarians vying for a strong central government based in Buenos Aires. It was a Federalist, Juan Manuel de Rosas, who eventually came out on top, ruling with an iron fist from Buenos Aires as a dictator who was looked upon unfavorably by the same European immigrants that the rest of the government was desperately trying to tempt into the country. His defeat came after 23 years of rule, when he lost the Battle of Caseros in 1852. The following year the Argentine constitution was written, leading to Buenos Aires seceding from the confederation for a few years. Upon its return, the ground was set for the first president of the unified country, Bartolomé Mitre.

DEVELOPING AUTONOMY

The fortunes of Buenos Aires soared, with its population exploding to over 200,000 by the 1870s and the grain and wool industries diversifying and developing to accommodate huge demand for exports. Further geopolitical disputes within Argentina led to

The Piramide de Mayo honors Argentina's independence.

the federalization of Buenos Aires, but this did little to harm the expansion of the city, becoming the first Latin American metropolis to reach one million inhabitants by the turn of the 19th century. During these years of expansion, Julio Roca conducted a campaign to remove the indigenous people from the central and southern regions of the country, leading to his eventual rise as president. He appointed Torcuato de Alvear as mayor of Buenos Aires, who was perhaps the person who most came to define the future of the city. The humble colonial streets were demolished to make room for larger boulevards and avenues, indicative of the optimistic visions that were held for Buenos Aires. Public buildings, monuments, and plazas sprouted up across the city, focusing development in the more wealthy areas of the city, such as Recoleta and Palermo, as opposed to the working-class, immigrant-based neighborhoods of La Boca and San Telmo.

PERONISM AND THE DIRTY WAR

Such divisions between the rich and poor began to fester, resulting in conflicts that often turned violent. This eventually led to the rise of Juan Domingo Perón, who became president in 1946. Both he and his wife, Eva Duarte (more commonly known as Evita), enjoyed huge popularity, especially from laborers, due to their championing of Argentina's working class and poor residents. His liberal tendencies ensured that he wasn't considered a dictator, but he maintained a firm hand over the country while implementing mammoth public works, which led to a coup d'état in 1955 and his exile to Spain.

After the country alternated between military dictatorships and civilian governments for a decade or so, Perón returned in 1973 and was greeted by a crowd estimated to be between two and four million people, clear evidence of his enduring popularity and idolization. Less than a year later, he died, and his third wife, María Estela Martínez (commonly known as Isabel), took over, whereupon things rapidly descended into chaos.

Having incorporated an increasing number of outlying towns beyond the city limits, Buenos Aires by this point counted over eight million inhabitants. The vast public expenditure, skyrocketing inflation, flailing economy, political disputes, and rise of domestic terrorism were all factors that led to the military ousting Isabel after less than two years, giving birth to what became known as the National Reorganization Process.

Lasting through a succession of dictators (mainly Jorge Rafael Videla, but also Roberto Eduardo Viola, Leopoldo Galtieri, and Reynaldo Bignone), the junta resorted to brutal measures to crush the guerrilla movements that had become increasingly violent over previous decades. They focused on destroying the social and intellectual heart of the movement, "disappearing" between 10,000 and 30,000 students, labor leaders, and intellectuals, many of whom had no ties to the guerrilla movements or violent insurgencies. Now known as the Dirty War, the conflict saw deaths on both sides, but those inflicted by the government, which involved the kidnapping, torture, and murder of its victims, is seen as the most offensive, perpetrated by the all-powerful state.

A group of mothers of disappeared citizens formed an unlikely alliance to take on the state. Protesting weekly in front of Buenos Aires's Casa Rosada, the Madres de Plaza de Mayo drew the attention of the world to Argentina's plight. With the enlightenment of the Argentine populace and international scrutiny of its behavior, the military junta struggled to maintain its footing in yet another period of economic woe.

On April 2, 1982, they invaded the Islas Malvinas (Falkland Islands), which lie some 500 kilometers east of the Argentine coast and had historically been a source of sovereignty squabbles by the Argentines and the British. The islands were easily occupied but the British response caught the young and poorly trained Argentine soldiers by surprise. Over a period of 74 days, 649 Argentines and 255 British soldiers lost their lives in the conflict, which ended in a decisive defeat for the military dictatorship. The junta folded in on themselves and handed back control of the country to the populace.

Raul Alfonsín was elected president in 1983 and surprised the world by taking the unusual step of prosecuting the military leaders that preceded him. After years of investigations and commissions, all the important figures and military generals of the Dirty War (including former president Jorge Videla) were convicted and given life prison sentences. They would eventually be pardoned by President Carlos Menem in 1990.

CONTEMPORARY TIMES

Democracy has managed to remain in place for longer than any other period in Argentina's volatile history, including during the economic and political collapse of 2001.

Buenos Aires is now one of the most important cities in Latin America—and indeed the world—continuing to draw huge numbers of immigrants with its liberal, bohemian, and vibrant tendencies. The city remains blighted with problems, including poverty, housing, health, and education, but it has emerged strong and unified from centuries of conflict.

Government and Economy

GOVERNMENT

Politics in Argentina is a divisive and hotly debated topic that has become largely polarized over the last decade or so. Great swaths of television airtime are given over to "debate," but such productions tend to be heavily biased one way or the other, as are the mainstream newspapers. Public opinion often rolls over into action, with tens of thousands of protesters regularly marching through and disrupting the city center.

Although operating under a representative democracy since 1913, there have been a number of military coups d'état that disrupted the country. The brutal and notorious dictatorships between 1976 and 1983 that ruled during the Dirty War led to widespread distrust of those in power and especially the military. Since then, the return to democracy has been more stable, albeit characterized by clashes of party ideologies and political figures. The economic crisis and resulting political collapse of the early 2000s led to five presidents holding office from late December 2000 into early January 2001, a period of protest and turmoil.

Lack of faith in institutions has led to a firm belief in "positive action" by the populace, which includes mass protests, strikes, and blockages, *escraches* (a tactic of publicly naming, locating, and shaming controversial figures), *cacerolazos* (spontaneous displays of discontent by whole neighborhoods that involve the banging of

The Argentine coat of arms adorns all public buildings.

saucepans out of windows and on the street), and the more worrying trend of public lynchings, notably against street thieves and looters.

ORGANIZATION

The president of Argentina is both the head of state and head of the government, while also being the only person to hold executive power. Below this, the legislative branch consists of two chambers, the highest being the Senado (Senate), which consists of 72 seats and is presided over by the vice-president. Below this comes the Cámara de Diputados (Chamber of Deputies) with its 257 seats. The judiciary is independent of the executive branch and the legislature, but interference and pressure are common, with Supreme Court judges appointed (and regularly leaned on) by the president.

The country is divided into 23 *provincias* (provinces) and one autonomous district, the Ciudad Autónoma de Buenos Aires. While each province has its own constitution, laws, and political structure, they must comply with the overriding national constitution and laws. Authorities in the city have historically enjoyed much less freedom than their counterparts in other provinces, suffering restrictions in a wide variety of areas, such as policing and trade. It wasn't until 1996 that the *jefe de gobierno* (head of government) in the city even became an electable post; until then the city mayor was appointed by the president. Perhaps unsurprisingly, this change has since resulted in some disagreements between the national government and its counterpart in the capital city.

As well as voting for their mayor, city residents elect three senators to the Senado and 25 *diputados* to the Chamber of Deputies.

POLITICAL PARTIES

After 12 years of Kirchnerismo, which included four years under President Nestor Kirchner before his wife, President Cristina Fernandez de Kirchner, took over for another eight years, the Argentine populace at the end of 2015 found itself as politicized and polarized as ever. The Kirchners headed Frente para la Victoria (Front for Victory), an electoral alliance that groups together the Peronists and a variety of other smaller left-wing parties. Traditionally known as the Justicialists, their roots harken back to Perón and the worker movements that still hold immense power. Their combined governance style was based on a vast centralized state machine, populist social welfare programs, the defense of human rights, and the nationalization of swaths of industry. The party enjoys unwavering support from a passionate and boisterous activist group known as the Campóra.

The traditional alternative to the Justicialistas or Peronistas are the Radicalists, who tend to appeal to a middle-class urban demographic. An amalgamation of different parties and ideologies, their inability to work together has arguably cost them recent elections.

With the country's history steeped in labor power and liberal politics, the rise of Mauricio Macri, first as mayor of Buenos Aires and, as of December 2015, as president of Argentina, at the head of the Cambiemos (Let's Change) party, bucks the trend. A former businessman and onetime president of the Boca Juniors soccer team, Macri is market-minded and conservative, much to the approval of North

America and Europe, who have had strained relations with the previous governments. Many Argentines fear that Macri and his government will lead the country drastically away from its historic ideology and bring it more into line with the orthodox politics and economics that have become the globalized norm.

the Argentine flag, designed by Manuel Belgrano

ELECTIONS

Since 1995, presidential elections have been held every four years, with presidents limited to two consecutive terms. The president is elected by a simple majority, although if no ticket achieves at least 40 percent of the vote along with a 10 percent lead over the next ticket, a second runoff vote between the top two settles the matter.

The Chamber of Deputies is formed by proportional representation, with the number of *diputados* for each province being decided by the share of the country's population. The Senate, on the other hand, has a standard of three senators per province, two of whom come from the majority party and one from the minority party.

The electoral process itself is complex and bewildering, with voting in national and local elections being universal for residents over 16 and compulsory for those between 18 and 70. To abstain, voters are required to submit a *voto en blanco,* which is an empty ballot paper, although for technical reasons such votes end up favoring the candidate with the highest number of affirmative votes.

JUDICIARY

Although independent, the judicial system in Argentina has historically suffered from heavy government interference. Recent changes have been made to limit this, but it remains difficult to successfully act against the executive. Courts operate on a federal and provincial level, depending on the character of each case and the origin of those involved. The country's civil law legal system is based on the 1853 constitution, and although juries are theoretically permitted, they are very rarely used.

CORRUPTION

Visitors to Buenos Aires are often surprised by the laid-back and nonchalant way that the police seem to go about their work. They very rarely hassle people on the street and they routinely let menial violations slide, such as driving through a red light or drinking on the street. While their tolerance is extensive in these matters, they will not hesitate to cause trouble when necessary or when they sense the chance to solicit a *coima* (bribe). The border police have historically been notably lax, but they are tightening things up and trying to reduce the number of long-term visitors who abuse the renewable three-month visa system. Customs is more relaxed with North Americans and Europeans than they are with returning Argentines and citizens of neighboring countries.

ECONOMY

The Argentine economy remains a mystery to most international observers because of its wild unpredictability and notorious mismanagement. With outstanding natural resources and a well-educated and multicultural population, Argentina has the potential for success, yet the country has repeatedly failed to take advantage of its years of growth.

In the buildup to World War I, when European and Asian immigrants were flocking to work on the plains that were driving the Argentine economic boom, the country's GDP was growing at a faster rate than any other country in the world—so much so that it quickly became one the richest nations in the world, above countries such as France, Germany, and Italy. Soon after that, the country's fortunes changed. A combination of forces (World War I and its resulting global depressions, World War II and Argentina's supposed neutrality, the military dictatorships that blighted the last 25 years of the previous century) can be considered to have played their part.

Some stability seemed to arrive in the 1990s when President Carlos Menem embraced the Washington Consensus style of government. Removing subsidies and privatizing state enterprises (airlines, railroad networks, utility companies) were the means to do this, while a fixed exchange rate of one U.S. dollar to one Argentine peso, replacing the temporary austral currency, encouraged the stability that was required. Inflation levels dropped and growth returned, but it was short-lived. A shrinking of the economy in 1995, caused by the Mexican Tequila Crisis, was temporarily overcome, but then unemployment increased, government expenditure dropped even farther, and the artificial value of the local currency began to severely harm Argentina's ability to participate in the global marketplace. By the end of 1998 the country had slumped back into a deep recession.

THE ECONOMIC CRISIS OF 2001 AND BEYOND

President Menem was replaced by Fernando de la Rúa in 1999 but the situation only worsened, with De la Rúa quickly pleading for help from the International Monetary Fund (IMF), who agreed to provide payments totaling US$7.2 billion but only on the condition of severe financial adjustments and increased growth, both of which the president was unable to comply with. By late 2001, investors were fleeing the country, and unpaid debt was going through the roof. When the Argentine populace began emptying their bank accounts out of fear, the government responded by severely limiting withdrawals, a move that enraged the population and breached conditions of the IMF payments, which then ceased.

Riots were staged across the country but especially in Buenos Aires, leading the president to declare a state of emergency when the military pointed out that they were legally no longer permitted to intervene in domestic matters, after the military dictatorships of the 1970s and 1980s. De la Rúa tried to censure the media and negotiate with the Peronists, but ultimately he was forced to flee the Casa Rosada by helicopter as the police struggled to hold off protestors. Five people died in Plaza de Mayo during those chaotic scenes on December 20, with a further 21 deaths across the country.

Adolfo Rodríguez Saá was placed into the vacant post (after two days under interim president Ramón Puerta) by Peronist governors. He immediately declared extreme economic adjustments, such as defaulting on foreign debt payments and introducing a third currency to the country. Although popular at first, he rapidly lost the support of the nation and the Peronists, abandoning the presidency on December 30, a mere seven days after taking office.

After three days under another interim president (Eduardo Camaño), Eduardo Duhalde was handed the position, becoming the fifth to bear it in just 12 days. He made withdrawal restrictions even more severe while also removing the fixed exchange rate. The value of the peso crashed. Middle-class families were thrown into poverty overnight, while industrialists came out none the worse for wear.

Despite the claims of corruption and cronyism, Duhalde lasted almost a year and a half as president. Former president Carlos Menem won the April 2003 election but with an insufficient lead to avoid a runoff ballot against newcomer Nestor Kirchner, which he decided to bow out of. President Kirchner continued Duhalde's basic economic plan at first. Hostile relations with the IMF ensured that international investors stayed clear of the country.

Such policies were emblematic of the patriotic populism that both Kirchner and his wife, Cristina Fernández de Kirchner, resorted to when serving as presidents. Championing the poor and the victimized, public spending and government infrastructure ballooned, helped at first by favorable international economic conditions but ultimately doomed to collapse as on so many other occasions in Argentine history.

EMPLOYMENT

After enjoying a low of 6 percent at the start of the 1990s, levels of unemployment exploded during the crisis, reaching a high of around 22 percent. There has been a downward trend ever since, with official statistics claiming it currently lies around 7 percent, although many independent observers believe it to be closer to 10 percent. As a result of decades of economic mismanagement, it's common in Argentina for employees to work *en negro* (off the books), which makes any kind of statistic on this topic dubious, given that such workers do not generally appear on tax records or other official databases.

The minimum wage in Argentina (around US$500 as of June 2016) is a monthly minimum that employers are obliged to pay, although such measures are hard to enforce when employees work *en negro* (off the books). Various sectors have their own minimum levels, and unions regularly arrange strikes across the country.

AGRICULTURE

Given the size of the country, its general flatness, favorable weather conditions, and rich soil, agriculture has always been important to Argentina. Creating around 10 percent of the overall GDP while employing 7 percent of the nation's workforce, agriculture draws in tens of billions of U.S. dollars per year.

The industry is in decline, with cattle producers turning to crop production. Industrial farming has increasingly been knocking smaller farms out of business and there are constant conflicts with large agrochemical companies such as Monsanto and the greater freedom that they have in using chemicals and techniques that are prohibited in the rest of the world.

INDUSTRY

Manufacturing is by far the greatest contributor to GDP (around 15 percent), although around half of the country's industrial exports are agricultural in nature. Motor vehicles and parts, petroleum and biofuels, pharmaceuticals, various metals, electronics, and home appliances are the main sectors, although many of the larger companies are Argentine branches of multinational organizations.

Recent governments, in a bid to stymie the decline in national industrial production, effectively banned the import of most goods in the hope that such measures would encourage local production. The results were largely negative and unproductive, and the measures are in the process of being reversed. Half of the industrial centers are to be found in Greater Buenos Aires, while the remainder are spread out mainly between Córdoba, Rosario, and Ushuaia.

TOURISM

Often considered a gateway to South America thanks to both its southern location and its great connections to North America and Europe, Buenos Aires is a regular starting point for travelers who plan to roam the continent. Just as often, it draws visitors who simply want to visit Argentina or the city itself. Receiving a far greater percentage of these travelers than the country's other provinces, Buenos Aires has always valued tourism for its importance to the city's economy.

Argentines themselves count for around 80 percent of the total tourists, but around five million foreigners also arrive per year, 30 percent from Brazil, 20 percent from Europe, and 10 percent from the United States and Canada. Although the vast majority arrive by air (48 percent) or land (40 percent), an increasing number arrive by cruise liners.

Local Culture

In a country of 40 million people, approximately 16 million live in Greater Buenos Aires, of whom 2.9 million live in the city itself. When Argentina started to encourage immigration in the mid-19th century, waves of people arrived in the city, with the majority coming from Europe, the Middle East, Russia, and Japan. The last few decades have seen a dramatic influx of Chinese immigrants as well. Today, the majority of *porteños* have European heritage, mostly Italian and Spanish. While there are still a small number of indigenous and *criollo* (of European descent, but born in South America) families in Buenos Aires, a greater number reside in more rural settings and smaller cities. The city has also always served as a magnet for citizens of surrounding countries, especially Bolivia, Paraguay, and Peru.

Certain neighborhoods attract more intense gatherings of nationalities, such as Peruvians in Congreso, Koreans in Flores, and Bolivians in

Liniers, where restaurants and supermarkets specialize in the respective nation's food. Europeans and North Americans tend to live in the central neighborhoods.

While ethnic conflict and racism are not as serious a problem as in other parts of the world, there are some ingrained sayings that are derogative. Citizens from neighboring countries, especially Bolivia and Paraguay often find their nation's name being used to describe something negatively, for example. Black people are habitually referred to as *negros,* but this Spanish word for black is considered as inoffensive as the standard nickname for anyone slightly overweight (*gordo,* meaning "fatty").

LANGUAGE

Spanish has been the national language since the country was officially founded, but it differs in some ways from Castilian Spanish (*castellano*), the *voseo* being the best-known example, with *vos* used instead of *tú* to mean "you." A study by the University of Toronto suggested that the *porteño* accent most closely resembles that of the accent in Naples, Italy, as opposed to any Spanish-speaking region. Indeed, Spanish here is spoken in a very Italian manner, with a lot of hand gesticulation and exaggerated flows of speech.

English is widely spoken and increasingly more so, especially in the center of Buenos Aires. Anyone working in the tourist industry can be expected to be passably fluent.

Lunfardo is a slang that was born around the turn of the 19th century in the criminal and working classes of Buenos Aires and later came to be accepted by all strata of society thanks to its regular use in tango. Many words have been adopted in the daily lexicon, such as *guita* (money), *pibe* (boy), and *laburar* (work). Some words are simple rearrangements of the correct word (e.g. *zapi* for "pizza"). Lunfardo words are generally considered to be crude and unsophisticated, but their widespread use and acceptance has survived for decades.

Religion

Argentine law guarantees freedom of worship, expression and speech, so the government does not meddle in the religious affairs of its citizens. Within the country's history of demographic diversity and tolerance, the various religions exist in almost total harmony.

CHRISTIANITY

Despite being constitutionally bound to financially support the Catholic Church, there's no obligation to follow the faith. However, Roman Catholicism is the official and most widespread religion, with an overwhelming 70 percent of the population claiming to be followers. Although the world was caught off guard when Jorge Mario Bergoglio, the Archbishop of Buenos Aires, was elected as the 266th Pope in 2013, the sheer dominance of Catholicism in Argentina suggested that it was a more than reasonable choice.

Approximately 15 percent of Argentines are Protestants, making

Christianity far and away the dominant faith. The next largest denomination would be those who claim to have no religion (including atheists and agnostics).

JUDAISM

Despite Argentina notoriously accommodating some of the highest-profile Nazi leaders at the end of World War II, the Jewish population in Buenos Aires has always been one of the highest in the world outside of the Middle East, with the country's total Jewish population adding up to some 400,000 people. Once and Abasto are the traditional Jewish neighborhoods, with numerous kosher supermarkets, synagogues, schools, and community centers. Abasto shopping center is also home to the only kosher McDonald's outside Israel, which picks up some lengthy queues on Saturday evenings after the end of the Sabbath. The oldest and most central synagogue is the Templo Libertad (Libertad 769, tel. 011/4123-0833, www.templolibertad. org.ar), which lies just a block away from Teatro Colón. Gran Templo Paso (Paso 423, tel. 011/4951-2306, www.grantemplopaso.org.ar), in the heart of Once, holds most importance in the local community.

ISLAM

The Muslim community remains somewhat of an enigma in Argentina, as despite the population of 500,000 to 700,000 Muslims, there is little evidence of Islam anywhere in Buenos Aires, where a quarter of the adherents reside. Indeed, there are Sunni, Shiite, Alawite, and Sufi Muslims, as well as other denominations. What is unusual compared to many parts of the Muslim world is that all these distinct communities live in complete harmony and tolerance.

There are three mosques in Capital Federal, and although they all have differing religious affiliations, all Muslims are welcome at each of the three. The largest, by far, is the Rey Fahd mosque (Av. Bullrich 55, tel. 011/4899-1144, www.ccislamicorey-fahd.org.ar), which can be found in Palermo. The Al-Ahmad mosque (Alberti 1541, www.islam.com.ar) in San Cristóbal is the most popular. The third, Al-Tauhid mosque (Felipe Vallese 3614, tel. 11/4672-7440, www.organizacionislam.org.ar), is in Floresta, a fair way out of the city center. Inquire at any of these mosques for the best way to obtain halal food.

OTHER RELIGIONS

Many other religions are practiced in Buenos Aires, although on a smaller scale than those previously mentioned. The worship of certain saints can be quite intense in certain localities and regions of the country. There are also some unconventional cults that stem from traditional folklore, such as Ceferino Namuncurá, a revered figure to the Machupe people, who received recognition from the Vatican. Gauchito Gil was an anti-establishment hero, akin to Robin Hood, who has shrines dedicated to him all around the country.

The Arts

With the Argentine population consisting of such a diverse mix of immigrants from all over the world and indigenous populations of very different types, it's unsurprising that different genres and styles of art have been fused to create authentic new ones. In Buenos Aires, the passion and talent of Argentine artists is evidenced all around, with street-art murals, artisans peddling their wares, and concerts being held in public spaces.

LITERATURE

Often described as the city with the most bookshops in the world, Buenos Aires has always held a deep passion for literature, both fiction and poetry. Spanish translations are available for locals of a wide variety of international writers, while many local writers have found their work translated into a multitude of other languages.

Although there are a number of bookstores that specialize in English books, nearly all have an English section. Secondhand books are available, but they are not sold for as low a price as is usual in other parts of the world. The annual book fair is huge and always pulls in some big international names to give talks.

Gauchesco literature (writings based on gaucho culture) was the first great wave of Argentine literature, with notable contributions from writers such as Bartolomé Hidalgo and Rafael Obligado, culminating in what is considered one of the country's finest and most important pieces of work, "Martín Fierro" by José Hernández, an epic poem (of 2,316 lines!) published in two parts during the 1870s that consolidated the gaucho tradition and embedded it in the nation's history.

This romanticism was replaced with realism, Domingo Faustino Sarmiento being one of many writers keen to repaint the importance of Buenos Aires and economic liberal development. Social issues have been present in writings throughout the country's history, and never was this more evident than in the stark differences between the writings of the rural Federalists and the liberal Unitarians. Ricardo Güiraldes, Miguel Cané, Almafuerte, Eugenio Cambaceres, and Benito Lynch were some of the biggest names of the following era, with Leopoldo Lugones writing what was the first Argentine foray into science fiction.

This all led to the arrival of the country's most renowned writer, Jorge Luis Borges, whose short stories, poems, and essays won him international acclaim (although, as was the case with all fellow Argentine writers, he was never bestowed with a Nobel prize for literature). His perspective of the world was presented through metaphor and philosophical debate, with the lyricism of his work fascinating readers to this day. Others, such as Oliverio Girondo, Leopoldo Marechal, and César Tiempo wrote in varying styles but also showed a predilection toward philosophical musing. Notable poets of the time were Ricardo Molinari, Olga Orozco, and Vicente Barieri, while Julio Cortázar, Silvina Ocampo, and María Granata took fiction toward idealism and the magic realism that was sweeping the continent at the time.

Some of the more appreciated writers of the second half of the 1900s and beginning of the 21st century include Silvina Bullrich, David Viñas, Alejandra Pizarnik, Manuel Puig, and Osvaldo Soriano. Many authors suffered during the cultural repression during the military dictatorships of the 1970s and 1980s, with many going into exile, such as Juan Gelman, and others being killed, such as Rodolfo Walsh. Modern writers continue to capture the attention of readers today, having reinvigorated a burgeoning scene in Buenos Aires, with writers such as Alan Pauls, Aníbal Cristobo, and Edgar Brau leading the way.

VISUAL ARTS

Artistic production in Argentina, both in painting and sculpture, did not really take off until after the heavy-handed ruling of Juan Manuel de Rosas ended in the mid-19th century, when artistic institutions began to be organized and exhibitions promoted. The resulting great wave of immigrants that arrived from Europe included painters such as Eduardo Schiaffino, Ernesto de la Cárcova, Eduardo Sívori, and Emilio Caraffa, who all painted in a mixture of realism and distinctive symbolism, with social issues being represented as much as the traditional landscapes and portraits. Benito Quinquela Martín helped introduce muralism in the early 20th century, a style that has been hugely influential on Argentine society to this day, while other artists such as Antonio Berni, Lino Spilimbergo, and Juan Carlo Castagnino developed a scene that is exemplified in the exceptional fresco on the Galerías Pacífico ceiling. Sculptors also rose in popularity in the early 20th century, largely thanks to the polemic works by Lola Mora, a student of Auguste Rodin, the French maestro. Rogelio Yrurtia, Erminio Blotta, and Ángel María de Rosa are some of the finest exponents of this genre. The more modern era has seen numerous painters, such as Xul Solar, Emilio Pettoruti, Raúl Soldi, and Leon Ferrari, excel in their genres.

The art museums and galleries of Buenos Aires are hugely varied and of excellent quality. Vast and comprehensive collections sit alongside small eclectic ones, and the city has never held back from exhibiting controversial pieces. Murals can be observed citywide, while *filete*, a flamboyant and colorful form of calligraphy, is also present across Buenos Aires. Annual festivals allow upcoming artists to display their work, while international artists regularly have their art shown in many of the city's spaces.

MUSIC

Argentina is associated worldwide with tango, an emotional, musically intricate genre that originated in Buenos Aires. Indeed, it is almost exclusively a *porteño* scene, with *milongas* (tango dance events) and tango concerts far rarer in other Argentine cities, but this is countered by a countrywide passion for other local music, such as folk and rock.

International acts regularly pass through Buenos Aires, but ticket prices are high. Festivals are held regularly, with jazz, classical, rock, and folk musicians descending on the city for days of concentrated enjoyment of their genre. Many such events are free and held in outdoor venues across the city.

CLASSICAL MUSIC

Home to the Orquesta Filarmónica de Buenos Aires, Teatro Colón has for many years been regarded as one of the finest and most important concert halls in Latin America and indeed the world. However, aside from the rich heritage and ongoing productions at Teatro Colón, there is less on offer than one would expect from such a cultured city, although some of the theaters and cultural centers in the city center stage concerts on a sporadic basis. The Orquesta Sinfónica Nacional has historically suffered from not having an official home to play in, but in 2015 they adopted the newly opened Centro Cultural Kirchner as their base.

Due to historically being the hub of the classical music scene in Argentina, Buenos Aires has produced most of the nation's most prominent composers, such as Juan José Castro, Alberto Williams, and Alberto Ginastera, many of whom suffered during the Juan Domingo Perón presidency and succeeding military dictatorships. Perhaps the most well-known Argentine performer of modern times is Martha Argerich, a flamboyant pianist who resides in Europe but returns to Buenos Aires most years to give wildly popular performances in her city of birth, often alongside Daniel Barenboim, another renowned pianist who also composes and conducts. José Cura, proud owner of one of the world's best tenor voices, is the best-known operatic performer, while prominent ballet dancers, such as Julio Bocca, perform regularly.

JAZZ

There aren't too many jazz venues around Buenos Aires, although the ones that do exist draw a passionate and knowledgeable crowd. In recent years, Thelonious and Notorious have been the two that draw the largest names, including endless international performers. The annual Buenos Aires Jazz, which has been put on by the city government since 2002, is also growing in stature and acclaim.

Many consider Ástor Piazzolla, a tango composer who fused tango with classical and jazz music, to be one of the central figures of the national movement. Indeed, Argentine jazz is notable for its willingness to incorporate aesthetics from other genres, including rock and, more recently, electronic music. Perhaps the country's best-known jazz musician was the late Leandro "Gato" Barbieri, a tenor saxophonist who exploded onto the international scene during the free jazz movement of the 1960s.

TANGO

Tango can be enjoyed in multiple forms in Buenos Aires. The most traditional and authentic place is at a *milonga,* a dance event steeped in tradition and held in dozens of bars, clubs, and venues across the city every night, where the public come to dance or merely sit and watch others take to the floor. A more traditional way is to attend one of the many *tanguerías,* where musicians play to rapt audiences without any dancing. Another way is via tango shows, which involve flamboyant dancers performing on stage, often in front of a live orchestra. The annual Tango Buenos Aires Festival y Mundial, which includes world dancing championships, draws thousands of passionate followers from across the world.

Tango originated in the working-class, immigrant neighborhoods of Buenos Aires and came about as a fusion of diverse musical genres from all over Europe, South America, and

Tango can be found as much on the street as behind closed doors.

even Africa from the mid-19th century onward. Originally a sordid scene frequented by the more violent sectors of society, by the 1920s and 1930s it had achieved recognition worldwide, notably in France, which led to it becoming more widely accepted. Legendary figures, such as Carlos Gardel and Francisco Canaro, brought their own interpretations and passions to the scene, moving it from being dance-oriented music to more an exposition of poetry and lyrics. The so-called golden age of tango, roughly coinciding with the U.S. jazz and swing golden age, was between 1930 and 1950, when *orquestas típicas,* often composed of over a dozen musicians, were led by figureheads such as Juan d'Arienzo, Aníbal Troilo, and Osvaldo Pugliese. After this, in an age largely dominated by Ástor Piazzolla, tango began to fuse with more mainstream genres, notably classical music and jazz, and in the last couple of decades, it was inevitably fused with electronic music, most successfully by groups such as Gotan Project and Bajofondo.

FOLK

From the very early days of the Spanish arrival in Argentina, European music was adopted and mixed with various other regional styles to produce eclectically different folk scenes across the country. While Buenos Aires has over the years been more associated with tango and rock, the rest of the country has developed its own hugely popular genres. *Chamamé* and *chacarera* are the two most widely played, both from the northern provinces of Argentina. Other forms are *charango, sobrepaso, malambo, cueca, contrapunto,* and *loncomeo.* Each has its own collection of instruments and specific dance and many are influenced by neighboring countries and indigenous traditions. Some of the most prolific folk musicians are Mercedes Sosa, Atahualpa Yupanqui, and León Gieco. Although the genre is more common outside of Buenos Aires, there are plenty of *peñas folklóricas* in the capital, where both music and dancing can be witnessed, as well as the Feria de Mataderos, a weekly market in the south of the city that has a gaucho culture and where musicians and dancers take to the street.

ROCK AND POP

Argentine rock gained traction in the 1970s, with artists such as Almendra and Los Gatos leading the way, followed by others that remain popular to this day, such as Soda Stereo and Charly García. The military dictatorships that cracked down on cultural activities in the late 1970s and 1980s brought a new style of music, *rock nacional,* which represented a form of urban resistance. Bands such as Sumo, Viejas Locas, Patricio Rey y sus Redonditos de Ricota, Flema, and Intoxicados were some of the most popular bands during this time.

Other well-known bands that emerged over the coming years, when rock started to give way to *cumbia* in popularity, are Almafuerte, Indio Solari, Andrés Calamaro, Callejeros, Turf, Bersuit Vergarabat, and Babasonicos. Influential musicians from throughout this time that have achieved huge followings among the Argentine populace are Charly García, Gustavo Cerati, Luis Alberto Spinetta, Andrés Calamaro, Indio Solari, Fito Paéz, Litto Nebia, and Luca Prodan.

an outdoor screening at a film festival

CUMBIA

Traditionally from the Caribbean coast of Colombia, *cumbia* became wildly popular in Argentina in the second half of the 20th century, especially during the 1990s, and is now the genre most listened to by young people. Bands generally play synthesizer keyboards and electronic sounds accompanied by percussion, voice, and any range of other instruments, such as guitar and trumpet, with a rhythm that is perfectly suited to dancing.

ELECTRONICA

There are some huge dance clubs in Buenos Aires that pump out electronic music to delirious crowds on a nightly basis, while large festivals, such as Creamfields BA, draw the biggest international names on the circuit. A number of drug-related deaths at high profile raves in 2016 led to the temporary closure of all nightclub venues until new drug laws were put in place, which increased awareness among the population regarding the scene. Most of the clubs have since reopened.

As with so much of Argentine music, the most internationally renowned of the country's electronic musicians emerged by fusing the genre with others, such as Gotan Project, who mix tango into their tracks, Juana Molina, with her folk-electronica, and rock legend Gustavo Cerati. More orthodox proponents, such as Hernán Cattáneo, Bad Boy Orange, and Diego Ro-K have all achieved a significant following outside Argentina.

CINEMA

The film industry in Argentina has arguably never been stronger than its current position, with students coming from across Latin America and the rest of the world to study at its prestigious film universities. The industry has historically received excellent state support. Local screens regularly sell out, and whenever one of the more renowned local directors releases a new film, hysteria surrounds the scene for a few weeks. Most international films are screened in their original language, but check the schedule before purchasing a ticket (*"Castellano"* means it will be dubbed in Spanish, while *"Subtitulos"* means that it will be the original language with Spanish subtitles). The exception to this rule is animated films, which are almost always dubbed.

The world's first animated film was created in Argentina in 1917, although live-action films had been produced in the country before this. In its early days, Argentine history and literature provided the themes for much of the output, with focus split between life in Buenos Aires and the gaucho culture. Toward the end of the 1920s, tango dancing, which was emerging from the working-class neighborhoods of Buenos Aires to a level of widespread popularity, began to appear in some films. Once sound began to be used, the use of tango music exploded, and the first Argentine film studios, Argentina Sono Film and Lumitón, were founded.

The 1930s to the 1950s are regarded as the golden age of Argentine cinema (coinciding, not incidentally, with the golden age of tango), when an average of 42 films were produced each year. José Ferreyra, Julio Irigoyen, Luis Maglia Barth, and Manuel Romero were some of the more influential directors of the time, and a lot of emphasis was put on the nobility of hard work and poverty, while political influence and agendas became staple. Indeed, president Juan Domingo Perón took advantage of the medium to promote his ideals and build support by attacking greed and promoting the working class.

From the late 1940s, a combination of political repression (including the exile of prominent directors and actors), religious censorship, and the rise of the U.S. film industry saw a waning in the movement, although the popularity of viewing films, albeit more international in origin, never wavered. A large proportion of the productions at this time continued to focus on local social and political issues. By the 1960s, comedy had taken a foothold, and slapstick was common. Some of the most popular directors of this time were Armando Bo, Leopoldo Torre Nilsson, Fernando "Pino" Solanas, and Jorge Porcel. The 1980s saw films

become heavily critical of society's excesses, be it with power, money, or prestige, with a notable decline in the use of humor. Once the country began to come to terms with what had occurred during the military repression, the subject became the theme of countless films and understandably dominated for the following decades.

Juan José Campanella, Damián Szifron, Santiago Mitre, and Pablo Trapero are some of the biggest names currently in Argentina cinema, with their films coming out to avid popularity among local audiences.

HANDICRAFTS

Argentine artisans specialize in leather and silver, both of which have been in great abundance throughout the country's history. Such craftsmen tend to be found in the vast countryside or smaller towns surrounding Buenos Aires, but their merchandise is easy to find in specialty stores and markets across the city.

Other artisans sell a wide variety of hand-crafted jewelry and clothing of all shapes, sizes, and colors as well as toys, accessories, and much more, with their products available at any of the artisanal markets that are held every weekend; two of the largest are the Feria Plaza Francia and the Feria de San Pedro Telmo.

ARCHITECTURE

The architecture of Buenos Aires is both stunning and confounding, with beautiful, ornate buildings sitting alongside inexplicably turgid constructions. Very little remains of the original colonial structures, although parts of the city center are clear examples of such times. The almost simplistic baroque style that is present in notable buildings such as the Casa

Rosada, Catedral Metropolitana, and Iglesia Nuestra Señora del Pilar began to be replaced in the 19th century by the elegant French and Italian styles brought over during periods of heavy European immigration, with whole neighborhoods, such as Retiro and Recoleta, filled with such buildings. The 20th century saw periodic popularity of brutalist, art deco, and futurist architecture, but their influences were limited to sporadic buildings, such as the Biblioteca Nacional.

CUISINE

The most popular dish in Argentina is the *asado*, a form of barbecue that involves multiple cuts of meat and a process of preparation and consumption that is filled with etiquette and tradition. Since Argentina is the world's greatest beef consumer, it's unsurprising that meat dominates Buenos Aires's restaurant scene.

Local specialities in Buenos Aires, unlike the rest of Argentina, are based on recipes brought over from foreign countries by immigrants, although many of them have since been adapted by Argentine chefs and cooks. These include the Genoan style of pizza, stuffed pastas, and *milanesas* (similar to schnitzel). The *porteño* cuisine is generally more sophisticated and cosmopolitan than Argentine cuisine.

The influence of the city's immigrant population, especially Italians, is heavy. Traditional *porteño* pizzas are deep-dish with huge portions of cheese on top. Ice cream is also very popular, with *heladerías* (ice cream parlors) staying open late into the night and offering an overwhelming selection of flavors.

Indigenous and *criollo* dishes, such as *locro* (a stewed mix of beans, corn, and various meats) and tamales are much more common in other parts of the country and remain relatively rare in Buenos Aires, although regional Argentine restaurants do serve them. More common local dishes are empanadas (stuffed pastries), *facturas* (Viennese-style sweet pastries), *dulce de leche* (a caramel spread), and *alfajores* (sandwich-style cookies filled with *dulce de leche* and encased in chocolate).

BEEF

Meat is usually cooked to well-done in Argentina, as fewer preservatives are added in the production process, given the speed at which it is consumed. While eating rare meat isn't implicitly dangerous, it is not particularly common for locals and is therefore necessary to ask. The levels of cooking are *bien cocido* (well done), *a punto* (medium), *jugoso* (medium rare), and *vuelta y vuelta* or *sangrante* (rare). The following are the most common cuts and all are worth trying. Sharing various cuts among the table is common:

- *Bife de Chorizo* (sirloin rump): The Argentine classic comes with a hefty piece of creamy fat along one side and more flavor than a spice rack.
- *Lomo* (tenderloin): This meat shouldn't have any fat and is the silkiest to cut through. The mild taste means it often comes with a sauce.
- *Vacío* (flank): Cows elsewhere in the world rarely offer up this juicy cut that comes sandwiched between two layers of chewy fat, which is usually cut off on the plate and discarded.
- *Tira de asado* (cross-cut ribs): Up to a meter long before serving, this cut contains bones (often sucked clean by locals) and a fair amount

of fat, all of which lend a strong flavor and make it the most popular for *asados*.

- *Cuadril* (rump): A cross between *lomo* and *bife de chorizo*, this cut is full of flavor and has an easy-to-remove piece of fat on the side.
- *Entraña* (skirt): A highly prized cut, this is exceedingly rich and juicy if skillfully cooked, with next to no fat.
- *Matambre* (thin flank): Either beef or pork, this cut is thin and should contain little or no fat. *Matambre a la pizza* is a common dish and is basically a pizza with a slab of *matambre* instead of a bread base.

Parrillas (steak houses) also include a section of the menu with items that are generally eaten as starters to be shared among the table. The most common of these are *chorizos* (sausages) and *morcillas* (blood sausages). After this come the *achuras* (offal), such as *chinchulines* (lower intestines), *mollejas* (sweetbreads), *higado* (liver), and *riñones* (kidneys). While these may sound unappetizing to those who are not accustomed to eating such parts, Argentines have been eating offal for centuries and often consider them to be the best part of the meal. Wait to order meat dishes after receiving the starter dishes. It's also worth asking for *chinchulines* and *mollejas* to be *bien cocido* (well cooked) and to season them with lemon and salt before eating. Most *parrillas* offer a *parrillada*, which is a shareable platter of a variety of cuts, usually including offal. *Parrillas* all have *pollo* (chicken) on the menu, as well as certain cuts of pork, such as *bondiola* (pork shoulder). *Provoleta* is a hard cheese that is put on the grill briefly and served molten hot. Typical sides are *papas* (fries), *pure de papa* (mashed potato), and *ensalada* (salad), which must usually be ordered separately.

MATÉ

Maté is the national drink. The drink consists of an infusion of dried leaves from the yerba maté plant. The drink originated in the Guaraní region, which occupies northeast Argentina, Paraguay, and the south of Brazil—and is the same area in which yerba maté is grown today. In the 16th century, swashbuckling Spanish colonizers took the drink with them down to the Río de la Plata region (today Uruguay and the surrounding Buenos Aires area), from where it rapidly spread across the country.

Drinking maté is steeped in tradition, although methods of preparing the drink differ. It is drunk from a gourd, also called a *mate*, which is traditionally made from dried butternut squash skins. The most important piece of equipment is the *bombilla*, a metal straw that filters the drink. The gourd is filled with yerba leaves, and the *bombilla* is placed firmly among them. Hot water is then added and the drink is ready, without much need for infusion.

The maté ritual is controlled by the *cebador*, who fills the gourd with water from a thermos or kettle before passing it to the first person. Once this person has drunk all the water, he or she returns the gourd to the *cebador*, who refills it and passes it to the next person. It is customary not to thank the *cebador* until you have had enough, upon which the gourd is returned with a polite *"gracias,"* signifying to the *cebador* that you can be omitted in subsequent rounds. It's considered bad form to move the *bombilla* around, as it disturbs the yerba leaves.

A common addition is sugar, which

is added by the *cebador*. Other additions like orange, grapefruit, mint, and spices are sometimes added to the infusion ahead of time. In summer, maté may be consumed cold. This is known as *tereré* and is more common in Paraguay and Brazil. *Mate cocido* is a weaker version of the drink in tea-bag form.

In plazas and parks, people of all ages sip maté at any time of day. Although it's the most common hot drink in Argentina, maté hardly ever appears on restaurant menus. When it does, the ritual never reaches traditional levels. Cheap *mate listo* kits are available in kiosks and gas stations for a few dollars and include a small polystyrene thermos, a *mate*, a *bombilla*, and a bag of yerba. Most bars or restaurants will fill the thermos with hot water for free, although some may charge a couple of pesos.

COFFEE AND TEA

Argentina is not a coffee-producing country, and yet coffee is drunk in vast quantities, at all times of the day. Old traditional cafés can be found all over the city, many of which are given special historic status by the government (referred to in this guide as *bares notables*), while international chains are becoming increasingly widespread.

Common options to choose from are *café solo* (single shot of espresso), *café doble* (double espresso), *café con leche* (latte), and *cortado* (equal amounts of espresso and milk).

Tea is generally drunk without milk, although a small jug should be served alongside. *Submarino* and *leche con chocolate* are both types of hot chocolate; the former is made with a bar of chocolate melting in hot milk while the latter is a blander, powder-based version.

WINE

Argentina is one of the world's top wine-producing countries, and much of the product is consumed domestically. Indeed, so great and appreciated is the production, it can be difficult to find wines from outside Argentina. Mainly based in the west and northwest regions of the country, the vast vineyards tend to use malbec or cabernet sauvignon grapes for *tinto* (red) and torrentés grapes for *blanco* (white). Many restaurants offer *vino de la casa*, which tends to be a cheap wine served in a jug, often in the shape of a penguin. It is not uncommon in Argentina to mix red wine with soda water or ice, a respectable way to improve the drinkability of lower-quality wines.

ESSENTIALS

Getting There

Subte station on Plaza de Mayo

Most visitors arrive in Buenos Aires via the international airport, Ezeiza, although for those coming from neighboring countries, buses tend to be the mode of choice. Ferries plow over the Río de la Plata from Uruguay, while only a few trains go in and out of the city, none of which arrive from outside Argentina.

AIR

Buenos Aires has two airports: Ministro Pizarini (EZE, Km. 33.5 Autopista Ricchieri, www.aa2000. com.ar), more commonly known as Ezeiza, and Aeroparque Jorge Newbery (AEP, Av. Costanera Rafael Obligado, www.aa2000.com.ar). Ezeiza is about 30 kilometers southwest of the city center, while Aeroparque sits snugly on the coast a few minutes from downtown. Most international flights land in Ezeiza, but travelers with a layover in Brazil often find themselves dropping into the city via the more convenient Aeroparque.

Only some airlines have representatives in the airports (more so in Ezeiza than Aeroparque), so if there's a problem with your return flight, go to the airline's office in town. Check the airline website for the office location.

GETTING TO THE CITY CENTER FROM EZEIZA AIRPORT

Ezeiza is relatively poorly connected to the city center, and all the available options have inflated prices. If you're traveling alone, a public bus or shuttle bus is the most economical way to reach the center. For groups of two or more, a taxi may be just as cheap or cheaper. No trains reach the airport, although a few car rental agencies are present.

Bus

Public bus 8 rolls through the suburbs and into the city center (Almagro, Balvanera, and Centro) in an epic two-hour trip. Costing less than US$0.50, it's by far the cheapest option and the favored choice of backpackers. Passengers need to pay either with a Sube transit card or coins—neither of which recent arrivals tend to have. Your best bet is to ask another passenger to pay for you with their own Sube card, in exchange for the equivalent amount in peso notes. The bus leaves approximately every 20 minutes during the day and hourly at night.

The bus stop can be reached by walking past Terminal B and following the road for 100 meters. Allow three hours if you're taking bus 8 back to the airport, which is the last stop on the line.

Shuttle

Shuttle bus company Manuel Tienda León (www.tiendaleon.com) charges US$12 for a ride from the airport to the company's station (Av. Eduardo Madero 1299) in Retiro, which takes approximately 50 minutes. Leaving from the entrance to terminal B, shuttles depart every half hour and run all night (although with less frequency at later hours).

Taxi

Taking a taxi is the most popular and efficient way to reach the city center. As soon as passengers leave the terminal they will find themselves faced by taxi drivers touting their services. While taking a lift from one of these drivers isn't hazardous, they are known to overcharge. It's better to approach the taxi stand outside the Arrivals terminal and arrange a car through the agent there. The trip should cost around US$25 and is a set price. Sometimes the driver will try to add a few dollars for the toll charges, so it's worth coming to an agreement before setting off.

Remis

A number of private companies offer *remises,* which are more spacious and well-maintained than taxis—the equivalent of a town car service in the United Sates. TaxiEzeiza (www.taxiezeiza.com.ar), Traslada (www.traslada.com.ar), and Go Airport Taxi (www.goairporttaxi.com.ar) are three options for taking a *remis*. Fares vary, but are generally a little more expensive than a taxi. Many companies offer deals, such as a half-price return journey to the airport at the end of your stay. Some can be booked in advance online and paid for in U.S. dollars.

GETTING TO THE CITY CENTER FROM AEROPARQUE JORGE NEWBERY

If you are fortunate enough to have a flight landing at Jorge Newbery, getting into town will be easy. No trains stop here. A few car rental agencies have offices in this airport.

FLIGHT-BOOKING TIPS AND DEALS

Most major international airlines introduce offers for flights to Buenos Aires at some point during the year, some of them quite extraordinary. To ensure the best deal, plan as far ahead in advance as possible. Don't rely exclusively on flight search engines or agencies such as Expedia or Kayak. Sometimes, the best deals can be found directly on the airline's website. Many third-party agencies also place severe restrictions on changes to the return flight or any other modifications.

The Argentine propensity to travel to Miami means that often many of the best deals originate from this city. Likewise, when traveling from Europe, flights from Spain are generally substantially cheaper than from other European countries. If you're coming from Europe, look into taking a budget flight to Spain before taking the transatlantic flight.

Bus

A number of public buses stop in front of the terminal, including **bus 33** (Retiro, Centro, Puerto Madero, San Telmo, and La Boca), **bus 37** (Palermo, Recoleta, and Balvanera), and **bus 160** (Palermo and Almagro). The fare is about US$0.50 and the trip takes 20-45 minutes.

If you're taking the bus to the airport at the end of your trip, check with the driver that it does actually stop there. Some lines have multiple routes, not all of which include the airport.

Taxi

A taxi stand can be found in front of the terminal. A taxi to the city center costs around US$8, and takes 10-30 minutes. There is usually someone who opens the taxi door and stows your luggage, for which he or she will expect some small change. If taking a taxi to Aeroparque at the end of your trip, ensure that the driver understands that you do not want to go to Ezeiza, the more common international airport.

The same *remis* services mentioned for Ezeiza also operate from Aeroparque.

TRAVELING BETWEEN AIRPORTS

Some passengers passing through Buenos Aires will arrive at one of the airports and have a connecting flight leave from the other. This is common when taking an ongoing domestic flight (to Ushuaia, for example).

Arbus offers a bus service every 90 minutes between the two airports (75 minutes, US$10). **Manuel Tienda León** does the same for US$13, but with greater frequency—every 30 minutes from 5am to 9pm, every 45 minutes from 9pm to midnight, and every hour from midnight to 5am.

A **taxi** costs around US$20 and takes 75 minutes to travel from one airport to the other. The same *remis* services mentioned for Ezeiza also operate between the two airports.

BUS

Argentine buses are of high quality, and are by far the most extensive form of long-distance public transportation both inside Argentina and connecting the country with neighboring nations. They are double-decker vehicles that usually come with televisions and meals included in the fares (although the quality of the food can vary wildly). There are two basic choices: *semi-cama* and *cama* (sometimes referred to as *cama ejecutivo*). The main difference between the two is that *cama* seats recline to almost horizontal, whereas *semi-cama* only recline about halfway. While Argentine buses are of an excellent standard, some of the services from other countries, such as Colombia, are not nearly as comfortable or efficient. Ticket prices are fixed, so booking two months in advance will cost the same as five minutes before departure.

Choosing which company to travel with can be confusing, as the main bus terminal in Retiro has almost 250 individual ticket offices to choose from. Although these are roughly separated by destination, it's usually necessary to comparison shop among several companies to find a trip that fits your budget and schedule. Some of the larger companies that also offer online booking are Nueva Chevalier (ticket office 67, www.nuevachevalier.com), Andesmar (ticket office 27, www.andesmar.com), and El Rápido Argentino (ticket office 1, www.rapido-argentino.com). Companies often share services, so buying a ticket through one company may mean traveling on a route operated by a different company. Your ticket indicates which company brand the bus will bear.

There are a couple of websites that allow travelers to sift through the various options, which is generally easier than making a decision at the bus terminal. However, these sites often don't list every service available. Plataforma 10 (www.plataforma10.com) allows you to book online as well as at one of their many outlets across the city. The website for the Retiro bus terminal (www.retiro.com.ar) also takes online reservations as well as listing the ticket office number for each company.

BUS TERMINAL

The sprawling Terminal de Ómnibus de Retiro (tel. 011/4310-0700, www.retiro.com.ar) is located in Retiro. It can be reached either by the C line of

city bus

the Subte or one of numerous bus services. Someone will load and unload your luggage, and they will expect a few pesos' tip each time. Beware of accepting a taxi from any of the touts waiting for disembarking passengers on the platform. Instead, head outside and take one from the taxi stand.

When you enter the terminal, you'll find a small information desk on the left. Staff at this desk offer answers to general inquiries and will refer any specific questions to the respective company's ticket office. The 200-plus ticket offices can be found on the second floor. They are roughly divided by geography, with the international section at the far end. It's worth preparing a list of the companies that serve your destination beforehand by visiting the terminal's website. The ground floor is filled with waiting areas, cafés, restrooms, and a collection of shops. The basement level is for cargo and freight and rarely used by tourists.

TRAIN

Although Argentina's railway system was once the envy of South America, the majority of tracks, tunnels, and bridges that connect the farthest points of the country are no longer functional. A handful of destinations around the country are served by rail through the national railway system, known as SOFSE (Operadora Ferroviaria Sociedad del Estado, www.sofse.gob.ar). Trains are very slow and their seats are uncomfortable. Travel by rail is very affordable, with tickets generally costing less than 10 percent of a bus ride. Given the outstanding value, they regularly sell out weeks or months in advance, making it complicated for international travelers to take advantage of the service. Nonetheless, tickets are sometimes returned close to the date, so it can be worth checking on the *larga distancia* (long distance) section of the SOFSE website. Satélite Ferroviario (www.sateliteferroviario.com) is an unofficial website that provides schedules and prices for all long distance services.

Ticket options on long journeys range from *turista* (cheapest), a glorified bench shared with other travelers, to *camarote* (most expensive), a private cabin with a bed. Shorter journeys offer *primera*, a regular train seat, up to pullman, a slightly more comfortable seat.

CAR OR MOTORCYCLE

Traveling from North America to Buenos Aires by private car or motorcycle means a mammoth journey across many kinds of terrain and numerous borders, the most complicated of which would doubtless be between Panama and Colombia. Once you arrive at the Argentine border (be it from Chile, Bolivia, Paraguay, Brazil, or Uruguay), you'll find no greater complications than on any of the previous crossings.

FERRIES

Regular ferry services run between Argentina and Uruguay, with the shortest trip leaving Colonia on the Uruguayan side. Bear in mind that many "ferries" from Montevideo are actually buses from the Uruguayan capital to Colonia, followed by boats to Buenos Aires.

Buquebus (www.buquebus.com), the company with the most experienced, highest frequency, and biggest boats, operates from the ferry terminal (Av. Antártida Argentina and Av. Córdoba) in Retiro with another ticket office at Avenida Córdoba 879. Seacat Colonia (www.seacatcolonia.com) operates smaller launches that bounce across the waves from the same port, with a ticket office at Avenida Córdoba 772. Colonia Express offers the cheapest voyages, including day trips, but its boats operate from a port (Pedro de Mendoza 330) on the edge of La Boca in the south of the city. All companies offer more crossings during the summer. It's always worth booking in advance to take advantage of discount offers.

CRUISE SHIPS

Cruise ships float through Buenos Aires regularly from December through February. They all deposit their passengers in the Retiro ferry port. Norwegian Cruise Line (www.

ncl.com), Princess Cruises (www.princess.com), MSC Cruises (www.msccruceros.com.ar), and Celebrity Cruises (www.celebritycruises.com) buzz up and down the east coasts of Argentina and Brazil, although a few hardy vessels make it around Tierra del Fuego before shooting back up the Chilean coast. Holland America Line (www.hollandamerica.com) and Crystal Cruises (www.crystalcruises.com) do all that as well as making it all the way down from the United States and other parts of North America. Costa (www.costa-cruise.com) breezes across from Europe and Cunard (www.cunard.com) makes the trip from Australasia. Prices vary depending on the company, time of year, length of trip, and scale of luxury.

Getting Around

Public transportation in Buenos Aires has excellent coverage and is dirt cheap, but the cleanliness and professionalism leave much to be desired. At any time of the day or night it's easy to travel between two locations, although working out the best way can be slightly confusing. Como Llego (www.mapa.buenosaires.gov.ar/comollego), an excellent website provided by the government, allows users to enter their location and destination to find the best way to travel between the two, including by foot, bicycle, public transportation, or car.

Public transit fares are heavily subsidized by the national government, much to the frustration of those who don't live in Buenos Aires. A bus

journey in any other Argentine city costs at least twice the price.

TRANSIT PASSES

Public transportation in Buenos Aires is paid for with a magnetic card called a Sube (www.sube.gob.ar), including the Subte (subway), buses, and overland trains. It is easy to obtain a Sube card from thousands of points across the city, including kioscos (newsstands), Subte stations, and lottery stores. Just present your passport and a US$0.75 fee. The card can then be topped up in Subte stations, kioscos, or other points around the city. It can be used for multiple travelers at once, so it's not necessary for each person in your group to obtain one. Friendly strangers are often happy to pay for your journey with their card in exchange for the fare in cash.

SAFETY ISSUES

On average, buses in Buenos Aires kill at least one pedestrian per week. Approaching an amber traffic light, they often speed up, toot their horn in warning, and then sail through the red light. Sometimes drivers will stick an arm out of the window telling cars behind to stop and let the bus pull out.

Cars rarely give way to pedestrians, so never step into the road without making sure it's clear. When disembarking from a bus, beware of passing bicycles or motorbikes if the bus doesn't stop directly next to the sidewalk. But even then you're not in the clear: Motorbikes and bicycles regularly take to the sidewalk, especially during rush hour.

BUS

Known locally as *colectivos*, the buses of Buenos Aires have an extensive network. More than 180 lines operate day and night. The frequency of buses during the day can be as little as a few minutes, but late at night this can reach up to 40 minutes.

Pay on board with your Sube card. Upon telling the driver your destination, he will tap a few buttons and wait for you to swipe your Sube over the card reader. Journeys cost as little as US$0.25, depending on the length of the trip.

Raise your arm to let an approaching bus know you want it to stop. Once onboard, it's necessary to press one of the Stop buttons to alert the driver that you want to disembark at the next stop. Although route maps are starting to appear at bus stops, they are few and far between. Bus stops are notoriously difficult to find, some signified by a

mere sticker on a tree, although these are slowly being replaced with more established structures. The *Guía T*, a small booklet available at most newspaper stands, lists all the lines with their routes marked out on maps.

Although the bus system has hundreds of lines crossing the city, a few stick to the main arteries and are of particular use to tourists.

- Route 8: Ezeiza airport, Almagro, Balvanera, Centro, and San Telmo
- Route 33: Aeroparque airport, Retiro, Centro, Puerto Madero, San Telmo, and La Boca
- Route 64: La Boca, San Telmo, Centro, Balvanera, Recoleta, and Palermo
- Route 152: La Boca, San Telmo, Centro, Retiro, Recoleta, and Palermo

Many buses in Buenos Aires bear a style of painting called *fileteado*, which involves ornate swirls, multiple colors, and occasionally drawings. The interiors of the *colectivos*, depending on the line and the driver, are often decorated with *fútbol* flags, pictures of saints, excessive collections of rearview mirrors, and sometimes even mood lighting. Jumping on a bus to cross the city can be a helpful means of transportation, but it can also be an experience in itself. Daniel Tunnard, an Englishman living in Buenos Aires, undertook a personal quest to ride them all, producing an excellent book, *Colectivaizeishon,* at the end of his mission.

SUBTE (SUBWAY)

The Subte (not to be confused with the Sube card) is the quickest way to travel, although it only runs between approximately 5am and 10pm daily. The service exists mainly to bring people in and out of the city

The Subte is the oldest underground train network in Latin America.

center, with six lines that shoot out from Plaza de Mayo. Although not very large, the system nonetheless reaches most places of interest to visitors. The most useful lines for tourists are the light blue A line, the red B line, the dark blue C line, and the green D line.

At only US$0.30, the Subte remains one of the cheapest metros in the world. The service can now only be paid for with a Sube card. Rush hour is heinous and often involves letting a few full trains pass before finding a space to squeeze into, although the interesting murals in most stations reduce the tedium. Vendors often stroll up and down Subte carriages placing items on passengers' knees before collecting them again a minute later if not wanted, while busking musicians also work their way along the vehicles.

TAXI

Taxis are generally a fairly quick and reasonably priced option. There always seem to be more taxis on the road than any other kind of vehicle, even in the dead of night. The wider *avenidas* are the best bet if hailing from the curbside, although it is safest, and no more expensive, to call a radio taxi company, who will have a cab at your door within minutes. Taxi Premium (tel. 011/5238-0000) is one option. If in doubt, restaurants and hotels will always call a taxi on your behalf. Bear in mind that the journey can take longer than expected during rush hour or if the driver decides to take a more circular route, as is often the case. It's worth establishing in advance the approximate cost of the journey, and always make sure that the driver doesn't "forget" to turn on the meter. The starting fare for a taxi is $20 (US$1.35) with the cost going up in increments of $2 (US$0.13). Between the hours of 10pm and 6pm, all costs increase by 20 percent. Taxi drivers do not expect tips, though rounding up to the nearest peso is appreciated. Expect every taxi in Buenos Aires to accept cash only.

CAR RENTAL AGENCIES IN BUENOS AIRES

A few car rental agencies, including **Alamo, Avis,** and **Hertz,** have offices in Ezeiza and Aeroparque airports. Others may not have an office but can arrange for a car to be waiting. The fee for picking a car up at the airport is much higher than picking up or dropping off in the city center, but not having to pay for a taxi ride into the city could make it worthwhile.

The following agencies often have multiple pickup and drop-off points. The contact information is for the central office:

- **Alamo:** Cerrito 1328, Retiro, tel. 011/4811-6903, www.alamo.com

- **Avis:** Cerrito 1535, Retiro, tel. 011/4326-5542, www.avis.com

- **Europcar:** Av. Antártida 821, Retiro, tel. 011/4316-6570, www.europcar.com.ar

- **Hertz:** Paraguay 1138, Retiro, tel. 011/4816-8001, www.hertz.com.ar

- **Sixt:** Cerrito 1366, Retiro, tel. 011/4815-2216, www.sixt.com

- **Tango Rent a Car:** Av. del Libertador 8580, Nuñez, tel. 011/5778-1333, www.tangorentacar.com

CAR

The city's grid structure may suggest an organized and methodical system, but that is far from the case. Driving in Buenos Aires can take some getting used to. Tempers flare easily, traffic violations are the norm, and parking is a challenge. Traffic jams can be horrendous. Having a car makes the most sense for those planning on excursions out of the city.

RENTING A CAR

To rent a car, drivers must present their original valid **driver's license** (International Driving Permits are not asked for and are not a valid document on their own) and a **credit card.** The **minimum age** is 21 years, regardless of the minimum driving age in the traveler's country of origin. Security deposits are usually taken from the credit card and then released upon return of the car, although some companies insist on retaining deposits for three months to ensure that no fines for traffic violations are served.

Rental agencies generally offer manual and automatic transmission vehicles. Always insist on giving the car a once-over before signing for it, as dents and scratches are common. To avoid problems when returning the car, point out preexisting damage beforehand.

For travel in and around Buenos Aires the *limitado* (limited) option, usually 200 kilometers per day on average with an extra charge for additional kilometers, is more than sufficient. If renting for travel to other cities, it is worth asking for the more expensive *ilimitado* (unlimited) option.

All agencies charge fees for pickup and drop-off, and this can vary drastically according to the time, day, and location. For example, the airport is always much more expensive than the central office. Most will also drop cars off at a private residence or hotel if requested.

ROAD RULES

Road signs at each junction indicate which direction cars should be heading, although the position of parked vehicles is also a good indication.

Some of the wider *avenidas* run in both directions, but these can be tricky to exit. When approaching a junction without traffic lights, the right-of-way belongs to the cars that are crossing from right to left, although this technicality is not taken very seriously. When driving on the *ruta* or *autopista* (highway), it is obligatory to have the headlights on at all times of the day. The speed limit on these roads can also change frequently, so pay attention to passing signs. Emergency vehicles often leave their lights flashing when cruising around (especially the police) and it is only necessary to move out of their way or pull over when the siren starts blaring. Control points are popping up all over the city. If the police wave you down at one, you will have to pull over and produce all relevant documents for the car and yourself, which include car registration and insurance, rental forms (if applicable), original driver's license, and personal ID (such as a passport). It is not uncommon for police to solicit bribes from drivers pulled over for minor infractions, but handing over your money in such a situation is risky. Instead, imply that you will contact your embassy for advice. Pretending that you don't understand Spanish can also be effective.

For maps, consult the headquarters of the Automóvil Club Argentino (ACA, Av. Libertador 1850, Palermo, tel. 011/4808-4000).

FUEL

Gasoline and natural gas are surprisingly expensive for a country so rich in petroleum deposits. Prices fluctuate wildly, but at the time of writing, a liter of standard gasoline (*super*) costs US$1, premium is US$1.20, and diesel is just under US$1. Natural gas is much cheaper, at only US$0.30 per liter, which means that many locals, especially taxi drivers, run their cars from large natural gas cylinders in the trunk or under the hood, which are prone to explode. Often when traveling by taxi, you will hear a dull thud coming from behind, which is a result of small (but not dangerous) explosions coming from inside the cylinder.

PARKING

Parking is notoriously difficult, with far too few spaces available. If you're lucky enough to find one, it is common for someone known as a *trapito* to sidle up and ask for money to "protect" your car. Refusing is not advised, as the vehicle is liable to suffer damage, or you might even find yourself physically accosted. If you're confident enough, suggest a "half now, half later" deal, but don't insist too hard. They will charge a flat rate, generally around US$2-3, although this can double in Palermo.

To avoid such confrontations and wasting time driving round in circles looking for a space, leave the car in any of the prolific *estacionamientos* (car parks), advertised with giant flashing "E" signs. Prices vary according to location and length of stay, with discounts given on weekly and monthly periods. Illegally parked cars are regularly towed and taken to a tow yard, where a fine of US$40 must be paid for the car to be returned.

BICYCLE

Since 2009, more than 160 kilometers of *bicisendas* (bike lanes) have been added to the almost completely flat streets of Buenos Aires, and the bicycle has become so popular that it is has become a fashion icon. It is common to come across a trendily dressed

BIKING BUENOS AIRES

The city government's **Ecobici** (www.buenosaires.gob.ar/ecobici) program provides thousands of vivid yellow bikes for public use. Found at about 100 stations around the city center, the bikes can be borrowed for up to an hour at no cost, although given the high number of thefts, it is probable that a charge will be enforced sometime in the future. The easiest way to register for the service is on the website, where information for visitors is also given in English. Another way is to download the BA Ecobici app onto your smartphone. Once registered, bikes are rented through the app and should be returned within an hour (to any station), or the user will be blocked.

Ecobici offers free bikes to residents and tourists.

While the Ecobici bikes can be used for exploring the city, the system is specifically designed for commuters. To rent a bicycle for a longer period and move freely at your own speed, a wide range of companies provide such services. **La Bicicleta Naranja** (www.labicicletanaranja.com.ar, US$20 per day) is one of the most experienced, with outlets in San Telmo and Palermo. **Rental Bike** (www.rentalbikeargentina.com, US$14 per day) in Centro is the cheapest. **Urban Biking** (www.urbanbiking.com, US$30 per day) in Retiro is another popular option. All of these companies offer guided bike tours as well as bike rentals, and they always advertise decent offers on their websites.

woman on a pastel-colored bike with flowers flowing down the handlebars as it is a bare-chested man on a wobbly number with no brakes. Popularity and trends aside, bicycles are often the fastest means of transportation, especially during rush hour.

Masa Crítica (Critical Mass) is held on the first Sunday of each month. Hundreds (on occasions thousands) of bike riders and skaters converge on the Obelisco by 4pm, although it often sets off closer to 5pm. An event held around the world, it is a celebration of the bicycle, and it offers a unique way to explore the city and meet a diverse range of characters.

BICYCLE SAFETY AND ROAD RULES

Drivers are still adjusting to the influx of two-wheeled vehicles, and riders should not assume that the presence of a bike lane guarantees safety. Taxis and buses in particular have been known to blithely cut in front of passing bikes without warning. Pedestrians also regularly step into bike lanes in the middle of a block without looking, often with children in tow. Technically, the order of priorities is pedestrian, then bicycle, then motor vehicle, but in practice each one of the three sets off at once. Patience and awareness are obligatory, helmets and lights are not, although they are of course strongly advised. When riding down a street without a bike lane, bikers should stay on the left side, mainly to avoid problems with the public buses that stop on the right side.

Bicicleterías are bike stores that either sell bikes and accessories or carry out repairs (more often than not they do both) and can mainly be found along the bike lanes.

THEFT

Bicycle theft is rife across the city. Bicycles should never be left unattended on the street and should always be locked up in as visible a place as possible, for example in front of an open business, or ideally near a patrolling police officer, with lights and all other accessories removed. The government has installed some 5,000 racks for chaining bikes, but these, ironically, are often a hotbed of thefts. *Estacionamientos* (car parks) charge a few pesos per hour to guard a bike, although bikes should still be locked up in such places. Most shopping malls provide a secure spot for bicycles in their parking lots for no charge.

MOTORCYCLES AND SCOOTERS

Despite the proliferation of scooters in Buenos Aires, there is not much trade in the short-term rental of these vehicles, but options are starting to appear. Motorcycles can also be found, but the cost involved suggests that they are intended for long-distance travel, and the agencies mostly operate on the outskirts of the city. Drivers must be over 25 (with at least three years' experience) and are required to present the same documents as for renting a car.

Ecomoving (Honduras 5164, tel. 011/3971-9045, www.ecomoving.com.ar) is located in Palermo and is generally the best option, renting scooters by the hour, day, or week. Motocare (Echeverria 738, tel. 011/4761-2696, www.motocare.com.ar) is in Vicente López, outside of Capital Federal, and has the widest range of more serious motorcycles. Officially partnered with BMW, Rentamoto (Av. Agustín García 6649, tel. 011/6261-5858, www.rentamoto.com.ar) can be found in Tigre.

WALKING

Despite crumbling sidewalks and perpetual construction, Buenos Aires is an ideal city for walking. The flat topography makes for easy movement, while the grid system makes navigation simple. Benches are frustratingly sparse outside of plazas and parks, and the only public maps on display are outside Subte stations, although these are quite detailed and extensive. The area between Avenida de Mayo and Avenida Santa Fe, to the east of Avenida 9 de Julio (colloquially known as Microcentro) is largely pedestrianized, although, unfortunately, it is one of the least interesting areas to walk around. Beware of vehicles at all junctions. Taxis, buses, and bicycles rarely heed the pedestrian's right-of-way.

Visas and Officialdom

PASSPORTS AND VISAS

While citizens from most other South American countries can enter Argentina with their respective identity cards, all other nationalities are required to carry a passport to enter the country. The standard visa given at entry is a tourist visa, which is valid for 90 days (strictly 90 days as opposed to 3 months) and is merely a stamp in the passport.

Officially, those arriving on a tourist visa are expected to have an already-booked onward or return journey ticket to present as documentation at border control. In reality, given that many visitors arrive with plans to travel through South America for a few months, such documents are never requested from North American, South American, or European citizens, although the request may be made for those arriving from Asian or African countries. Unfortunately, some airlines take the official line seriously and refuse to let passengers board without the onward journey booked, regardless of their nationality or starting destination. If this happens to you shortly before your flight is due to leave, the best solution is to try to book a day trip online to Uruguay, less than 90 days ahead, for around US$40. You may never take the trip, but the ticket will placate the airline and ensure that travel on the flight is not refused.

A reciprocity fee is currently charged to all visiting citizens from United States (US$140), Australia (US$100), and Canada (US$70). This was introduced after those countries started charging Argentine citizens those amounts. The fee must be paid in cash or by credit card before passing customs. Once paid, the fee is valid for ten years, during which the traveler is free to travel in and out of Argentina without incurring further fees. Everyone crossing the border is now required to have their photo and right thumbprint taken. This happens every time you enter the country and is not optional.

EXTENDING YOUR TOURIST VISA

To extend your tourist visa an additional three months, make a request in **Dirección Nacional de Migraciones** (Av. Antartida Argentina 1355, Retiro, 8am-2pm Mon.-Fri.). Passport photocopies and a US$40 fee are required. Overstaying the visa will result in the US$40 extension fee being enforced as a fine of the same amount when leaving the country, be it by bus, boat, or plane.

Making this request at Dirección Nacional de Migraciones can be time-consuming and frustrating. An alternative option is to take a boat to Uruguay, then return to Buenos Aires. Travelers will be given another 90-day visa when reentering Argentina. Although Argentine immigration has started to crack down on those who repeat this process for years on end, there are no problems doing it for the first time. Three ferry companies offer day trips ideally suited to this need, most of which include a guided tour around the interesting Uruguayan town of Colonia del Sacramento: **Buquebus** (www.buquebus.com), **Colonia Express** (www.coloniaexpress.com.ar), and **Seacat Colonia** (www.seacatcolonia.com). With fares for less than US$40 (if booked in advance), such a trip may be cheaper and much more enjoyable than a few hours spent in the immigration office.

CUSTOMS

While it may be unnerving to see customs guards picking through the suitcases of returning Argentines and querying them about electronic goods, this practice largely relates to strict importation laws and is unlikely to affect visitors. Nonetheless, bringing a wealth of new phones, computers, or cameras into the country may raise suspicions at the border and is not advised. Such searches are most common on flights arriving from other continents. Flights from other South American countries provoke more concern over drugs and fresh produce. A maximum of US$10,000 can be brought into the country in cash or traveler's checks; any excess is liable to confiscation. Strictly speaking, this rule is per family, not per person, so US$2,500 per person in a family of four.

LOST OR STOLEN PASSPORTS

A foreign visitor whose passport is lost or stolen must obtain a new one from his or her embassy or consulate. Such a document tends to be excessively expensive and only temporary, meaning that it will only be valid for returning to the holder's native country. Once obtained, it must be taken to the Dirección Nacional de Migraciones to arrange a new visa stamp.

Conduct and Customs

GREETINGS

Men routinely greet male friends (and even strangers) with a peck on the cheek. The same is the case with women. This is a standard greeting.

TOBACCO

Argentina remains laissez-faire in its attitude toward smoking, even though smoking in confined places and on public transportation is illegal. The interior of any restaurant, bar, hotel, or entertainment venue should be expected to be smoke free, but this is not always the case. Bus drivers often light up with a busload of passengers, and taxi drivers may behave similarly. Expressing displeasure at their action will rarely cause problems, but it will often be ignored.

The vast majority of smokers in Argentina smoke pre-rolled *cigarillos* (cigarettes). The major international brands are available at all *kioscos*. For pipe or rolling tobacco, smokers need to visit one of the few *tabaquerías,* such as Tabaquería Inglesa (Paraguay 553, Retiro) or La Covacha (Charcas 5182, Palermo).

DRUGS

Hard drugs are illegal in Argentina. With much nightlife kicking off after midnight and lasting until dawn, however, it is unsurprising that the city's nightclubs are rife with drugs.

It's legal for residents to grow a couple of marijuana plants at home for private use, but that is exactly where the police expect it to be smoked: at home. Although it's technically illegal to smoke in public, it is not uncommon to smell marijuana smoke when walking down the street or see someone smoking a joint in the park.

PROSTITUTION

Prostitution is legal in Argentina, but there are strict regulations. Prostitutes are not allowed to advertise themselves within 100 meters of schools or residences, meaning that many head to either the Bosques de Palermo or the dimly lit streets of Puerto Madero, where late at night it is not uncommon to pass a semi-naked (sometimes completely naked) person leering through car windows. On the tourist-filled streets of Florida and Lavalle, hustlers furtively shove business cards offering sexual services into the hands of unsuspecting passersby. Many of them will demand money before allowing customers to leave their premises. Strip clubs, cabarets, brothels, swinger clubs, erotic massage parlors, sex shops, and escort services are widespread across the city.

Health and Safety

Buenos Aires offers no major health risks beyond the normal maladies of any metropolis. Currently no immunizations are required before travel to Buenos Aires, although this could change. Before traveling, check the website of the Centers for Disease Control and Prevention (www.cdc.gov) for up-to-date information.

Mosquitoes are rife during the hotter months in Buenos Aires. While malaria is not an issue, dengue fever persists. Beyond the possibility of contracting this disease, the mere presence of the devilish pests is frustrating. Repellents are widely available in supermarkets and pharmacies, with Off being the most popular local brand, available as a cream or spray. If you're particularly bothered by mosquitoes, it can be worth seeking out accommodations above the third floor, a height they rarely reach.

FOOD AND WATER

The water of Buenos Aires is perfectly drinkable and safe. Nonetheless, visitors to the city often react badly to it merely because their bodies are unaccustomed to it. It's worth drinking only bottled water for at least the first few days of your stay while your body acclimates. Also be wary of ice in restaurants and bars, and food like salad that comes into contact with water, and use bottled water while brushing your teeth.

Meat in Argentina rarely sits for very long, so it is not treated against bacteria the same way as in the United States and Europe. The Argentine tendency to order beef well-done is not just a taste preference; it's a way of ensuring that any bacteria is neutralized. While eating undercooked beef will not necessarily cause problems, it certainly increases risk of illness and should be avoided. All fruits and vegetables should be washed before consumption, as they are hardly ever sold prewashed.

COMMON AILMENTS
TRAVELER'S DIARRHEA (TD)

The most common affliction for travelers across the world, TD is a fairly self-explanatory illness that is often the result of consuming contaminated food or water. It tends to last for up to four days. Sufferers find themselves feeling queasy, passing liquid feces, vomiting, or experiencing general weakness. To reduce the risk of TD, be wary of the cleanliness of what you consume, especially water and things that have come in contact with water, such as ice or salads. Bottled water is widely available and is advisable for visitors to Buenos Aires, at least for the first week or so when travelers are most prone to this particular affliction.

Visit a doctor in the case of extreme symptoms or if a child is showing symptoms. Over-the-counter and prescription drugs are available, but such treatments only serve to reduce the diarrhea (although this can be sufficient enough treatment for those who don't want to ruin a short holiday by sitting on the toilet for four days). You can pick up Pepto-Bismol, Lomotil, and Imodium from any pharmacy, but these medications are liable to produce side effects. Antibiotics require a prescription from a doctor.

DENGUE FEVER

Although malaria is no longer an issue in Buenos Aires, mosquitoes are everywhere during the summer. Some years they bring an epidemic with them, usually dengue fever. Rarely fatal, the disease usually takes a few days for the body to overcome naturally, as there is no treatment available. Symptoms are similar to flu, with fever, headaches, joint pains, nausea, and vomiting. The dreaded *Aedes egypti* mosquitoes, which carry this disease as well as yellow fever, are distinguishable by white markings on their legs and body, although being bitten by one of these mosquitoes does not imply infection, which is fortunate, as you are liable to be bitten by quite a few if visiting between October and April.

YELLOW FEVER

Known as *fiebra amarilla* in Argentina, yellow fever need not concern visitors to Buenos Aires. That said, if you're planning to head to rainforest areas (Iguazú Falls, for example), a vaccination will be necessary and even obligatory if there is

an outbreak at the time—check the website for the CDC before your trip. When obligatory, free vaccines are available to the public at hospitals.

SUNBURN AND SUNSTROKE

The effect of the sun's rays in Buenos Aires are similar to those in the northern hemisphere. While not as dangerous as in the far south of Argentina, where holes in the ozone layer allow the sun to pound down with all its force, it is still advisable to take precautions during hot months, even if the locals seem to be constantly challenging the sun to burn them. Sunscreen is essential. Beware that *bronzeador* (tanning lotion) is sold widely alongside *protector solar* (sunscreen), and it does very little, if anything, to protect against the sun's rays.

If hit by dizziness when in the sun, immediately seek shade, sit down, and drink cold water if possible.

RABIES

A disease carried by the saliva of a contaminated animal, rabies is not a common problem in Buenos Aires. Nonetheless, unvaccinated stray dogs are common, and bats screech around at night. If bitten by a dog (or a bat), seek medical attention immediately, regardless of any reassurances the dog owner may profess.

MEDICAL SERVICES

The proud home of Dr. René Favaloro, the heart surgeon who developed the coronary bypass procedure, Argentina has an extensive and skilled medical sector. The public hospitals of Buenos Aires are the most highly regarded in the country, and are known for having most of the top doctors. People flock to them from all parts of the country to receive treatment. This can mean that patients seeking to book appointments have to queue from 6am to be allocated a *turno* (appointment) for later in the day. Queuing in the *guardia* (emergency department) can also last a while, although attending doctors are often intrigued by the opportunity to treat foreigners and bump them up the order.

The largest public hospitals include Hospital Rivadavia (Av. Las Heras 2670, Recoleta, tel. 011/4809-2000) and Hospital Argerich (Pi y Margall 750, San Telmo, tel. 011/4123-3100), although there are plenty dotted around the city.

Fees charged at private hospitals are reasonable by Western standards, even for foreigners with or without insurance. Private hospitals are generally more modern and cleaner than the public ones. Hospital Italiano (Juan D. Perón 4190, Almagro, tel. 011/4959-0200) and Clínica Bazterrica (Billinghurst 2072, Recoleta, tel. 011/4821-1600) are two of the most respected.

Doctors in both the public and private sector usually speak English, at least sufficiently well to deal with patients.

PHARMACIES

Large green crosses that signify the presence of a pharmacy are in wide abundance, especially around hospitals and clinics. Greater freedom is given in Argentina with regard to the necessity of prescriptions, and many drugs that require authorization by a doctor in the United States and other countries are available over the counter here (for example, diazepam). If taking medications from home during your travels, make sure to bring

clear information on what it is in case replacements are needed; the original packaging is ideal. Be wary of advice from pharmacists, and check the expiration date on drugs before purchasing them.

In every neighborhood, one pharmacy will be open through the night; this information is posted in the window of each pharmacy, so patients will know where to go.

CRIME

Argentines are obsessed with *seguridad,* which strictly speaking means "security" or "safety," but in this context refers more specifically to safety from crime. If the newspapers were to be believed, you could barely step out on the streets for fear of being robbed, beaten, kidnapped, or killed. In reality, Buenos Aires is a remarkably safe city, especially the central areas. The constant high density of people, even in the dead of night, means that you are unlikely to find yourself alone on a dark street, and a strong police presence provides deterrence. Statistically speaking, you are more likely to run into trouble on the streets of New York or London than in Buenos Aires.

There are certain areas that travelers should stay clear of—namely, the *villas* (shantytowns), the most central of which is Villa 31, alongside the Retiro bus station. Pay attention when using public transit, as much in the area surrounding the station or terminal as in the vehicle itself, where pickpocketing is rife. Be wary of people asking you for directions or help in central neighborhoods, as this is a common distractive ploy used by thieves working in groups. When sitting in a sidewalk café or restaurant, ensure that any bags are secure and can't easily be grabbed by passersby.

A common crime in Buenos Aires is for thieves to wait outside banks and then follow people who have made withdrawals for a while before accosting them and relieving them of the cash. Be cautious when using ATMs, and do not flash your cash around. If confronted by someone carrying a weapon at any time, be it a gun or a knife, it is inadvisable to do anything other than submit to their demands, as robberies are perhaps more prone to turn violent than in some other parts of the world, and a lost phone, wallet, or bag can always be replaced.

POLICE AND MILITARY

Argentina has a complicated history with its security services following the military dictatorships and extrajudicial killings that have blighted the country's history. To this day, witnesses in police trials and high-profile cases occasionally "disappear" or simply turn up dead shortly before giving testimony, joining the tens of thousands that were killed in the 1980s. On top of this, the police are notorious for corruption and derided for incompetence, although the latter is often merely a result of the former.

Police officers are easy to spot with their luminous jackets. Widely scorned by the populace, they try not to get too involved if they can at all help it. The orange-jacketed Policía Federal (Federal Police) are held in slightly higher esteem than the yellow-jacketed Policía Metropolitana (Metropolitan Police, limited to Capital Federal) and notorious Bonarense (police covering the rest of the province), although any are likely to be seen smoking or chatting on their phones while working.

It is not uncommon for police to solicit bribes, especially with drivers pulled over for minor infractions or visitors unsure of local laws and protocol. It is rarely advisable for visitors to part with their money in such situations. Instead, imply that you will contact the embassy for advice, although without being too insistent or obtuse. Despite what they may claim, a police officer on the beat is not going to have you thrown out of the country for drinking beer in the park. Offering a bribe to a police officer, however, is highly risky and likely to worsen any situation. Often the easiest and most effective solution is to pretend you don't understand a word of Spanish. This will get the officer worked up, but eventually they will get bored and give up.

The military is also widely derided by the populace, although anything that is connected to the Malvinas (Falklands) War wins the sympathy and support of the nation. Aside from this perpetual conflict with the United Kingdom, which is more a diplomatic spat than an armed confrontation, Argentina maintains entirely peaceful, if somewhat strained, relations with surrounding countries.

Travel Tips

WHAT TO PACK

Visitors from the northern hemisphere must remember that seasons in Buenos Aires are reversed—winter in the United States is summer in Argentina. Argentines tend to be fairly well-dressed, especially when going out at night, so those wearing stereotypically casual traveling clothes will stick out like a sore thumb. A rain jacket is highly advisable if visiting during the summer, which is prone to sudden heavy thunderstorms.

Many Argentine women are small in size and therefore it can be very difficult for women larger than size 8 to find clothing that fits. If planning on trying a bit of tango dancing, women should bring shoes with heels, as the moves are much harder without a pivot to swing on—although such footwear is not advisable for walking around the city's uneven sidewalks.

The voltage in Argentina is 220 volts, which differs from the United States (although not from most of Europe), so it is worth bringing a voltage converter. Adapters will also be necessary but can be easily purchased in Buenos Aires. It is worth checking that your electronic equipment is fully functioning before departing for Argentina, as replacements for imported goods, such as Apple products, can be expensive and hard to find.

WOMEN TRAVELERS

Despite having had a female president for the last decade, Argentine society continues to openly display strong signs of *machismo* (chauvinism). The *porteño* hobby of *piropos* (sexual innuendos muttered to passing females)

is as popular as ever, as is the custom of wolf-whistling, although some men believe that gentle applause instead of an insinuating whistle is somehow more respectful. Such people can sometimes be quite insistent in what they see as harmless advances, often finding amusement in their victim's timidity. To escape such approaches, enter any nearby business, or even just place yourself closer to other people.

Most Argentines have naturally dark hair, and female travelers with blond or dyed hair may find themselves attracting more attention, although this should not in itself be of concern. There is also a very small black population in Argentina, so women of African descent or other nonwhite backgrounds may experience similar extra attention.

Aside from this, women travelers should have no greater concerns in Buenos Aires than in any other large city. Standard advice, such as the following, applies: Don't walk the streets alone at night; call for a taxi instead of hailing one on the street; and be wary of drinks offered by strangers. In the event of trouble, call the police immediately. A 24-hour phone line is dedicated to sexual and family violence (137). The police also run a 24-hour emergency center (Pasaje Angel Peluffo 3981, tel. 011/4958-4291) in Almagro for victims of sexual violence.

GAY AND LESBIAN TRAVELERS

In many respects, Argentina is one of the most advanced countries in the world regarding rights and social attitudes toward LGBT people. Same-sex marriage was legalized in 2010, thus strengthening Buenos Aires's popularity as a global destination for LGBT travelers after flourishing during the previous decade. While there are no parts of the city that are specifically frequented by gays, in the city center there are no neighborhoods where gays need feel threatened. Most *porteños* accept gays and lesbians as they would any other part of society. That being said, Argentina remains a Roman Catholic country, and overt public displays of affection may be greeted with disparaging remarks, generally from older members of the population.

The Marcha del Orgullo (Gay Pride Parade) is held on the first Saturday of November and turns the whole of Centro into a colorful and jubilant party during the day and evening. The Gay Travel Guide to Buenos Aires (www.thegayguide.com.ar) is a great source for information on the gay and lesbian scene in Buenos Aires.

TRAVELING WITH CHILDREN

In many regards, Argentine children are granted far greater freedom than their North American or European counterparts. Bedtime is a flexible concept, with toddlers and even babies often roaming around until midnight and beyond. It is also common to come across unsupervised children on the street, in plazas, and on public transit. This may appear strange in a society that is largely hysterical about crime, but it's a part of everyday life in Buenos Aires, and even more so in Argentina's smaller towns and cities.

Breast-feeding in public is common, even in confined spaces such as buses. *Porteños* have a habit of habit of showing interest in the babies and young children of strangers, sometimes even stroking them without seeking permission. This custom is common on public transit. It should not necessarily cause alarm to traveling parents, as it is generally indicative of the friendliness between strangers in Argentina.

Many of the city's plazas and parks have play areas for children. A lot of them are based in sand pits, but these are increasingly being replaced by more sanitary surfaces. Parque Tres de Febrero, Parque Las Heras, and Parque Centenario are notable parks that are ideal for children.

TRAVELERS WITH DISABILITIES

Most of the city's museums and attractions are adapted for people with limited mobility, although this rarely extends to the restroom facilities. Most offer reduced rates or free entry upon presentation of documents proving a disability, but such documentation is rarely actually asked for. All major hotels and increasingly the smaller ones are fully adapted for wheelchair use, but this should be confirmed before booking.

The woeful state of the city's sidewalks can complicate movement around the city for travelers with disabilities, although nearly all intersections now provide slopes on both sides of the road. The newer Subte stations are fitted with lifts that go straight from the street to the platform, but the older lines (those most frequented by visitors) rarely have such facilities. Many buses have a lower access door halfway down the vehicle, with some providing a ramp, although both these facilities depend on the line. Other travelers are accustomed to hopping off to help bring a wheelchair on board, so don't be afraid to ask *"Me ayudarías, por favor?"* ("Would you help me, please?"). Every bus includes an area adapted for wheelchairs, including safety belts.

While it is always acceptable for people with disabilities to ask to skip a queue, this unfortunately often provokes complaints by others in the queue, who may start claiming imaginary disabilities of their own. Such situations can be uncomfortable, but other members of the public usually shout down the complaints and offer assistance. Cash machines and banks are the worst for this, while the larger supermarkets always have a checkout lane where people with disabilities or reduced mobility have priority.

STUDENT DISCOUNTS

Discounts for students are not widespread in Buenos Aires and are rarely advertised. Museums are the exception. Most offer reduced rates upon presentation of documentation (a student card, for example). Some even offer free entry on a certain day of the week. The same is the case with some events. It is worth obtaining an International Student Identity Card (www.isic.com.ar) before traveling. This card provides a fairly extensive range of discounts for restaurants, bars, travel, and accommodations that are not necessarily given when presenting alternative student identification.

VOLUNTEERING

Traveling to Buenos Aires for a few months to carry out volunteer work is popular, especially for North Americans. While it receives a fair amount of criticism from the locals for distorting wage levels and taking away paid jobs, in many cases it provides a helpful source of labor for projects that otherwise struggle to survive. Buenos Aires Volunteers (www.bavolunteer.org.ar), Techo (www.techo.org), Expanish (www.expanish.com), and BA Placement (www.baplacement. com) offer ideas and help in searching for such projects.

LUGGAGE STORAGE

Lockers are not common in Argentina, and in most bus stations across the country you would be lucky to find a room where a small fee is charged to leave a bag. (Valuables should *never* be left in such circumstances.) Retiro bus station does have some lockers, paid for with tokens sold in the *kiosco* in front of them. Train stations do not provide lockers.

When leaving Buenos Aires on an excursion for a few days, many hotels are happy to hold whatever luggage you don't need to take free of charge (apart from perhaps expecting you to stay with them upon your return). If not, Storage BA (De la Carcova 3528, tel. 011/4793-3496, www.storageba. com, from US$20/week) is a private storage company that will pick up, drop off, and keep your luggage safe for as long as you need.

Money

The Argentine economy can only be described as volatile and fragile, with the populace having suffered ruinous currency crashes over the last few decades. Heavy inflation over the last decade has seen prices rise by over 1,000 percent on many goods, such as meat. Although the exchange rate has also risen drastically, it has not done so as quickly, meaning that while Buenos Aires used to be a remarkably cheap city for foreigners to visit, it now often surprises with its high costs.

CURRENCY

Argentina uses the Argentine peso, which is divided into 100 *centavos*. The notes currently in circulation have a value of 2, 5, 10, 20, 50, and 100 pesos, although the government has announced that notes worth 200, 500, and potentially 1,000 pesos will be introduced over the next few years. Some of these notes seem to crumble upon touch, so handle with care.

In theory, the coins in circulation are 5, 10, 25, and 50 *centavos* (cents) as well as 1- and 2-peso coins, but given the currency's collapse, coins have become largely worthless, and anything less than 50 *centavos* is rare. Coins are notoriously rare across Argentina, the rumor being that they are worth more when melted down and sold as crude metal in Chile, a practice carried out on industrial scale by unknown people. Whether or not this is true, there are never enough coins in circulation, and shopkeepers can become enraged if you do not have sufficient change. The banks do not provide them with coins, meaning that the little change they have comes from customers.

Often shop owners will offer candy instead of change.

Be cautious when handling U.S. dollars in Argentina, where forgery is rife, and some fake notes are of high quality. While fake notes may slip past the general public, businesses and exchange houses have fine-tuned detection techniques. If there is any doubt, the note will be flatly refused (although note that the supposed fake note should always be returned to its owner rather than destroyed or handed to the police). Despite being of noticeably lower quality than many other currencies, there do not seem to be great problems with forged peso notes. As long as the peso note is complete (not missing any corners, for example) it would be very unlikely to come across any forgeries.

EXCHANGE RATES

The Argentine peso, worth US$1 during the 1990s, had crashed to a mere US$0.07 at the time of writing. Many businesses accept payment in U.S. dollars, and to a lesser extent euros, pounds sterling, and a few other currencies, but the exchange rate offered is rarely favorable, and change will be given in Argentine pesos (if at all).

As a result of rampant inflation and a volatile currency, a parallel and unofficial exchange rate, known as the *dolar blue* emerged alongside the *dolar oficial,* or the official rate. The appearance of the *dolar blue* over the last few years has been a constant problem in the government's attempts to wrest control of Argentina's economic woes. The *dolar blue* is basically decided by the speculators and traders who run the country's vast, murky underworld of currency exchange and is widely considered to be closer to the true value of the peso. In the past, it has reached double the value of the *dolar oficial* and also experiences wild fluctuations. Websites such as www.dolarblue.net publish current rates for both the *oficial* and *blue,* but these should be taken as guides rather than exact figures. The exact, real value of the peso is seemingly unknown.

The Argentine obsession with U.S. dollars has led to the North American currency being overvalued here, sometimes quite excessively. This means that travelers from Europe actually end up with more pesos in their pocket if they first change their original currency (e.g., pound sterling, euros, etc.) into dollars before traveling to Argentina. Indeed, many exchange houses either refuse to change anything other than U.S. dollars or will only do so for a poor rate.

EXCHANGING MONEY

Essentially illegal for the past few years, currency exchange is a serious problem in Argentina. Getting your hands on pesos in Buenos Aires can be difficult or expensive, and trying to find them in other countries often proves no easier, with many exchange houses reluctant to deal in what is an unreliable and volatile currency. The situation is easing now, with the new government starting to lift the ban on selling and buying U.S. dollars.

Since withdrawing money from ATMs incurs exchange fees that could mean losing up to 50 percent of the intended amount, visitors are essentially forced to change their money at *cuevas,* which are informal exchange houses (they are also illegal, but tolerated by authorities). Some of these

are respectable affairs, some are not. Walking along Florida street, every few meters someone will mutter *"Cambio?"* ("Change?") at you, asking if you want to exchange money. If you say yes, they will lead you to a *cueva,* often at the back of a shop, where the transaction will be carried out. No identification is needed. Such places are not known for causing trouble for travelers beyond offering a scandalous exchange rate, which can be countered by establishing the current exchange rate (for both the *dolar blue* and the *dolar oficial*) beforehand, then asking for a few quotes before entering the *cueva.*

The hope is that banks will start operating in the exchange markets again, but currently their services are restricted to those who hold an account with the bank. When they do start up again, identification will be necessary to make any currency exchange.

Because of the difficulties in exchanging currencies, it's best to obtain a sufficient amount to ensure travel from the airport to your lodgings while still in your home country. If this is not possible, a better exchange rate is generally given when withdrawing cash from the ATM at the airport than when changing money at one of the airport's exchange houses.

DEBIT AND CREDIT CARDS

Whether or not it is advisable to use a foreign credit or debit card will depend on the current distortion between the *oficial* and *blue* dollar rates, so make sure to check these rates prior to use. If they are practically the same, there is not much problem using the card, but if there is much of a difference, the card issuer will always be charged at the *oficial* rate, which means that you will end up paying more dollars than the value of the transaction. This is the case whether paying by card or using the card to withdraw cash from an ATM.

Card issuers may block unexpected payments and transactions in a foreign country. To reduce the likelihood that you'll face this problem, let your bank or card issuer know in advance that you will be traveling to Argentina. Also, establish your card's daily limit along with what fees will be charged for foreign purchases.

ATMS

Many ATMs charge fees to foreign cards on top of the standard withdrawal fee, sometimes in excess of US$5. To reduce fees, try and find a branch of your bank if at all possible. International banks like Citibank, Santander, and HSBC all have a presence in Buenos Aires.

Cash withdrawals are limited to 2,400 pesos (currently around US$160), although multiple withdrawals can be made until the card issuer's limit is reached. Note that transaction and withdrawal fees will be implemented on *each* withdrawal.

PAYING WITH DEBIT AND CREDIT CARDS

During debit- and credit-card transactions in Argentina, it is standard for the card owner to be asked for identification, and sometimes the number of a document (if asked, suggest your passport number). Card payments are often declined in supermarkets, but this is usually due to problems with the payment system as opposed to the card. Many businesses like restaurants or hotels don't accept cards, so always confirm in advance that cards are accepted if that's how you plan to pay. Taxis don't accept cards, although

some *remis* (private car, akin to a town car) companies do.

WIRING MONEY AND BANK TRANSFERS

Due to the currency exchange issues, wiring money is often complicated and sometimes impossible. Agencies are currently not allowed to distribute any currency other than Argentine pesos, which means that if U.S. dollars or euros are sent, they must be picked up in pesos. The pesos are given at the *oficial* exchange rate, which means that a substantial loss is usually incurred when sending money this way. Most small agencies that previously wired money have gone out of business as a result. Western Union (www.western-union.com) and MoneyGram (www.moneygram.com) remain the best options for sending money to Argentina, with countless branches around the city. Another option for citizens outside North America is the European wiring company Azimo (www.azimo.com), with the money being picked up from Argenper (www.argenper.com.ar), an Argentine money wiring company, in Buenos Aires.

BANKING HOURS

Banks are open 10am-3pm Monday-Friday and closed the whole weekend. ATMs often run out of cash on Sunday, especially if there are national holidays that mean banks are closed for more than two days in a row. The machines are also filled up shortly after banks close, meaning that trying to withdraw cash in the middle of the afternoon can be impossible, as the banks are locked during the procedure.

TIPPING

Tipping in restaurants is not obligatory but is largely expected, especially in classier establishments (though if service or quality has not reached expectations, it is perfectly acceptable to leave without tipping). The standard is 10 percent, less in relaxed environments. Delivery people are generally tipped a few pesos, but is not necessary to offer anything close to 10 percent if making larger orders.

Some restaurants charge *cubiertos,* which is basically a per-person cover charge. It is not equivalent to a tip, nor is it optional. While in some places it covers extras such as bread, sauces, or "free" drinks while queuing, in others it is merely an extra charge.

Taxi drivers do not expect tips, but they always appreciate customers who round up to the nearest peso or suitable amount. Occasionally when getting into or out of a taxi (outside the airport or bus station, for example), your door will be opened by someone who may or may not also offer to stow your luggage. They will expect a tip (regardless of whether or not they help with your luggage); a peso or two is sufficient.

When traveling by long-distance bus, a bag handler will stow your suitcase. Definitely tip them, if only to ensure the safe arrival of your luggage, but only a small amount, such as the smallest note in your possession. Bear in mind that another bag handler will unload your bag upon arrival. They will be equally expectant of a tip, and the lack of one can be tense or awkward.

BARGAINING AND DISCOUNTS

Unlike many other Latin American countries, bargaining is not common in Argentina. Offering a lower price than the one indicated will usually result in a bewildered look followed by a shake of the head. Some vendors in open-air markets may consider lowering their price, but this is far from the norm and is not worth considering unless the price seems particularly inflated. On the other hand, businesses often drop prices by up to 20 percent when paying in cash, so this is definitely worth asking for, especially in clothing and accessory shops, where this practice is common.

Communication and Media

POSTAL SERVICES

After passing through a few years of experimentation in the private sector, Correo Argentino (www.correoargentino.com.ar), the national postal service, is back in state hands. While mailing postcards and letters is a straightforward affair, sending parcels can be complicated and time-consuming. Those mailing parcels must declare exactly what is inside and adhere to the agent's demands for how the package is sealed or packed. Restrictions on what can be sent (e.g., food, items of value, etc.) are constantly changing and should be checked beforehand, either on the postal service's website or inside a branch office. Consider paying extra for letters or parcels to be *certificada* (registered), as Argentine customs agents have notoriously long fingers. A standard postcard or letter weighing less than 20 grams costs US$2.50 for standard delivery and US$7 for registered delivery, with prices increasing according to weight. Two easily accessed outposts are in Centro (Av. de Mayo 770) and Palermo (Av. Santa Fe 3882).

Alternative local services, such as OCA (www.oca.com.ar), offer a more reliable but also more expensive option. DHL International (www.dhl.com.ar) operates widely in Buenos Aires; FedEx (www.fedex.com/ar) less so, but both are available for international and national deliveries.

TELEPHONE

The country code for Argentina is 54, while the area code for Buenos Aires (including the surrounding region) is 11 for *fijos* (landlines) and 15 for mobiles. All numbers in the capital, whether mobile or landline, contain eight digits after the area code. When calling an Argentine cell phone from outside the country, dial 54+9+11 before the eight-digit number, as the 15 prefix is only used within the country, and the 11 in this case is the area code for Buenos Aires.

PUBLIC PHONES

Public phones are abundant, although many of them do not work. Most accept coins. It is also possible to buy phone cards from *kioscos* and *locutorios*. Certain cards are suited to domestic calls, while others offer huge discounts on international calls. State the country that you are calling, so that the vendor ensures you buy the right card.

Locutorios are small telephone centers, often with just a couple of booths, from where you can make calls that are slightly more expensive than the public phones, paying the total cost at the end of the call. While direct international calls can be made from

these phones, costs can be high, and it is worth checking with the attendant beforehand. Calls are cheaper outside peak hours (8am-10pm Mon.-Fri. and 8am-1pm Sat.). The attendant may also be able to sell you a phone card that will make the call cheaper.

CELL PHONES

If you own an unlocked smartphone, consider obtaining a free SIM card from any of the major phone operators: Claro (www.claro.com.ar), Movistar (www.movistar.com.ar), or Personal (www.personal.com.ar). With this SIM card, your phone will be permanently connected to the Internet for as little as US$0.30 per day. Ensure that your phone is unlocked before traveling, as doing so in Buenos Aires can be unreliable and expensive. All of the major phone operators have multiple branch locations across the city.

Standard cell phones with a prepaid SIM card (*prepago*) can be bought in Buenos Aires for as little as US$20, which usually works out cheaper than renting one. Many hotels lend cell phones as part of their rates.

INTERNET ACCESS

With the rapid advance in mobile telephone technology, Internet access in Buenos Aires has become easier and more widespread. Most bars, restaurants, and hotels now have free Wi-Fi, while many public spaces are starting to offer the service. If a network is password protected, ask for the *contraseña* (password).

There are plenty of Internet cafés dotted around the city, especially in Centro and along the *avenidas*. *Locutorios* (small telephone centers) often provide a handful of computers. To produce the "@" symbol on most

Argentine keyboards, hold down the Alt key while typing 64.

MEDIA

The whole spectrum of Argentine media is deeply politicized. Government criticism of some journalists and outlets borders on the extreme.

NEWSPAPERS AND MAGAZINES

Newspaper stands abound across the city. Green metal affairs that sit on the sidewalk, most operate only during the day. *Clarín* (www.clarin.com) is by far the most read daily. It is the flagship paper of a mammoth media conglomerate that dominates the Argentine press, television, and radio. It generally tries bridge political divides but descended into all-out war with the previous government. The widely acclaimed *Ñ* (www.revistaenie.clarin. com) is a cultural magazine included in the Saturday edition. Another newspaper that they print is *Olé* (www.ole. com.ar), a sports daily that fills dozens of pages on *fútbol* every day.

La Nación (www.lanacion.com.ar) is the next most widely bought daily and tends toward the right on the political spectrum. *Página 12* (www.pagina12.com.ar) is staunchly left-wing and offers intellectual analysis on current issues but struggles to surpass party political lines. *Perfil* (www. perfil.com), printed on the weekend, is as close to an objective opinion as you are likely to find, although one of its high-profile journalists, Jorge Lanata, became embroiled in a highly personal spat with President Cristina Fernández de Kirchner, which warped its neutrality significantly. *Diario Popular* (www.diariopopular.com. ar) and *Crónica* (www.cronica.com.

ar) are the country's sensationalist tabloids.

The main English-language newspaper is the decades-old *Buenos Aires Herald* (www.buenosairesherald.com), which is revered for taking on the military dictatorship during the 1980s. Unfortunately, it tends to be filled with errors and articles bought from other news agencies. For visitors, it's a decent introduction to current issues in Argentina, but rarely offers much insight. It can be a good source for finding out about cultural events. The *Argentina Independent* (www.argetinaindependent.com) was a free monthly newspaper that is currently out of print but still active online.

Foreign newspapers such as the *New York Times, Le Monde,* and *El País* as well as a few international magazines such as *Time* can occasionally be found in some newspaper stands in Centro, although prices tend to be excessive. Newspapers from the United Kingdom are rarely sold anywhere.

A huge number of magazines are sold alongside the newspapers. *Caras* and *Gente* are popular celebrity gossip rags. *Barcelona* offers satire, and *Hecho en Bs. As.* is the Argentine version of the *Big Issue,* a magazine that supports homeless people. Most also offer a surprisingly large selection of sudoku and Spanish *sopa de letras* (word searches, literally translated as "letter soup") magazines.

TELEVISION AND RADIO

Cable channels are quite vast in selection. Many hotels place great importance on having cable, although regular TV channels offer a decent range of programs. Loud programs, mostly not of particularly high quality, are the norm, and watching news channels or debates about current issues can mean trying to listen to four conversations at once. Dubbing is not very popular in Argentina, and most foreign films and TV shows, of which there are many, are shown in their original language with Spanish subtitles.

There are numerous FM and AM radio stations in Buenos Aires. FM channels, such as Rock & Pop (95.9), Aspen (102.3), which plays pop and rock, and the purely tango playing 2x4 (92.7), are more musically oriented, while AM channels offer more diversity, like Radio Nacional (870), which broadcasts programs on Argentine news, culture, and history.

Tourist Information

WEIGHTS AND MEASURES
TIME
Argentina decides whether to enforce daylight saving time on a year-by-year basis. Its geographical location would imply a time zone of UTC-4 during daylight saving time and UTC-5. In 2016, the standard was UTC-3.

MEASUREMENTS AND ELECTRICITY
The metric system (kilometers, meters, liters, kilograms, etc.) reigns in Buenos Aires.

Argentine electric outlets operate on 220 volts, 50 hertz. While older plugs included round pins, these have been banned and selling adaptors for them is illegal, although widespread. These older plugs do not have grounding capabilities, making them a safety hazard.

Generally speaking, travelers from North America will need adapters for all electronic devices, but they're easy to locate in Buenos Aires (as well as the airport). Many European devices (with two round sockets) will work without an adapter. *Ferreterías* (hardware stores) are your best bet for finding adapters and converters, although they can often be found being sold on the sidewalk for cheaper. If you're concerned about whether to take a power converter for your computer or laptop, it is always worth asking the manufacturer before traveling.

TOURIST OFFICES
The Ministerio de Turismo (Ministry of Tourism, www.turismo.gov.ar) is the national government department charged with drawing tourists to Argentina and ensuring that they get the most out of their time once they arrive. Their central office (Av. Santa Fe 883, tel. 011/4312-2232, 9am-5pm Mon.-Fri.) is located in Retiro. There is also an outlet in each airport, open 8am to 8pm daily.

The city government (www.turismo.buenosaires.gob.ar) offers advice that is more extensive and specifically dedicated to the city of Buenos Aires from six different points around the city: Centro (Florida 50, no phone, 9am-6pm daily), La Boca (Pedro de Mendoza 1821, no phone, 10am-5pm Tues.-Sun.), Puerto Madero (Av. Alicia Moreau de Justo 200, no phone, 10am-6pm daily), Retiro (Florida and Marcelo T. de Alvear, no phone, 9am-6pm daily), Retiro Bus Station

(Terminal de Omnibus, Local 83, no phone, 7:30am-4:30pm daily), and Recoleta (Av. Quintana 596, no phone, 9am-6pm daily). Opening times change regularly with these information offices, so check in advance.

MAPS

Free foldout street maps of Buenos Aires can be obtained at any of the above tourist offices, and many hostels and hotels provide guests with maps on request. An excellent resource for exploring the city is the *Guía T,* available from most newspaper stands. This pocket-size booklet covers all the streets of Capital Federal in a methodical pattern and includes all the bus routes as well as listings for buildings such as hospitals, churches, and police stations. Stalls and newspaper stands running down the center of Florida street often sell a variety of maps.

Topographic maps are notoriously hard to come by in Argentina. Inquiries should be made at the Instituto Geográfico Militar (Av. Cabildo 301, Palermo, tel. 011/4576-5576).

Librería Turística (Paraguay 2457, Recoleta, 9am-7pm Mon.-Fri., 9am-1pm Sat.) is a bookshop that specializes in guides and maps for Buenos Aires, Argentina, and the rest of the world.

RESOURCES

Glossary

alfajores: sandwich-style cookie filled with *dulce de leche* (caramel), mousse, or jam

asado: traditional slow-cooked barbecue

avenida: avenue

autopista: freeway

bandoneón: type of accordion used in traditional Argentine music, especially tango

bar notable: historic bar or café

barra bravas: soccer hooligans (fervent, sometimes violent, fans)

barrio: neighborhood

bombilla: straw used to drink maté

calle: street

carne: meat; generally used to refer to beef

cebador: the person who pours maté at the official ceremony

chopp: draft beer

colectivo: local bus

confitería: shop that sells pastries, which sometimes also serves as a café

costanera: road or walkway along a coastline

desaparecido: term used to describe someone who was "disappeared" by the military dictatorship

empanada: savory pastry stuffed with a wide range of fillings, such as meat, cheese, and vegetables

estación fluvial: port

feria: outdoor market

fileteado: flamboyant style of signage traditional to Buenos Aires

kiosco: a kiosk or newsstand that sells sweets, refreshments, and cigarettes

IVA: the Argentine equivalent of value-added tax (VAT)

locutorio: business that provides enclosed phone booths and fax and internet services

maté: traditional hot drink, similar to tea, usually drunk as a part of a ceremony

milonga: tango dance event

parrilla: steak house; also the name of the grill used for barbecuing meat

peña folklorica: traditional folk party, with music, food, and dancing

picada: platter of cold meats and cheeses, often eaten as a meal in itself

porteño: someone or something originating from Buenos Aires

práctica: when used in regard to a *milonga*: an informal tango dance event

tabaquería: tobacco store

Spanish Phrasebook

Argentine Spanish is one of the most unique and identifiable dialects of the world's second most-spoken language. Referred to as *"castellano,"* Spanish spoken in Buenos Aires sounds rougher than most other Spanish accents, while also being more animated—akin to Italian. It is rare to come across anyone working in the Argentine tourism industry that does not speak English, however, and a large percentage of locals are also able to hold conversations in English.

One of the more distinctive aspects of *porteño* Spanish is the use of the *"voseo,"* where the second person singular pronoun (the informal form of "you") is *"vos"* instead of *"tú."* As a result, irregular verb conjugations are made simpler. For example, *tienes* (you have) becomes *tenes.* Likewise, the conjugation of *ser* (to be) becomes *sos* instead of *eres,* meaning that *tú eres* (you are) is actually *vos sos.*

The local slang, known as *lunfardo,* includes many words that are used in everyday life, such as *guita* (money), *laburar* (to work), *mina* (young woman), and *quilombo* (chaos). Some other common *porteño* phrases are *viste* (you know) and *che* (hey/mate).

PRONUNCIATION

Once you learn them, Spanish pronunciation rules—in contrast to English—don't change. Spanish vowels generally sound softer than in English. (*Note:* The capitalized syllables below receive stronger accents.) The pronunciation of "ll" and "y" both differ from the standard Spanish pronunciation.

VOWELS

a   like ah, as in "hah": *agua* AH-gooah (water), *pan* PAHN (bread), and *casa* CAH-sah (house)

e   like ay, as in "may:" *mesa* MAY-sah (table), *tela* TAY-lah (cloth), and *de* DAY (of, from)

i   like ee, as in "need": *diez* dee-AYZ (ten), *comida* ko-MEE-dah (meal), and *fin* FEEN (end)

o   like oh, as in "go": *peso* PAY-soh (weight), *ocho* OH-choh (eight), and *poco* POH-koh (a bit)

u   like oo, as in "cool": *uno* OO-noh (one), *cuarto* KOOAHR-toh (room), and *usted* oos-TAYD (you); when it follows a "q" the u is silent; when it follows an "h" or has an umlaut, it's pronounced like "w"

CONSONANTS

b, d, f, k, l, m, n, p, q, s, t, v, w, x, y, z, and ch pronounced almost as in English; h occurs, but is silent—not pronounced at all

c   like k as in "keep": *cuarto* KOOAR-toh (room), *casa* CAH-sah (house); when it precedes "e" or "i," pronounce c like s, as in "sit": *cerveza* sayr-VAY-sah (beer), *encima* ayn-SEE-mah (atop)

g   like g as in "gift" when it precedes "a," "o," "u," or a consonant: *gato* GAH-toh (cat), *hago* AH-goh (I do, make); otherwise, pronounce g like h as in "hat": *giro* HEE-roh (money order), *gente* HAYN-tay (people)

j   like h, as in "has": *Jueves* HOOAY-vays (Thursday), *mejor* may-HOR (better)

ll   like zh, as in "leisure": *toalla* toh-AH-zhah (towel), *ellos* AY-zhohs (they, them)

ñ   like ny, as in "canyon": *año* AH-nyo (year), *señor* SAY-nyor (Mr., sir)

r is lightly trilled, with tongue at the roof of your mouth like a very light English d, as in "ready": *pero* PAY-roh (but), *tres* TRAYS (three), *cuatro* KOOAH-troh (four)

rr like a Spanish r, but with much more emphasis and trill. Let your tongue flap. Practice with *burro* (donkey), *carretera* (highway), and Carrillo (proper name), then really let go with *ferrocarril* (railroad)

y identical to "ll"; like zh, as in "leisure." An exception when it's being used as the Spanish word for "and," as in "Ron y Kathy." In such case, pronounce it like the English ee, as in "keep": Ron "ee" Kathy (Ron and Kathy).

ACCENT

The rule for accent, the relative stress given to syllables within a given word, is straightforward. If a word ends in a vowel, an n, or an s, accent the next-to-last syllable; if not, accent the last syllable.

Pronounce *gracias* GRAH-seeahs (thank you), *orden* OHR-dayn (order), and *carretera* kah-ray-TAY-rah (highway) with stress on the next-to-last syllable.

Otherwise, accent the last syllable: *venir* vay-NEER (to come), *ferrocarril* fay-roh-cah-REEL (railroad), and *edad* ay-DAHD (age).

Exceptions to the accent rule are always marked with an accent sign: (á, é, í, ó, or ú), such as *teléfono* tay-LAY-foh-noh (telephone), *jabón* hah-BON (soap), and *rápido* RAH-pee-doh (rapid).

BASIC AND COURTEOUS EXPRESSIONS

Most Spanish-speaking people consider formalities important. Whenever approaching anyone for information or some other reason, do not forget the appropriate salutation—good morning,

good evening, etc. Standing alone, the greeting *hola* (hello) can sound brusque.

Hello. *Hola.*

Good morning. *Buenos días.*

Good afternoon. *Buenas tardes.*

Good evening. *Buenas noches.*

How are you? *¿Cómo está usted?*

Very well, thank you. *Muy bien, gracias.*

Okay; good. *Bien.*

Not okay; bad. *Mal* or *feo.*

So-so. *Más o menos.*

And you? *¿Y usted?*

Thank you. *Gracias.*

Thank you very much. *Muchas gracias.*

You're very kind. *Muy amable.*

You're welcome. *De nada.*

Goodbye. *Adios.*

See you later. *Hasta luego.*

please *por favor*

yes *sí*

no *no*

I don't know. *No sé.*

Just a moment, please. *Momentito, por favor.*

Excuse me, please (when you're trying to get attention). *Disculpe* or *Con permiso.*

Excuse me (when you've made a boo-boo). *Lo siento.*

Pleased to meet you. *Mucho gusto.*

How do you say . . . in Spanish? *¿Cómo se dice . . . en español?*

What is your name? *¿Cómo se llama usted?*

Do you speak English? *¿Habla usted inglés?*

Is English spoken here? (Does anyone here speak English?) *¿Se habla inglés?*

I don't speak Spanish well. *No hablo bien el español.*

I don't understand. *No entiendo.*

My name is . . . *Me llamo . . .*

Would you like . . . *¿Quisiera usted . . .*

Let's go to . . . *Vamos a . . .*

TERMS OF ADDRESS

When in doubt, use the formal *usted* (you) as a form of address.

I *yo*
you (formal) *usted*
you (familiar) *vos*
he/him *él*
she/her *ella*
we/us *nosotros*
you (plural) *ustedes*
they/them *ellos* (all males or mixed gender); *ellas* (all females)
Mr., sir *señor*
Mrs., madam *señora*
miss, young lady *señorita*
wife *esposa*
husband *esposo*
friend *amigo* (male); *amiga* (female)
sweetheart *novio* (male); *novia* (female)
son; daughter *hijo; hija*
brother; sister *hermano; hermana*
father; mother *padre; madre*
grandfather; grandmother *abuelo; abuela*

TRANSPORTATION

Where is . . . ? *¿Dónde está . . . ?*
How far is it to . . . ? *¿A cuánto está . . . ?*
from . . . to . . . *de . . . a . . .*
How many blocks? *¿Cuántas cuadras?*
Where (Which) is the way to . . . ? *¿Dónde está el camino a . . . ?*
the bus station *la terminal de autobuses*
the bus stop *la parada de autobuses*
Where is this bus going? *¿Adónde va este autobús?*
the taxi stand *la parada de taxis*
the train station *la estación de ferrocarril*
the boat *el barco*
the launch *lancha; tiburonera*
the dock *el muelle*
the airport *el aeropuerto*
I'd like a ticket to . . . *Quisiera un boleto a . . .*

first (second) class *primera (segunda) clase*
roundtrip *ida y vuelta*
reservation *reservación*
baggage *equipaje*
Stop here, please. *Pare aquí, por favor.*
the entrance *la entrada*
the exit *la salida*
the ticket office *la oficina de boletos*
(very) near; far *(muy) cerca; lejos*
to; toward *a*
by; through *por*
from *de*
the right *la derecha*
the left *la izquierda*
straight ahead *derecho; directo*
in front *en frente*
beside *al lado*
behind *atrás*
the corner *la esquina*
the stoplight *la semáforo*
a turn *una vuelta*
right here *aquí*
somewhere around here *por acá*
right there *allí*
somewhere around there *por allá*
road *el camino*
street; boulevard *calle; bulevar*
block *la cuadra*
highway *carretera*
kilometer *kilómetro*
bridge; toll *puente; cuota*
address *dirección*
north; south *norte; sur*
east; west *oriente (este); poniente (oeste)*

ACCOMMODATIONS

hotel *hotel*
Is there a room? *¿Hay cuarto?*
May I (may we) see it? *¿Puedo (podemos) verlo?*
What is the rate? *¿Cuál es el precio?*
Is that your best rate? *¿Es su mejor precio?*
Is there something cheaper? *¿Hay algo más económico?*
a single room *un cuarto sencillo*

a **double room** *un cuarto doble*
double bed *cama matrimonial*
twin beds *camas gemelas*
with private bath *con baño*
hot water *agua caliente*
shower *ducha*
towels *toallas*
soap *jabón*
toilet paper *papel higiénico*
blanket *frazada; manta*
sheets *sábanas*
air-conditioned *aire acondicionado*
fan *abanico; ventilador*
key *llave*
manager *gerente*

FOOD

I'm hungry *Tengo hambre.*
I'm thirsty. *Tengo sed.*
menu *carta; menú*
order *orden*
glass *vaso*
fork *tenedor*
knife *cuchillo*
spoon *cuchara*
napkin *servilleta*
soft drink *refresco*
coffee *café*
tea *té*
drinking water *agua pura; agua potable*
bottled carbonated water *agua mineral*
bottled uncarbonated water *agua sin gas*
beer *cerveza*
wine *vino*
milk *leche*
juice *jugo*
cream *crema*
sugar *azúcar*
cheese *queso*
snack *antojo; botana*
breakfast *desayuno*
lunch *almuerzo*
daily lunch special *comida corrida* (or *el menú del día* depending on region)

dinner *comida* (often eaten in late afternoon); *cena* (a late-night snack)
the check *la cuenta*
eggs *huevos*
bread *pan*
salad *ensalada*
fruit *fruta*
mango *mango*
watermelon *sandía*
papaya *papaya*
banana *plátano*
apple *manzana*
orange *naranja*
lime *limón*
fish *pescado*
shellfish *mariscos*
shrimp *camarones*
meat (without) *(sin) carne*
chicken *pollo*
pork *puerco*
beef; steak *res; bistec*
bacon; ham *tocino; jamón*
fried *frito*
roasted *asada*
barbecue; barbecued *barbacoa; al carbón*

SHOPPING

money *dinero*
money-exchange bureau *casa de cambio*
I would like to exchange traveler's checks. *Quisiera cambiar cheques de viajero.*
What is the exchange rate? *¿Cuál es el tipo de cambio?*
How much is the commission? *¿Cuánto cuesta la comisión?*
Do you accept credit cards? *¿Aceptan tarjetas de crédito?*
money order *giro*
How much does it cost? *¿Cuánto cuesta?*
What is your final price? *¿Cuál es su último precio?*
expensive *caro*

cheap *barato; económico*
more *más*
less *menos*
a little *un poco*
too much *demasiado*

HEALTH

Help me please. *Ayúdeme por favor.*
I am ill. *Estoy enfermo.*
Call a doctor. *Llame un doctor.*
Take me to . . . *Lléveme a . . .*
hospital *hospital; sanatorio*
drugstore *farmacia*
pain *dolor*
fever *fiebre*
headache *dolor de cabeza*
stomach ache *dolor de estómago*
burn *quemadura*
cramp *calambre*
nausea *náusea*
vomiting *vomitar*
medicine *medicina*
antibiotic *antibiótico*
pill; tablet *pastilla*
aspirin *aspirina*
ointment; cream *pomada; crema*
bandage *venda*
cotton *algodón*
sanitary napkins use brand name,
  e.g., Kotex
birth control pills *pastillas
  anticonceptivas*
contraceptive foam *espuma
  anticonceptiva*
condoms *preservativos; condones*
toothbrush *cepilla dental*
dental floss *hilo dental*
toothpaste *crema dental*
dentist *dentista*
toothache *dolor de muelas*

POST OFFICE AND COMMUNICATIONS

long-distance telephone *teléfono
  larga distancia*
I would like to call . . . *Quisiera llamar
  a . . .*

collect *por cobrar*
station to station *a quien contesta*
person to person *persona a persona*
credit card *tarjeta de crédito*
post office *correo*
general delivery *lista de correo*
letter *carta*
stamp *estampilla, timbre*
postcard *tarjeta*
aerogram *aerograma*
air mail *correo aereo*
registered *registrado*
money order *giro*
package; box *paquete; caja*
string; tape *cuerda; cinta*

AT THE BORDER

border *frontera*
customs *aduana*
immigration *migración*
tourist card *tarjeta de turista*
inspection *inspección; revisión*
passport *pasaporte*
profession *profesión*
marital status *estado civil*
single *soltero*
married; divorced *casado; divorciado*
widowed *viudado*
insurance *seguros*
title *título*
driver's license *licencia de manejar*

AT THE GAS STATION

gas station *gasolinera*
gasoline *gasolina*
unleaded *sin plomo*
full, please *lleno, por favor*
tire *llanta*
tire repair shop *vulcanizadora*
air *aire*
water *agua*
oil (change) *aceite (cambio)*
grease *grasa*
My . . . doesn't work. *Mi . . . no sirve.*
battery *batería*
radiator *radiador*
alternator *alternador*

generator *generador*

tow truck *grúa*

repair shop *taller mecánico*

tune-up *afinación*

auto parts store *refaccionería*

VERBS

Verbs are the key to getting along in Spanish. They employ mostly predictable forms and come in three classes, which end in *ar, er,* and *ir,* respectively:

to buy *comprar*

I buy, you (he, she, it) buys *compro, compra*

we buy, you (they) buy *compramos, compran*

to eat *comer*

I eat, you (he, she, it) eats *como, come*

we eat, you (they) eat *comemos, comen*

to climb *subir*

I climb, you (he, she, it) climbs *subo, sube*

we climb, you (they) climb *subimos, suben*

Here are more (with irregularities indicated):

to do or make *hacer* (regular except for *hago,* I do or make)

to go *ir* (very irregular: *voy, va, vamos, van*)

to go (walk) *andar*

to love *amar*

to work *trabajar*

to want *desear, querer*

to need *necesitar*

to read *leer*

to write *escribir*

to repair *reparar*

to stop *parar*

to get off (the bus) *bajar*

to arrive *llegar*

to stay (remain) *quedar*

to stay (lodge) *hospedar*

to leave *salir* (regular except for *salgo,* I leave)

to look at *mirar*

to look for *buscar*

to give *dar* (regular except for *doy,* I give)

to carry *llevar*

to have *tener* (irregular: *tengo, tiene, tenemos, tienen*)

to come *venir* (similarly irregular: *vengo, viene, venimos, vienen*)

Spanish has two forms of "to be":

to be *estar* (regular except for *estoy,* I am)

to be *ser* (very irregular: *soy, es, somos, son*)

Use *estar* when speaking of location or a temporary state of being: "I am at home." *"Estoy en casa." "I'm sick." "Estoy enfermo."* Use *ser* for a permanent state of being: "I am a doctor." *"Soy doctora."*

NUMBERS

zero *cero*

one *uno*

two *dos*

three *tres*

four *cuatro*

five *cinco*

six *seis*

seven *siete*

eight *ocho*

nine *nueve*

10 *diez*

11 *once*

12 *doce*

13 *trece*

14 *catorce*

15 *quince*

16 *dieciseis*

17 *diecisiete*

18 *dieciocho*

19 *diecinueve*

20 *veinte*

21 *veinte y uno* or *veintiuno*
30 *treinta*
40 *cuarenta*
50 *cincuenta*
60 *sesenta*
70 *setenta*
80 *ochenta*
90 *noventa*
100 *ciento*
101 *ciento y uno* or *cientiuno*
200 *doscientos*
500 *quinientos*
1,000 *mil*
10,000 *diez mil*
100,000 *cien mil*
1,000,000 *millón*
one half *medio*
one third *un tercio*
one fourth *un cuarto*

TIME

What time is it? *¿Qué hora es?*
It's one o'clock. *Es la una.*
It's three in the afternoon. *Son las tres de la tarde.*
It's 4 a.m. *Son las cuatro de la mañana.*
six-thirty *seis y media*
a quarter till eleven *un cuarto para las once*
a quarter past five *las cinco y cuarto*
an hour *una hora*

DAYS AND MONTHS

Monday *lunes*
Tuesday *martes*
Wednesday *miércoles*
Thursday *jueves*
Friday *viernes*
Saturday *sábado*
Sunday *domingo*
today *hoy*
tomorrow *mañana*
yesterday *ayer*
January *enero*
February *febrero*
March *marzo*
April *abril*
May *mayo*
June *junio*
July *julio*
August *agosto*
September *septiembre*
October *octubre*
November *noviembre*
December *diciembre*
a week *una semana*
a month *un mes*
after *después*
before *antes*

(Courtesy of Bruce Whipperman, author of *Moon Pacific Mexico*.)

Suggested Reading

HISTORY AND GENERAL INFORMATION

Chatwin, Bruce. *In Patagonia*. London: Jonathan Cape, 1977. When Chatwin traveled to Argentina and the deepest regions of Patagonia, he likely never expected that his travels would culminate in one of history's most important and acclaimed travel books. Although not about Buenos Aires, its relevance and authority on Argentina make it an excellent choice for anyone visiting the country.

Crassweller, Robert. *Perón and the Enigmas of Argentina*. New York: Norton, 1987. Taking on the unenviable task of trying to explain the complex roots of Peronism, Crassweller has produced an excellent account of where Perón and his wife, Evita, came from and how they were converted into the figureheads worshipped across the country long after their deaths.

Darwin, Charles. *The Voyage of the Beagle*. London: Penguin, 1989. Darwin's account of his five-year voyage aboard Robert Fitzroy's HMS Beagle remains one of the most fascinating travel books of all time, combining his scientific studies, geographic discoveries, and anthropologic observations from visits to Buenos Aires and the surrounding region.

Goñi, Uki. *The Real Odessa*. London: Granta Books 2002. Goñi refuses to hold back on a topic that many fear to even broach in this astonishing book that carefully chronicles the process that allowed Nazi war criminals to live out their lives anonymously in Argentina after the end of the war, implicating the Vatican, Peronist regime, and many European figures in the scandal.

Nouzeilles, Gabriela & Montaldo, Graciela (editors). *The Argentina Reader*. Durham, NC: Duke University Press, 2002. A 600-page compendium on Argentina's history, society, and culture, this book is a diverse collection of articles, short stories, essays, poems, songs, and photos, which make it the stand-out introduction to Argentina.

Verbitsky, Horacio. *The Flight: Confessions of an Argentine Dirty Warrior*. New York: New Press, 1996. Based on interviews conducted with a soldier who personally pushed dozens of political prisoners out of airplanes above the Rio de la Plata, Verbitsky's chilling book breaks the steadfast silence of the murderous practices of the military dictatorship during the Dirty War (1976-1983).

CULTURE

Denniston, Christine. *The Meaning of Tango: The History and Steps of the Argentinian Dance*. London: Anova Books, 2008. Tracing the history of tango from the dingy streets of La Boca, through the salons of Parisian high-society, and back to the concert halls of Buenos Aires, Denniston paints a wonderful picture of how tango is not merely a genre of music or dance but is in fact a way of life.

Gardner, James. *Buenos Aires: The Biography of a City*. New York: St. Martin's Press, 2015. Ostensibly a book about the varied and eclectic architecture of Buenos Aires, Gardner's writings discuss the history of the city and its culture, formation, and residents, all of which ended up influencing the look of the city as we know it today.

Kogan, Gabriela. *The Authentic Bars, Cafés, and Restaurants of Buenos Aires*. New York: The Little Bookroom, 2008. A guide to 70 of the city's bars, cafés, and restaurants that fight to maintain the traditions and spirit of old Buenos Aires in the face of modernity and economic streamlining. Delightful black-and-white photos accompany the passionate text.

Wilson, Jonathan. *Angels with Dirty Faces: The Footballing History of Argentina*. London: Orion, 2015. One of the world's most respected soccer writers, Wilson covers in great detail the history of football in Argentina from its earliest introduction by the British through to its current state with the world's best player as its captain.

FICTION

Borges, Jorge Luis. *Labyrinths*. New York: New Directions, 1962. One of the world's most important 20th-century writers, Borges was a master of short stories, 23 of which are compiled in this collection. Many appeared in his more renowned earlier compendiums in their original language, but his greatest classics, such as "The Garden of Forking Paths" and "The Library of Babel" are gathered in this outstanding English-language collection.

Cortázar, Julio. *Blow-up and Other Stories*. New York: Pantheon Books, 1985. A collection of 15 short stories written by one of Argentina's most celebrated writers. Part of the magic realism literary movement that blossomed in Latin America during the mid-20th century, Cortázar fused surrealism with realism; this collection is a great introduction to his renowned works.

Hernández, José. *Martín Fierro*. Albany, NY: State University of New York Press, 1967. This epic poem by Hernández defined the idea of the gaucho culture in Argentina as well as becoming the authoritative text in the *gauchesco* genre of literature, originally written in 1879. An alternative translation can be viewed for free online at www.sparrowthorn.com.

Martínez, Tomás Eloy. *The Tango Singer*. London: Bloomsbury, 2004. Forced into exile during the military dictatorship in the 1970s, Martínez wrote this fiery novel about Buenos Aires, tango, and Jorge Luis Borges in a story that is set during the Argentine economic crisis of the early 21st century, making it an excellent contextual preparation for visitors to Buenos Aires, along with the rest of the author's titles.

Sabato, Ernesto. *On Heroes and Tombs*. Boston: David R. Godine, 1981. Writing only three novels in his lifetime, Sabato focused more on essays, holding an open dislike to the magic realism movement so widespread at the time. This, his second novel originally written in 1961, stands up as one of the finest of his contemporaries, with vivid and elegant depictions of Buenos Aires during some of its most desperate moments.

Internet Resources

GENERAL

Buenos Aires City Government
www.turismo.buenosaires.gob.ar/en

An excellent resource for tourists, the website run by the city government provides information on a wide range of attractions, accommodations, transportation, activities, and events, while being particularly up-to-date with fresh and reliable content.

NEWS AND MEDIA

Buenos Aires Herald
www.buenosairesherald.com

English-language newspaper that has been providing news and information since 1876, providing easy access to information on current stories.

The Argentina Independent
www.argentinaindependent.com

English-language news outlet that provides articles of general interest and in-depth analysis.

Uki Goñi
www.ukinet.com

As the Argentine correspondent for international newspapers, including *The New York Times* and the *Guardian,* Uki collects much of his writing on Argentina on this website, including in-depth analysis of a broad spectrum of topics.

TRANSPORTATION

Buenos Aires Ciudad
www.mapa.buenosaires.gov.ar

A government website that helps find the best route between any two locations across the city, including public transportation, driving, biking, or walking.

EMBASSIES AND VISAS

Immigration and Border Control
www.migraciones.gov.ar/accesibleingles

Official website for the national government department that deals with visa issues, as well as immigration and imports.

RESTAURANTS AND BARS

Oleo
www.guiaoleo.com.ar

A website with comprehensive coverage of the city's bars and restaurants, including customer reviews/ratings, opening hours and price indications (largely in Spanish).

ENTERTAINMENT

Cultural Agenda
www.disfrutemosba.buenosaires.gob/ar

Although in Spanish, the visual and simple layout allows for easy navigation to find current and up-coming cultural events, including tours, exhibitions, and festivals, most of which are free.

Vuenos Airez
www.vuenosairez.com
A comprehensive listing of upcoming events, including concerts, exhibitions, festivals, parties, and theater productions, all presented in an easy-to-use website that allows for searching by date or genre.

Hoy Milonga
www.hoy-milonga.com/en
A website that provides schedules for city-wide *milongas* (tango dance events) and classes, as well as providing extra information on the scene for those looking to buy tango-related products.

BLOGS

Pick Up the Fork
www.pickupthefork.com
Run by American blogger Allie Lazar, Pick Up the Fork offers extensive insight into the Buenos Aires food and restaurant scene, with excellent suggestions and an informal attitude.

Gringo in Buenos Aires
www.gringoinbuenosaires.com/blog
A website that offers extensive insight into Buenos Aires neighborhoods as well the city's culture, nightlife, and gastronomy.

The Real Argentina
www.therealargentina.com/en
A blog that provides articles on tourism, culture, food, and wine in Buenos Aires and beyond, The Real Argentina offers its readers ideas for places to visit in the city.

Hand of Pod
www.handofpod.wordpress.com
A soccer blog run by a group of English and Argentine football fans, who produce weekly podcasts in English about Argentine football, providing a knowledgeable introduction to the local scene.

Buenos Aires Expats
www.baexpats.org
A forum run by foreigners living in Buenos Aires, this is a great resource for travelers or visitors to the city who need a quick answer from someone who knows the city and culture.

Buenos Aires Gay Guide
www.thegayguide.com.ar
A comprehensive look at the gay and lesbian scene in Buenos Aires, including nightlife, accommodation, culture, while also offering other general help for travelers.

Index

Restaurants Index

Nightlife Index

Shops Index

Hotels Index

Photo Credits

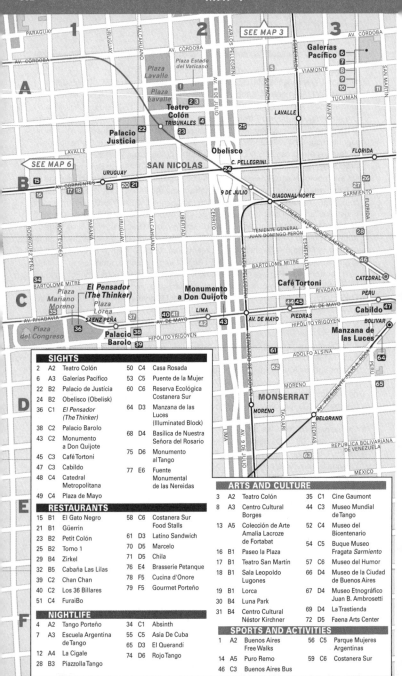

SIGHTS

2	A2	Teatro Colón	
6	A3	Galerías Pacífico	
22	B2	Palacio de Justicia	
24	B2	Obelisco (Obelisk)	
36	C1	*El Pensador (The Thinker)*	
38	C2	Palacio Barolo	
43	C2	Monumento a Don Quijote	
45	C3	Café Tortoni	
47	C3	Cabildo	
48	C4	Catedral Metropolitana	
49	C4	Plaza de Mayo	
50	C4	Casa Rosada	
53	C5	Puente de la Mujer	
60	C6	Reserva Ecológica Costanera Sur	
64	D3	Manzana de las Luces (Illuminated Block)	
68	D4	Basílica de Nuestra Señora del Rosario	
75	D6	Monumento al Tango	
77	E6	Fuente Monumental de las Nereidas	

RESTAURANTS

15	B1	El Gato Negro
21	B1	Güerrin
23	B2	Petit Colón
25	B2	Tomo 1
29	B4	Zirkel
32	B5	Cabaña Las Lilas
39	C2	Chan Chan
40	C2	Los 36 Billares
51	C4	FuraiBo
58	C6	Costanera Sur Food Stalls
61	D3	Latino Sandwich
70	D5	Marcelo
71	D5	Chila
76	E4	Brasserie Petanque
78	F5	Cucina d'Onore
79	F5	Gourmet Porteño

NIGHTLIFE

4	A2	Tango Porteño
7	A3	Escuela Argentina de Tango
12	A4	La Cigale
28	B3	Piazzolla Tango
34	C1	Absinth
55	C5	Asia De Cuba
65	D3	El Querandí
74	D6	Rojo Tango

ARTS AND CULTURE

3	A2	Teatro Colón
8	A3	Centro Cultural Borges
13	A5	Colección de Arte Amalia Lacroze de Fortabat
16	B1	Paseo la Plaza
17	B1	Teatro San Martín
18	B1	Sala Leopoldo Lugones
19	B1	Lorca
30	B4	Luna Park
31	B4	Centro Cultural Néstor Kirchner
35	C1	Cine Gaumont
44	C3	Museo Mundial de Tango
52	C4	Museo del Bicentenario
54	C5	Buque Museo Fragata *Sarmiento*
57	D4	Museo del Humor
66	D4	Museo de la Ciudad de Buenos Aires
67	D4	Museo Etnográfico Juan B. Ambrosetti
69	D4	La Trastienda
72	D5	Faena Arts Center

SPORTS AND ACTIVITIES

1	A2	Buenos Aires Free Walks
14	A5	Puro Remo
46	C3	Buenos Aires Bus
56	C5	Parque Mujeres Argentinas
59	C6	Costanera Sur

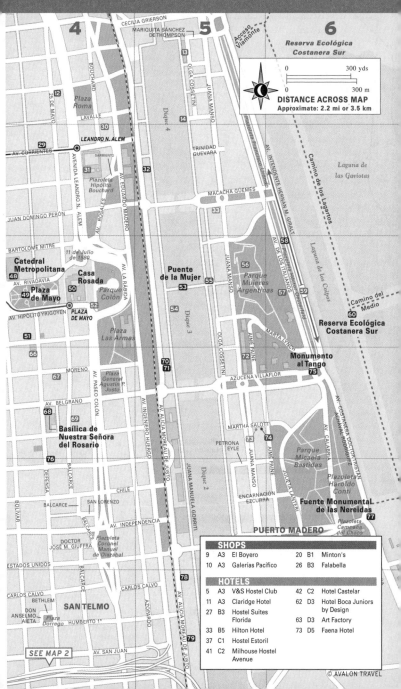

4 CECILIA GRIERSON
MARIQUITA SÁNCHEZ
DE THOMPSON
5
Acceso
Viamonte
6
*Reserva Ecológica
Costanera Sur*

6
| 0 | 300 yds |
| 0 | 300 m |
DISTANCE ACROSS MAP
Approximate: 2.2 mi or 3.5 km

12 *25 DE MAYO*
BOUCHARD
*Plaza
Roma*
LAVALLE
30
29 *LEANDRO N. ALEM*
AV. CORRIENTES
SARMIENTO
31
*Plazoleta
Hipólita
Bouchard*
32
Dique 4
OLGA COSSETINI
JUANA MANSO
13
14
TRINIDAD
GUEVARA
AV. FRANCIA VÉLEZ
Laguna de
las Gaviotas
Camino de los Lagartos

JUAN DOMINGO PERÓN
AVENIDA LEANDRO N. ALEM
AV. EDUARDO MADERO
MACACHA GÜEMES
33
AV. DE LOS ITALIANOS
AV. INTENDENTE HERNÁN M. GIRALT
Laguna de los Coipos

BARTOLOME MITRE
**Catedral
Metropolitana**
48
AV. RIVADAVIA
49 **Plaza
de Mayo**
*11 de Julio
de 1580*
AV. LA RÁBIDA
**Casa
Rosada**
50
*Parque
Colón*
**Puente
de la Mujer**
53
JUANA MANSO
56
*Parque
Mujeres
Argentinas*
57
58
59
Laguna de los Coipos

52
*PLAZA
DE MAYO*
AV. HIPÓLITO YRIGOYEN
51
*Plaza
Las Armas*
54
Dique 3
OLGA COSSETINI
AIMÉ PAINE
55
60
Camino del
Medio
**Reserva Ecológica
Costanera Sur**

66
MORENO
67
AV. PASEO COLÓN
*Plaza
General
Agustín P.
Justo*
70
71
AZUCENA VILLAFLOR
72
MARTA LYNCH
**Monumento
al Tango**
75

AV. BELGRANO
68
69
**Basílica de
Nuestra Señora
del Rosario**
76
AV. INGENIERO HUERGO
AV. ALICIA MOREAU DE JUSTO
MARTHA SALOTTI
PETRONA
EYLE
73
JUANA MANSO
AIMÉ PAINE
74
AV. CALABRIA
AV. COSTANERA DOCTOR TRISTÁN ACHÁVAL RODRÍGUEZ
*Parque
Micaela
Bastidas*
JULIETA LANTERI

DEFENSA
BALCARCE
CHILE
SAN LORENZO
Dique 2
JUANA MANUELA GORRITI
ENCARNACIÓN
EZCURRA
*Plazoleta
Haroldo
Conti*
**Fuente Monumental
de las Nereidas**
77

BOLÍVAR
BALCARCE
AV. INDEPENDENCIA
PUERTO MADERO
*Plazoleta
Campaña
del Chaco*

DOCTOR
JOSÉ M. GIUFFRA
*Plazoleta
Coronel
Manuel
de Olazabal*

ESTADOS UNIDOS
BALCARCE
78

CARLOS CALVO
BETHLEM
CARLOS CALVO
SAN TELMO
DON
ANSELMO
AIETA
*Plaza
Dorrego*
HUMBERTO 1°
AZOPARDO
AV. ALICIA MOREAU DE JUSTO
79

SEE MAP 2
AV. SAN JUAN

© AVALON TRAVEL

SHOPS					
9	A3	El Boyero	20	B1	Minton's
10	A3	Galerías Pacífico	26	B3	Falabella

HOTELS					
5	A3	V&S Hostel Club	42	C2	Hotel Castelar
11	A3	Claridge Hotel	62	D3	Hotel Boca Juniors by Design
27	B3	Hostel Suites Florida	63	D3	Art Factory
33	B5	Hilton Hotel	73	D5	Faena Hotel
37	C1	Hostel Estoril			
41	C2	Milhouse Hostel Avenue			

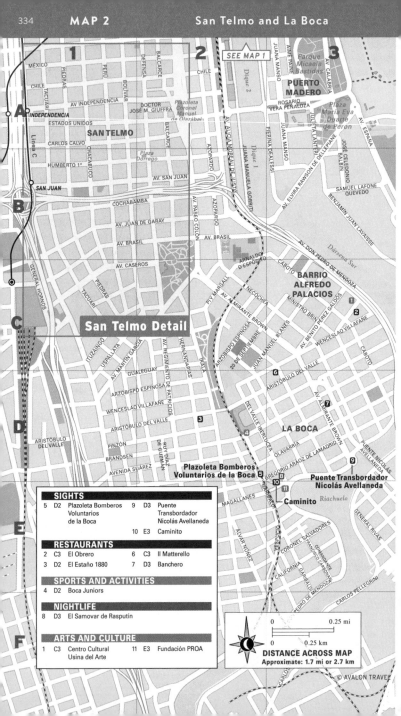

SEE MAP 1

Parque
Micaela
Bastidas

PUERTO
MADERO

Plaza
María Eva
Duarte
de Perón

SAN TELMO

Plazoleta
Coronel
Manuel
de Olazábal

Plaza
Dorrego

Dique 1

Dársena Sur

San Telmo Detail

BARRIO
ALFREDO
PALACIOS

LA BOCA

Plazoleta Bomberos
Voluntarios de la Boca

Puente Transbordador
Nicolás Avellaneda

Caminito

Riachuelo

SIGHTS

| 5 | D2 | Plazoleta Bomberos Voluntarios de la Boca | 9 | D3 | Puente Transbordador Nicolás Avellaneda |
| | | | 10 | E3 | Caminito |

RESTAURANTS

| 2 | C3 | El Obrero | 6 | C3 | Il Matterello |
| 3 | D2 | El Estaño 1880 | 7 | D3 | Banchero |

SPORTS AND ACTIVITIES

| 4 | D2 | Boca Juniors |

NIGHTLIFE

| 8 | D3 | El Samovar de Rasputín |

ARTS AND CULTURE

| 1 | C3 | Centro Cultural Usina del Arte | 11 | E3 | Fundación PROA |

0   0.25 mi
0   0.25 km

DISTANCE ACROSS MAP
Approximate: 1.7 mi or 2.7 km

© AVALON TRAVEL

DISTANCE ACROSS MAP
Approximate: 0.8 mi or 1.3 km

0   200 yds

0   200 m

MÉXICO

MÉXICO

CHILE

CHILE

El Zanjón de Granados

AV. INDEPENDENCIA

SAN LORENZO

Plazoleta Coronel Manuel de Olazábal

DOCTOR JOSÉ M. GIUFFRA

Canto al Trabajo

ESTADOS UNIDOS

INDEPENDENCIA

CARLOS CALVO

SAN TELMO

BETHLEM

DON ANSELMO AIETA

Plaza Dorrego

HUMBERTO 1°

Pasaje de la Defensa

AV. SAN JUAN

COCHABAMBA

Iglesia de la Santísima Trinidad (Cathedral of the Most Holy Trinity)

AV. JUAN DE GARAY

BRASIL

Parque Lezama

AV. CASEROS

A   B   C   D   E

Linea E

Linea C

TACUARI   PIEDRAS   CHACABUCO   PERU   BOLIVAR   BALCARCE   DEFENSA

SIGHTS

8	A3	El Zanjón de Granados
23	B3	Canto al Trabajo
30	C3	Plaza Dorrego
34	C3	Pasaje de la Defensa
41	D3	Iglesia de la Santísima Trinidad (Cathedral of the Most Holy Trinity)

RESTAURANTS

5	A2	El Baqueano
6	A2	La Poesía
7	A3	Don Esculapio
11	B2	Nacional
15	B2	El Federal
16	B2	El Banco Rojo
18	B2	Mercadito Latino
19	B2	Nonna Bianca
20	B2	Desnivel
25	B3	Naturaleza Sabia
27	C1	Untertürkheim
39	D3	Mash
40	D3	Bar Británico
44	E3	1880

NIGHTLIFE

2	A1	La Puerta Roja
13	B2	Gibraltar
21	B3	El Viejo Almacén
24	B3	Bar Sur
26	C1	Escuela Mariposita
31	C3	La Milonga del Indio

ARTS AND CULTURE

9	B1	Museo Argentino del Titere
33	C3	Museo Penitenciario Argentino
36	C3	Museo de Arte Moderno de Buenos Aires (MAMBA)
37	C3	Museo de Arte Contemporáneo de Buenos Aires (MACBA)
42	E3	Museo Histórico Nacional

SPORTS AND ACTIVITIES

14	B2	Biking Buenos Aires
22	B3	La Bicicleta Naranja
43	E3	Parque Lezama

SHOPS

4	A2	La Libre
12	B2	Walrus Books
17	B2	Mercado de San Telmo
29	C2	Cualquier Verdura
32	C3	Feria de San Pedro Telmo
35	C3	Artesanos de Argentina

HOTELS

1	A1	Telmotango
3	A2	America del Sur
10	B1	Mansión Dandi Royal
28	C2	Circus Hostel & Hotel
38	D2	Bonito

© AVALON TRAVEL

1

2

3

Parque Carlos Thays

A

RODRÍGUEZ PEÑA

AVENIDA DEL LIBERTADOR

CALLE 6

B

MONTEVIDEO

POSADAS

LIBERTAD

CERRITO

SAN TELMO

PADRE C

AV. 9 DE JULIO

Plazoleta Dr. Ruiz Moreno

2

6

AVENIDA DEL LIBERTADOR

3

SUIPACHA

4

C

PARERA

ALVEAR

Plaza de Cataluña

ARROYO

5

7

ESMERALDA

Plazoleta Dr. Carlos Pellegrini

ARROYO

Plazoleta Pierre de Coubertin

10

RETIRO

13

JUNCAL

SUIPACHA

D

Palacio de San Martín

12

BASAVILBASO

AVENIDA MAIPÚ

ARENALES

9

ARENALES

11

SARGENTO CABRAL

SAN MARTÍN

21

17

19 **Palacio Paz**

E

AV. SANTA FE

MARCELO T. DE ALVEAR

20

18

SUIPACHA

MAIPÚ

29

30 31

TACUARÍ

Plaza Libertad

LIBERTAD

CERRITO

PARAGUAY

27

F

AV. 9 DE JULIO

CARLOS PELLEGRINI

ESMERALDA

Línea C

AV. CÓRDOBA

28

AV. CÓRDOBA

SEE MAP 1

◄ SEE MAP 4

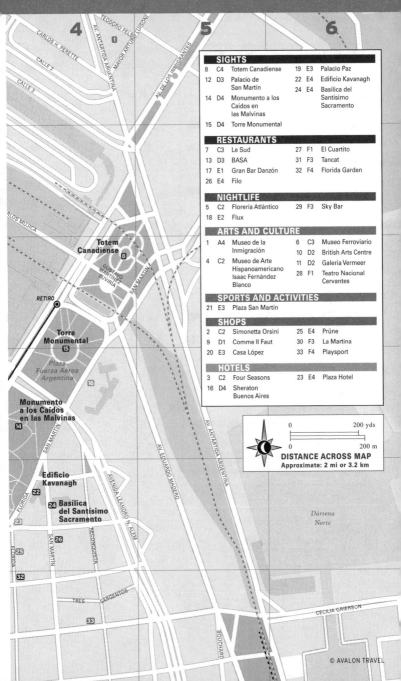

SIGHTS

8	C4	Totem Canadiense	19	E3	Palacio Paz
12	D3	Palacio de San Martín	22	E4	Edificio Kavanagh
14	D4	Monumento a los Caídos en las Malvinas	24	E4	Basílica del Santísimo Sacramento
15	D4	Torre Monumental			

RESTAURANTS

7	C3	Le Sud	27	F1	El Cuartito
13	D3	BASA	31	F3	Tancat
17	E1	Gran Bar Danzón	32	F4	Florida Garden
26	E4	Filo			

NIGHTLIFE

| 5 | C2 | Florería Atlántico | 29 | F3 | Sky Bar |
| 18 | E2 | Flux | | | |

ARTS AND CULTURE

1	A4	Museo de la Inmigración	6	C3	Museo Ferroviario
4	C2	Museo de Arte Hispanoamericano Isaac Fernández Blanco	10	D2	British Arts Centre
			11	D2	Galería Vermeer
			28	F1	Teatro Nacional Cervantes

SPORTS AND ACTIVITIES

| 21 | E3 | Plaza San Martín | | | |

SHOPS

2	C2	Simonetta Orsini	25	E4	Prüne
9	D1	Comme Il Faut	30	F3	La Martina
20	E3	Casa López	33	F4	Playsport

HOTELS

| 3 | C2 | Four Seasons | 23 | E4 | Plaza Hotel |
| 16 | D4 | Sheraton Buenos Aires | | | |

0   200 yds
0   200 m

DISTANCE ACROSS MAP
Approximate: 2 mi or 3.2 km

© AVALON TRAVEL

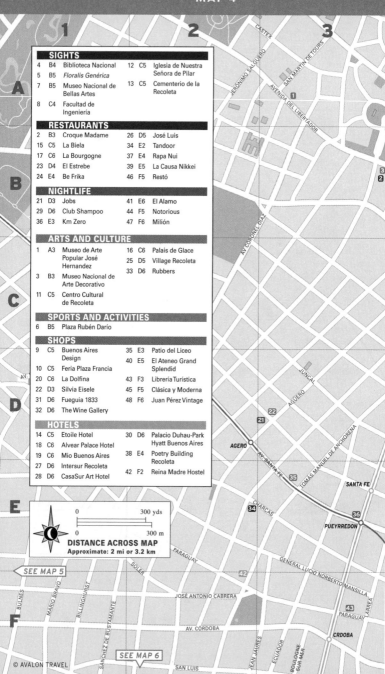

SIGHTS

4	B4	Biblioteca Nacional	12	C5	Iglesia de Nuestra Señora de Pilar
5	B5	Floralis Genérica	13	C5	Cementerio de la Recoleta
7	B5	Museo Nacional de Bellas Artes			
8	C4	Facultad de Ingeniería			

RESTAURANTS

2	B3	Croque Madame	26	D5	José Luis
15	C5	La Biela	34	E2	Tandoor
17	C6	La Bourgogne	37	E4	Rapa Nui
23	D4	El Estrebe	39	E5	La Causa Nikkei
24	E4	Be Frika	46	F5	Restó

NIGHTLIFE

21	D3	Jobs	41	E6	El Alamo
29	D6	Club Shampoo	44	F5	Notorious
36	E3	Km Zero	47	F6	Milión

ARTS AND CULTURE

1	A3	Museo de Arte Popular José Hernandez	16	C6	Palais de Glace
3	B3	Museo Nacional de Arte Decorativo	25	D5	Village Recoleta
11	C5	Centro Cultural de Recoleta	33	D6	Rubbers

SPORTS AND ACTIVITIES

6	B5	Plaza Rubén Darío

SHOPS

9	C5	Buenos Aires Design	35	E3	Patio del Liceo
10	C5	Feria Plaza Francia	40	E5	El Ateneo Grand Splendid
20	C6	La Dolfina	43	F3	Librería Turística
22	D3	Silvia Eisele	45	F5	Clásica y Moderna
31	D6	Fueguia 1833	48	F6	Juan Pérez Vintage
32	D6	The Wine Gallery			

HOTELS

14	C5	Etoile Hotel	30	D6	Palacio Duhau-Park Hyatt Buenos Aires
18	C6	Alvear Palace Hotel	38	E4	Poetry Building Recoleta
19	C6	Mio Buenos Aires	42	F2	Reina Madre Hostel
27	D6	Intersur Recoleta			
28	D6	CasaSur Art Hotel			

0 300 yds

0 300 m

DISTANCE ACROSS MAP
Approximate: 2 mi or 3.2 km

SEE MAP 5

SEE MAP 6

© AVALON TRAVEL

4 5 6

Floralis Genérica 5

Museo Nacional de Bellas Artes 7

Biblioteca Nacional 4

Parque Carlos Thays

GUSTAVO MARTINEZ ZUVIRIA

AV. FACUNDO QUIROGA

EDUARDO J. COUTURE

AV. PRESIDENTE FIGUEROA ALCORTA

JUAN A. BIBILONI

JUAN VICTOR GONZALEZ

FRANCISCO ROMERO

DR. CARLOS VAZ FERREIRA

AVENIDA DEL LIBERTADOR

AUSTRIA

AGÜERO

GALILEO

DOCTOR LUIS AGOTE

DOCTOR RICARDO LEVENE

POSADAS

PERITO LUCHA

ACCEL LEON YACANO

AV. GENERAL GELLY Y OBES

AV. PUEYRREDON

AZCUENAGA

9

10

16

LAS HERAS

Iglesia de Nuestra Señora de Pilar 12

11

PRESIDENTE EDUARDO VICTOR HAEDO

15

14

FR. ROBERTO ORTIZ

JUNIN

AYACUCHO

AV. ALVEAR

17

18

19

AV. CALLAO

POSADAS

Facultad de Ingeniería 8

PASAJE CANTILO

AV. GENERAL LAS HERAS

VICENTE LOPEZ

25

Cementerio de la Recoleta 13

26

27

28

29

AV. PRESIDENTE QUINTANA

20

RODRIGUEZ PEÑA

30

31

32

MONTEVIDEO

33

23

PEÑA

JOSE A. PACHECO DE MELO

RECOLETA

FRENCH

JUNIN

AZCUENAGA

PRESIDENTE JOSE EVARISTO URIBURU

JUNIN

24

38

JUNCAL

JUNCAL

Plaza Vicente López y Planes

SEE MAP 3 ▷

GUIDO

PARERA

37

ARENALES

39

AV. CALLAO

RODRIGUEZ PEÑA

ARENALES

41

AV. SANTA FE

PARANA

47

40

MONTEVIDEO

48

MARCELO T. DE ALVEAR

URUGUAY

TALCAHUANO

44

PASAJE PIZZURNO

46

PARAGUAY

45

FACULTAD DE MEDICINA

CALLAO

AV. CORDOBA

SEE MAP 1

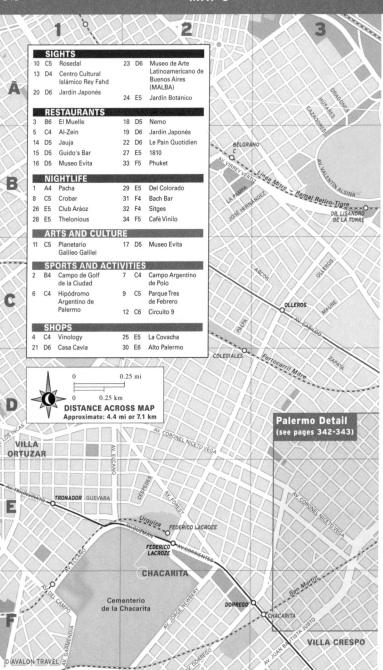

SIGHTS

10	C5	Rosedal	
13	D4	Centro Cultural Islámico Rey Fahd	
20	D6	Jardín Japonés	
23	D6	Museo de Arte Latinoamericano de Buenos Aires (MALBA)
24	E5	Jardín Botánico	

RESTAURANTS

3	B6	El Muelle	18	D5	Nemo
5	C4	Al-Zein	19	D6	Jardín Japonés
14	D5	Jauja	22	D6	Le Pain Quotidien
15	D5	Guido's Bar	27	E5	1810
16	D5	Museo Evita	33	F5	Phuket

NIGHTLIFE

1	A4	Pacha	29	E5	Del Colorado
8	C5	Crobar	31	F4	Bach Bar
26	E5	Club Aráoz	32	F4	Sitges
28	E5	Thelonious	34	F5	Café Vinilo

ARTS AND CULTURE

11	C5	Planetario Galileo Galilei	17	D5	Museo Evita

SPORTS AND ACTIVITIES

2	B4	Campo de Golf de la Ciudad	7	C4	Campo Argentino de Polo
6	C4	Hipódromo Argentino de Palermo	9	C5	Parque Tres de Febrero
			12	C6	Circuito 9

SHOPS

4	C4	Vinology	25	E5	La Covacha
21	D6	Casa Cavia	30	E6	Alto Palermo

0   0.25 mi

0   0.25 km

DISTANCE ACROSS MAP
Approximate: 4.4 mi or 7.1 km

Palermo Detail
(see pages 342-343)

VILLA ORTUZAR

TRONADOR   GUEVARA

CHACARITA

Cementerio de la Chacarita

DORREGO

FEDERICO LACROZE

VILLA CRESPO

© AVALON TRAVEL

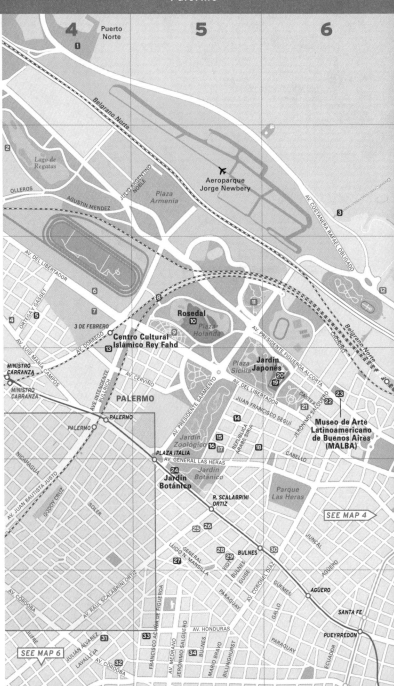

4

Puerto
Norte

1

5

6

2

Lago de
Regatas

OLLEROS

Belgrano Norte

JULIO ARGENTINO NORTE

AGUSTIN MENDEZ

Plaza
Armenia

Aeroparque
Jorge Newbery

AV. COSTANERA RAFAEL OBLIGADO

3

AV. DEL LIBERTADOR

4

ORTEGA Y GASSET

6

7

8

3 DE FEBRERO

Rosedal
10

9

Plaza
Holanda

11

12

Belgrano Norte

CHENUT

Centro Cultural
Islámico Rey Fahd
13

AV. DORREGO

AV. PRESIDENTE FIGUEROA ALCORTA

MINISTRO
CARRANZA

AV. LUIS MARIA CAMPOS

AV. CERVIÑO

AV. INTENDENTE BULLRICH

PALERMO

PALERMO

AV. PRESIDENTE SARMIENTO

Plaza
Sicilia

Jardín
Japonés
20

19

AV. DEL LIBERTADOR

JUAN FRANCISCO SEGUI

CASTEX

21

22

JERÓNIMO SALGUERO

23

Museo de Arte
Latinoamericano
de Buenos Aires
(MALBA)

MINISTRO
CARRANZA

Jardín
Zoológico

14

15

REPUBLICA ARABE SIRIA

16

17

18

CABELLO

PLAZA ITALIA

NICARAGUA

AV. JUAN BAUTISTA JUSTO

GODOY CRUZ

SOLER

Jardín
Botánico

AV. GENERAL LAS HERAS

24

Jardín
Botánico

Parque
Las Heras

SEE MAP 4

R. SCALABRINI
ORTIZ

JUNCAL

25 26

AGÜERO

AV. RAUL SCALABRINI ORTIZ

GENERAL
LUCIO N. MANSILLA

28

27

29

BULNES

VIDT

GUISE

BULNES

30

CORONEL DIAZ

GÜEMES

GALLO

PARAGUAY

AGÜERO

AV. CORDOBA

JUFRE

JULIAN ALVAREZ

31

LAVALLEJA

32

SEE MAP 6

FRANCISCO ACUÑA DE FIGUEROA

33

AV. MEDRANO

JERÓNIMO SALGUERO

34

AV. HONDURAS

BULNES

MARIO BRAVO

BILLINGHURST

PARAGUAY

PARAGUAY

SANTA FE

PUEYRREDON

ECUADOR

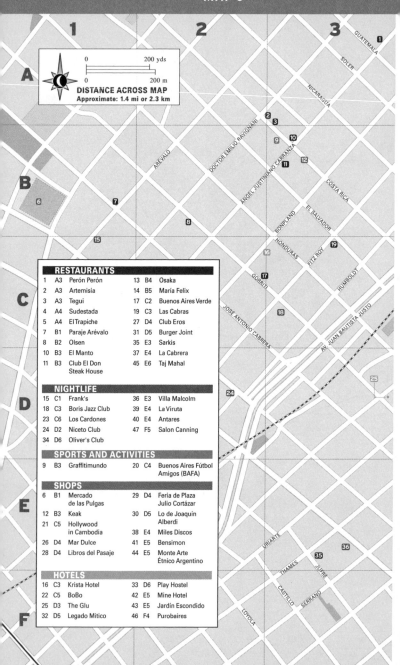

DISTANCE ACROSS MAP
Approximate: 1.4 mi or 2.3 km

0		200 yds
0		200 m

RESTAURANTS

1	A3	Perón Perón	13	B4	Osaka
2	A3	Artemisia	14	B5	María Felíx
3	A3	Tegui	17	C2	Buenos Aires Verde
4	A4	Sudestada	19	C3	Las Cabras
5	A4	El Trapiche	27	D4	Club Eros
7	B1	Paraje Arévalo	31	D5	Burger Joint
8	B2	Olsen	35	E3	Sarkis
10	B3	El Manto	37	E4	La Cabrera
11	B3	Club El Don Steak House	45	E6	Taj Mahal

NIGHTLIFE

15	C1	Frank's	36	E3	Villa Malcolm
18	C3	Boris Jazz Club	39	E4	La Viruta
23	C6	Los Cardones	40	E4	Antares
24	D2	Niceto Club	47	F5	Salon Canning
34	D6	Oliver's Club			

SPORTS AND ACTIVITIES

9	B3	Graffitimundo	20	C4	Buenos Aires Fútbol Amigos (BAFA)

SHOPS

6	B1	Mercado de las Pulgas	29	D4	Feria de Plaza Julio Cortázar
12	B3	Keak	30	D5	Lo de Joaquín Alberdi
21	C5	Hollywood in Cambodia	38	E4	Miles Discos
26	D4	Mar Dulce	41	E5	Bensimon
28	D4	Libros del Pasaje	44	E5	Monte Arte Étnico Argentino

HOTELS

16	C3	Krista Hotel	33	D6	Play Hostel
22	C5	BoBo	42	E5	Mine Hotel
25	D3	The Glu	43	E5	Jardín Escondido
32	D5	Legado Mitico	46	F4	Purobaires

MAP 6

SEE MAP 5

DISTANCE ACROSS MAP
Approximate: 3 mi or 4.8 km

0   0.25 mi
0   0.25 km

Monumento a Osvaldo Pugliese

Parque Centenario

ALMAGRO

CASTRO BARROS

LORIA

Basílica de San Carlos y María Auxiliadora

SIGHTS

1	A1	Monumento a Osvaldo Pugliese
17	A4	Museo Casa Carlos Gardel
19	A6	Palacio de las Aguas Corrientes
46	C5	Iglesia de Nuestra Señora de Balvanera
48	C6	Casa de los Lirios (House of Lilies)
49	C6	Palacio del Congreso
50	C6	Confitería del Molino
53	D3	Basílica de San Carlos y María Auxiliadora

RESTAURANTS

3	A2	Melão
4	A2	Arepera
7	A3	Lucuma
8	A3	Lo de Mary
13	A4	Pierino
16	A4	La Viña del Abasto
27	B3	Doña Cocina Tipo Casa
33	B4	La Reina Kunti
37	B4	Carlitos
41	C3	Las Violetas
43	C4	Don Ignacio
44	C4	Damblee
45	C4	La Conga
47	C6	Café de los Angelitos
52	C6	La Americana

NIGHTLIFE

2	A2	La Cava de Jufré
5	A2	Club Cultural Matienzo
6	A2	Amerika
9	A3	Dni Tango
12	A3	El Banderín
14	A4	Club Atlético Fernández Fierro
20	B1	Casa Brandon
24	B2	La Tribu
26	B3	La Catedral
28	C3	Lo de Roberto
30	B4	Tango Escuela Carlos Copello
31	B4	Casona Humahuaca
35	B4	Esquina Carlos Gardel
36	B4	Konex
39	B6	El Beso
42	C3	Señor Duncan
55	D5	Complejo Tango

ARTS AND CULTURE

10	A3	El Camarín de las Musas
18	A6	Museo de la Deuda Externa
21	B1	Museo Argentino de Ciencias Naturales
38	B4	Teatro Ciego (Blind Theater)
40	C3	The Actors Studio

SPORTS AND ACTIVITIES

22	B1	Parque Centenario
32	B4	Torre Blanca
57	F6	Asociación Ornitológica del Plata

SEE MAP 4

SEE MAP 1

Palacio de las
Aguas Corrientes

FACULTAD
DE MEDICINA

Museo Casa
Carlos Gardel

PASTEUR-
AMIA

Confitería
del Molino

ONCE
TRAIN
STATION

Iglesia de Nuestra
Señora de Balvanera

Casa de los Lirios
(House of Lilies)

CONGRESO

ONCE-
30 DE DICIEMBRE

BALVANERA

PLAZA
DE MISERERE

Palacio del
Congreso

Plaza
Primero
de Mayo

SAN CRISTOBAL

Plaza
Boedo

SHOPS				
11	A3	Calzados Correas	34	B4	Mercado del Abasto
29	B3	La Percalina	56	E1	Feria del Parque Rivadavia

HOTELS				
15	A4	ChillHouse	51	C6	Apart Hotel & Spa Congreso
23	B1	La Taba	54	D3	Racó
25	B2	Lecer Apart			

© AVALON TRAVEL

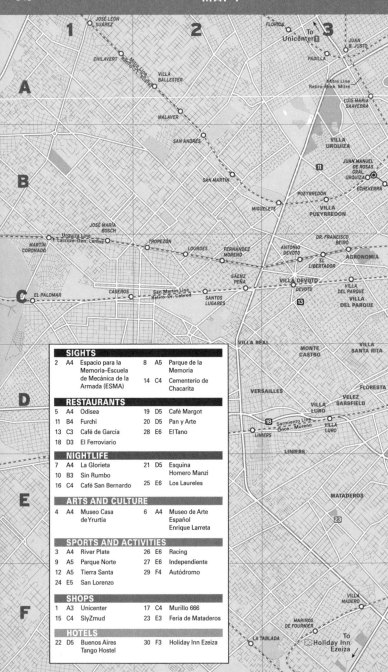

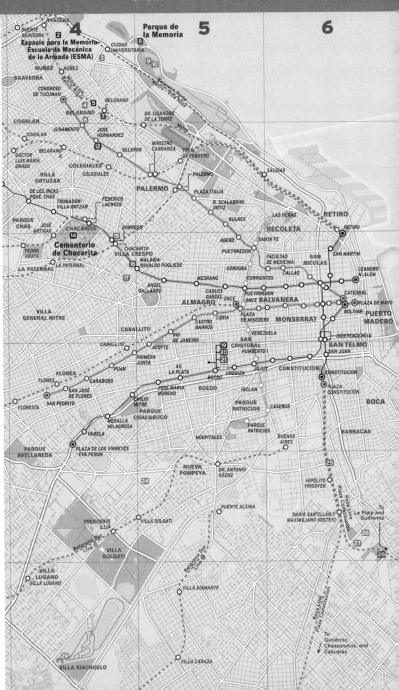

RIVADAVIA

PUENTE
SAAVEDRA

2

4

Espacio para la Memoria—
Escuela de Mecánica
de la Armada (ESMA)

CIUDAD
UNIVERSITARIA

3

Parque de
la Memoria

5

6

NÚÑEZ   NÚÑEZ

SAAVEDRA

CONGRESO
DE TUCUMAN

9 10

Belgrano Norte
Retiro – Villa Rosa

COGHLAN

JURAMENTO

BELGRANO

4 5

7

BELGRANO

6

DR. LISANDRO
DE LA TORRE

RETIRO

COGHLAN

JOSÉ
HERNANDEZ

Mitre

RETIRO

DOCTOR
LUIS MARÍA
DRAGO

BELGRANO

12

OLLEROS

MINISTRO
CARRANZA

TRES
DE FEBRERO

SAN MARTIN

SALGUAS

VILLA
ORTÚZAR

COLEGIALES
COLEGIALES

PALERMO

PALERMO

PLAZA ITALIA

LEANDRO
N. ALEM

DE LOS INCAS
PQUE. CHAS

FEDERICO
LACROZE

R. SCALABRINI
ORTIZ

LAS HERAS

RETIRO

PARQUE
CHAS

TRONADOR—
VILLA ORTÚZAR

BULNES

RECOLETA

RETIRO

JOSÉ
ARTIGAS

CHACARITA

DORREGO

AGERO

SANTA FE

SAN MARTIN

14

Cementerio
de Chacarita

15

CHACARITA
VILLA CRESPO

PUEYRREDON

FACULTAD
DE MEDICINA

SAN
NICOLAS

SAN MARTIN

PEDRO
ARATA

MALABIA—
OSVALDO PUGLIESE

CÓRDOBA

CORRIENTES

CALLAO

LEANDRO
N. ALEM

LA PATERNAL   LA PATERNAL

15

MEDRANO

CALLAO

CATEDRAL

VILLA
GENERAL MITRE

17

ANGEL
GALLARDO

CARLOS
GARDEL

PUEYRREDON

CORRIENTES

PLAZA DE MAYO
BOLIVAR

PUERTO
MADERO

ALMAGRO   ONCE   BALVANERA

PLAZA
DE MISERERE

MONSERRAT

CABALLITO

CASTRO
BARROS

LORIA

VENEZUELA

INDEPENDENCIA

CABALLITO

RIO
DE JANEIRO

19

SAN
CRISTOBAL

SAN TELMO

PRIMERA
JUNTA

ACOYTE

20

HUMBERTO I

SAN JUAN

FLORES

PUAN

21

AV.
LA PLATA

URQUIZA

JUJUY

CONSTITUCION

FLORES

CARABOBO

BOEDO

CONSTITUCION

SAN JOSÉ
DE FLORES

JOSÉ MARIA
MORENO

INCLAN

PLAZA
CONSTITUCIÓN

FLORESTA

SAN PEDRITO

EMILIO
MITRE

BOEDO

BOCA

MEDALLA
MILAGROSA

PARQUE
CHACABUCO

PARQUE
PATRICIOS

CASEROS

VARELA

PARQUE
PATRICIOS

BARRACAS

PARQUE
AVELLANEDA

PLAZA DE LOS VIRREYES
EVA PERÓN

HOSPITALES

BUENOS
AIRES

25

24

NUEVA
POMPEYA

DR. ANTONIO
SÁENZ

HIPÓLITO
YRIGOYEN

PRESIDENTE
ILLIA

Belgrano Sur
Line G

VILLA SOLDATI

PUENTE ALSINA

DARÍO SANTILLÁN Y
MAXIMILIANO KOSTEKI

Roca Line
Plaza Constitución

To
La Plata and
Gutiérrez

26

VILLA
SOLDATI

Belgrano Sur
Line M

27

28

VILLA
LUGANO
VILLA LUGANO

VILLA DIAMANTE

29

VILLA RIACHUELO

VILLA CARAZA

Roca Line
Plaza Constitución

To
Gutiérrez,
Chascomús, and
Cañuelas

Also Available

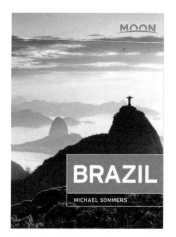

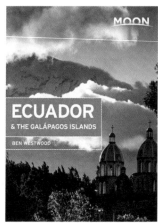

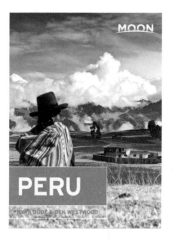